EGYPT

Economic Management in a Period of Transition

*The report of a mission sent
to the Arab Republic of Egypt by the World Bank*

Khalid Ikram
Coordinating Author

D1357784

Published for the World Bank
The Johns Hopkins University Press
Baltimore and London

Fired. 35.00/31.50/10/28/83

Library of Congress Cataloging in Publication Data

International Bank for Reconstruction and Development.
    Egypt, economic management in a period of transition.
    Includes index.
    1. Egypt — Economic policy. 2. Egypt — Economic
conditions — 1952-   I. Ikram, Khalid, 1938-   II. Title.
HC830.I57   1980   338.962   80-552
ISBN 0-8018-2418-4
ISBN 0-8018-2419-2 (pbk.)

EGYPT

A World Bank Country Economic Report

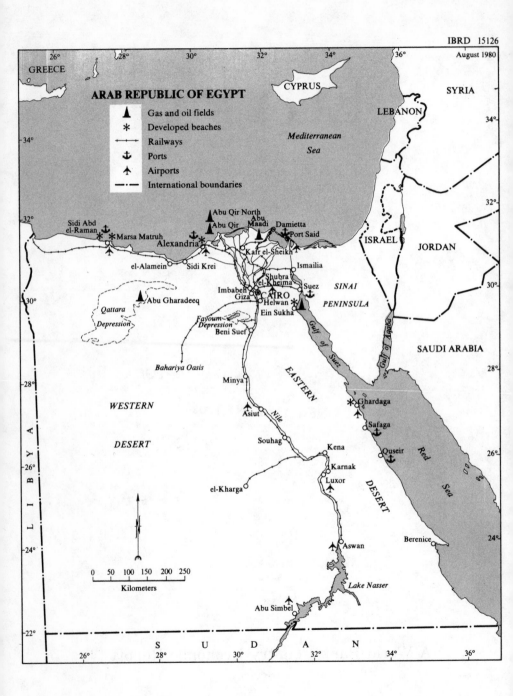

IBRD 15126

August 1980

GREECE

ARAB REPUBLIC OF EGYPT

🔺 Gas and oil fields
✳ Developed beaches
✛ Railways
⚓ Ports
✈ Airports
–·–·– International boundaries

CYPRUS

SYRIA

LEBANON

Mediterranean
Sea

ISRAEL

JORDAN

Sidi Abd
el-Raman

✳ Marsa Matruh

Alexandria

Abu Qir North

Abu Qir

Abu
Maadi

Damietta

Port Said

el-Alamein

Sidi Krei

Kafr el-Sheikh

Ismailia

SINAI
PENINSULA

Imbabeh

Giza

Shubra
el-Kheima

CAIRO

Helwan

Ein Sukha

Suez

Abu Gharadeeq

Qattara
Depression

Fayoum
Depression

Beni Suef

SAUDI ARABIA

Bahariya Oasis

Minya

EASTERN

Gulf of Suez

Gulf of Aqaba

WESTERN

Asiut

Nile

Ghardaga

Safaga

DESERT

Souhag

Kena

Quseir

Red

el-Kharga

Karnak

Luxor

DESERT

Sea

L I B Y A

Berenice

Aswan

0 50 100 150 200 250
Kilometers

Lake Nasser

Abu Simbel

S   U   D   A   N

Foreword

This is the nineteenth in the current series of World Bank country economic reports, all of which are listed on the following page. They are published, in response to a desire expressed by scholars and practitioners in the field of economic and social development, to facilitate research and the interchange of knowledge.

The Bank regularly prepares economic reports on borrowing countries in support of its own operations. These surveys provide a basis for discussion with governments and for decisions on Bank policy and operations. Many governments use the reports as an aid to their economic planning, as do consortia and consultative groups of governments and institutions providing assistance in development. All Bank country reports are published subject to the agreement of — and several have been published by — the governments concerned.

Hollis B. Chenery
Vice President for Development Policy
The World Bank

WORLD BANK COUNTRY ECONOMIC REPORTS

Published for the Bank by The Johns Hopkins University Press

Egypt: Economic Management in a Period of Transition
Yugoslavia: Self-management Socialism and the Challenges
  of Development
Korea: Policy Issues for Long-Term Development
The Commonwealth Caribbean: The Integration Experience
Ivory Coast: The Challenge of Success
Korea: Problems and Issues in a Rapidly Growing Economy
Kenya: Into the Second Decade
Yugoslavia: Development with Decentralization
Nigeria: Options for Long-Term Development
Economic Growth of Colombia

Published by the World Bank

Papua New Guinea: Its Economic Situation and Prospects
  for Development
The Philippines: Priorities and Prospects for Development
Lesotho: A Development Challenge
Turkey: Prospects and Problems of an Expanding Economy
Senegal: Tradition, Diversification, and Economic Development
  (also published in French)
Chad: Development Potential and Constraints (also published
  in French as Le Développement du Tchad: Possibilités
  et Limites)
Current Economic Position and Prospects of Peru
Current Economic Position and Prospects of Ecuador
Employment in Trinidad and Tobago

Contents

Part IV. Financial Resources and Infrastructure

Figures

xi

Tables

Acknowledgments

The groundwork for this report was initiated by economic missions which visited Egypt in May–June 1976 and June–July 1977. The first mission consisted of: Khalid Ikram (chief of mission), Shu Chin Yang, Shahid Chaudhry, and Salem Gafsi (general economists), Gabriel Sciolli (public finance), Lance Taylor (income distribution), William Cuddihy (agriculture), Jayanta Roy (econometrics), Keith Marsden (manpower and employment), Andrew Loewenthal (urbanization), Malvina Pollock (external debt), Roberto Benjerodt (tourism), and Ozana Apkarian (secretary).

The second mission consisted of: Khalid Ikram (chief of mission), Shahid Chaudhry and Adil Kanaan (general economists), Robert Mabro (industry and general economics), Malvina Pollock (external debt), Judy O'Connor (human resources), and Betty Dow (programmer).

The report was amplified and updated in 1978 and 1979 in the course of the World Bank's regular economic missions led by Khalid Ikram, and by drawing on the Bank's continuing sector and project work. The final report has benefited from the Bank's review procedures and from the contributions of Mehdi Ali, Hasan Imam, and S. Rangachar (general economists), Vineet Nayyar (petroleum), and Shail Jain and Karen Brown (research assistants).

Jane H. Carroll edited the manuscript for publication. James Silvan and Ralph Ward indexed the text, Christine Houle corrected proofs, and Raphael Blow prepared the charts. The frontispiece map was compiled by Ulrich Boegli and drawn by Larry Bowring under the supervision of the World Bank's Cartography Division.

Khalid Ikram

xix

Unified Exchange Rate

1 Egyptian pound (LE)	=	US$1.43
1 U.S. dollar	=	LE0.699

Fiscal Year

January 1 - December 31

Weights and Measures

1 hectare	=	2.379 feddans
1 feddan	=	1.038 acres
1 acre	=	0.963 feddans
1 square kilometer	=	238 feddans
1 ardeb (metric)	=	198 liters
	=	160 kilograms (kg) of lentils
	=	157 kg of clover
	=	155 kg of beans, chick peas, lupine, and fenugreek
	=	140 kg of maize, millet
	=	120 kg of cottonseed, barley, and sesame
	=	60 kg of groundnuts
1 qintar	=	157.5 kg of seed cotton
	=	50 kg of cotton lint
	=	45 kg of onions and sugarcane

EGYPT

Overview

The geographical and demographic characteristics of Egypt delineate its basic economic problem. Although the country contains about 386,000 square miles — about the size of France and Spain together — only a narrow strip in the Nile Valley and the Delta is usable. This area of 15,000 square miles — less than 4 percent of the land — is but an elongated oasis in the midst of desert. Without the Nile, which flows through Egypt for about a thousand miles without being joined by a single tributary, the country would be part of the Sahara. Crammed into the habitable area is 98 percent of the population, estimated at more than 40 million, giving a density of more than 2,600 per square mile (about 1,000 per square kilometer). The population has been growing rapidly and is estimated to have doubled since 1947.

Despite some land reclamation, the cultivated area has increased by less than 5 percent since 1947. More intensive cultivation has to some extent moderated the effects of the deterioration in the man-land ratio, but even so the cropped area has increased only from 9.1 million feddans to 10.8 feddans (less than 20 percent) in the same period.[1] Each feddan is now expected to support 3.5 persons, compared with 2.1 in 1947. Of itself this change may not be unusual, but it fixes a lower limit to the increase in factor productivity required in the absence of significant structural change in the economy at large. These two themes — the relatively fixed amount of the usable land and the rapid growth of the population — will be seen as leitmotivs in the discussion of Egypt's economic problems.

The resolution of these problems — difficult even under the most favorable circumstances — is complicated by the fact that Egypt was at war from 1967 on. As a concomitant, the physical infrastructure has deteriorated considerably because of inadequate investment. These material difficulties are intensified by the prevalence of institutions, policies, attitudes, and expectations that are not always appropriate to the post-1973 circumstances of the economy.

---

1. The cropped area is the cultivated area times the cropping intensity. A feddan is equal to 1.038 acres or 0.42 hectares.

3

But the present and the future are not without opportunities.
There are prospects of earnings from petroleum, revenues from
a widened Suez Canal, and rapidly increasing remittances from
Egyptians working abroad. Other assets include the opportunities
for tourism, the cultural and political links with the capital-surplus
Arab countries, the location of the country (in the Middle East but
well placed for European markets), and a reasonably well-trained
labor force. The Egyptian economy thus possesses considerable
potential in the longer term.

The realization of this potential, however, will require many
policy reforms and structural changes. The broad framework of
a fundamental change toward a more open and market-oriented
economy was enunciated in April 1974 by President Anwar el-Sadat
in his October Working Paper. This process will take time and is
likely to generate considerable stress and pressure throughout the
economic system. A major problem is, therefore, the management
of the Egyptian economy during the period of transition, which is
expected to occupy most of the next decade. This volume focuses
on the major policy issues (both macroeconomic and sectoral) that
are likely to be confronted.

OVERALL DEVELOPMENT, 1952-76

The performance of the Egyptian economy has been uneven in the
twenty-five years since the 1952 revolution. In the early 1950s the
economy was suffering from the inevitable uncertainties of a major
change in the political regime and from the effects of the worldwide
downturn in the business cycle after the boom of the Korean War.
Recovery followed, with a stretch of ten years of significant economic growth, after which there was a steady decline. Then in 1973
the oil price revolution opened up new opportunities for investment
and development in Egypt, but it also triggered off a phase of recession combined with inflation in the world economy, which had adverse
repercussions on all developing countries.

The economic development of Egypt in these years may be divided
into two periods. The 1955-65 decade witnessed fairly rapid and
sustained economic growth as well as a major structural transformation of the economy. Industry and services increased their
shares of both total output and employment, and within industry the
composition of output shifted in favor of intermediate goods and consumer durables. At the same time, the transition was made from
a free, private enterprise system to an economy characterized by
state planning, public ownership of modern means of production,
and wide-ranging administrative control and policy interferences.

In the decade after 1965, the economy could no longer sustain
the pace of high economic performance, largely because resources
were being diverted to defense, and aid flows from the West were

interrupted. The rate of economic growth declined steadily, with
a marked fall in the rate of investment and domestic saving. Though
the decline was arrested in the last years of the 1960s, there was
no dramatic improvement nor sign of sustainable recovery. Egypt
was suffering from a multitude of problems: the consequences of
earlier economic policies that failed to push up the rate of saving
in line with the rate of investment; the impact of the Yemen war and
the Arab-Israeli war of 1967; a heavy defense burden; the inefficiencies of the public sector and the maladministration of prices, foreign
trade, and investment programs; and the cumulative effects of the
population explosion.

Between 1960 and 1976 the gross domestic product (GDP) at market prices increased at an average annual rate of just over 5 percent. Much of the increase, however, was eroded by the rate of
population growth, so that the per capita income improved only from
about LE65 to LE100 (in 1965 prices) over the sixteen-year period,
that is, at about 2.7 percent a year.[2] This growth in per capita income occurred at an uneven rate: between 1960 and 1965 the average rate was 4.2 percent annually, but it dropped to less than 1
percent a year between 1966 and 1973; in 1966-68 and 1972 there
was actually a fall in real per capita income.

Because of the differential rates of growth in the three major
sectors — agriculture, industry, and services — a familiar pattern
of structural change emerged in which the share of agriculture in
GDP declined rapidly. In the 1950s industry increased its share
of real GDP at the expense of both agriculture and the services.
In the 1960s the rapid growth of the services sector overshadowed
that of industry. Normally, when secondary (industrial) activities
decline in relation to tertiary (service) activities, it is a sign of
economic development. In Egypt, however, it is in fact a sign of
economic problems — arising from the population explosion, the
indiscriminate expansion of education, and the unsatisfactory performance of agriculture and industry.

ISSUES FOR DEVELOPMENT STRATEGY

The developmental problem is essentially a question of the quantity, quality, and proportion of resources to be devoted to development on the one hand, and to economic management on the other.
Any viable development strategy for Egypt will have to address this
question in terms of several fundamental issues.

Population growth has been ignored by policymakers for too long;
government policy has approached it only tentatively and with too
little means. Though the demographic trends of the past decade

2. In 1973 the Egyptian pound was the equivalent of US$2.30 at the official rate
and US$1.70 at the "parallel" market rate.

have been slightly more encouraging, Egypt will continue to face a major employment problem. Moreover, the cost of providing the basic needs of the population — food, clothing, shelter, education, and health — may rise to unmanageable levels. Emigration is not a satisfactory solution because it introduces imbalances in the skill structure of manpower supplies. Nor is using government employment to absorb potentially redundant workers an attractive choice because it involves economic costs.

An important issue for the future is the role of agriculture. Since the 1950s Egypt's price and exchange rate policies have squeezed resources out of agriculture in order to develop other sectors. This strategy was perhaps inevitable when agriculture was the only sector capable of yielding a significant surplus. But the effect was to weaken and distort incentives for production and make it difficult for small farmers to adopt much needed technological advances. Now that resources are readily available from petroleum, workers' remittances, tourism, the Suez Canal, and external assistance, the former attitude toward agriculture is neither necessary nor desirable. Egypt must encourage a greater degree of accumulation within agriculture, particularly by medium-size and small farmers, to foster the wider dissemination of technical change. Within agriculture is the need for a qualitative transformation. In the past twenty or thirty years increasingly costly schemes of land reclamation have been directed toward "horizontal expansion." Yet despite high yields and apparent constraints on the intensive margin of cultivation, much remains to be done on the old land. The far-reaching transformation of agriculture could involve drainage, new crop patterns, new methods of irrigation, improved cultivation techniques, and the linking of new kinds of agricultural production with industry and exports.

Policymakers also face deficiencies in the structural transformation brought about by industrialization — that is, the accumulation of physical capital for the production of material goods — and educcation — that is, the formation of human capital. Industrialization went on far too long behind protective walls, and the process was, at times, marred by wrong investment decisions that loaded the manufacturing sector with inefficient industries. Education has suffered from the sacrifice of quality in favor of quantity. Because government policies in Egypt established a nexus between education and guaranteed employment, some of the benefits expected from the investment in human resources have been lost.

Fiscal policy has been little used as an instrument, despite the extensive share of the public sector in the economy. Monetary policy has also been largely passive — the banking sector has expanded credit to finance the overall budget deficit, while interest rates have changed slowly and lag well behind the rate of inflation. The government has relied on other instruments to pursue its objectives for prices, employment, and balance of payments. Thus, for example, the authorities have sought to stabilize prices through direct controls on the prices of "supply" (that is, essential) commodities and the output of public enterprises, combined with an extensive system of subsidies.

The mobilization of resources, both external and domestic, is thus another area on which economic strategy will have to focus, and where fundamental choices of both means and ends need to be made. Will external funds be available at the required levels? Will they be available on terms that will not exacerbate the debt problem? Would a slower-growth strategy, which required a smaller inflow of foreign saving, be preferable to a high-growth, high-aid option? What would be the costs of the slower-growth strategy in income and employment forgone? Even if the external funds were available, could the complementary domestic resources be mobilized in a non-inflationary manner and without adversely affecting income distribution? Some of these considerations are addressed in this report, but the ultimate choices have to be made by the Egyptian authorities, and their decisions need not coincide on all points with the views of external donors.

Economic growth and development are significantly related to investment. Productivity growth, a main source of income increases, also depends in part on investment. Much remains to be done in Egypt to improve the methods of project appraisal, project selection, and the implementation of investment programs. Uneconomic projects, once begun, are difficult to close down, especially when employment or prestige is at stake. The economy generally lives with them and subsidizes the inefficiencies. In Egypt the public sector has selected many projects that turned out to be costly to the economy. Because the institutional framework is still weak, and because the public sector will continue to be responsible for a significant share of total investment, such errors might be repeated. Whether private investment carries less risk of inefficient selection is not evident. The private sector, too, could easily be given the type of protection and incentives that allows inefficiencies to creep in and take their toll.

There are major issues of economic policymaking and coordination. Because of the long and extensive involvement of the government in the economy, the issues are not limited to improving or modifying any specific measures. A complete overhaul of the whole system of policy intervention is called for. The dilemma is that such an overhaul may be ineffective if attempted piecemeal, but perhaps impossible to implement in a swift and radical manner. The liberalization of the price system, for example, may have to be extensive in range and yet gradual and accompanied by measures to protect the poorer sections of the community. Industry cannot be suddenly exposed to the high winds of international competition. Here again, the gradual lowering of tariff walls may have to be associated with other measures, such as special incentives to improve technological and managerial efficiency (or what is sometimes referred to

as X-efficiency). The fundamental principle is that tinkering with
prices, exchange rates, and fiscal and monetary measures, however
necessary, would rarely be sufficient in the present Egyptian context.
Any realistic program of reform, moreover, will have to take into
account the limitations on implementation imposed by the cumbersome
workings of the bureaucracy.

Egypt's economic system will undoubtedly remain mixed, with a
very large public sector and a strengthened private sector. The de-
mise of the public sector is not politically feasible, nor is it an objective of government policy. And while liberalization policies may
influence, perhaps superficially, the modes of operation and the organization of the public sector, it will not affect state ownership in
petroleum, mining, and transport. The expansion of these activities will therefore counteract any decline in the relative size of the
public sector in manufacturing. "Ownership," however, may not be
important. Liberalization is really a matter of freer access to domestic and foreign markets and less administrative interference
with the mobility of factors of production and the functioning of markets — in short, it concerns the management of the economy at both
the macro and the micro level.

The problem of the government is to devise policies which, while
proceeding with liberalization, will continue the modest protection
hitherto granted to the poor and will check the operation of forces
that aggravate income disparities. The inherent difficulty is that
liberalization might remove many administrative interventions that
were introduced to improve income distribution. The government
will have to continue trying to strike a balance between the conflicting objectives of liberalization for the sake of productivity growth
and intervention for the sake of an equitable distribution of income.

Exercises with a simulation model indicate that given certain assumptions regarding the balance of payments, and if most of the policy reforms discussed in this report were undertaken, the Egyptian
economy could grow at an annual rate of about 6 to 7 percent in real
terms over the coming decade. To some extent a relatively high-
growth strategy would make it easier to tackle the employment question and also generate a higher level of domestic saving. Aiming at
too high a rate of growth, however, could create a number of serious problems, unless policy actions were consciously devised to fore-
stall them or to alleviate their impact. The most important of these
problems are that the relative distribution of incomes between rural
and urban areas is likely to deteriorate, that extremely high rates
of saving would be required out of additions to per capita incomes,
and that there would be greater dependence on external capital and
an increased burden of servicing the foreign debt.

PART ONE
General Assessment

1
Historical Background

During the first half of the nineteenth century Egypt was ruled by
Muhammad Ali, an Albanian officer who managed to seize supreme
power and be recognized by the Ottoman sultan as pasha of Egypt
in 1805. His policies had far-reaching consequences for the economic development of the country.[1] Cotton was introduced in the
1820s and cotton exports developed, major irrigation works such as
the Nile barrage and the Mahmudia Canal were executed, railway
and telegraph lines were begun, the administration was reorganized,
and the educational system was reformed to incorporate modern technical subjects such as medicine and engineering. Between 1816 and
the late 1830s Muhammad Ali attempted to establish a modern and
diversified industrial structure in Egypt, owned entirely by the state,
but for a variety of reasons the experiment failed.[2] The next major
thrust toward industrialization did not come until the interwar years
of the twentieth century.

THE CENTURY BEFORE THE 1952 REVOLUTION

Under Muhammad Ali's successors Egypt's external indebtedness increased steeply. Although this debt was incurred partly for
economic purposes (including the construction of the Suez Canal), a
large part of it was for noneconomic ends, such as the rulers' consumption of luxury goods, the purchase of a measure of independence

1. A vivid account of the life of the people during this time is provided by Edward
William Lane, The Manners and Customs of the Modern Egyptians, first published
in 1836. We have used the fifth edition (1860) edited by E. Stanley Poole (London:
J. M Dent and Sons, 1923).
2. Robert Mabro and Samir Radwan, The Industrialization of Egypt, 1939-1973 (Oxford: Clarendon Press, 1976), pp. 17-18. See also Ahmed Abdel-Rahim Mustafa,
"The Breakdown of the Monopoly System in Egypt after 1840," in P. M. Holt, ed.,
Political and Social Change in Modern Egypt (London: Oxford University Press,
1968), pp. 291-307.

from the Ottoman sultan, or the financing of military expeditions into Africa. Difficulties in servicing the growing debt could not be
staved off even by selling Egypt's shares in the Suez Canal to
Britain in 1875.[3] The major powers, who represented the chief
creditors, created a Caisse de la Dette in 1876, an organization responsible for controlling all the fiscal receipts of the government and
for supervising their disposal in the repayment of external loans.

An army revolt against the increasing foreign interference led to
direct intervention and the occupation of the country by the British
in 1882. While Egypt continued to be legally a part of the Ottoman
Empire, the effective power passed into the hands of the British,
whose policies were implemented through a consul general. The
most powerful and well known of these consuls general was Sir Eve-
lyn Baring, later Lord Cromer. His long tenure (1883-1907) was
marked, on the one hand, by substantial measures of financial consolidation, improvement of the physical infrastructure, and administrative reform but, on the other, by a neglect of education and rather
heavy-handed dealing with rising nationalist aspirations.[4]

The outbreak of World War I, with Turkey (the nominal suzerain
of Egypt) on the side of Germany, enabled Britain openly to declare
its protectorate over Egypt on December 18, 1914. After the war,
the movement for independence gained strength, and on February 21,
1922, Britain recognized Egypt as an independent sovereign state.
The major questions of communications, defense, foreign affairs,
protection of foreign interests, and the Sudan, were still under Britain's control, however, and the British army continued to occupy
the country.

Immediately after World War II the struggle intensified against
the foreign occupation and the corruption and extravagance of the
royal court. Strikes, demonstrations, and violent outbreaks increased rapidly, culminating in the outbreak of guerrilla warfare
between the Egyptians and the British forces in the Suez Canal
Zone in December 1951 and the riots of January 26, 1952, in
Cairo. Between February and late July there were five governments. Public order continued to deteriorate until the Free
Officers, led by Lieutenant-Colonel Gamal Abd el-Nasser, seized
power on July 23, 1952, in what has come to be known as the
1952 revolution.

4. Cromer's own side of the story is detailed in Earl of Cromer, Modern Egypt,
2 vols. (London: Macmillan and Co., 1908). For a modern Egyptian assessment,
see Afaf Lutfi Al-Sayyid, Egypt and Cromer (New York: Frederick A. Praeger,
1969).

ECONOMIC EVOLUTION

With the collapse of Muhammad Ali's industrial policies and programs, one important phase of Egypt's economic development ended, and future developments were oriented in a totally different direction. As Issawi expressed it: "The attempted leap from a subsistence to a complex economy had failed, and instead the country had landed on the road leading to an export-oriented economy. Egypt could now be integrated, as an agricultural unit, in the worldwide economic system."[5]

The integration of Egypt into the world economy, spurred on by Muhammad Ali and based largely on the cotton trade, necessitated many structural changes. First, the rapid expansion of the irrigation system increased the cultivated area from 4.16 million feddans in 1852 to 5.28 million in 1913. Cotton production went up from 501,000 qintars in 1860 to 2.14 million in 1865 and to 7.64 million in 1913.[6] Cotton exports rose from an average of 360,000 qintars in 1848-52 to 1.69 million qintars in 1863-67 and 6.72 million qintars in 1908-12; in the latter period cotton accounted for about 89 percent of total exports.

Second, there was a great improvement in transport and communication facilities, both internal and external. The first railway was opened in 1853, and by 1858 Cairo had been linked with Alexandria and Suez; the Suez Canal was opened on November 17, 1869; the port of Alexandria was rapidly expanded and new ports were constructed at Suez and Port Said; and an extensive network of telegraph lines was laid down.

Third, the restrictions on private ownership of land were slowly removed, a system of private landownership gradually developed, and with it a class of large landowners and a concomitant concentration of landholding. In 1897, it is estimated, 1.5 percent of the landowners held 44 percent of the total agricultural land area, while 80 percent of the owners held only 20 percent. By 1913 the situation had worsened, and 0.8 percent of the landowners held 44.2 percent of the land, while 91 percent of the proprietors owned only 26 percent of the land.[7]

Fourth, the integration of Egypt into the world economy was accompanied by a rapid increase in indebtedness to foreign private

5. Charles Issawi, Egypt in Revolution (London: Oxford University Press, 1963), p. 24. The following discussion also draws on Issawi, pp. 25-27.
6. A qintar is a unit of measure that varies with the product; it is the equivalent of 157.5 kilograms of seed cotton or 50 kilograms of cotton lint.
7. Mabro and Radwan, Industrialization of Egypt, p. 24; see also Gabriel Baer, A History of Landownership in Modern Egypt, 1800-1950 (London: Oxford University Press, 1962).

banks. This debt was incurred partly to pay for the irrigation and other works that were necessary for the expansion of cotton production and partly for the rulers' extravagant expenditures. It is estimated that in 1880 the public debt had reached a level of nearly Ł100 million and was growing. In the early 1900s the servicing of the public debt and the tribute to the Sublime (Ottoman) Porte represented about 30 percent of the country's export proceeds and 37 percent of government revenues, a drain of some 4 to 5 percent of Egypt's national income at that time.[8] Moreover, some calculations suggest that had irrigation and infrastructural projects yielded a minimum annual net return of 14 to 15 percent, it would still have taken about eighty years to pay off the debt. It is very doubtful whether many investment projects performed nearly so well.[9]

The new phase of industrialization did not begin until the interwar years. This industrial renaissance was sparked by many factors, the most important of which were the accumulation of saving and the profitability — indeed, the possibility — of import substitution.

The interruption of maritime communications during World War I led to the stockpiling of cotton and to a decrease in imports. With the reopening of communications the price of these stocks increased.[10] Much of this accumulated saving was drained off by a new indigenous institution, the Bank Misr, which was founded in 1920. The development of the nontraditional sectors of the Egyptian economy in the interwar years is largely the story of the growth of the Misr group. In addition to its banking activities, the group began to branch out into other enterprises: printing, cotton ginning, paper, navigation, cotton spinning and weaving, cinema and theater, commercial enterprises, and insurance, to name only the principal ones. The Misr group also developed political connections with the Wafd party, which espoused nationalist principles.

Until World War I Egypt had followed an export-led growth strategy, with cotton exports as the "engine of growth." In the 1920s a series of agricultural crises culminated in the Great Depression of 1929-32. Because of its extreme dependence on a single crop, Egypt suffered more than other countries; the price terms of trade deteriorated sharply and this deterioration continued for more than twenty years.[11] It was evident that the economy needed to be diversified to reduce its vulnerability to fluctuations in external markets.

8. Mabro and Radwan, Industrialization of Egypt, p. 20; Robert Mabro, The Egyptian Economy, 1952-72 (Oxford: Clarendon Press, 1974), p. 21, and see the references cited in notes 19 and 21 on p. 236. See also David S. Landes, Bankers and Pashas (Cambridge, Mass: Harvard University Press, 1958), and John Marlowe, Spoiling the Egyptians (London: Andre Deutsch, 1974, for a more accessible account of Egyptian indebtedness.
9. Mabro, Egyptian Economy, p. 20.
10. Cotton prices rose from an average of US$38 a ton in 1916 to US$90 in 1919.
11. Samir Radwan, Capital Formation in Egyptian Industry and Agriculture, 1882-1967, (London: Ithaca Press, 1974), p. 243.

In 1930 Egypt regained the fiscal autonomy which had been taken away by the Capitulations,[12] and a tariff reform gave a measure of protection to domestic industry. Until that time, the tariff system had been looked upon as a source of revenue, not of protection. Tariffs were very low; the conventions signed by the Sublime Porte — of which Egypt was technically a dependency — limited import duties to 5 percent ad valorem (later increased to 8 percent), with only a few exceptions which varied from time to time. Even as late as the end of the 1920s, a uniform 8 percent ad valorem rate was applied to almost all imports; direct controls were virtually nonexistent, with the exception of a ban on imports of raw cotton from 1916.[13] In 1930 the general rate of 8 percent ad valorem was replaced by specific rates ranging from 12 to 30 percent on imports of manufactured products. Some other incentives were also provided; for example, in state purchases the government favored domestically produced items even if their prices exceeded by 10 percent those of foreign products. The tariff did not have an immediate impact because it coincided with the Great Depression. As Radwan points out, however, it was important as a change in the environment and in attitudes toward industrialization.[14] The existing industries, such as cotton textiles, expanded rapidly by the end of the 1930s, and new industries, such as cement, kerosene, and petroleum products, were established.

The next major impetus to industrialization was provided during World War II, when Egypt was largely cut off from foreign supplies. This protection, coupled with the increased expenditures of the Allied military establishment, encouraged the growth of many economic activities, such as repairs, metal manufacturing, and construction. After the war, the protectionist policies were continued and still newer industries, such as nitrogenous fertilizers, were set up. This was the situation at the time the regime was ousted by a group of army officers in July 1952.

12. The Capitulations were a series of treaties between the sultan of Turkey and the European powers that defined the conditions under which European nationals lived and traded in Ottoman dominions.
13. Bent Hansen and Karim Nashashibi, Foreign Trade Regimes and Economic Development: Egypt (New York: National Bureau of Economic Research, 1974), pp. 3-4.
14. Radwan, Capital Formation, pp. 189-91.

2
Economic Philosophy and Policies since 1952

The Free Officers took power in July 1952 without any clear economic philosophy.[1] This was not surprising because since the nineteenth century Egypt had known — sometimes through choice and sometimes by accident — a variety of economic systems. Under Muhammad Ali the ruler was identified with the state as the major economic agent. Government monopolies existed in agriculture, industry, and foreign trade, and an attempt was made at import substitution under the aegis of the state. A later period of free trade and laissez-faire stretched from the 1880s to the 1930s. The government still played a major role in economic development, however, because of its special responsibilities for irrigation. Successive regimes have consistently seen the regulation of the Nile and the development of a network of dams, barrages, canals, and drains as falling in the public domain.

The government's direct involvement with other sectors of the economy is relatively recent. In 1930 a cascading tariff structure thought to be favorable to industry was adopted. During World War II a battery of controls on foreign trade, supplies of necessities, prices, rents, foreign exchange, and the like were introduced because of the emergency. After the war liberalization was never complete. The government continued to fix prices of basic consumer goods, using subsidies in an attempt to keep down the cost of living. Tariff levels were raised in the late 1940s and again in the 1950s to implement specific import-substitution objectives. Yet private enterprises continued to operate in a relatively free environment, deriving benefits from protectionist policies which probably outweighed the cost of, say, the price controls.

---

1. Gamal Abd el-Nasser, The Philosophy of the Revolution (Cairo: Dar Al-Maaref, 1954); see also Panagiotis J. Vatikiotis, The Egyptian Army in Politics (Bloomington: Indiana University Press, 1961), pp. 67-68.

16

PREDOMINANCE OF THE PRIVATE SECTOR, 1952-56

In 1952 the economic role of the state was virtually confined to investment in infrastructure (chiefly in the irrigation system) and social services. The main productive sectors — agriculture and industry, internal and foreign trade, banking, insurance, urban transport, and even a number of utilities, such as electricity and water — were in private hands. It is estimated that the public sector accounted for only 13 percent of the gross domestic product, while the private sector provided the remaining 87 percent.[2]

Rather surprisingly, the 1952 revolution seemed favorable to private enterprise in the initial years. During the first four years of the new regime the government's pronouncements on economic ideology emphasized the importance of the private sector. Official policies were also intended to reassure private enterprise. For example, the government consulted frequently with the Federation of Egyptian Industries and agreed to the federation's demand for lower taxes and higher protection by lowering customs duties on raw materials and capital goods and raising tariffs. Taxes on profits and undistributed dividends were also reduced. The government repeatedly insisted that it would act as the partner of private enterprise and confine itself to heavy, or basic, industry. The rest of the manufacturing sector was explicitly reserved for private enterprise. Government investment continued to be directed largely toward the traditional area of irrigation, drainage, and land reclamation. The main theme of the economic policy debate during this period was not the respective responsibilities of the public and private sectors, but rather the role of foreign investment. The government partially reversed the Egyptianization policy of the former regime by allowing foreign shareholders to hold a majority interest and control in any domestic company.[3]

Perhaps the most significant restraint of the private sector was the agrarian reform of August 1952, which limited individual ownership to a maximum of 200 feddans. The main purpose was not to attack the principle of private ownership — the excess feddans were distributed to landless peasants — but to curtail the political power of the large landowners by weakening their economic base. In fact, the most radical component of the agrarian reform was the introduction of agricultural cooperatives. To obtain inputs or agricultural credit, a farmer had to become a member of a cooperative and

2. Donald C. Mead, Growth and Structural Change in the Egyptian Economy (Homewood, Ill.: Richard D. Irwin, 1967), pp. 272-73.
3. Patrick O'Brien, The Revolution in Egypt's Economic System (London: Oxford University Press, 1966), pp. 71, 72.

abide by its rules concerning crop rotation, output pricing, marketing, and so forth. Since the cooperatives were directed by the government, this was an effective, if indirect, method of control.

In the early days of the revolution there were indications of a new economic orientation, however. Decisions in 1952-54 did not at first seem to attack private enterprise, but merely revealed the government's intention to intervene in the economy to foster important developmental objectives. It was decided to build the Aswan High Dam at about this time, and, though the execution was much delayed, the government engaged immediately in ambitious land reclamation projects. Some partial planning was introduced in 1953 through the creation of the Permanent Council for the Development of National Production, which consisted of representatives of both the government and the private sector. The council studied projects, coordinated the public works program and the state investment budget, and paved the way for government participation as an equity owner in new industries for the first time since the 1860s.

GROWING GOVERNMENT INTERVENTION, 1957-60

The transition from a free, private enterprise system (with the government mainly in charge of law and order and public works) to a planned economy with a dominant public sector took place between 1954 and the early 1960s. The first small step was the government's decision to take an equity stake in two or three new industrial companies established in 1954. The public sector then expanded in 1957 through the nationalization of British and French economic interests and public investment in industry, in 1960 through the nationalization of Bank Misr, and soon after through massive waves of nationalization of other financial and industrial enterprises. Planning became more comprehensive than the limited attempts under the Permanent Council. In 1957 the government launched two sectoral five-year plans, one for agriculture and one for industry, and in 1960 adopted the First Five-Year General Plan for Economic and Social Development (1960-61 to 1964-65).

The second phase of government policy (1957-60) was aptly described by President Nasser as "controlled capitalistic economy."[4] The government moved toward greater intervention in economic activity along four major paths. First, although private sector activity was still encouraged, the 1956 Constitution adumbrated the ideological framework within which such activity was expected to be conducted.

4. Ibid., p. 85.

Second, the Suez war of 1956 led to the sequestration of British and French assets, largely concentrated in banking and insurance. A special state Economic Organization was set up in early 1957 to manage these and other assets in which the government already had a share. This agency thus acquired considerable influence as a vehicle for promoting the government's economic policies. By 1958 the Economic Organization controlled all the specialist banks in Egypt, seven commercial banks which accounted for nearly half of all commercial bank loans, and five insurance companies responsible for 68 percent of all insurance business transacted in Egypt. It is estimated to have been responsible for roughly a third of aggregate output produced by the organized industrial sector, and it employed about 20 percent of the labor force in that sector.[5]

Third, there was a vigorous move to Egyptianize the main arteries of the national economy. All foreign banks, insurance companies, and commercial agencies were required to be converted into domestically owned joint stock companies within five years. The major banks and insurance companies were placed under the control of the Economic Organization.[6]

Fourth, comprehensive economic planning was introduced and pushed through vigorously at the highest levels. In January 1957 a National Planning Committee was set up to prepare a long-term plan for social and economic development; this plan was to come into effect July 1, 1960. In 1958, however, a five-year plan for industry was launched, in which the state was to provide 61 percent of the finance, mainly for heavy industry. The industrial plan required a rapid acceleration in investment from the annual average of LE34 million of gross investment in the previous quinquennium to an annual average of LE45 million of net investment between 1957 and 1961.[7]

In this phase of economic management the government moved away from letting the private sector act as the main vehicle of growth, and state intervention and influence became increasingly important. This was felt most strongly in the area of capital formation. Thus, in 1952 the public sector accounted for about 13 percent of GDP and 28 percent of gross capital formation; by 1959-60, while still accounting for only 18 percent of GDP, the public sector undertook nearly 74 percent of gross investment.[8]

5. Ibid., pp. 95, 90.
6. Ibid., pp. 95-96.
7. Ibid., p. 86.
8. Mead, Growth and Structural Change, pp. 272-73; O'Brien, Revolution in Egypt's Economic System, pp. 100, 107; see also Peter Mansfield, Nasser's Egypt (London: Penguin Books, 1965), p. 136. These figures understate the share of the government in GDP, but even after correcting for this, O'Brien

Although a socialistic ideology was starting to be invoked, most
nationalizations were still ad hoc, in response to political and other
considerations, and were justified on a variety of nonideological
grounds.[9]

Perhaps the biggest indicator of the change in the government attitude toward the private sector was the introduction of comprehensive economic planning. The restrictions placed on private economic
activity appear to be closely related to successive efforts to make
the planning process more comprehensive. Although the biggest
waves of nationalization did not occur until 1961, even during the
late 1950s the government began to feel that a high rate of planned
investment could not be attained with a predominantly private sector economy. Moreover, as O'Brien points out, the introduction
of a comprehensive five-year plan in 1960 compelled the policymakers to become much more specific about the kind of economic system
they wished to create, and it showed up the incompatibilities between
central planning and private enterprise.[10]

CENTRAL PLANNING, 1961-73

The first harbinger of the government's new direction in economic policy came on February 13, 1960, when Bank Misr and the
National Bank were taken into public ownership. The step was
significant because, whereas previous nationalizations had been
of foreign firms, these banks were owned mainly by Egyptian
nationals. The National Bank, although privately owned, performed
all the normal functions of a central bank; for example, it had a
monopoly of the note issue, it was the lender of last resort, and it
had control of the bank rate. Bank Misr was not only the largest
commercial bank left in the private sector, but also a most important holding company, whose twenty-nine affiliated companies accounted, according to some estimates, for 20 percent of Egypt's
industrial output, including half of all textile production. The precise reasons for the nationalization are not entirely clear, but apparently differences had arisen between the government and the Bank
Misr group. At issue were the targets allocated to Misr companies
under the first industrial plan — the group was made responsible for

(pp. 107-08) concludes that at least two-thirds of GDP took place outside the
government's contribution. (To anticipate the story a little: in 1976, 50 percent
of GDP originated in the public sector, while another large part — agriculture —
was subject to extensive government control.)

9. See Galal Amin, "The Egyptian Economy and the Revolution," in Panagiotis
J. Vatikiotis, ed., Egypt since the Revolution (New York: Praeger, 1968), p. 41.

10. O'Brien, Revolution in Egypt's Economic System, p. 103.

nearly half of all activity undertaken by private enterprises — and the investment policy of the group.[11] No ideological reason was explicitly advanced by the authorities.

The biggest waves of nationalization occurred in June and July 1961 in what has come to be called in Egypt the "Socialist Revolution." First, the Alexandria cotton futures market was closed and the state Cotton Authority given the exclusive right to purchase cotton; subsequent laws Egyptianized all companies dealing with the cotton trade and brought all firms engaged in external trade under state control. Second, in the most massive of the nationalization measures, the remaining banks and insurance companies were taken over, as were 44 companies in basic industries (such as cement, electricity, and copper); half the capital of 86 firms, mainly in commerce and light manufacturing, was expropriated; and the shareholders of another 147 firms were dispossessed of a large part of their assets by a law that limited individual holdings to a market value of LE10,000 — all shares in excess of that amount passed into public ownership. The nominal capital of the companies affected by the nationalization laws of 1961 was put at LE258 million, about two-thirds the total share capital of companies then registered in Egypt.[12] Third, after the secession of Syria from the United Arab Republic, in October the property of 167 wealthy Egyptians was sequestrated for political reasons, and in November that of about 500 others.

After the 1961 nationalizations, the private sector was relegated to a relatively minor role. Private property was not abolished, but the opportunities for private economic activity and decisionmaking, especially in investment and production, were severely circumscribed. The takeovers were later justified as part of the "Arab Socialism" that was a cardinal element of the National Charter presented to the National Congress of the Popular Powers by President Nasser in May 1962. This document described the rationale for the economic system in some detail.[13]

According to the Charter, economic development could not be left to individual efforts motivated by private profit, but must be based on socialism:

11. The Misr group wanted to invest largely in the textile industry, while the government wanted it to invest elsewhere. See Bent Hansen and Girgis Marzouk, Development and Economic Policy in the UAR (Egypt) (Amsterdam: North-Holland, 1965), p. 171. See also O'Brien, Revolution in Egypt's Economic System, pp. 92-93, 125; Amin, "The Egyptian Economy," p. 41.

12. O'Brien, Revolution in Egypt's Economic System, pp. 130-31, 153.

13. United Arab Republic, The Charter (Cairo: Information Department, n.d), especially pp. 49-74. For a summary of the economic sections, see O'Brien, Revolution in Egypt's Economic System, pp. 132-36; and Mansfield, Nasser's Egypt, pp. 130-32.

- The economic infrastructure should be publicly owned, as should the majority of heavy and medium industries and mining.
- Banks and insurance companies should be only in the public sector.
- The entire import trade should be in the public sector, as should three-quarters of the export trade; the private sector could be responsible for the rest.
- The ownership and control of internal trade could be in the private sector, but the public sector should take charge of at least one-quarter of internal trade over the following eight years.
- Apart from internal trade, the sphere of private ownership and control was defined as land, buildings, construction, and light industry. The application of land reforms, rent control legislation, and taxation measures would help to prevent any "exploitation."
- The Charter also spelled out the "basic rights" of citizens to social welfare that the state would provide. The framework included medical care, education, employment, minimum wages, and insurance benefits in old age and sickness.

Thus, in the decade after assuming power, the Egyptian government moved through successive stages, from encouragement of the private sector, to gradually increased restrictions and controls, and finally massive nationalizations and state intervention throughout the economy. Although this was later justified as "Arab Socialism," the ideological basis was rather tenuous in the earlier instances. The process was frequently hesitant and often ad hoc; in the words of Hansen and Marzouk, much of it "just happened."[14] The National Charter did, however, fix the main lines of economic structure and policy direction until the next major turning, the el-Infitah (the "opening up" or open-door policy) of President Sadat.

In the First Five-Year General Plan, which was in a sense the first and the last of its nature to be implemented, the public sector accounted for some 90 percent of total (monetized) investment throughout the 1960s and until 1973. This proportion has not declined very significantly since the liberalization measures of 1974. Annual investment programs have been the main planning instrument since 1965.[15] The public sector owns most of modern industry; all banks, insurance companies, and financial intermediaries;[16] and a

14. Hansen and Marzouk, Economic Policy in the UAR, p. 169.
15. They include projects which had begun to be implemented earlier and are not yet completed, as well as new projects.
16. Other than the foreign banks that have established branches or representative offices in Cairo since 1974.

large proportion of construction firms, modern transport, and whole-sale trade. Despite liberalization, the bulk of foreign trade operations has remained in the public sector. In agriculture, old land is privately owned within the ceilings defined by the agrarian reform laws, but the new land is largely in public ownership. The state has considerable influence in agriculture, not only because of its traditional responsibilities for the hydraulic system, but also because of the cooperative system and the control it exercises in selling inputs and buying the major crops. In the 1960s the private sector also retained ownership of both rural and urban dwellings, small-scale industry, most of the retail trade, certain transport, construction, and manufacturing activities (leather, wood, printing), and part of wholesale trade. In petroleum, the state has been for some time in partnership with foreign oil companies. Liberalization is beginning to encourage entrepreneurial talent in some industries, but its main impact has been in the promotion of a service sector related to tourism, consultancies, real estate, foreign investment, and to some extent foreign trade.

An important feature of the economic system is an extensive system of cost and price controls. Price control originated during World War II but covered few commodities; it became extensive in the 1960s. Since then price administration has affected all the major sectors of the economy, such as agriculture, housing, and industry. Allocative efficiency suffers considerably in such a system. The stated objectives of price administration were to improve income distribution and resource mobilization. But these goals are sometimes contradictory. Price controls and subsidies are used to check possible rises in the cost of living, but price administration is also used as a form of excise on certain necessities to raise revenues for the Treasury. In the industrial public sector, prices are usually calculated on a cost-plus basis, but they are varied for many reasons — to increase revenues, clear stocks, or depress demand. Price administration has important implications for both the budget and the balance of payments. The ramifications of the price system remain complex and widespread and may not be amenable to quick attempts at liberalization.

The welfare-oriented policies of the first two decades had two broad aims: greater equity in the distribution of income and wealth, and increased consumption of goods and services. The principal measure for redistributing wealth was the land reform law of September 1952.[17] Just before the land reform, about 2,000 owners (out

17. President Sadat later described the land reform as the measure which, more than any other, gave the Free Officers' movement the character of a genuine revolution rather than a mere coup d' etat. See Anwar el-Sadat, In Search of Identity (New York: Harper and Row, 1978), p. 130.

of a total of about 2.8 million) held about 20 percent of the land; at
the other end of the spectrum, more than 2.6 million owners (about
94 percent of the total) held about 36 percent of the land. In 1965,
at the highest end of the scale, about 4,000 owners (out of 3.2 million) held about 7 percent of the land, while at the lowest end about
3 million (about 95 percent of the total) held 57 percent of the land.

The land reform achieved a number of results. The average size
of small properties increased from 0.8 to 1.2 feddans in 1965; the
very large estates (which had covered about 20 percent of the area
in 1952) disappeared; and the medium-size landowners retained their
share of the cultivated area. As Mabro points out, the reform did
not aim to satisfy the land hunger of all tenants and landless workers — indeed, given the scarcity of land, such an aim would not have
been practicable. Rather, "the Egyptian land reform sought limited
improvements in the distribution of wealth, and benefitted the upper
section of the low-income group."[18]

The other major factor in improving the distribution of wealth
was the nationalization of the large industrial enterprises. Nationalization did not, in itself, increase the wealth of the poorer groups,
because the measures were "essentially privative rather than distributive,"[19] but it did reduce the concentration at the upper end of
the spectrum, opened up opportunities for promotion, and allowed
wider participation by those who had hitherto been excluded. Moreover, nationalization enabled the government to legislate substantial
benefits to workers and to police the legislation.

Other socialist reforms of the government were in labor legislation, education, health, and employment. The minimum wage in
industry was raised from LE0.125 a day to LE0.250 in 1953, but it
was seriously enforced only from the early 1960s; until then real
wages were raised mainly by increasing fringe benefits. Strikes
were made illegal, but labor conditions were improved by an insurance scheme for industrial workers financed by contributions from
the employer, profit-sharing schemes whereby 25 percent of the net
profit was distributed among the workers and employees, increased
sickness leave and higher sick pay, and effective constraints on the
employer's ability to dismiss workers.

Public education expanded rapidly after the revolution. Government expenditure on education rose from about 3 percent of GDP in
1952-53 to about 5 percent in 1969-70, despite the increased diversion of resources to defense following the 1967 war. Public investment in education increased from approximately 2 percent of total
investment in 1952-53 to about 6 percent twenty years later. With

18. Robert Mabro, The Egyptian Economy, 1952-72 (Oxford: Clarendon Press,
1974), p. 222.
19. Ibid.

these increased expenditures the number of students rose sharply: twenty years after the revolution, the number of primary and preparatory students had tripled, secondary students had increased by about 165 percent, and the number of university students had more than quadrupled. (The population increase during this period was about 62 percent.) This expansion, however, was not without its cost. The quality of education appears to have deteriorated, with both pupil-teacher and pupil-classroom ratios increasing significantly.

Expenditures on health rose from about 0.5 percent of GDP in 1952-53 to about 1.9 percent in 1975. The number of hospital beds more than doubled, from a little less than 36,000 in 1952 to about 77,000 in 1975; the ratio of beds to a thousand of the population thus increased from about 1.7 to nearly 2.1 over the period. There were also steady rises in the availability of medicine at subsidized prices and in the number of pharmacies and public health centers, although health services continued to be severely imbalanced in favor of urban over rural areas.

Finally, the rate of economic growth coupled with the distributive policies permitted the per capita consumption of the main staples to increase. Thus, the per capita consumption of calories increased from about 2,300 a day in 1952 to nearly 2,600 twenty years later; that of protein from 35 to 45 grams a day; and of cotton textiles from 2 to 3 kilograms a year.

EL-INFITAH (THE OPENING): AFTER 1973

Since the war of October 1973 Egypt has had three main policy objectives: defense preparedness, reconstruction and economic development, and the preservation of the social welfare framework. After the war the political and economic milieu — within Egypt, in the region, and internationally — had changed dramatically, and to take advantage of the new environment, a fresh economic strategy needed to be articulated. This is what President Sadat did in his October Working Paper.[20]

This document was presented to the People's Assembly in April 1974 and approved by a national referendum in May. It laid out a comprehensive outline for a major redirection of both political and economic policies. The arguments for a change in economic strategy and the new direction that it outlined were essentially as follows:

20. President Anwar el-Sadat, The October Working Paper (Cairo: Arab Republic of Egypt, Ministry of Information, May 1974).

- The war of October 1973 had unified all sections of Egypt's society. This unity must be harnessed for the "construction battle" to modernize Egyptian society by the year 2000.
- The basic element in the modernization process was an acceleration of economic growth. This would require changes in the roles of the different sectors. Moreover, since Egypt would require considerable financial and technological assistance from abroad, it would have to adopt an "outward-looking" economic policy.
- The public sector had played a crucial role in Egypt's past development, but experience had revealed some shortcomings. In particular, the sector suffered from an excess of bureaucracy, and some of the activities that had been "annexed" were not compatible with the public sector's mission and should have been left to the private sector. In the final analysis, however, the public sector had been effective, especially in carrying out major projects, increasing production, and implementing Egypt's policy of full employment and stabilized prices. Reorientation was required to rid the sector of obstructions and increase its efficiency. In the future, the public sector would concentrate on carrying out the development plan (it was the only sector directly committed by the plan), undertaking basic projects that other sectors would not or could not take up, and providing essential services to private and foreign investment.
- "Contradictory policies" in the past had neutralized the private sector as a productive agent. It was now time to eliminate those conditions and to provide stability and encouragement to the private sector to maximize production.
- Although the main burden of development would fall on its own shoulders, Egypt would still require a great deal of foreign resources. Changing world conditions made it extremely likely that, given a proper response, the necessary amounts of external capital would be forthcoming. The Arab world would wish to invest a part of its vastly increased financial resources in Egypt because of cultural and historical links and because Egypt would provide a sound economic haven. The status of Egypt after the October war would induce other countries to take its goals and efforts seriously and to want to invest in it. The Egyptian response should be to grasp these new opportunities — as the October Paper put it, "our national responsibility does not permit us to miss such an opportunity." To avail itself of this, Egypt was prepared to adopt an outward-looking policy by providing foreign investors with all the necessary legislative guarantees.
- The development effort could not be a haphazard affair, but must take place in a planned framework. The priorities set

for the plan emphasized a modernized industry, an intensive,
high-value agriculture, oil and energy development, and
tourism.

- The October Paper stressed that social goals would not be
neglected and that "economic development cannot proceed
soundly forth unless accompanied by a social development at
compatible rates." As part of a better balanced social development, there would be more equitable growth between the
regions, thereby reducing the disparities that had developed
between the capital and the provinces.

Policies enacted in the years following the October Working
Paper were largely inspired by its principles and attempted to
implement them.   The economy faced difficult circumstances in
the external sector, however, especially in 1974.   The prices
of foodstuffs and of some other essential commodities that dominate Egypt's import bill rose very sharply and created significant imbalances in both the trade accounts and the government budget.   The external debt became a much heavier burden, and the
disbursements from new aid commitments were affected by familiar
lags.   In short, the liberalization policies were introduced at a time
of considerable difficulties, and their success in transforming the
economic system must be assessed in the framework of these circumstances.   The period since 1973 can be regarded as representing the beginning of a fairly long transition, which may well take a
decade to complete.

3
Principal Changes in the Economy since 1952

Egypt's economic performance has been uneven because of the magnitude of the developmental problems, the impact of external factors such as wars, world recession, and imported inflation, and because of defects in the policies adopted to meet developmental challenges and external crises. The problems that Egypt faces in the immediate future are in part those of the past, some seemingly perennial, some transitory and amenable to quick solution. But Egypt has considerable assets. It enjoys a privileged place in the Middle East; it can rely on significant financial contributions from major aid donors; it is aware of the urgent need to reform the economic setup and to correct defective policies; it possesses resources that are in short supply in neighboring countries — mainly, an agriculture with potential for a qualitative transformation and a skilled labor force which could contribute directly to production and provide workers' remittances to help the balance of payments. In the coming years, new sources of wealth (petroleum, phosphates, and perhaps other minerals) are likely to contribute significantly to income growth. These are the constraints and opportunities that will affect Egypt's economic performance.

POPULATION AND MIGRATION

The demographic characteristics of Egypt are typical of most developing countries. The natural rate of population growth rose substantially in the 1940s and 1950s, reaching an average of 2.3 percent a year and a peak of 2.5 percent in the early 1960s; but it declined slowly until about the mid-1970s and then began again to increase. Typically, the population explosion was the result of a sudden fall in the deathrate unmatched by a decline in birthrates. The crude birthrate, which has been falling steadily from 42.3 per thousand in 1964 to 34.4 per thousand in 1972, has still a long way to go.[1] Mortality, now at about 12 per thousand, is fairly high — especially infant mortality, which is as high as 115 or 120 per thousand. Egypt is thus in transition from a situation of high birth- and death-rates to a stage where both these rates tend to be low.

Movements of population between rural areas and towns and within both rural and urban sectors have been of economic and demographic significance for the past thirty or forty years. The share of urban population increased from some 32.6 percent in 1947 to 44 percent in 1976. The rate of urban growth at present is close to 3.0 percent, while the rate of natural increase is about 2.5 percent The factors influencing this migration are well understood. The expansion of employment in Egyptian agriculture is constrained by both the supply of land and the labor-intensive nature of the technology already in use. There is little scope for creating employment by increasing either the cultivated area or the labor intensity of cultivation. The spread of education also spurs migration, since the countryside offers neither the range of jobs nor the amenities to which the educated aspire. Rural-to-urban migration is often considered a major problem for developing countries because it puts pressure on urban infrastructure and affects urban unemployment. These, however, are only symptoms of a more fundamental economic and demographic problem that concerns the whole country, rather than the urban areas exclusively — the problem of resources which are insufficient to provide a livelihood for the population.

The emigration of Egyptians abroad is also of some demographic importance, particularly for the quality of the labor force. The brain drain to the West of a few professionals — medical doctors, engineers, scientists, and economists — began in the early 1960s. Emigration to Arab countries, especially oil-exporting countries, has involved a broader range of professions and skills — teachers, construction workers, and skilled artisans as well as engineers and doctors. But its quantitative significance seems to have increased in two jumps, first in the late 1960s when Libya exerted a strong pull and then, after 1973, when Saudi Arabia, Iraq, and all the Gulf countries began to absorb large numbers of migrant workers. The consequence of large-scale migration for Egypt are twofold. A positive contribution is made to the balance of payments through foreign exchange remittances.[2] But since migration is selective and tends to remove from the domestic labor force some of the best elements across the full range of professions and skills, a cost is

1. After 1973 there was a slight increase in the birthrate.

2. Remittances in 1978 were US$1,761 million, including US$839 million of imports under the "own exchange" scheme, that is, goods sent to Egypt that are financed largely from the earnings of Egyptians working abroad.

incurred. Migration tends to aggravate shortages of skills that are
scarce — from the good manager to the experienced carpenter or
welder — and does little to alleviate unemployment or underemployment of those who are genuinely in excess supply.

Some of the structural and qualitative aspects of Egypt's population are reminiscent of other developing countries. The age structure has a broad base with some 40 percent of the population aged
less than fifteen years in 1970. The life expectancy at birth is lower
than in industrialized nations (51.6 years for males and 53.8 years
for females in the population census of 1960).[3] Endemic parasitic
diseases — bilharzia and anklostoma — are still prevalent in rural
areas and may have increased since the extension of perennial irrigation in Upper Egypt. Finally, despite the remarkable expansion
of education after World War II, especially in the 1950s and early
1960s, much remains to be done to eradicate illiteracy.

INDICATORS OF ECONOMIC GROWTH

There are problems with the estimates of GDP at factor cost
and their subaggregates (see Statistical Appendix tables 7 and 8).
First, the time series are not very consistent. In the course of
time the methods of estimating the contribution to GDP by certain
sectors, the coverage, and definitions have changed, but no retro-
active adjustment has been made to estimates of previous years;
an example is the treatment of the housing component of the GDP
series after 1967-68. Second, it seems that the contribution of certain sectors (especially construction and services) is often understated because of incomplete coverage or (in the case of housing
before 1967-68) because of defective valuation of imputed services.
The contribution of others, notably manufacturing, may be overstated. Third, there are well-known problems relating to the methods used to obtain estimates for manufacturing (insufficient data on
the small-industries sector) and agriculture (undervaluation of both
inputs and of nonmarketed output). In addition, the constant price
series (see Statistical Appendix table 8) has major shortcomings
owing to a lack of adequate price adjustment indexes.

"Current price estimates of GDP should always be understood to
mean current official prices."[4] This warning must be kept in mind
because it explains to some extent why the GDP implicit deflator
appears to be so modest. Price administration has ensured a large
measure of stability in official prices. Were the current price GDP

---

3. These details from the 1976 census are not yet published.
4. Bent Hansen, "Planning and Economic Growth in the UAR (Egypt), 1960-65,"
in Panagiotis J. Vatikiotis, ed., Egypt since the Revolution (London: Allen and
Unwin, 1968), p. 28.

TABLE 3-1. GDP AT CURRENT AND
CONSTANT MARKET PRICES, 1950-78
(millions of Egyptian pounds)

Year	Current prices	Growth rate (percent)	Constant 1965 prices	Annual growth rate (percent)
1950	929.9	—	1,228.7	—
1955	1,056.0	2.6	1,344.1	1.8
1960	1,443.2	4.3[a]	1,695.0	3.3[a]
1965	2,340.1	8.3[b]	2,340.1	5.7[b]
1966	2,473.8	5.7	2,353.5	0.6
1970	3,058.4	7.9	2,682.8	6.3
1973	3,644.6	7.5	2,925.0	2.8
1975	4,861.0	15.8	3,447.0	8.9
1976	5,828.0	19.9	3,770.0	9.4
1977	7,551.0	29.6	4,147.0	10.0
1978	8,602.0	13.9	4,624.0	11.5

a. Average annual growth rate for 1950-60.
b. Average annual growth rate for 1955-65.

Source: Statistical Appendix table 6.

to be estimated at black market prices or at prices adjusted for certain manifestations of scarcity — such as queues and rationing — higher absolute figures would be obtained.

There were significant turning points in the movements in real GDP from 1950 to 1975 (see table 3-1). A study by Hansen and Mead suggests stagnation at the beginning of the period with high rates of growth (5 percent a year and over) starting in 1957 or 1958.[5] According to both the Hansen-Mead and the official estimates, annual increases in real GDP continued to remain significant every year (except 1961-62) until 1965, when a peak seems to have been reached. The rate of growth then began to decline until it reached a negative value in 1967. This was followed by a short-lived recovery, with small GDP increases in 1972 and 1973. The performance from 1974 onward stands in sharp contrast to the sluggish behavior of the preceding decade.

SECTORAL DEVELOPMENTS

The different sectors in the economy vary greatly in their resource endowments and in the degree to which they have been affected by circumstances and policy actions. It is therefore not surprising

5. Bent Hansen and Donald Mead, "The National Income of the UAR (Egypt), 1939-62," in Simon Goldberg and Phyllis Deane, eds., Studies in Short-Term National Accounts and Long-Term Economic Growth, Income and Wealth Series 11 (London: Bowes and Bowes, 1965), p. 255.

TABLE 3-2. STRUCTURE AND GROWTH OF GDP BY SECTOR, 1955-56 TO 1978
(percent)

Sector	Share of GDP at constant prices					Average annual growth rate at constant prices				
	1955-56	1961	1970	1976	1978	1955-56 to 1960-61	1960-61 to 1965-66	1966-71	1971-75	1975-78
Agriculture	34	32	28	28	25	3.5	3.7	1.6	2.0	2.7
Manufacturing, petroleum, mining	18	20	21	22	24	8.0	6.6	4.7	4.2	12.7
Electricity	...	1	2	2	2	...	14.0	15.3	15.0	9.4
Construction	2	3	5	5	5	9.3	16.6	3.0	2.0	8.7
Transport and communication	6	7	5	8	9	9.4	11.3	-6.0	13.9	34.0
Trade and finance	11	10	9	13	13	4.0	2.2	3.4	9.0	13.9
Housing	7	6	5	2	2	2.6	1.5	2.1	2.0	4.7
Other services	22	21	25	20	20	4.0	7.6	5.6	7.3	3.0
Total (average)	100	100	100	100	100	(5.3)	(6.1)	(2.9)	(5.5)	(8.6)

... Zero or negligible.
Note: 1955-70 at 1964-65 prices; 1970-75 at 1970 prices; 1975-78 at 1975 prices.
Source: Statistical Appendix table 8.

32

that economic growth has proceeded as unevenly across sectors as
it has over time (see table 3-2). In the following sections are described the salient aspects of the major economic sectors and their
contribution to growth from 1950 to 1978.

Agriculture

Egypt's main resource is the rich alluvial soil of the valley and
Delta, which enabled one of the world's oldest agrarian societies to
emerge and flourish. The twin characteristics of the arable land
are fertility and limited supply. A wide range of crops can be, and
indeed are, cultivated. The yields are usually high, but there is
scope for still higher returns through greater use of improved inputs and better cultivation techniques. The qualities of the soil and
the climate enable multicropping whenever water is available. The
average cropping intensity in Egypt is close to 1.8 crops a year.
That figure is naturally sensitive to the crop pattern — cotton and
sugarcane, for example, have longer growing periods than do cereals or vegetables — and to the nature of the irrigation system. Beyond a certain limit the cultivated area cannot be extended without
a sudden and sharp rise in reclamation costs. That limit has been
one of the major resource constraints on the economic development
of the country in the past sixty or seventy years.

The agricultural development of Egypt since the 1920s is related
to these characteristics of the land endowment. First, new crops
were introduced, and second, cultivation was expanded at the extensive margin (through costly reclamation projects) and then at the
intensive margin (through increased cropping intensity, which is
detrimental to soil fertility). The favorable physical conditions of
soil and climate facilitated the introduction of a variety of crops and
rewarded innovation. The most notable innovation, of course, was
long-staple cotton discovered by Jumel in 1820 and developed by
Muhammad Ali, a ruler with great entrepreneurial talent. But many
other field crops, fruit trees, and vegetables were introduced at
different times, all contributing to growth through the shift from
low-value to high-value crops. The second dimension of agricultural development was expansion. The extensive margin was expanded
in the valley and Delta through simple reclamation works and a network of canals. By the end of the nineteenth century all the useful
area of the Nile basin was under cultivation, which left for further
reclamation the salty marshes in the north and land at the edge of
the valley in Upper Egypt and in some pockets in the Delta.

The British, who occupied Egypt in 1882, turned their attention
toward the end of the nineteenth century to the intensive margin.
Perennial irrigation makes multicropping possible, but it depends
in turn on the regulation of the Nile flow. Part of the flood water
must be made available for crops grown during the summer season

when the Nile is low. The old Aswan Dam was built in 1902, and its height raised in the 1910s and again in the 1930s, for precisely that purpose. Thanks to the reservoir at Aswan and the complementary infrastructure of regulators and canals, perennial irrigation and multicropping was extended to most of Lower and Middle Egypt. During the six decades or so between the construction of the Aswan Dam and that of the Aswan High Dam in the 1960s, expansion at both the extensive and the intensive margin continued but at a slow and irregular pace.

Construction of the High Dam started in 1960, power generation commenced in 1968; the dam was completed in 1970 and commissioned in January 1971. It was expected to add 1.2 million feddans to the cultivated area; to add 850,000 feddans to the cropped area by converting Upper Egypt from basin to perennial irrigation; to increase net agricultural output by changing cropping patterns; and to provide flood protection, additional electric power, and other advantages, such as the establishment of a fishery industry on Lake Nasser.[6] Not all these expected benefits are likely to be realized in their entirety, although substantial gains have been made. For example, it is estimated that about 650,000 feddans out of the 805,000 reclaimed between 1960 and 1970 are related to the dam; the conversion from basin to perennial irrigation of 850,000 feddans has virtually been completed, but for a variety of reasons only about 490,000 feddans can be multicropped. Other significant contributions of the dam are that it reallocated water in favor of high-value summer crops such as rice and maize and protected Egypt in the early 1970s from the potentially disastrous effects of a severe drought. Further advantages can be realized only over many years and will require additional investment.

Long-staple cotton has historically been the chief catalyst of growth in the Egyptian economy.[7] Introduced in 1820, cotton became significant during the American Civil War (1861-64). The volume of cotton exports rose in steps in the early 1870s, again in the late 1880s, and by significant amounts in 1890 to 1910, the period in Egypt's economic history that corresponded most closely to the theoretical model of export-led growth. Cotton never occupied in agricultural production the same dominant place it has in exports. Agricultural output is and has always been diversified, including cereals for human consumption, clover for livestock, and a variety of other products. Cotton acreage rarely exceeded 2 million feddans, less than 40 percent of the cultivated area and between 20 and 25 percent of the cropped area. Today cotton acreage has shrunk to less

6. An excellent short discussion of the issues related to the Aswan High Dam is in Robert Mabro, The Egyptian Economy, 1952-72 (Oxford: Clarendon Press, 1974), pp. 83-106.

7. For a detailed account, see E. R. J. Owen, Cotton and the Egyptian Economy 1820-1914 (Oxford: Clarendon Press, 1969).

than 1.5 million feddans, and other agricultural products — onions, rice, oranges, vegetables — have acquired a share of the export basket.

Between 1952 and 1978 agriculture was a slow-growing sector with average rates of 3.5 percent in the 1950s and of 2.5 to 3.7 percent in the 1960s and the first half of the 1970s. Agricultural production may have expanded at a slightly higher rate, though the evidence from various sources is contradictory. In developing agriculture, gross output tends to expand at a higher rate than value added because the share of material inputs in output generally rises over time. Agricultural growth may thus have barely kept up with population growth. Such a situation, when incomes are rising and income elasticities of demand are positive, implies growing imbalances between the domestic supply of and demand for food and other agricultural products. Employment in agriculture may have been rising at about 1 percent a year over the period, which suggests a rate of productivity growth of between 1.0 and 1.5 percent a year. The disturbing feature, however, is a marked decline in the average rate of agricultural growth between the 1950s and the next decade.

Industry

Egypt has natural resources outside agriculture, but their contribution to the economy has not yet been very significant. This situation will change because of the rapid development of petroleum resources and the increase in petroleum prices, the discovery of natural gas reserves in the late 1960s which now provide a valuable input to the fertilizer industry, and the discovery of significant quantities of phosphate at Abu Tartour. Crude petroleum production may approach 600,000 barrels a day by 1980 and could be a little higher a couple of years later. Although the quality of the Abu Tartour deposits is somewhat uncertain, there is serious hope that phosphates will follow petroleum as a major earner of foreign exchange in the 1980s. Egypt's other mineral resources include limestone, used in both the cement and the fertilizer industries, and iron ore for the expanding basic metal industry. There are problems, however, with the Bahariya ore, and its impurities are now being studied so that the operations of the Helwan Iron and Steel plant can be improved.

The structure of the Egyptian economy is characterized by the large but declining share of agriculture, the growing share of the industrial sectors (manufacturing, mining, and electricity), and the predominant place occupied by tertiary (service) activities. In 1952 agriculture accounted for about 35 percent of GDP at factor costs, industry for 15 percent, construction for less than 3 percent, and the tertiary sector for some 47 percent. In 1978 the respective shares were 29 percent (agriculture), 24 percent (industry), 4 percent (construction), and 43 percent (tertiary). A part of the structural shift toward industry and away from agriculture is actually a statistical illusion — the pattern of relative prices created by the system of protection overstates the contribution of industry and undervalues that of agriculture, compared with a valuation at international prices. As in most developing countries, the share of agriculture in employment is much larger than its share in GDP, while that of industry is much lower. In 1978 agriculture provided employment to 41 percent of the civilian labor force and industry gave employment to only 18 percent.

Although industry has grown faster than agriculture in recent decades, this does not necessarily signify that manufacturing has been the leading sector in recent development. The expansion of Egyptian industry is the result of protectionist policies pursued in a variety of ways under successive economic systems since 1930. Large segments of Egyptian industry still cannot compete in world markets. Some of it would not fare well in the domestic market should protection be removed. Further, industrialization in Egypt does not seem to have imparted any sustained momentum to sectors other than the services. There is considerable validity in the view that "the kind of industrialization via import substitution employed in Egypt has contributed positively to industrial output and employment expansion, but negatively to resource allocation and the growth of manufactured exports."[8]

There are strong backward linkages with agriculture because textiles and food processing make up a large proportion of industry. But industry does not appear to have stimulated major new demands from the agricultural sector. It simply diverted output away from direct exports (for example, cotton) or direct consumption (foodstuffs) into a different use, namely, the domestic manufacture of textiles and processed food. Industry supplies agriculture with fertilizers and little else, with import substitution the dominant theme. Egyptian industry has so far not attempted to contribute more directly to productivity growth in agriculture by developing inputs and implements adapted to local conditions. Although industry has helped to train a skilled labor force, its main contribution has been direct increases in national income and indirect increases in employment, especially in construction, transport, trade, banking, and government.

Between 1952 and 1978 industry tended to grow faster than agriculture, a natural outcome of development strategies consistently pursued since World War II. The annual rate of growth of manufacturing and mining was about 8 percent in 1955-56 to 1960-61. This is to be compared with 6.6 percent between 1960-61 and 1965-66, 4.7 percent between 1965-66 and 1970-71, 4.2 percent in 1971-75,

8. Maurice Girgis, Industrialization and Trade Patterns in Egypt (Tubingen: J. C. B. Mohr [Paul Siebeck], 1977), p. 1.

and 12.7 percent in 1975-78. The period of fast industrial growth
stretched in fact from 1955-56 to 1964-65 with an average annual
rate of around 7.3 percent. Industrial growth began to slow down
after 1965-66 with an annual rate of 0.7 percent in 1966-67 and -4.7
percent in 1967-68. Whether industry pulled down the rate of GDP
growth (which declined in a similar way, albeit less dramatically,
in these years) or whether industry suffered together with other
sectors from the adverse impact of external variables is a matter
of some dispute. There were problems of performance within industry, arising in part from the disruptive effects of nationalizations,
the employment drive, and state interference with foreign trade.
But the economy as a whole also had problems relating to the management of large balance of payments deficits and to the delayed effect on the labor market of the population explosion of the 1940s.

Industrial growth picked up in 1968-69 after emerging from the
trough of 1967-68. Annual rates of increase were as follows:

Year	Percent
1968-69	9.8
1969-70	6.4
1970-71	10.7
1971-72	1.6
1973	-0.4
1974	3.8
1975	11.9
1976	14.0
1977	13.7
1978	12.1

The recovery from 1968-69 to 1970-71 was of short duration, and
between 1970 and 1974 the growth of industry was as slow as in
1964-65 to 1967-68. Average rates of growth for 1966-67 to 1976
are raised by the inclusion of 1975 and 1976. In those two years
foreign aid reactivated excess capacity and brought rapid increases
in petroleum production so that industrial output increased significantly. It is too early to judge whether the achievements of the manufacturing component in these years are sustainable. There is
marked contrast between the growth performance of manufacturing
between 1956-57 and 1963-64 and the following ten years.[9] If the
growth of industrial output had to be correlated with a single variable, it would almost inevitably be identified as the availability of
foreign exchange. In fact, several factors influence output growth,
and the full story must take them all into account (see chapters 11
and 12).

9. Unfortunately, the data for the industrial sector include petroleum production
(including crude oil).

Services

The structure of the Egyptian economy cannot be understood without reference to the role of services. The tertiary sector grew at a slightly slower rate than GDP between 1956 and 1965 and then at a faster rate after 1965. The rate of growth of employment in the services since 1960 has been markedly faster (3.0 percent a year) than in the whole economy (1.5 percent). Much of that growth reflects in part natural adjustments and in part the effects of policy responses to the population and employment problems. In Egypt an informal urban sector has been expanding because agriculture fails to absorb new entrants to the labor force. But though the informal sector is a haven for certain categories of rural migrants and for many groups of urban dwellers, it does not provide attractive opportunities for the growing number of educated in search of jobs.

To avoid massive unemployment of the educated, the government stepped in early in the 1960s with a policy commonly referred to as the "employment drive." In principle, the government guaranteed every university student a job on graduation. In practice, the gates were opened in government administration and in the organizations and companies of the public sector for other than university graduates, such as secondary school leavers and people with lesser qualifications. As a result of that policy, the share of public consumption in national expenditure increased significantly at a time when the defense budget was also expanding because of the external situation. Such a policy has adverse effects on both the balance of payments (which, especially in Egypt, tends to feel the repercussions of budgetary deficits) and economic growth (which suffers from a fall in the investment ratio that tends to accompany the rise in the share of public consumption). The further danger is that the employment guarantee will increase the demand for education, and the increased supply of educated people will in turn force the government to expand the number of redundant jobs in the public sector. Part of the additional government workers are employed in providing education, health, and social services and hence contribute to the formation of human capital.

The services were a slow-growing sector until radical changes transformed the nature of the economic system in the early 1960s, and the rapid growth of the services sector then overshadowed that of industry. In a planned economy with a very large public sector, and in which social welfare objectives dominate policymaking, the service sector is bound to grow fast. Moreover, part of the recent growth in Egypt is attributable to the rapid increase in military capabilities after the 1967 war. An interesting aspect of the problem is that the expansion of services has meant growth in employment rather than output.

Some Smaller Economic Sectors

Movements in the output index of construction reveal movements in investment. Value added at constant prices in construction has been growing at a fairly fast rate throughout the period — 9.3 percent between 1955-56 and 1960-61 at 1964-65 prices and 16.6 percent between 1960-61 and 1965-66. The official figures suggest growth of only 3 percent between 1965-66 and 1970-71, followed by an annual average increase of about 12 percent between 1970-71 and 1978.

The figures for the construction sector seem to exaggerate the amplitude of movements in the gross value added at different constant prices. It is certain that the sector expanded very fast in the first half of the 1960s because of the construction of the High Dam and the projects of the first plan. But all other indicators suggest that this pace was not maintained; in fact, output in construction declined almost continually between 1963-64 and 1967-68. The existence of a short recovery in 1968-69 and 1969-70 is borne out by the data on construction as it is for industry and the whole of GDP. But it is also evident that after this very short recovery, investment activity in real terms declined until 1974 because resources were being diverted to military construction along the Suez Canal front and elsewhere.

The growth behavior of the transport sector is dominated by the Suez Canal. Expansion of traffic through the canal meant very high rates of growth: 7.1 percent (1952-53 to 1959-60) and 11.3 percent (1960-61 to 1965-66). The closure of the canal in 1967 is marked by a discontinuity in the transport series, with a drop in the growth rate of about 6 percent during 1965-70. Between 1970-71 and 1976 — the Suez Canal was closed for most of this period — the average annual rate of growth of the transport sector was 8.9 percent.

USE OF RESOURCES

The main macroeconomic developments are illustrated in figures 3-1 and 3-2. Total resources available to the economy in a given year are GDP at market prices plus net imports. Net imports are defined as the difference between all current expenditures and all current receipts from abroad. The total resources are disposed of as consumption (private and public) and investment (gross fixed accumulation and stock changes). Domestic saving is equal to the difference between investment and net imports (see table 3-3).

The striking features of macroeconomic developments may be summarized as follows:

Figure 3–1. Percentage Share of Total Investment, Public and Private Consumption, and Domestic Saving in GDP, 1952-53 to 1978

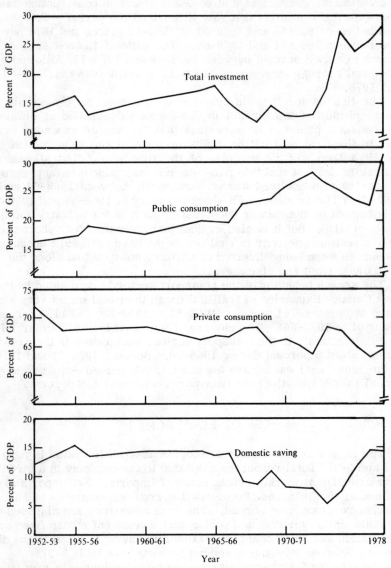

Figure 3–2. Exports and Imports as a Percentage of GDP, 1952-53 to 1978

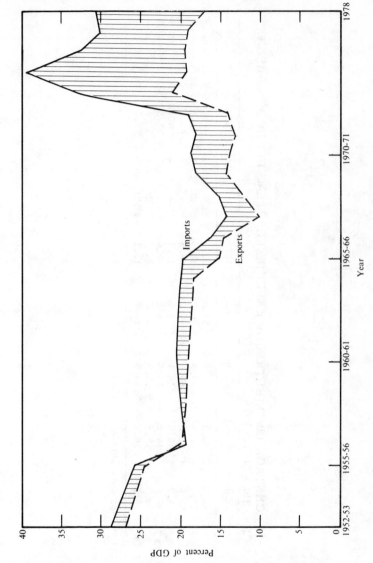

Source: Statistical Appendix table 5.

TABLE 3-3. PERCENTAGE DISTRIBUTION OF EXPENDITURE ITEMS IN GDP AT CURRENT MARKET PRICES, 1955–56 TO 1978

Item	1955–56	1960–61	1965–66	1970–71	1973	1974	1975	1976	1977	1978
Consumption	84.9	85.9	86.4	91.8	92.0	84.6	92.7	88.5	85.7	85.8
Public	17.3	17.6	19.8	25.6	28.2	26.2	25.0	23.3	22.5	35.4
Private	67.6	68.3	66:6	66.2	63.8	68.4	67.7	65.2	63.2	64.6
Gross investment	16.3	15.5	18.1	13.0	13.1	17.4	27.3	24.1	25.3	27.9
Domestic saving	15.1	14.1	13.6	8.2	8.0	5.4	7.3	11.5	14.3	14.2
Exports	24.5	19.2	15.3	14.0	14.0	21.2	19.5	19.6	19.2	17.1
Imports	25.7	20.5	19.8	18.7	19.1	33.2	39.5	32.3	30.1	30.7

Source: Statistical Appendix table 5.

- The share of public consumption in GDP at market prices had a marked tendency to rise throughout the 1952-78 period, while the share of private consumption moved around a declining trend line.
- The share of investment displayed a cyclical pattern of large amplitude, with an upward movement between 1955-56 and 1965-66 followed by a sharp decline in the next five years. A new upward movement seems to have begun in 1973.
- The sectoral distribution of investment shows some interesting features (Statistical Appendix table 9). The major part of fixed investment has consistently gone to industry, petroleum, and mining, averaging over one-third of the total during the last decades. This, of course, reflects the government's development strategy, which emphasized setting up a manufacturing sector aimed principally at import substitution, and which included a significant component of heavy industry in the form of the Helwan Iron and Steel Works. The share of agriculture (including irrigation and drainage) flucuated markedly, exceeding 20 percent of the total fixed investment in the mid-1960s, when the construction work on the Aswan High Dam and its ancillary structures was at its peak, but declining continuously since then; by 1978 it constituted only about 8 percent of the total. These figures are in current prices; there has been an absolute fall in real terms in this sector. Housing received about 12 percent of total investment from 1960-61 to 1967-68; the effect of the 1967 war was to divert the major part of construction materials to defense purposes, with a resulting fall in the allocation to the housing sector. A recovery in allocation in 1968-69 was followed by an almost continuous decline, and the 1978 allocation was only about 7 percent. Transport and communication has accounted for an increasing amount of the total.
- The share of domestic saving remained fairly stable between 1950 and 1965, but then began to move along a declining trend line until a recovery in 1975.
- The share of exports in GDP fell from some 25 percent in 1955-56 to as low as 14 percent in 1970-71. An upward tendency is noticeable thereafter, reflecting a rise in the export prices rather than an increase in export volumes.
- The import share follows movements that are fairly closely associated with those of investment: a decline between 1955-56 and 1970-71, and a very considerable increase after 1973. The latter movement reflects price as well as quantity increases.
- The shaded area in figure 3-2 shows changes in the export-import gap (expressed as a percentage of GDP). Clearly shown are the emergence of a large deficit since the mid-1950s,

the attempt to reduce the relative size of this gap between 1964 and 1967, the reemergence of sizable deficits after 1967, and the unprecedented gaps of 1974 and 1975.

These developments, when related to the preceding analysis of changes in the rates of economic growth, suggest a very simple explanation of macroeconomic behavior in Egypt since the early 1950s. The critical variables which seem to determine the rates of real output growth in the short, and perhaps medium, term are investment and imports. In Egypt the nexus between investment, imports, and growth is very strong, and the recent economic history of the country can be viewed as attempts and failures to raise the investment ratio. The first attempt to raise the ratio from an average rate of about 14 percent of GDP to 18-20 percent was made through planning and public control of the means of production during the first five-year plan between 1960 and 1964. The rise in the investment ratio was not accompanied by a commensurate increase in the rate of domestic saving, but was financed from abroad, mainly by the United States and the Soviet Union. It was short-lived and failed when foreign financial assistance became harder to obtain after political difficulties with the United States.

Both the investment and import ratios were bound to fall when external financing ceased to be forthcoming at the previous rate. The rate of economic growth — as mentioned earlier — followed the same plunge between 1964 and 1968. Rises in the share of public consumption, which became sharper in the early 1960s than in the 1950s, made things worse. Private consumption took the brunt at first (1961-63), but sooner or later something else had to give way: the investment share declined more than it would have done had public consumption remained stable.

The 1967 war and the defense burden made things worse. The investment ratio stabilized from the late 1960s until 1973 at around 13 percent of GDP, while the share of public consumption continued to rise as did that of private consumption, though not as steeply as public consumption. The external gap widened to finance an increase not in investment, but in public consumption. The rates of economic growth were high in the interwar years (1967-73), but much of that growth was accounted for by services, a sector in which real output expansion is overstated by the statistics.

After 1973 both the investment and the import ratios rose to very high levels. In 1975 and 1976 the rate of economic growth was also high; so was the import-export gap — as defined here it was equivalent to 20 percent of GDP in 1975. Part of this gap, especially in 1974, can be attributed to very unfavorable movements in the external terms of trade. Since then the gap has narrowed, largely as a consequence of sharply rising petroleum exports, and in 1978 it was equivalent to about 15 percent of GDP.

4
Present Development Issues

This chapter discusses the major issues that are likely to loom large for policy purposes in the coming decade and that Egypt's development strategy must address. The emphasis is chiefly on the macroeconomic management of the economy, but "macroeconomic" is broadly interpreted to encompass issues, such as the efficiency of public enterprises, which have substantial implications for other sectors of the economy. The salient problems of individual sectors are also discussed.

STRUCTURAL BREAKS IN 1973

The problems of economic management are compounded by the uncertainties arising from the structural breaks that occurred in 1973. Their full implications have not yet unfolded, but it may be useful to distinguish four main areas of discontinuity.

The first was in international politics. The October 1973 war changed many of the parameters which define the Middle East conflict and opened up real opportunities for peace. Though the final outcome is uncertain, Egypt has moved from being actively engaged in war to making serious bids for peace. This change is an important discontinuity, and yet Egypt's present position in the Middle East conflict is best characterized as transitional. The quest for peace is accompanied by some of the defense expenditures incurred when countries prepare for war, and some of the expectations of smooth economic development that is one of the benefits of settled peace.

The second discontinuity occurred in the economic system. In 1973, following the October war and the oil revolution, the government announced liberalization measures and an intention to pursue an open-door policy. It can be argued, of course, that some rather timid liberalization had begun as early as 1967 and that the forces working to open up the economic system in favor of the private sector had already acquired some momentum before 1973. The October Paper nevertheless represents such a significant shift in

45

perspective that it constitutes a discontinuity. A page of the economic history book has been turned, but it is not certain that Egypt has irrevocably entered a new chapter of its economic history. The aim of the liberalization policy — to create a new economic system in which public and private sectors match one another in weight and in which the government severely limits the degree of its interference in the economy — cannot be immediately achieved. Many characteristics of the old economic system remain: a large concentration of the ownership of modern means of production in the public sector, and extensive state intervention in the operations of product and factor markets. But the system has some new features. The private sector — domestic, Arab, and foreign — is being encouraged to invest, produce, and export. Imports are being allowed in a liberal fashion. Foreign exchange controls have been relaxed, and the private sector now has easy access to free foreign exchange in the parallel market.

Transitional situations can often be messy. The least desirable characteristics of the public sector may well prove to be the most stubborn, the longest to survive. At the same time, the private sector may cause problems and tensions. It is difficult to assess the medium-term prospects for moving toward a system that is "mixed" not only in the sense of including public and private sectors of comparable strength, which provide checks and balances to each other, but also in the sense of being both liberal in relation to the allocation of resources and equitable in terms of the distribution of income. The transformation is unlikely to be smooth. The risk of policy reversals cannot be discounted; they may occur for a variety of reasons, and some may be the result of the liberalization process itself. Unless carefully and gradually implemented, liberalization creates social and political tensions that could force the government to abandon or change drastically the policy.[1]

Third, in 1973 there was a break in the continuity of the behavior of the balance of payments. Before 1973 Egypt had been chronically suffering from balance of payments deficits; yet the current account deficits never exceeded 6 or 7 percent of GDP, and this upper limit was rarely reached. After 1973 the deficit expressed as a proportion of GDP moved in the range of 15-20 percent instead of 0-7 percent. In 1978 the deficit was equivalent to 15 percent of GDP; the prospects are for an improvement in the early 1980s, but a subsequent deterioration unless the longer-term outlook for the petroleum sector improves. There is a discontinuity here, a marked change from one pattern to another. The difference in the size and share of the balance of payments deficit is not one of degree but of kind, so

---

1. For instance, the riots of January 1977 stemmed from the hasty attempts to cut subsidies on a number of items. The resulting disturbances forced a restoration of the subsidies and froze all movement on prices for the entire year.

large is the change in magnitude and so significant the economic implication of that change.

The discontinuity may be attributed to a variety of causes.
There was an adverse movement in the external terms of trade in
1973-76, largely because of a fourfold increase in the price of imported wheat, unmatched by comparable rises in the price of cotton
exports. In 1974 and 1975 the prices of both imports and exports
rose unevenly but significantly. Relative prices moved against Egyptian exports by 12 percent between 1973 and 1974. A more telling
indicator is the movement in the cotton exports-agricultural imports
price ratio, which dropped by some 35 percent between 1973 and
1974. Yet the adverse movement in the terms of trade is not the
sole, and probably not the most important, explanation for the
deterioration in the balance of payments.[2] Both import and export
volumes moved very unfavorably for the balance of payments. At
first sight one would have expected import price rises to reduce the
volume of imports and export price rises to lead to real export expansion. But import volumes increased after 1973 and exports decreased. The expansion of domestic demand (for both consumption
and investment) — the "income effect" working in the opposite direction to the "price effect" — has been the dominant force. The
increase in local demand seems to have stimulated imports and diverted exports (other than petroleum) away from foreign into
domestic markets.

Balance of payments deficits must be financed in one way or another. Egypt was receiving sizable grants after 1973, but loans
were also needed on a large scale.[3] Though foreign indebtedness
is an old phenomenon, the rate of debt accumulation after 1973 is
unprecedented. The direction of capital inflows also changed: at
the end of 1974 the main creditors (in order of size) were the Soviet
Union, the Federal Republic of Germany, Kuwait, and the United
States; at the end of 1976 they were Kuwait, Saudi Arabia, the United
States, the Soviet Union, and the Federal Republic of Germany. It
is possible, of course, to look at these issues the other way round
and to stress not the indebtedness but the change in world circumstances. The surplus of Arab money, the new pattern of international alliances, and other results of the political events of 1973 gave
Egypt access on a considerable scale to new sources of finance. If
indebtedness is one side of the coin, the other side is the enhanced
ability to effect a transfer of resources from abroad.

To sum up, the October 1973 war and the oil revolution, with
other factors, have created a new situation for the Egyptian economy.

2. Particularly after 1976, when petroleum began to provide a substantial share
of total exports.

3. At the end of 1973 Egypt's nonmilitary medium- and long-term debt (disbursed
and outstanding) stood at US$2,485 million; at the end of 1978 it had risen to
US$9,968 million.

The quest for peace with its economic implications, liberalization, significant external imbalances, and changes in the patterns of foreign indebtedness characterize this situation. All these changes are recent, and the adjustments to a series of structural breaks are still being made. To take advantage of the transformed milieu, a fresh economic strategy has to be articulated. The strategy has been formulated, but the management of the economy within the new framework requires, as a concomitant, a revised set of policies.

The emphasis given here to structural breaks and to the emergence of a new situation should not distract attention from the weight of the past. Elements of continuity between the periods before and after 1973 are pervasive. The present Egyptian economy, despite changes in some important variables, is in other respects molded by the past. The capital stock of today in the productive sectors and the infrastructure is the result of past investments (in both good and bad projects); more important perhaps, the institutions, the administrative structure, the policy framework, the modes of production and organization, the vested interests, and the habits of thought and work are a collective inheritance that determines many of the features of the economy today and colors its prospects. The management of the medium term will have to take account of these continuities.

POVERTY AND INCOME DISTRIBUTION

The distribution of income in Egypt is examined in the appendix to this chapter. Subject to the caveats mentioned there, it is estimated that in 1974-75 the lowest 40 percent of the households in both rural and urban areas accounted for about 16 percent of the income originating in the sector. The income distribution per person was considerably more egalitarian, with the distribution in rural areas being more equitable than its urban counterpart, but of course at a lower average level. In the rural areas the lowest 40 percent of the personal distribution accounted for about 25 percent of total incomes in the sector, compared with about 21 percent for the urban areas; however, the average annual income in the rural areas was about LE65, while in urban areas it was LE128. Comparisons in the mid-1970s with previous studies indicate that the distribution had not noticeably deteriorated since the mid-1950s, despite the rapid growth of the population and changes in the economy. Much of the credit for this is due to the policies of land reform, taxation, and employment that successive governments have followed in pursuit of a more equitable distribution of income and wealth since the 1952 revolution. A vital issue for economic management will be to pursue the aims of rapid economic growth, without jeopardizing the goals of social equity toward which the government has labored for so long.

Recent developments in the economy, coupled with the rapid rate of inflation since 1973-74, threaten to disrupt this pattern of distribution. Many of the gains since 1973 have been made by income groups and activities that do not contribute commensurately to the national exchequer. A reform of the system of taxation is needed in four main areas. First, since the bulk of Egypt's tax revenues now comes from indirect taxes, which in general have a regressive impact, the system should be redesigned so that direct taxes bear a much larger share of the total revenue, on the ground of equity and because direct taxes generally possess a higher growth elasticity. Second, the opening up of the economy to external influences has been partly responsible for the sudden increase in the value of assets, especially in the case of real estate. A capital gains tax would seem appropriate to capture a part of this windfall. Third, while income differentials may be important sources of incentives, too great differences in visible consumption can cause friction. A considerable part of the expenditure of the richer class in Egypt currently appears to be on imported items. This suggests that the proposed tax reform should pay close attention to a review of import duties, with a view to increasing those that impinge on luxury commodities. Fourth, in recent years farmers who grow fruit, vegetables, and berseem (Egyptian clover) have greatly increased their incomes because of the absence of price controls on these products. The agricultural tax, however, is based not on income but on the rentable value of the land. Although these values are supposedly recomputed every ten years, the present ones were fixed in 1952. Much of the increase in the income of those farmers not subject to the government-imposed cropping patterns appears to have escaped the tax net. The system of agricultural taxation should be reformed, and the rental value should be reassessed at more frequent intervals.

Another question concerns the absolute level of poverty: What proportion of the population is below some minimum level of income, defined so as to cover the typical diet and nonfood costs of lower income groups?[4] According to World Bank estimates, in 1975 the absolute poverty level in urban areas was about LE300 annually per household, while in rural areas it was about LE240. These figures put about 19 percent of the urban population and 27 percent of urban households, and 25 percent of the rural population and 35 percent of

4. The many and difficult problems related to this subject are discussed in Richard Webb, On the Statistical Mapping of Urban Poverty and Employment, World Bank Working Paper no. 227 (Washington, D.C., January 1976).

rural households below the absolute poverty line in that year.[5] This underlines the importance that the system of subsidies has had in maintaining real incomes.

Subsidies, particularly on the so-called supply commodities (the items of mass consumption), rose dramatically following the increases in international commodity prices in 1973. In that year, the subsidy on the supply commodities amounted to LE89 million, two years later it had risen to LE409 million; if the administrative and other costs are included, the distribution of the supply commodities cost LE491 million. The decline in wheat prices in 1976 helped to lower the subsidy bill in that year, but even then the cost of distributing the supply commodities stood at about LE322 million. In 1978 the net subsidy on the supply commodities amounted to LE423 million, of which the wheat and flour component accounted for LE223 million, and total subsidies amounted to 8 percent of GDP.

Two conclusions follow from these developments. First, Egypt can continue to sustain this diversion of resources to consumption only at the cost of seriously affecting the level of public saving and investment, and the growth rate of the economy. This, in turn, would lower the capacity to provide employment and meet welfare goals in the future. Second, the level of subsidies is now so high that it could be counterproductive to eliminate them all at once. A sudden drop in real incomes of the magnitude implied by the subsidy elimination could trigger major social tensions and lead to disturbances, as occurred in January 1977. An abrupt curtailment in purchasing power, amounting to 10-15 percent of the national income, could cause a substantial disruption in aggregate demand, which in turn could lead to material changes in the level and distribution of incomes.

What, then, should be the strategy? The goals of equity and internal resource balance would be best served by a gradual restructuring of the system of subsidies. First, the use of subsidies should be more selective. At present, there is no correlation between income and subsidies. The subsidized bread is available to both the rich and poor; the fertilizer subsidy is given equally to the cotton grower, who must sell a part of his output at prices fixed by the government, and to the fruit and vegetable farmer, who also benefits from uncontrolled prices. Second, the heavy subsidization of some items can lead to waste or uneconomic use. It would be worthwhile, therefore, to extend dual pricing so that essential quantities are made available at low prices, while the excess is sold at economic prices. Third, attention must be given to subsidies in the form of pricing below economic cost, especially for petroleum products, public utilities, and public transport. Fourth, it would be

---

5. At the income levels corresponding to the poverty line, the average household sizes were 5.2 for urban and 5.8 for rural areas, compared with the overall averages of 5.6 and 6.0 respectively.

useful for formulating policy to bring together in the budget all the
subsidies, direct and indirect, to make explicit the total cost of subsidization and focus attention on alternative uses of those resources.

These steps would cut down the subsidy bill in a measured manner, and at the same time direct the available assistance toward
the most vulnerable groups in the population. It would thus recognize the economic wisdom of not abruptly depressing aggregate demand. Moreover, by cushioning the impact on the poorest sections
of society, it would recognize the humanitarianism as well as the
political wisdom of tempering the wind to the shorn lamb, and thus
give the necessary measures a better chance of acceptance.

MANAGEMENT OF THE EXTERNAL SECTOR

The performance of the external sector is crucial for Egypt's
economic management and future prospects. Between 1973 and 1975
the import bill more than doubled, rising from US$1,664 million to
US$4,538 million. Between 1973 and 1978 payments for services
almost tripled. Although earnings from the export of merchandise
and services (including workers' remittances) increased considerably, the deficit on goods and services in 1978 was about 2.7 times
that in 1973. Moreover, the import requirements of the Egyptian
economy are likely to remain high in the future, because the main
import items are food, intermediate goods needed to utilize existing industrial capacity, and capital goods required for investment.

One can hardly argue that imports should be sharply reduced at
the cost of lower standards of living, idle capacity, and curtailed
investment. What, then, can the authorities do? First, the growth
of imports could be limited in accordance with a set of targets for
average consumption growth, capacity utilization, and future rates
of economic growth. As analyzed in chapter 15, the pricing policy
for food and fiscal policy in general cause waste. Moreover, there
is scope for curtailing the import of nonessentials, such as soft
drinks and expensive motor cars. The importation of intermediate
goods for industry has been maladministered, causing imbalances
in the composition of import orders — a surplus of some items and
insufficient supply of others (see chapter 12). In addition, investment projects have been poorly chosen, which means that expenditures on imported capital goods do not yield as high a rate of
economic growth as they would under other, more optimal conditions. In other words, foreign exchange is wasted both directly
and indirectly, and the growth of imports can be curtailed by policy
reforms and improvements in import management and project
selection.

Second, policies are required to deal with other important trade
issues. Egypt's nonpetroleum exports are dominated by cotton,

in both raw and manufactured forms; in 1978, for example, cotton
and cotton textiles accounted for about 40 percent of total commodity exports.[6] The authorities regard this degree of concentration
as a weakness, and they have tried to stimulate the export of non-
cotton manufactures, but without much success.

This underlines the fact that there is no coherent overall strategy for encouraging exports. Some ad hoc measures have, indeed,
assisted the development of certain types of export commodities,
but their cumulative impact has not been significant.[7] The most
important measure was the creation of the "parallel market" in
September 1973, in which exporters of specified commodities were
given a premium of 50 percent over the official exchange rate,
which produced an effective exchange rate of LE0.58 to the U.S. dollar (compared with LE0.39 at the official rate). In 1976 the parallel rate was altered in successive steps to LE0.70, while the scope
of the market was steadily widened to cover all export commodities,
except for a few insignificant items in bilateral trade (see chapter
16 for details). As a result of these measures, the exchange rate
for both imports and exports was depreciated.

Changes in the effective exchange rate, however, do not, in themselves, constitute a comprehensive export promotion policy. Egypt's
exports are seriously handicapped by the erosion of the exportable
surplus owing to rising domestic consumption, the nature and effects
of bilateral trade, problems of institutional change and marketing in
agricultural products, and low factor productivity and poor quality
in manufacturing. This litany of ills points up the wide range of reforms that will be necessary to stimulate exports to the required
level for the coming decade. The government will have to evolve an
explicit strategy that incorporates appropriate movements in the exchange rate and a shift from bilateralism, and that takes advantage
of the Arab Common Market. More basic changes will be required
in the institutional and policy framework for both agriculture and industry, so as to induce more efficient use of factors in producing
higher outputs. Some of these issues are discussed later in this
chapter, and in more detail in chapters 10 and 12.

Export diversification will acquire particular importance in the
1980s. The danger is not that in its absence exports would not grow
(they would), but that they would likely be as dominated by a single
commodity — petroleum — during the next decade as they have been
by cotton until the present. The simulation exercises undertaken by
the World Bank (see chapter 5) suggest that, even with vigorous policies to push the growth of nonpetroleum exports, petroleum (mainly crude) could account for around 50 percent of commodity export

6. Petroleum exports accounted for a further 28 percent.

7. This refers only to the effect on merchandise exports; the parallel rate has
had a significant impact on remittances from Egyptians working abroad.

earnings in the mid-1980s. The diversification strategy will have to encompass both agricultural and industrial exports. Among the former, the prime candidates appear to be fruits, vegetables, and possibly flowers, primarily for the Middle East market. These possibilities are being explored, but much more systematic and concerted efforts at marketing and quality control will be required.

In view of the pressure on the land, the authorities have in practice not appeared too sanguine about the prospects of a vast increase in agricultural exports, but have pinned their expectations on the growth of manufactured exports. Egypt's development strategy calls upon industry, especially sophisticated engineering goods, to spearhead the thrust toward higher growth rates in both production and exports. But for these goods, price competitiveness is not enough. Other important considerations are quality, design, reliability, running costs, the availability of spare parts, and the provision of credit to potential buyers. Thus a major structural change in the direction and composition of exports will require many additional measures, quite apart from the rationalization of the exchange rate. The successful implementation of a comprehensive policy package, even if vigorously pursued, can be expected to occupy at least the next five to ten years. Moreover, as Egypt will be aiming chiefly at the rich Middle East market, the improvement of quality will have to be a continuing process.

For successful management of the economy through the 1980s, priority must be given to formulating a strategy for handling external indebtedness. Egypt's nonmilitary medium- and long-term external debt (disbursed and outstanding) quadrupled between 1973 and 1978; at the end of 1978 it stood at US$9,968 million (about 50 percent of GDP)[8] compared with US$2,485 million (26 percent of GDP) at the end of 1973. Moreover, during the 1973-78 period Egypt passed through a liquidity crisis occasioned by heavy short-term borrowing. The short-term debt, represented by 180-day banking facilities, increased from US$497 million at the end of 1973 to US$1,533 million in May 1977 (including US$710 million of arrears). The outstanding amounts were paid off in late 1977 through a long-term loan from the capital-surplus Arab countries, and thereafter the authorities have held down this type of borrowing — at the end of 1978 the amount was US$443 million.

There are three major aspects of the debt problem. First, in view of the rapidly increasing amounts it is essential to ensure that debt is incurred only for really important uses and on the best possible terms. It would thus be advisable to lay down guidelines regarding the minimum terms on which fresh medium- and long-term debt could be incurred. Such guidelines could indicate, for example,

8. At the official exchange rate; at the parallel market rate the ratio would be about 89 percent.

a minimum grant element in the loan, or a minimum period of grace or maturity, in addition to specifying an acceptable interest rate. Second, although the terms on the new commitments of borrowing have been extremely concessional,[9] there still has been a drop in the proportion of outright grants. This trend, together with the effects of loans previously contracted, could lead to a substantial "hump" in debt service payment even by the mid-1980s. Thus, efforts must be made to lengthen the debt profile; of the disbursed and outstanding debt at the end of 1978, about 31 percent was due for repayment in the next four years.[10] Third, the message conveyed by the short-term debt crisis of 1976-77 was that a slight deterioration in the environment or in economic management could trigger a liquidity crisis and possibly damage the country's creditworthiness. Hence, continued tight control over the incurring of short-term debt has to form an important plank in debt management policy.

DOMESTIC RESOURCE MOBILIZATION

The savings-investment gap has widened enormously since the mid-1960s, largely because of the deterioration in the domestic savings effort. This, in turn, was mainly the result of a decline in government saving and, as elaborated in chapter 15, rapid increases in government consumption which outstripped even the very commendable revenue effort. The restoration of balance between domestic resources and expenditures will bulk large among the policy priorities for the coming decade, particularly since increased self-reliance has been officially pronounced a major strategic objective. An improvement in the resource balance will require a wide range of measures; the major issues and recommendations are discussed below.

Government Saving

Gross domestic saving reached a high point of about 14 percent of GDP in 1965; thereafter it declined until in 1974 it formed only 5 percent of GDP. The major reason for this trend was the decline in government saving after 1967, and even more so after 1973. Public sector saving dropped from 12.5 percent of GDP in 1970-71 to about 2.7 percent in 1978. This secular decline in public saving attests to the relative fixity of the two main items of public expenditures: defense and administration. Of course, as discussed earlier,

---

9. The grant element on commitments in 1978 is estimated at 47 percent.
10. This excludes nearly US$2,000 million of deposits by Arab countries in the Central Bank of Egypt, which are expected to be rolled over for several years. If these amounts are included, the proportion of debt to be repaid by 1982 increases to 48 percent.

after 1973 subsidies also became an important claimant on resources. This trend in saving will need a major reversal if the government is to realize its objectives of growth and reduced dependence on external sources.

What are the prospects for achieving a substantial rise in domestic saving, and what would be the main policy issues? First, the tax system will have to be made more responsive to the current realities of the economy. Because the economic framework for which it was designed is rapidly changing, the present tax system is unable to capture a due proportion of the increases in income and wealth that, in general, are arising from new activities. Thus, the system will have to be restructured to cover gains from the appreciation of assets, the large profits on real estate dealings, the increased agricultural incomes generated from the sale of products (such as fruits, vegetables, berseem, poultry, and meat) whose prices are not controlled, rents on furnished apartments, and the import and sale of consumer goods and durables. In line with the earlier remarks, it is also clear that the tax system will have to be revised in the direction of providing a minimum of exemptions, and of incorporating as many ad valorem (rather than specific) rates as possible.

A second important reform must be the strengthening of the tax administration. Despite the impressive gains in the collection of some taxes, there are shortfalls in others owing to weaknesses in the tax administration. In particular, considerable arrears have built up in the collection of import duties. This, of course, also affects equity because it implies that certain individuals and organizations contribute less than their share to the national exchequer.

Third, the public sector enterprises will have to increase their saving, and hence their efficiency, substantially. Although specific recommendations in this area depend on the sector in which the enterprise is located and the responsibility it bears, there is nevertheless a body of policy recommendations that can be applied in common to virtually all public economic enterprises, as discussed in the following section.

Fourth, over the longer term we would expect the level of defense spending to decline. This would make an important contribution to public saving, since this type of expenditure (including the deficit in the Emergency Fund) has accounted for more than a third of current revenues in recent years.

Fifth, the government guarantee of employment in the public sector to all graduates of universities and higher educational institutions has resulted in the large expansion of the bureaucracy and overstaffing. As part of the effort to increase public saving the government will have to curtail the growth of its expenditures and hence to reconsider its policy of acting as the employer of last resort.

Sixth, the system of subsidies merits close investigation. It covers a very large number of items, even if the account is confined to

items affected by "financial" subsidies. The total bill in 1978 is
estimated at nearly US$1,350 million,[11] or about 27 percent of the
current expenditure in the budget. Many of these items cannot
strictly be considered "essential" to meet basic needs. Indeed, for
some of them — for example, macaroni, biscuits, and sweets — it
is difficult to find any cogent argument for subsidization. No "means
test" is applied to individual or family income or to family size to
determine qualification for the grant of a subsidized item; all commodities are available equally to both the rich and the poor. Some
items are available in unlimited amounts. The examples most frequently cited are bread and transportation fares, but others, such
as water and electricity, can easily be added. Many prices have
been left unchanged since at least 1973, although costs have risen
drastically. In some cases the subsidies may not even reach the intended beneficiaries. There are indications that for some items
(for example, cloth and meat) a flourishing black market exists
whereby middlemen sell off these commodities at higher than official prices and reap handsome profits.

In view of the foregoing, it would indeed be surprising if significant savings could not be effected by rationalizing the system. While
a detailed examination of the subsidy system is beyond the scope of
this work, some fruitful ways of approaching the problem can be
indicated. The coverage of the system should be made much more
selective by restricting the number of commodities that are made
available and by limiting the access of individuals and groups to
them. Limiting access would require the implementation of a means
test, possibly by widening the rationing system (which, incidentally,
is already reasonably well developed). To prevent waste and possible misallocation, it might be desirable to reexamine the subsidized
goods and services that are offered in unlimited amounts. Some,
in particular bread, are politically sensitive, in addition to present-
ing administrative problems of distribution under a rationing system.
The political decision must, of course, properly rest with the government, which must determine the timing and scope of any reform.
The administrative difficulties could be overcome, however, and
rationed bread supplies made available to the deserving (however
defined) through a variety of mechanisms. For example, the existing cooperatives could contract with the bakeries for bread and sell
to individuals the amounts allowed on their ration cards. Alternatively, bread could be sold at its economic price, and individuals
who were eligible under a means test could be issued bread stamps
to use in (perhaps part) payment. More attention could also be paid
to what in Egyptian terminology are called implicit and hidden
subsidies. Again, there are many possible ways to redirect the
subsidies; for example, gasoline prices and upper-class railway

---

11. At an exchange rate of LE1 = US$1.496.

fares could be raised to economic levels while bus fares and lower-
class tariffs remained more or less at present levels. This would
effectively reduce the implicit subsidies to the middle- and upper-
income groups, but retain them for those at the lower end of the
income distribution.

It is important to distinguish the macroeconomic impact of subsidies from how effectively they are targeted. For example, subsidies could be abolished while the overall level of economic activity
was maintained by increases in some other expenditure category,
say, public investment. But what would be the micronutritional implications of such a policy change? Some calculations suggest that
food consumption per capita among the poor might drop by 100 to
200 calories a day if subsidy reductions were imposed together with
offsetting macroeconomic policies. [12] (Of course, calorie consumption would drop even more were the compensating policies not applied.) For groups at major risk, such as small children and preg-
nant or lactating mothers, such population-wide average reductions
in food intake could easily translate into perceptible increases in
acute undernutrition. These calculations suggest that food subsidies
provide part of the "safety net" protecting the poorest Egyptians
from major deprivation. The thrust of this argument, therefore,
is not that the subsidy system should be abolished, but that it should
(and could) be better targeted and made more discriminating.

Seventh, much of the projected growth in revenues is predicated
upon the substantial increases in returns expected from the petroleum sector and from an expanded Suez Canal. Since these revenues
will accrue directly to the government, it is very important that
they be earmarked for productive purposes. If this is done, it would
be possible to sustain high marginal rates of saving in the public sector without increasing either tax rates or the burden of taxation.

Eighth, the level of public saving is not likely to be independent
of the government's growth strategy; rather, the rate of growth of
the economy will have a feedback effect on saving. The simulation
exercises sketched in chapter 5 indicate that a fast growth strategy
would help to support itself through the generation of higher tax and
other revenues. These could be translated into higher saving if government consumption expenditures did not similarly increase.

Public Enterprise Saving

In accordance with government policy, the share of GDP originating in the public sector increased from 13 percent in 1952 to 53
percent in 1978. This share is, of course, concentrated in certain
sectors of the economy. Since public enterprises are required by
law to transfer to the central government budget 65 percent of the

12. See the appendix to chapter 15.

surplus available for distribution, an increase in their efficiency could contribute substantially to improving the domestic resource balance. Some public enterprises are already extremely efficient, for example, the Suez Canal Authority, but many others, particularly in the field of industry, are in need of urgent policy reform and attention.

Public enterprises are so prevalent that the problem of their efficiency is exceedingly complicated and varies with each sector and the responsibilities (such as production or marketing) of the enterprise. Even within a single sector, such as manufacturing, the underlying causes may be multiple. A strategy can be fashioned, however, to tackle the broad set of issues that are common to most public sector enterprises.

To increase resource mobilization two sets of measures could be taken: one designed to protect the surplus for investment, the other to increase the surplus through internal reform of the enterprise or sector and through reform of the general environment in which public enterprises function.

The internal measures to boost the financial surplus are similar to those that would improve the efficient functioning of the enterprise. First, the large-scale overstaffing must be reduced and capacity utilization increased. Second, the authorities must grant a greater measure of decisionmaking to enterprise management; in return, some targets for annual productivity increase could be set, especially if action on overstaffing and capacity utilization were taken at the same time. Third, the system will have to make financial surplus a more important indicator of efficiency. If it were linked with financial advantages and perhaps social recognition for enterprise managers, there might be greater efforts to increase the surplus. Fourth, the emphasis on increased productivity implies a strengthening of management in its dealings with labor, giving it authority to dismiss workers for unsatisfactory performance and to pay production-related bonuses. On the Egyptian income scale, industrial workers are a fairly privileged group, and the authorities should not be averse to introducing the concept of payment by results.

The reform of the environment within which the public sector operates will have to begin with the price policy. Prices of products supplied by the public sector have been arbitrarily fixed for several years and are subject to change only gradually and after considerable scrutiny. It is not argued here that public enterprises should be permitted to increase prices at will, or that prices be increased automatically if certain elements of cost have risen. However, with the freeing of the economy, the rise in international and domestic prices, and the transfer to the parallel market of all imports, there has been a considerable surge in costs, and holding down prices by fiat will continue to squeeze public sector surpluses or increase losses. Hence, a major review of price policy is a

prime condition for improving public sector performance. Future
increases in prices could take account of increases in costs, on the
one hand, and on the other, the productivity targets set by the authorities in consultation with management.

Among other reforms, the government will have to make some
decision on enterprises that continuously register a loss. Unless
there are weighty strategic or national reasons, it is proposed that
the subsidy to such enterprises be stopped. In addition, the government will have the responsibility for ensuring easy access to foreign
exchange for inputs and capital investment. In the absence of this,
many of the measures suggested earlier for improving the efficient
functioning of enterprises (such as better capacity utilization) would
be rendered nugatory. The government must also take the lead in
transferring the appropriate technology to the country or developing
it domestically.

There is an overwhelming need for the government to reexamine
the working of the public sector and the future strategy for it. Perhaps the first area to focus on would be public industrial enterprises.
The government has yet to evolve an overall long-range industrial
strategy that takes account of Egypt's comparative advantage (see
chapter 12). Its main advantage (as measured by the effective rates
of protection) appears to lie in cement, fertilizers, some petroleum
products, furniture and food items, and some engineering goods. Textiles and wearing apparel could also become important if they were
upgraded; at present both the quality and the prices of textile products are considerably below the potential offered by Egyptian long-
staple cotton.

To increase the public sector's contribution to resource mobilization it is suggested that the surplus generated in public enterprises
not be transferred to the general resources of the budget. Instead
it should be earmarked for investment in the public sector, thus
ending the mandatory transfer of this surplus and encouraging greater self-financing by public enterprise of at least the domestic component of investment. As an alternative, the authorities could lay
down a target or minimum rate of return on capital invested in an
enterprise. This amount would be transferred to the exchequer,
while the rest of the surplus could be invested either in interest-
bearing bonds issued by the banking system or reinvested in the enterprise, depending on the circumstances. This would help to create a capital market for public enterprises, increase capital mobility,
and underline the principle that the enterprise's own funds have a
high opportunity cost.

Private Sector Saving

The new economic strategy favored by the Egyptian authorities requires a considerable increase in the rate of saving. The strategy

emphasizes the role of the private sector, which is expected to generate a large part of the overall increase in domestic resources. Private saving is currently low because of the expectations of inflation; the level of interest rates on available instruments, especially in relation to inflation expectations, and the merits of nonfinancial saving; the lack of awareness of the potential of savings instruments and their merits[13] and, indeed, the lack of sufficient instruments; and the high level of taxation on saving — at present both low-income and high-income savers appear to be penalized by the tax rates on all financial instruments, except some government bonds that are exempt from all taxes.

There are a number of avenues for boosting private saving. First, the interest rate policy can be deployed as a more aggressive instrument to mobilize savings. For a considerable period, the ceiling on interest rates was fixed by the civil code at 7 percent a year; given the "normal" spread between borrowing and lending rates in Egypt, the result was a maximum interest rate on savings deposits of only 4.5 percent a year. Moreover, the interest payment was subject to a withholding tax of 40 percent, which further reduced the effective interest rate to a level of about 2.7 percent. Since January 1976 the interest rate structure has been increased and the withholding tax eliminated; the current effective interest rate on savings deposits has consequently increased to about 8 percent a year. Even this is hardly an attractive yield in view of a current rate of inflation of perhaps 15 to 20 percent a year and the returns that are available from holding nonfinancial assets.

Second, the authorities must clarify their structural objectives and make their policies for encouraging the appropriate type of saving consistent with their overall strategy. If the aim is to increase saving in order to finance the public sector, and especially budget deficits, the present policy of totally exempting interest from government bonds would be appropriate. If it is to promote short-term saving of the banking system for the public sector and for financing trade and working capital, the elimination of the withholding tax on interest from savings accounts is a realistic measure. But if the primary policy is to promote ownership of stock in private companies, stock dividends should receive more favorable tax treatment than that accorded other instruments. If policies with regard to public sector and private sector development are neutral, it would be logical to treat all investment the same for tax purposes. Whatever actions are taken, the wider policy regarding the distribution of incomes might suggest that an upper limit be established on tax exemptions on investment income.

Third, in the medium run, the domestic resource balance could be considerably improved by encouraging self-financed private investment; this would also be consonant with the government's

---

13. This may be termed the lack of adequate marketing of savings instruments.

development strategy.[14] The government can influence private investment, both domestic and foreign, in four main ways. (1) It can help ensure the profitability of investment by permitting greater flexibility in setting prices and by maintaining a realistic exchange rate for exports. It is important to adjust the parallel rate regularly. (2) High priority must be accorded to the improvement of infrastructure, especially telecommunications and power distribution, and the rapid development of the construction sector. In fact, the limitations in construction capacity might be the greatest single bottleneck to the acceleration of investment, both private and public. If construction capacity is not increased, the attempt to increase the rate of investment might merely push up costs and prices, without having much impact on the real level of investment. (3) The government can cut down on the red tape that is encountered in obtaining the licenses and permissions necessary for investment. (4) Penalties could be levied against foreign enterprises that obtain permission to invest (both in the free-trade zones[15] and in inland projects) but do not take up this option within a reasonable time. As of March 1, 1977, the authorities had approved 527 such projects with a total capital of over US$6,000 million (of which nearly US$2,000 million was for free-trade zone projects), but only a handful had been taken up.

Fourth, the government could play an indirect role in increasing private saving. Policies to moderate the rate of inflation could increase the attractiveness of financial instruments. Less reliance on deficit financing could help reduce the preemption of domestic credit by the government sector and release funds for the more productive private sector, actions which could evoke complementary saving by that sector. The public sector captures — through the tax system, the social security, and postal savings schemes — a substantial amount of private saving. As the private sector grows in size, its needs for financing will increase. Future savings strategy will have to develop mechanisms which would obviate the need to siphon off a growing proportion of such private saving.

Fifth, considerable scope exists for increasing the availability of financial instruments and, concordantly, financial institutions. At present, commercial banks offer the usual spectrum of deposits, as do certain of the specialized banks and the post office savings system. Government bonds, bonds of previously nationalized companies, and some stocks of private companies are also available, but in limited supply. Adding savings deposits linked to housing mortgages and mortgage bonds would be a useful addition to the

14. Some of the issues involved in encouraging private sector investment in industry are discussed in connection with the small industry sector in chapter 12.

15. Free-trade zones are areas in which economic activities, principally manufacturing and warehousing, are exempt from taxes.

spectrum. More sophisticated instruments would be shares of investment trusts and units of mutual funds. Commercial banks' certificates of deposit and enterprises' commercial paper could also be added as short-term instruments, which might be used to develop a better use of short-term saving and a higher level of efficiency in the management of enterprises. In practice, not all these instruments could be added at once, nor could savers be educated to understand them quickly. There is thus merit to a systematic approach to broadening the spectrum.

The "marketing" of saving is a function of the availability of financial instruments, satisfactory effective rates of return, and overall confidence in the financial system. While it is up to the government to establish the broad policy which builds a positive attitude to saving, it is the financial institutions which must carry out the day-to-day work of marketing savings instruments. The broader the range of financial institutions (commercial banks, savings banks, mortgage banks) plus insurance companies, pension plans, investment trusts, and mutual funds, as well as the financial market intermediaries (investment banks, stockbrokers, and so on) and the more such institutions there are, the more the private sector is likely to be aware of the savings opportunities available and encouraged to save.

At present in Egypt financial institutions are few in number and limited in type. Consequently, in accordance with a broad and consistent strategy to increase saving, the spectrum of financial institutions should be expanded along with the increase in types of financial instruments. Establishing "lead institutions" of each new type would set an example for others and encourage a proper pattern of operation. Again, as with the development of new instruments, this will involve policy considerations and possibly new legislation along with appropriate — but minimal — government supervision.

Sixth, it is important to encourage saving in long-term financial instruments more than short-term saving. For this reason, instruments for contractual saving should be encouraged, as should the development of the securities markets. In the context of income distribution, broader ownership of the stock of profitable enterprises would give lower-income individuals an opportunity to earn the same high rate of return on their saving that is usually available only to the rich. As a step in this direction, the corporate income tax rate might favor companies that have a large proportion of their voting stock in the hands of a certain minimal, but large, number of individual investors.

Seventh, more widespread dissemination of the economic and financial results of both public and private entities would help make the public at large aware of which enterprises are more efficient and thus more worthy investments. Such information would also encourage managements to improve their efficiency.

ECONOMIC COORDINATION AND PLANNING

Egypt possesses the entire gamut of institutions and mechanisms that are required for both short- and medium-term management of the economy. These include the five-year plan, the annual plan, the domestic budget, the foreign exchange budget, the controls of the Central Bank of Egypt, import and export controls, committees to regulate the prices of all the major commodities, the Supreme Planning Council, and of course the ownership and direction of virtually the entire industrial and banking structures. There appears to be a problem, however, in coordinating the policies and recommendations of the different agencies.

The new economic order will require a fundamental change in the methods of guiding and regulating the economy. Hitherto, the predominant methods have been administrative controls and various directives. Much of this apparatus will need to be dismantled and more indirect and sophisticated measures substituted. Economic management will have to be more selective and differentiated, because large-scale projects or centrally run programs may not be able to solve such basic problems as how to increase agricultural production and employment. In the liberalized setup the government will have to rely chiefly on fiscal, monetary, price, and exchange rate policies to achieve its aims. Some goals, however, may continue to require direct methods; for example, a wage policy could be directly administered.

Some of the problems of short-term economic coordination spring from the frequent changes in high-level personnel in the major economic ministries. These range from rapid changes at the cabinet level to movements at senior undersecretary level.[16] Although these changes may be necessary, they create a hiatus during which the new incumbent has to learn the dimensions of the problems confronting him, develop a set of policies to deal with them, and establish a working rapport with his new colleagues. Many of the administrative changes might be avoided if the present salary structure were made sufficiently attractive to retain the most able civil servants and high-level technicians and keep them from moving to the private sector or to other countries.

Another difficulty in short-term economic management is the lack of timely data. Egypt has a well-developed statistical system that generates a considerable body of numbers. These are not always conceptually useful, however, and often are not available at

---

16. To cite only some major examples, from 1974 to 1978 there were five ministers of planning, five finance ministers, and three ministers of economy. Sectoral ministries have not fared much better; there were, for example, four ministers of agriculture in the same period.

the appropriate time. For example, the formulation of a satisfactory price and subsidy policy is hindered in part by the fact that official price indexes continue to rely on official prices, which are not very meaningful for many products. The budget is exceedingly intricate and contains much double-counting; this confuses the statistical picture and makes it of limited usefulness for analyzing financial policy or assessing its impact. Major weaknesses concern data for policies that will result in long-term structural changes. Income distribution data are particularly fragmentary, hence the distributive effect of various policies cannot be ascertained. Moreover, data relating to land distribution are obsolete and even predate the 1969 land reform.

There appears to be insufficient interaction between ministries, particularly when policies are being discussed. This has perhaps shown up most clearly in the annual plans which, up to now, have been seriously deficient in a discussion of policies.

In the last several years, particularly owing to the balance of payments exigencies, the authorities have been concerned primarily with the day-to-day management of foreign exchange resources. This explains in large part the emphasis on short-term management and the absence of serious attention to medium-term planning. In nearly two decades, Egypt has had only one medium-term plan (from 1960 to 1965) that was seriously pursued; subsequent attempts were disrupted by wars and other emergencies. A fresh start toward medium-term planning was made with the 1978-82 plan, which therefore represents a considerable achievement. A number of issues important to Egyptian medium-term economic management can be flagged, as they are likely to recur during the 1980s.

A major issue is that the government has consistently spread its resources too thinly over a large number of projects. Instead of ruthlessly cutting out some projects and focusing on a narrow set of priorities, the authorities have generally preferred to initiate a great many projects and then spend too little to achieve a satisfactory rate of completion. The problem is apparently compounded when these ongoing projects acquire a prior claim on resources in subsequent investment allocations. The lengthening of the completion period not only deprives the economy of the benefits from these projects, but also proliferates the opportunities for cost increases.

The setting of priorities and coordination of the economy is sometimes impeded when enterprises obtain an informal commitment from external sources for part of the project funding, and then put pressure on the Planning and Finance Ministries to come up with the rest, particularly local financing.[17] This, of course, accentuates the pressure toward overextension.

17. A former minister of planning expressed this vividly: "They bring me a button and ask me for a coat to sew onto it."

Likely to increase in importance in the coming decade, because of the large share of investment expected to be financed by foreign assistance, is the need to coordinate the priorities of aid donors and those of Egypt. To some extent this can be done through the institution of the Consultative Group,[18] in which both sides have an opportunity to discuss development strategy, sectoral priorities, and financing availabilities. It is, however, important for the government to develop an adequate portfolio of high-priority projects and to begin discussing them sufficiently early with aid donors so that the projects can come on stream (after their gestation periods) as planned, appropriate linkages can be developed, and delays and bottlenecks avoided. In most cases this will require looking ahead at least three to six years.

Another issue that has become important and may continue to be so for some time is the extent of the domestic currency component of investment expenditures. Measures to improve the domestic resource balance have been discussed earlier, but another consideration is the extent to which recurring or current expenditures on key economic projects ought to be included in the development plan. There is a danger, otherwise, that insufficient amounts will be allocated from the budget and the projects will be used below their capacity. The development plans of countries such as Pakistan do not employ a strict investment concept, but use one of "development expenditure," in which expenditures on scholarships, subsidies on fertilizers, and the like are included in the plan's total requirements.

With a large part of planned investment to be financed from abroad and with the political uncertainties in the region, medium-term planning in Egypt will remain a somewhat difficult exercise. The case for a medium-term plan is based largely on the presumption that the quality of current decisions would be improved if there were a fairly good idea of the likely outcome of events and the direction of policy for, say, three to five years in the future. A fixed medium-term plan in effect negates this basis of planning, because in a relatively short time the three- to five-year time frame no longer exists. Furthermore, the actual performance of the economy in any year could diverge significantly from the original forecast, and the once-for-all nature of a fixed-term planning exercise would preclude the possibility of reassessing the projections for subsequent years. Medium-term planning in Egypt could be rendered more effective by a system of "rolling" five-year plans, whereby each year the planning horizon is extended by one year so as to encompass five years, and the medium-term plan is updated to take account of actual implementation and changing priorities.

18. The Consultative Group for Egypt comprises Arab countries, members of the Organisation for Economic Co-operation and Development (OECD), and international and bilateral institutions under the chairmanship of the World Bank. It was formed in 1977 to institutionalize assistance.

These arguments have found favor with the authorities, who have decided to adopt a series of rolling five-year plans, with the first covering the period 1978-82. This plan projected an annual growth of GDP of 12 percent in real terms. The ratio of investment to GDP was expected to rise from 20 percent in 1976 to 28 percent in 1982; if the investments by the oil companies are taken into account (to make the magnitudes comparable with our simulation runs) the ratio exceeds 35 percent in 1982. The marginal rates of saving implied in the plan were extremely high, at about 45 percent for the period as a whole. As the previous chapters have shown, such rates are unprecedented in Egypt's history since at least 1950 and could come about only as the result of some fortunate and fortuitous circumstances, such as a much faster rate of petroleum production or a much more efficient use of capital. Moreover, attempts to sustain an annual investment rate of the magnitude posited in the plan are liable to run into severe constraints on absorptive capacity, such as the inadequacies of the project portfolio, delays in project preparation and weaknesses in selection and evaluation, physical limitations of the ports for imports of machinery and other capital goods, and shortages of domestic funds as a counterpart to foreign exchange inflows.

The precise magnitudes, however, are not crucial; the first serious exercise in medium-term planning since the mid-1960s was bound to contain some exploratory ideas, and the virtue of a rolling plan is that targets can be reset in the light of actual developments. Among the more general issues connected with planning that can be raised here are, first, that overoptimistic projections of the growth of GDP can permit planners to assume high rates of both consumption and saving. The authorities can thus avoid facing up to the difficult choice between consumption and further growth that would have to be made if the plan's assumptions did not materialize. Second, this could leave the government's development strategy vulnerable. The experience of several countries has shown that if a plan's assumptions are invalidated, the reaction is generally to make hasty ad hoc cuts in investment allocations, without considering the effects on welfare and income distribution. This risk can be minimized by formulating a "basic needs" component of the plan so that a minimum level of food, clothing, shelter, and access to health and educational services would be protected even if other goals had to be lowered because of unfavorable circumstances, such as a shortfall in resources. It is particularly important to strengthen the sociopolitical component of economic policy if, under the open-door strategy, economic activity is to be guided more and more by the market. Such an approach would require the identification of target groups and sectors that need particular attention, as well as institutional and administrative changes that would have to be made. Third, the large volume of investment proposed (perhaps not altogether realistically) for the plan period could easily dilute the thrust toward greater selectivity in project approvals and more rigorous setting of priorities. Fourth, the plan should include greater discussion of the specific policies required for a sustained transformation of the performance of the Egyptian economy to a degree unprecedented in Egypt's modern history. In particular, the role of the private sector must be more fully elaborated if the plan is to act as an operational document for implementing the open-door strategy.

The mixed economy at which Egypt is aiming will be more complex than at present. In addition to public investment, which can easily be directed into designated channels, the economy will include a large private sector whose investment decisions are more amenable to incentives and disincentives than to prescriptions. Thus, planning will have to incorporate a new dimension, namely, indicating targets for the private sector. Moreover, planning for the private sector will have to take account of the difference between negative and positive injunctions. In other words, although the authorities can always stop private enterprise from doing something — by rejecting a license, denying access to foreign exchange, or other means — they might find it impossible to make it take certain actions. Alternatively, it might turn out that the authorities could ensure that the private sector would meet a given target, but only by giving it a degree of profitability (through protection or other measures) that was not acceptable to society. The possible divergence between social and private profitability resulting from proposed economic policy and strategy will have to be carefully monitored.

SECTORAL POLICIES

The following sections do not substitute for the more detailed discussions of sectoral issues in the later chapters; rather, the aim here is to highlight only the issues that are likely to be important for the management of the economy in the medium to long term.

Human Resources

Population. Egypt's population in 1976 was estimated to have reached a level of 38 million and to have grown at an average annual rate of 2.31 percent since the previous (sample) enumeration of 1966. At this rate, about 900,000 persons are being added annually to the population. The population size and the current rate of growth imply that even if the growth rate is reduced in the near future, a large absolute number will continue to be added. Although the birthrate had been falling until the early 1970s, it began to rise again between 1973 and 1978. This may represent a temporary aberration from the long-term trend, but in any case the crude birthrate is high enough to warrant taking action to limit it. The attitude of the government has been that the birthrate could best be brought down by socioeconomic changes, which in turn would alter attitudes and behavior. It is, however, extremely unlikely that such a passive approach would bring useful results within the medium term. The authorities will have to initiate a well-designed, active program that will motivate people to adopt family planning and provide access to the necessary facilities.

Manpower and employment. Open unemployment is relatively low, but a major issue in the medium term is disguised unemployment and underemployment. This is most prevalent in the public sector — in the overstaffing of enterprises and in the growing bureaucracy — and is caused in large measure by the government's policy of assuring employment to graduates of universities and institutes of higher education. Another area of disguised unemployment is the service sector in urban areas. The problem is likely to grow with the growth in the population, the continuing migration to the cities, the increased participation of women in the labor force, and the demobilization of at least part of the armed forces once a permanent peace settlement is arranged for the region.

The solution is not likely to be simple, but the elements of a viable approach can be indicated. The planned faster growth of the economy will help absorb the labor force in productive jobs, although much of this growth is expected in sectors, such as petroleum, the Suez Canal, and heavy industry, which are not employment intensive. Industrial policy, especially, has been aimed primarily at reducing the foreign exchange gap and has not had explicit employment goals. Hence, more attention will have to be paid in the future to small-scale industry (see chapter 11) and to services such as tourism (see chapter 14), which could offer productive employment on a much wider scale.

Continued migration to neighboring oil-rich countries could offer a "safety valve" for some of the increase in the labor force. It is, however, a double-edged weapon, for the migrants may be precisely those with the greatest initiative or proficiency in their fields. In addition, migration may be concentrated among those with certain skills, so that the home economy is subjected to shortages in those areas. This appears to have started to affect Egypt. Wages in the construction sector have been rising rapidly, and there are repeated reports of shortages of masons, bricklayers, carpenters, electricians, and plumbers. Teachers, doctors, engineers, and technical specialists are also in demand in the neighboring countries, and Egypt has begun to experience shortages in some of these fields. Although quantitatively perhaps quite small, the movement of experienced high-level civil servants and administrators is also important, as referred to earlier. The government policy for expanding the supply of particular skills must explicitly take into account the

foreign demand for them. An important goal in the employment strategy should be to link employment goals with other development objectives; for example, unemployed and underemployed labor could be
mobilized in off-harvest seasons to improve rural infrastructure by
clearing irrigation canals, repairing bridges, and maintaining roads.
Such rural works programs have been extremely productive and successful in creating employment in several countries. [19]

Urbanization. Egypt is highly urbanized, with nearly 44 percent
of the population in 1976 living in centers with more than 20,000 inhabitants. Moreover, between 1966 and 1976 the urban population
increased at an average annual rate of 3 percent compared with 2.3
percent for the population as a whole. The rapid rate of urbanization has created problems of employment, housing, water supply,
and public transport and made large demands on the budget in the
form of a growing subsidy bill.

Cairo dominates the urban hierarchy, as shown by practically
all available indicators. Between 1947 and 1976 Egypt's urban population increased from 38 to 44 percent of the total population, that
of Greater Cairo from 11 to nearly 22 percent of the population
present in the country on the census date; in 1976 Greater Cairo
accounted for nearly half the total urbanized population. [20] In the
mid-1960s over half the nation's skilled tradesmen resided in Cairo,
as did 36 percent of its production workers. The city contained 66
percent of all television receivers, 52 percent of the telephones, 33
percent of the medical doctors and pharmacists, and at least two-
thirds of all university graduates. More recent data are not available on a comparable basis, but there is a strong presumption that
this concentration has intensified over the last decade as Cairo has
claimed a growing proportion of the total population.

What can the authorities do to contain the expansion of the urban
areas, or at least slow down the concentration in the two biggest
centers, Cairo and Alexandria? In the next decade a coherent strategy for rural development is needed to promote more rapid growth
in agriculture, improve the rural infrastructure, develop nonfarm
productive activities and employment opportunities, and provide greater access to social and cultural affairs. The implementation of such
a strategy would help to slow down migration to the urban areas.

Regional development, particularly of industry, must emphasize
areas away from Cairo and Alexandria. This could be done by consciously locating major public sector projects in the less developed

19. See, for example, John Thomas, "Rural Public Works and East Pakistan's
Development," in Walter Falcon and Gustav Papanek, eds., Development Policy
II: The Pakistan Experience (Cambridge, Mass.: Harvard University Press,
1971), pp. 186-236.

20. Greater Cairo comprises the governorate of Cairo, the cities of Giza and
Imbabeh in the Giza governorate, the city of Shubra el-Kheima in the governorate
of Kalyubia, and several surrounding settlements.

areas; by ensuring that future development of the free-trade zones is not near the two major cities; by urgently building up the infra-structure in the more backward areas; and by inducing the private sector to forgo the "soft option" of investing in or near the two ma-jor cities and instead to invest in other areas. These inducements could be positive or negative, and could take the form of denying permits to locate in the Greater Cairo and Alexandria areas; giving substantial tax holidays for investing in designated (less developed) regions; or even imposing a higher tax or levy on activities in the more developed cities and using the proceeds to provide subsidies for investment in other areas. For the coordinated and effective use of the wide variety of mechanisms available, an overall policy is needed for regional development.

The government must seriously consider moving some of the ministries and general authorities away from Cairo. At present, all the ministries are located in the capital with the exception of the Maritime Ministry, which is in Alexandria. Many general au-thorities which have a national function are also located in Cairo. The experience of many developing countries has been that private trade and industry tend to cluster near the seat of government, be-cause propinquity facilitates their requests for licenses, acquisi-tion of information, lobbying for protection, and other activities that depend on official action.

In urging a strategy for controlling and directing future urban growth, we are not arguing that all activities in the coming decade be channeled into the undeveloped areas. But continued rapid ur-ban growth, particularly in the most populous cities, is likely to exacerbate the problems of poverty and inequality. It would prob-ably also increase the pressures on the budget and the balance of payments (through the importation and distribution of supply com-modities), without contributing equivalent gains in productivity and growth. In articulating an urban strategy, the government has sev-eral options, from developing large villages, to building new cities in the virgin desert, to expanding existing small towns and cities; in fact, the most economical solution may well be the expansion of cities with a population of between 200,000 and 400,000.

Agriculture

Egypt needs an annual growth rate in total agricultural production of around 4 percent in real terms for at least ten years to feed a population growing at more than 2.3 percent, narrow the food supply deficit, and contribute resources for the development of other sec-tors. After this initial period, growth of the expanded base at an an-nual rate of 2 percent would feed the population, which could then be growing at less than 2 percent a year, and the surplus would continue to provide funds for other sectors.

What are Egypt's chances of achieving these figures? Because the supply of arable land is inelastic, growth in total product will have to come very largely from increases in the output per hectare. Some cross-country analyses of economic growth in agriculture have found that the maximum sustained by both developing and developed countries since the 1940s has been 2 percent a year per hectare, and that the critical difference in performance has been in the output per worker, which in the less developed countries is growing at 1.5 percent a year and in the developed at 4.5 percent a year.[21] This 2 percent increase in yield should be taken as the maximum that can be expected for long-run sustained growth. Whether it can be maintained, and what its effect will be, will depend on the growth in output per worker and on whether the increased product is consumed or invested.

It is estimated that Egypt could have an annual growth rate in total agricultural production of 4 percent for a period of about ten years, if the adjustments discussed in chapters 9 and 10 are carried out. The country could also sustain a long-run increase in output per worker of around 2 percent a year by investment in technology. Whether these targets will actually be achieved will depend on basic policy changes, developments outside the sector, and reasonable luck.

To manage the development of agriculture it will be necessary to grapple with the pricing system, investment policies, and the organization of the sector.

Price system and structure. A major constraint on the quantity and level of agricultural output is the administered price system. Its impact is especially pronounced on old valley farmers and settlers on reclaimed land because they are also subject to the administered cropping pattern. The large state farms on reclaimed land produce according to agronomically established cropping patterns, and the operating costs and losses are financed through the central government budget.

A major implication of past government policy has been that agriculture would transfer resources to other sectors. This transfer has come about through an indirect tax on agriculture, effected by maintaining producer prices for the major exported crops (chiefly cotton and rice) at levels lower than international prices and by applying an overvalued exchange rate.[22] In addition, a lower consumer

21. See, for example, Vernon W. Ruttan, "The Future of Agriculture," Fifteenth International Conference of the International Association of Agricultural Economists (IAAE), Oxford University, 1973.

22. Translated into farm-gate terms — with allowance made for handling, transport, and processing (ginning) costs — it is estimated that in the mid-1970s farmers received less than two-thirds of the export price for cotton, around half the export price for rice, 70-80 percent of the import price for wheat, and 40-50 percent of the international price for sugar.

price level has been maintained for basic foods, especially wheat. Prices of these commodities are fixed at the retail level and then allowed to work their way back to the producer level. This policy, combined with the administered price of cotton and inputs, effectively determines the cost and profitability relationships that dominate old valley production. The only prices essentially uncontrolled at the farm level are those for livestock products, berseem, vegetables, and fruits. Not surprisingly, over the past decade the prices of these commodities have risen rapidly.

In the face of these large discrepancies in income-earning possibilities, there have been persistent pressures to increase the area of fruits, vegetables, and berseem.[23] Once a permanent orchard is established, a farmer is freed from following the required cropping pattern on that land. Because of the high price of berseem, farmers have taken advantage of the short season for this crop to obtain a second cutting before planting cotton. The delay in planting cotton, however, increases its susceptibility to insects and pests. On the one hand, the farmer is thus induced to move out of traditional crops but is constrained from doing so by the imposed cropping pattern and the lack of inputs. On the other hand, he is required to grow traditional crops but has limited inducement to do so. These two competing forces are an important explanation for the slow growth of yields in Egypt in the past decade.

What are the implications for the management of agricultural policy in the coming period? A major precondition for increasing production is a reform of the pricing policy to reduce the discrepancies between the social and private profitabilities of the different crops. Such a policy would enable the authorities to drop many of the direct controls, especially those defining the acreage for various crops. If the policy is phased in gradually, there should be interim adjustments between relative price movements and the compulsory quota deliveries. The implication of this proposal is not that the government should abdicate its role in influencing agricultural prices, but that it should use indirect means, such as adjustments in government stockpiles, rather than direct controls.

The profitability of one crop in relation to that of others and the need to feed his own family and animals are more important to a farmer than the output price alone. Therefore, output prices cannot be set in isolation but must be treated within price sets. If one crop is to be encouraged at the expense of others, then more than one crop price will usually have to be adjusted. Fine tuning of cotton prices in relation to wheat is not of much use if berseem prices are left free. Similarly, controls will have to be balanced among all competing crops.

If the sector indeed generates a surplus, ways of taxing this sur-

23. During the period of controls, the cotton and wheat area declined in absolute terms by nearly 700,000 feddans. In relative terms the decline was even greater, as extra land became available, and berseem, fruit, and vegetable plantings expanded to take up the difference.

plus other than through price manipulation need to be examined.
For example, fixed costs that do not vary with production levels or
combinations of crops would not distort production incentives in the
manner of unbalanced price manipulation. One method would be to
increase the land tax, which was last set in 1952 on 1949 values,
and to allow output prices to rise. The increased tax receipts would
offset part of the higher subsidies that may be required because of
raising producer prices. Higher producer prices would also permit
input subsidies to be lowered or eliminated.

Another major shortcoming of the present price policy is its complexity, which sends conflicting signals to producers, with results
that are impossible to predict. The cotton farmer, for example, is
simultaneously subject to a heavy export tax and domestic tax on output prices, a buffer stock price support, a subsidy on pest control,
a tax or subsidy on fertilizer, a subsidy on water supplies, a seed
subsidy, physical controls over input use and minimum area planted,
and incentive payments to expand acreage and plant earlier. The net
effect of this melange of policy instruments has been the opposite of
the stated aims — cotton plantings have continuously declined, quota
evasion is widespread, and efficiency has suffered. There is, therefore, a good case for making the system of agricultural taxes and
subsidies more "transparent" — that is, with a minimum of concealed instruments.

Investment policies. The two main issues for investment policy
are the level and direction of investment in the agricultural sector.
The flow of public funds into the sector has been less than the outflow caused by the implicit taxation of the price policy; the price
policy has also affected the ability and willingness of the private sector to invest. The share of agriculture, irrigation, and drainage in
total investment has fallen from around 25 percent in the mid-1960s
(when the allocations for the Aswan High Dam and its ancillary works
were at their peak) to 12 percent in 1971-72 and is projected at 8.6
percent for 1978-82. The absolute amount, adjusted for inflation,
has also declined. Precise figures on private investment are not
available, but the data available on monetized fixed investment suggest that it is very low. The unwillingness or inability of the private
sector to invest can be explained in part by the fact that because the
small farms provide most of the output, they also bear most of the
implicit tax, which is levied per unit of output via the price per unit.

The available public investment has largely been directed toward
reclaiming the so-called new lands. Over the last decade, the new
lands have received around 50 to 60 percent of total public investment in agriculture, although they contribute only about 2 to 3 percent of production. Given Egypt's shortage of arable land, adding
to the cultivable acreage must be an important element in the long-
term strategy, but there is considerable doubt whether the current
distribution of investment between the old and the new lands is consonant with the aim of rapidly raising agricultural output. The old

lands, which could quickly increase their productivity with investment in drainage and support services, are being starved of allocations.   Instead, investment is being directed into the new lands,
which are expected to require a minimum of fifteen years' capital
absorption before they can earn annual income sufficient to cover
even operating expenses, and which probably produce no more than
5 percent of agricultural output in the early 1980s.   It is evident
that if the agricultural growth target is to be attained the investment
in the sector must be increased and a larger part of that investment
must be channeled into the old lands.   Moreover, the new lands
would yield quicker results if investment were concentrated in small
demonstration areas rather than being spread thinly across the
900,000 feddans that are being reclaimed.   Since an important aim
of the reclamation project is to increase the living space of Egypt,
there is a good case for regarding it as multisectoral regional development, the costs of which do not have to be covered exclusively,
or perhaps even primarily, from agricultural production.

Planning, management, and organization.   Planning for the agricultural sector consists essentially of drawing up a detailed production program in which the assumptions about crop yield and area
are predicated on physical investment in improvements such as irrigation and drainage.   The original proposal for the investment
program is developed by the departments, agencies, and authorities
within the Ministry of Agriculture and then submitted to the Ministry of Planning for review.   Because of staff limitations, the review procedure is somewhat cursory, but the Ministry of Planning
usually imposes overall constraints on the resources available for
use in the sector, which means the original proposal has to be re-
defined.   The discussion between the two ministries focuses on the
physical aspects of the project: its overall costs and physical characteristics (for example, the number of feddans to be drained).

The pattern of the investment program is dictated by the many
autonomous or semi-autonomous agencies of the Ministry of Agriculture, which have their own objectives and internal priorities.
The overall plan for the Ministry of Agriculture is an aggregation
of the plans of individual units and often depends on the strength of
a given subunit rather than on national priorities for the sector.

These institutional subdivisions seriously constrain the agricultural sector in four other ways: (1) They make it difficult to develop projects that would best utilize the resources in agriculture,
either in general or in a given area, because the availability and
utilization of resources are usually considered within an administrative rather than regional, national, or economic context.   In the
capital-intensive state farms, capital is subsidized by the government and qualified labor is scarce.   In the cooperatives, capital is
extremely limited, and though labor is plentiful there seem to be
few productive activities to employ it.   (2) Separate administrative

jurisdictions render it extremely difficult to develop regions along the best lines. (3) Small subunits, even with merit in their case, are unable to compete with the larger units for resources. (4) Subunits also compete at the wholesale and retail market levels. For example, subsidized public sector production competes with cooperative and private sector production of poultry, livestock, fruits, and vegetables.

Industry

The industrial scene is dominated by public sector enterprises, which account for around two-thirds of value added in manufacturing and are responsible for about 90 percent of fixed investment. Much of what was said earlier in this chapter about public enterprise efficiency is relevant for this section. However, the private sector, especially small-scale enterprises, is the major employer in manufacturing; in 1975 it provided about 54 percent of employment in industry. Employment objectives thus make it essential to take policy action in this area and to adopt a strategy for the development of small-scale industry.

The major issue in the manufacturing sector in the coming decade is to increase factor productivity. This will require a reform of the very complex system of tariffs and other (especially quantitative) controls that sets high and widely varying effective rates of protection for the production of consumer goods and discourages the manufacture of capital goods.[24] Another drawback is that the system has not furnished incentives for manufactured exports. To promote efficiency in factor use, it would be necessary to remove gradually the quantitative restrictions on imports, in order to stimulate cost-consciousness in domestic industry by the threat of external competition; to impose a uniform tariff on all imports, so as to end the bias against particular industries; to provide an open subsidy to industries that appear to have a comparative advantage (see chapter 12); to improve quality, particularly in cotton manufactures; and to redirect export markets.

A number of direct measures could be taken to promote the efficient use of labor and capital. As discussed above in connection with public sector efficiency, the object of these measures is to make financial surplus a more important criterion in judging the performance of enterprises and to give management greater incentives and authority to increase this surplus. At the same time, the reform of the institutional system would gradually remove some of the artificial props and make enterprises accountable for their performance. Such management reforms ought to be acceptable

---

24. For a description, see Robert Mabro and Samir Radwan, The Industrialization of Egypt, 1939-1973 (Oxford: Clarendon Press, 1976), pp. 51-59.

because they would not affect the ownership structure, but would generate larger resources for deployment toward socially directed goals.

The relevant measures would include greater financial and social recognition to management for good performance and sanctions for poor performance; a wider use of payment to workers on the basis of results; and a reform of the labor laws and employment policy that grant security of tenure and other advantages to workers for social welfare reasons. The point is that the welfare burden should be carried by the state rather than the firms, and distributional considerations should be separated as much as possible from the allocative mechanism for products and factors of production. Such measures should perhaps be introduced gradually in pilot enterprises. It might help if workers were to participate with management in setting goals, such as the increase in productivity to be achieved during a given period, and were represented in decisions regarding dismissals. Fuller utilization of installed capacity, including the renovation of equipment where necessary, and better project preparation would also increase efficiency. On a more macro level, the policy package should include the adjustment of interest rates to levels that better reflect the scarcity of capital, and the reform of the price structure and the system of price administration in the economy.

In the 1980s the ever increasing complexity in the structure of Egyptian industry will require serious efforts to coordinate investment and production activities in three areas. First, because control over the public industrial sector has become fragmented, an overall policy is required to set priorities. In recent years responsibility for the production of a great many items — such as cement, paper, medical supplies, petrochemicals, ginned cotton, and baked goods — has been transferred from the Ministry of Industry to other ministries, for example, the Ministries of Housing and Reconstruction, Culture, Health, Petroleum, Commerce, and Supply. Second, since joint ventures with foreign partners are the responsibility of the Ministry of Economy's Arab and Foreign Investments and Free Zones Authority, another agency will be introduced when there is foreign investment. Third, the expected growth of the domestic private sector will add to the difficult problems of coordination, especially in view of the paucity of information regarding this sector and the lack of clearly defined goals for it. Perhaps the best that the authorities can do initially is to indicate targets for production and investment, based on demand studies for the major industrial products, and closely monitor them to see whether over- or underinvestment is likely to occur. A shortfall could be made up by having the public sector step in or by increasing the profitability to the private sector (if this is not too far out of line with social profitability). Similarly, it will be necessary to check overinvestment in the more profitable items, as failure to do this would leave capacity unutilized, perhaps in substantial amounts.

The orderly encouragement of private enterprise, which is largely concentrated in small-scale manufacturing, will require the articulation of a strategy for small industry. Small-scale industries should be perceived as complementing the larger public and private enterprises. To promote small industry, developmental policies should aim for efficiency, adaptation to new circumstances, and growth, rather than protection of out-of-date methods of production against the competition of more modern techniques. The effectiveness of this effort would be greatly enhanced if financial and technical assistance could be combined. Support of small-scale industries should not imply the creation of a privileged situation — a sort of discrimination in reverse. Rather, it should put small industry on an equal footing with the public sector and establish conditions for equal opportunities.

In devising a strategy, two major and parallel objectives are employment generation and the alleviation of constraints on the growth and development of small-scale industries, essentially by improving productivity. A youthful and growing population and labor force make the creation of employment opportunities an important consideration for the next five to ten years. Open unemployment in Egypt is reportedly low, however — although underemployment is common — and shortages of particular skills are becoming increasingly evident. Under these circumstances employment generation is not the dominant need. Equally important is the need to improve productivity, which can be achieved primarily by modernizing equipment and upgrading small manufacturing establishments through a properly tailored technical assistance program that includes the training of skills. The introduction of more sophisticated and specialized equipment at this stage of Egypt's development should not be cavalierly dismissed. Nor should it lead to an indiscriminate choice of highly capital-intensive techniques and equipment. Given the scarcity of capital and foreign exchange and wages that are low by world standards, a conscious effort should be made to adopt technologies appropriate to the local circumstances.

In essense, the strategy should direct private investment and extend support primarily to small-scale industries with a relatively high probability of survival and success, and it should promote the gradual integration of these enterprises into the rest of the industrial sector. Viability and self-sustained growth are most likely to be found among industrial activities with growth potential and with rather insignificant economies of scale — those that cater to specialized or low-priced markets, or that are in areas where rapid changes in tastes are likely to occur, or that display complementarity with the activities of larger firms, including efficient import substitution. Such a conscious approach, effected through the lending procedures of financial intermediaries, would ensure that small-scale industries fill interstices, command an interlocking position within the industrial structure, and constitute vital parts of a functionally integrated whole.

The Infrastructure

During the last decade, Egypt's infrastructure has deteriorated steadily as resources were diverted to other uses. As a result, serious weaknesses in the infrastructure have begun to affect productive efforts and could gravely discourage investment, especially foreign. To attract large-scale foreign financing Egypt needs not only to extend attractive financial inducements, as it is doing through Law 43 of 1974 and its revision, but also to improve the supporting facilities required to make the investment profitable. The government has recognized the urgency of rehabilitating the infrastructure and has allocated to it around 50 percent of total public investment in the 1978-82 plan.

The efficient provision of infrastructure services is inhibited by a number of factors. First, the price of virtually all products and services has been set at an uneconomic level, with little or no flexibility to change in response to changing conditions of cost or demand. Second, all the infrastructure enterprises possess labor forces considerably in excess of their requirements — one more instance of the public sector's acting as the guarantor of full employment. Third, most facilities suffer from a lack of adequate investment. Frequently it is insufficient to maintain the original level and quality of service, and it is especially needed to keep up with the requirements of an expanding economy and a growing population. Fourth, there has been an absence of comprehensive planning and evaluation of alternatives, particularly in sectors such as transport and energy where the same service can be provided through different modes. Fifth, in common with public industrial enterprises, the infrastructure agencies have been given little incentive to improve their performance. While almost all sections of the infrastructure require attention, the main need appears to be in energy, transport, and communications.

At present there is no formal national energy policy in the sense of an explicit statement of national objectives and specific plans for attaining them. Implicitly, however, the aim appears to be to develop and exploit indigenous energy resources as rapidly as possible and to supplement them with nuclear power in the early 1980s. Because the issues are numerous and complex, it is important to formulate a clearly defined national energy strategy. The completion of the Aswan High Dam has increased the hydroelectric potential of the country, and with the discovery of gas and oil fields, Egypt has become a surplus producer of petroleum. The availability of various types of energy and the possibility for substitution among them raises the question of the socially and economically optimal mix. Another issue concerns the optimal rate of development of additional energy sources, such as the associated natural gas that is now being flared, the additional hydropower that could be developed from the Nile between Aswan and Cairo, and the possibility of nuclear power. The location of new power generation plants relative to load fields and the related question of transmission and distribution networks must be addressed. The Aswan High Dam now gives Egypt a surplus of generating capacity, but investment is needed to correct deficiencies in transmission and distribution facilities. In addition, the energy tariff structure needs revision. For allocative efficiency, the marginal cost of producing electricity should provide the basis for electricity tariffs. The marginal cost calculations, in turn, should price the fuel inputs at their opportunity cost, which would be the export price for oil. At present, oil is made available to the Electricity Authority and to a large part of the industrial sector at prices well below the export price.

The transport sector has suffered from the investment squeeze of the last decade. Underinvestment in railway maintenance has so seriously constrained capacity that roads are used for some traffic that could be more economically moved by rail. Waterways have also been neglected in recent years, and the transport strategy will have to consider to what extent this mode could be economically developed. The most efficient use of resources in the transport sector would thus be in rehabilitating and improving the railway system, followed by investment in waterways.

More feasibility studies are needed before a decision can be taken on the construction of additional ports. There is a strong case, however, for the immediate improvement and expansion of the port of Alexandria, which is seriously congested because of insufficient equipment to handle cargo. Railways, roads, and the port could perhaps be better maintained if a certain amount of recurring expenditure for maintenance were ensured by being included in the development budget.

The telecommunications sector has also suffered from underinvestment and a lack of overall planning. This area is ripe not only for investment but also for a number of other reforms, especially of tariffs, which have not been changed since 1966. Moreover, the sector appears to be considerably overstaffed owing to the mandatory requirements of the government.

No discussion of improvements in the infrastructure, or indeed of investment generally, would be complete without underlining the vital role of the construction sector. The building boom in the neighboring capital-surplus countries has drawn Egyptian construction workers both directly and in connection with the activities of Egyptian construction companies in these areas. Shortages of many construction skills are beginning to be serious in Egypt and could act as a brake on the country's ambitious investment plans. Unless construction capacity is rapidly increased, attempts to accelerate the implementation of projects would only result in bidding up their costs.

The construction sector faces an amalgam of shortages — of skills, technology, materials, and finance. One way to tackle them would be to set up joint ventures with foreign construction companies to facilitate the transfer of modern building technology to Egypt. Projects financed under external aid programs could be designed to attract foreign construction firms to form joint ventures with Egyptian companies in order to bid for contracts. The industrialization plan should give priority to alleviating the shortage of materials, especially of construction steel and cement. And training programs for the construction sector must rapidly be enlarged to offset the drain on the reservoir of skills caused by emigration.

APPENDIX: INCOME DISTRIBUTION AND CONSUMPTION PATTERNS

No single data source can be used to estimate income distribution in Egypt. The most consistent numbers come from a series of three consumer budget surveys undertaken by the Central Agency for Public Mobilization and Statistics and predecessor agencies in 1958-59, 1964-65, and 1974-75. The expenditure distributions from the first two surveys have been described in an article by Osman A. el-Kholie.[25] These, plus some results from the first round of the 1974-75 survey, are described here.

In general, the surveys and other sources seem to indicate that the Egyptian income distribution is fairly egalitarian by the standards of developing countries and has not deteriorated noticeably over time. These conclusions, of course, depend on the overall quality of the expenditure survey data. A thorough statistical analysis would require access to the unprocessed survey results (instead of the summary statistics used here) and much more time than was available. Crude tests, however, suggest the coverage is fairly good. The major omissions in income and expenditure surveys in underdeveloped countries usually comprise income in kind and similar payments at the bottom end of the income distribution, and unreported profit income at the top. Outside of agriculture,

25. "Disparities of Egyptian Personal Income Distribution as Reflected by Family Budget Data," L'Egypte Contemporaine, vol. 64, no. 354 (October 1973), pp. 358-72.

profits go largely to the state in Egypt (at least in the initial accounting), so that omissions on this score may be fairly small. And since a blowup of total expenditure for the 1974-75 survey agrees well with the aggregate consumption estimates obtained separately, omissions at the bottom may be fairly small as well.

Results from the Consumer Expenditure Surveys

Distributions of consumer expenditure from the household surveys are shown in figure 4-1 for the three sample periods. The striking thing about the Lorenz curves is how closely they lie to one another. There was apparently a small improvement in the rural distribution between 1958-59 and 1964-65 and a somewhat larger deterioration in the decade ending in 1974-75, but the movements were quite small. At the scale of the figure, there is no observable difference between the 1958-59 and 1964-65 urban distributions; the 1974-75 urban distribution is slightly more egalitarian than the other two. Rough estimates of Gini coefficients based on the Lorenz curves for 1974-75 are 0.39 for the rural household expenditure distribution and 0.36 for the urban. Given the proximity of the curves, estimates of Gini coefficients for the other years would be very close to these values.

The slightly less egalitarian rural expenditure distribution is an uncommon but not startling result, and it disappears when savings are taken into account. Less unexpected is a generally higher level of expenditure in urban households, where annual expenditures per person averaged LE99.8 during 1974-75, as opposed to LE63.0 in rural households. This difference in per capita expenditure is explained by the facts that average expenditure per household is substantially lower in rural areas than in urban (LE375.4 compared with LE556.8), and rural households are on the average larger than those in urban areas (6.0 persons per household as opposed to 5.6).

Egypt does not differ greatly from most underdeveloped countries in having relatively low spending levels and large families in the countryside. The low spending is usually explained by incomplete monetization of the rural economy and lower markups on food. The larger families presumably reflect the usefulness of children as farm laborers and insurance against future mishaps. Somewhat more surprising is the positive association between household size and expenditure level. This observation runs contrary to the notion that well-to-do families are less fertile, but in fact the income and expenditure data in many underdeveloped countries show a positive association. The growth in family size with income undoubtedly reflects the remaining power of the extended family in poor regions. It makes the income distribution of persons much more egalitarian than that for households, especially in rural areas.

Figure 4–1. Lorenz Curves for Rural and Urban Household
Expenditure, 1958-59 to 1974-75

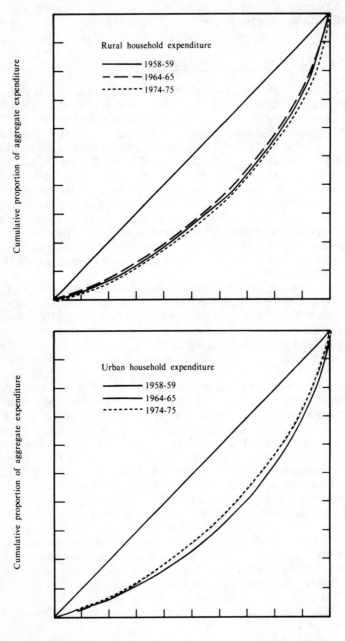

Cumulative proportion of households, in order by size of expenditure

Source: Osman A. el-Kholie, "Disparities of Egyptian Personal Income Distribution as Reflected by Family Budget Data," *L'Egypte Contemporaine,* vol. 64, no. 354 (October 1973); and Central Agency for Public Mobilization and Statistics.

Inferences about the Size Distribution of Incomes

To reveal something about the household distribution of income in Egypt, the expenditure distribution must be blown up to take into account household saving and direct taxes. The expenditure survey, of course, deals with a sample of households, but when rural and urban average expenditures per household from the 1974-75 survey are multiplied by the number of households in agriculture and nonagricultural activities respectively, the results are close to the total consumption expenditures estimated separately, as shown below:

| | Expenditure per household (Egyptian pounds) | Number of households (millions) | Total expenditures (millions of Egyptian pounds) | |
			Survey estimate	Independent estimate
Rural	375.4	2.87	1.078	1.024
Urban	556.8	3.84	2.138	2.160

A transformation of expenditure into income was attempted first from estimates of total household saving. Household saving was assumed to have an elasticity of 1.5 with respect to consumer expenditure, and levels of saving per household were inferred for the various consumption expenditure classes. These calculations suggest that savings shares of disposable income range from 5.2 to 30.8 percent in urban households and from 2.0 to 17.1 percent in rural households. The savings share at low income levels may be overestimated, but for high incomes the estimates take into account the saved component of social security contributions and may be fairly realistic.

The calculations of income distribution also accounted for direct taxes, which were assumed to affect only high urban incomes. The frequency distributions for the final estimates of rural and urban income distributions are shown by the Lorenz curves in figure 4-2. Because of the positive association of household size with expenditure, the per person distributions are considerably more egalitarian. The relevant Gini coefficients are:

	Household expenditure	Household income	Personal income
Rural	0.39	0.40	0.27
Urban	0.36	0.40	0.33

Figure 4–2. Lorenz Curves for Rural and Urban Income
Distribution, 1974-75

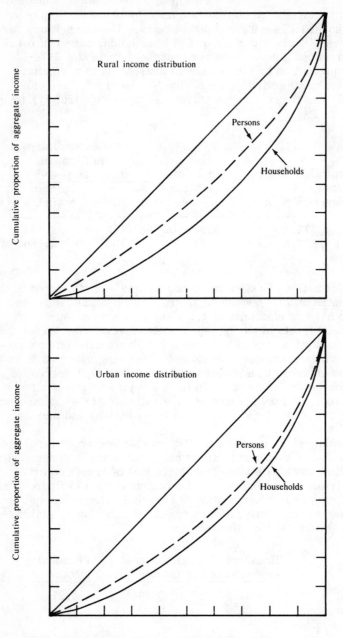

Cumulative proportion of income-receiving units, in order by size of income

Source: Central Agency for Public Mobilization and Statistics; distribution by persons is based on World Bank
estimates.

For households, the estimated Lorenz curves for income practically overlap. The per person distribution for rural households is
more egalitarian than its urban counterpart, but of course at a lower average income level.

Consumption Patterns in Egypt

Data from several sources are available regarding consumption
patterns in Egypt. Some are reviewed here, beginning with time
series information from the Ministry of Planning on the "disappearance" (that is, production plus imports less nonconsumption uses)
of certain items. Some results from the 1974-75 household expenditure survey, especially on food comsumption, are then presented,
followed by a discussion and comparison of different estimates of
Egypt's current consumption levels of major staples.

Changes in consumption over time. In the Ministry of Planning's
compilations of the disappearance of important consumption goods
over time, several points stand out. There have been no substantial increases in the amounts of staple grains consumed per capita
over the 1963-75 period (table 4-1). If flour is included with wheat,
kilogram consumption per capita increased only 16.9 percent over
thirteen years, or 1.2 percent a year. (The 1964-74 growth rate
was 0.8 percent per year.) Trend increases in consumption of
other grains are no more favorable. Consumption of meat and
poultry seems to have risen, however, along with vegetables and
fruits.[26]

These consumption trends are broadly consistent with what is
known about changes in agricultural productivity. Growing imports
of wheat and maize have supplied the greater part of the increase
in consumer demand, and in recent years meat and fish imports
have been a noticeable share of total supply. On the other hand,
although total meat, poultry, and vegetable consumption has gone
up rapidly, it is still largely supplied from within the country. The
production of vegetables and of inputs such as berseem into meat
production must have increased substantially (see chapter 9).

Consumption of cotton textiles and leather products has increased
steadily, reflecting the high income elasticities of demand for these
products (table 4-2). Similarly, as table 4-3 indicates, total consumption of durable goods has increased steadily, especially in the
1970s. These trends in part reflect the appearance of new products
on the market.

26. The Planning Ministry estimates of consumption of meat and similar products, milk and milk products, and vegetables are much higher than those of other
agencies. The sources of the biases in the various calculations are not apparent,
but presumably the ministry ommitted some important uses of vegetables and especially milk in calculating its estimates of disappearance.

TABLE 4-1. ESTIMATES OF STAPLE FOOD CONSUMPTION PER CAPITA, 1963-64 TO 1975
(kilograms)

Item	1963-64	1964-65	1965-66	1966-67	1967-68	1968-69	1969-70	1970-71	1971-72	1973	1974	1975
Wheat	117.7	115.5	106.1	109.4	107.2	110.9	111.3	118.2	120.3	114.1	115.3	119.9
Flour[a]	—	—	—	—	—	—	—	—	—	15.4	11.3	17.7
Nili maize	74.8	71.5	69.7	76.4	68.3	70.0	69.7	67.5	64.0	69.3	77.4	80.3
Maize	24.0	18.8	25.4	26.5	26.2	25.2	22.3	23.2	22.2	21.6	20.4	20.5
Barley	1.7	2.0	1.3	1.5	2.3	2.6	1.8	1.4	2.0	1.5	1.3	1.3
Rice	31.1	35.2	25.6	20.8	22.1	25.0	28.4	31.4	30.6	33.5	35.3	36.2
Beans	7.5	8.4	7.4	9.6	3.5	4.8	6.4	4.6	7.3	6.9	7.9	9.2
Lentils	1.5	1.6	1.9	1.4	1.1	1.1	1.1	1.7	1.5	2.2	1.8	2.2
Sesame	0.1	0.1	0.1	0.06	0.06	0.03	0.1	0.1	0.1	0.1	0.2	0.2
Meat and poultry	10.3	6.3	6.5	7.6	7.5	7.2	10.9	10.9	11.0	12.6	13.8	13.3
Fish	5.0	5.5	5.5	5.5	4.5	2.9	3.4	3.3	3.2	3.5	3.7	4.1
Eggs	1.3	1.2	1.2	1.2	1.2	1.3	1.4	1.4	1.5	1.6	1.7	1.7
Vegetables	104.9	140.6	147.5	135.5	133.5	153.5	148.9	140.3	137.0	153.4	158.8	158.1
Fruits	31.2	25.2	25.6	24.0	27.7	24.9	26.6	21.1	34.9	37.0	39.3	39.9
Tea	9.0	1.1	1.0	1.1	0.7	0.7	0.7	0.7	0.7	0.7	0.7	1.0
Coffee	0.1	0.2	0.2	0.2	0.1	0.1	0.1	0.1	0.1	0.1	0.1	0.2

a. Flour was included with wheat from 1963-64 to 1971-72.
Source: Ministry of Planning.

TABLE 4-2. ESTIMATES OF TEXTILE CONSUMPTION PER CAPITA, 1963-64 TO 1975

Item	1963-64	1964-65	1965-66	1966-67	1967-68	1968-69	1969-70	1970-71	1971-72	1973	1974	1975
Cotton textiles (meters)	14.338	16.489	17.322	15.239	13.541	12.328	11.696	18.117	17.654	17.818	22.109	22.633
Wool textiles (meters)	0.241	0.292	0.285	0.248	0.207	0.217	0.223	0.258	0.255	0.253	0.195	0.193
Satin textiles (meters)	1.852	2.410	2.688	2.662	1.968	2.085	1.934	1.830	1.766	1.737	1.635	1.653
Leather shoes (pairs)	n.a.	0.088	0.099	0.148	0.154	0.143	0.149	0.249	0.249	0.421	0.436	0.438

n.a. Not available.
Source: Ministry of Planning.

TABLE 4-3. ESTIMATES OF ANNUAL CONSUMPTION OF DURABLE GOODS, 1963-64 TO 1976
(thousands of units)

Item	1963-64	1964-65	1965-66	1966-67	1967-68	1968-69	1969-70	1970-71	1971-72	1973	1974	1975	1976
Refrigerators	30.0	30.9	44.3	23.6	12.6	36.1	52.0	40.3	48.9	40.1	61.2	63.6	65.8
Washing machines	16.8	17.0	14.3	11.0	9.2	8.3	16.1	19.2	20.5	22.2	31.5	32.4	33.3
Butane heaters	11.9	16.1	16.6	10.9	12.4	13.3	13.1	13.1	13.4	11.9	14.1	14.5	14.6
Butane stoves	78.8	80.0	81.9	68.7	64.0	69.6	78.1	54.9	56.0	124.1	128.9	134.0	139.3
Sewing machines	14.6	9.5	8.8	11.1	12.6	27.9	14.2	15.0	15.5	22.9	32.4	33.3	34.2
Radios	245.9	229.1	142.4	155.5	119.5	102.2	148.0	191.8	207.5	172.2	105.2	109.4	113.5
TV sets	51.9	76.4	40.4	48.1	54.7	41.9	60.5	77.0	75.8	77.7	87.9	89.6	90.8
Automobiles	6.3	5.9	4.3	1.6	3.3	6.3	10.3	17.7	10.9	13.1	25.8	26.3	26.8
Bicycles	40.0	39.6	53.9	61.9	48.6	54.6	47.5	52.6	46.1	50.4	51.9	54.4	57.1

Source: Ministry of Planning.

The 1974-75 consumer budget survey. Tables 4-4 and 4-5 present compilations from the first round of the 1974-75 household expenditure survey and break down household expenditure by major classes of goods and by expenditure groups. Since the sample sizes are small (1,001 rural households and 2,000 urban) the results must be regarded as tentative. As in most poor countries, the budget share devoted to food consumption is high. In the rural data the food share ranges from 74 to 27.5 percent and is more than 50 percent for all consumer groups except the very richest. The range for urban families is 70 to 34 percent, with only the top four groups dropping below 50 percent.

Among the nonfood items, there is a sharp increase in expenditures on transport and communications (especially on automobiles in the top income groups) and on categories such as culture and entertainment and "Other expenditures." These increases simply reflect growing diversity in the consumption basket as income goes up. The share of textiles and clothing also goes up by about 5 percent in the income range of the tables, suggesting that clothing subsidies in Egypt will have to be carefully directed if they are really to benefit the poor.

The household expenditure survey data give information only on the value of purchases, not on quantities. A discussion of the physical amounts of commodities actually consumed requires the use of price information, but the data are not completely satisfactory, for the quality of the product is not specified. For example, the wheat price is known, but not the extraction rate of the flour from which bread is made. Similarly, the household expenditure data are not classified finely enough to tell how the shares of wheat and flour change in the consumer basket as household incomes go up.

These problems must be kept in mind when looking at table 4-6, which gives quantity food consumption as inferred from tables 4-4 and 4-5, using the Ministry of Planning prices (with grain and starch prices weighted according to the 1975 final demand breakdown of table 4-1, to give an average price of LE39.54 a metric ton). Food consumption per capita clearly rises with income, and in most cases the implied elasticities are reasonable. For example, consumption of dry beans — a major Egyptian staple — goes up by between one-third and one-half, while total expenditure increases by a factor of twenty; the near zero income elasticity is quite plausible. Arc elasticities in the vicinity of one-half for meat and milk also look reasonable. The main problem is with grain and starch consumption in rural areas, where the apparent consumption of 500 kilos a year would strain physical limits. There is surely an omitted price effect here — rural families eat Nili maize and rich families eat at least some fine bread. Valuing both forms of grain at the same price clearly introduces error into the computation.

TABLE 4-4. ANNUAL EXPENDITURE OF RURAL HOUSEHOLDS, 1974-75
(Egyptian pounds)

Expenditure	Less than 50	50- 74	75- 99	100- 149	150- 199	200- 249	250- 299
				Expenditure intervals			
Food and beverages							
Grain and carbohydrate	230	418	849	2,647	4,616	6,321	7,801
Dry beans	28	46	98	283	559	682	838
Fresh and preserved vegetables	44	101	198	562	1,082	1,261	1,654
Fresh and preserved fruit	14	41	98	228	473	641	860
Meat and poultry	57	213	344	1,061	2,054	2,830	3,692
Fish and seafood	8	19	82	173	393	478	630
Eggs	3	11	30	93	182	262	370
Milk and dairy products	25	43	98	276	598	842	1,119
Oil and fat	36	100	184	620	1,192	1,655	2,057
Sugar and sweets	36	56	126	374	852	1,162	1,376
Other food	46	58	100	270	533	586	851
Tea and coffee	15	49	79	286	523	815	920
Other beverages	...	4	2	12	57	141	213
Subtotal	542	1,159	2,288	6,885	13,114	17,676	22,381
Textiles, clothes, and footwear	24	70	120	657	1,692	2,141	3,734
Housing, fuel, and light	143	260	417	1,328	2,307	3,148	4,005
Furniture and household services	17	37	78	230	448	552	788
Medical care and medicine	5	7	24	54	153	200	271
Transport and communications	1	10	16	51	177	325	284
Education	...	...	4	16	74	112	158
Culture and entertainment	...	...	...	12	34	59	56
Other	14	123	139	619	1,346	2,366	2,775
Total consumer expenditures	746	1,666	3,086	9,852	19,345	26,579	34,452
Gifts	...	1	5	47	38	123	224
Advance payments	...	...	...	...	...	...	30
TOTAL	746	1,667	3,091	9,899	19,383	26,702	34,706
Total families (number)	20	27	35	78	112	118	126
Total persons (number)	26	52	106	289	504	626	756
Persons/family	1.300	1.926	3.029	3.705	4.500	5.305	6.000

... Zero or negligible.
Source: Household Expenditure Survey, 1974-75.

				Expenditure intervals					
300-349	350-399	400-499	500-599	600-799	800-999	1,000-1,399	1,400-1,999	2,000 or more	Total
6,862	6,842	9,497	4,200	7,637	4,474	3,055	2,554	978	68,981
867	753	1,139	567	960	639	603	266	195	8,523
1,657	1,491	2,270	936	1,884	1,020	993	693	245	16,091
999	893	1,432	611	1,446	840	927	850	238	10,591
3,912	3,715	5,926	2,653	4,724	2,793	2,968	2,148	1,748	40,838
612	485	997	415	860	420	690	345	131	6,738
353	319	550	265	511	282	291	253	145	3,920
1,003	898	1,656	729	1,630	913	985	885	272	11,972
2,184	2,148	3,040	1,286	2,501	1,599	1,379	932	346	21,259
1,307	1,330	1,945	977	1,545	887	841	740	277	13,831
790	869	1,108	639	829	467	500	275	145	8,066
836	840	1,232	593	1,035	596	488	454	165	8,926
266	306	402	240	426	305	506	294	407	3,581
21,648	20,889	31,194	14,111	25,988	15,235	14,226	10,689	5,292	223,317
3,627	3,647	6,117	3,088	7,134	3,740	4,862	2,975	2,040	45,668
3,369	3,634	4,626	2,272	4,206	2,086	2,207	1,494	683	36,185
730	642	1,151	629	1,086	692	1,250	1,347	2,769	12,446
304	270	494	228	499	454	414	319	120	3,816
350	408	677	408	678	569	836	302	5,871	10,963
182	185	586	270	618	479	588	199	243	3,714
31	33	112	239	221	75	457	80	81	1,490
2,747	2,763	4,053	2,331	3,880	2,302	2,307	1,805	993	30,563
32,988	32,471	49,010	23,576	44,310	25,632	27,147	19,210	18,092	368,162
146	536	382	176	532	654	1,667	1,603	1,166	7,300
22	6	60	25	30	70	90	...	...	333
33,156	33,013	49,452	23,777	44,872	26,356	28,904	20,813	19,258	375,795
102	89	113	44	65	30	24	13	5	1,001
672	596	804	340	551	269	193	138	46	5,968
6.588	6.697	7.115	7.727	8.477	8.967	8.042	10.615	9.200	5.962

TABLE 4-5. ANNUAL EXPENDITURE OF URBAN HOUSEHOLDS, 1974-75
(Egyptian pounds)

Expenditure			Expenditure intervals				
	Less than 50	50-74	75-99	100-149	150-199	200-249	250-299
Food and beverages							
Grain and carbohydrate	68	135	320	1,809	3,285	4,998	7,198
Dry beans	7	16	55	311	415	705	1,094
Fresh and preserved vegetables	19	45	90	631	1,167	1,725	2,792
Fresh and preserved fruit	11	20	27	290	581	914	1,484
Meat and poultry	19	63	157	984	1,847	2,721	4,394
Fish and seafood	6	18	35	200	436	690	1,176
Eggs	...	3	13	86	163	224	341
Milk and dairy products	11	23	41	344	606	1,078	1,747
Oil and fat	10	36	93	470	934	1,476	2,276
Sugar and sweets	11	30	59	433	685	1,110	1,671
Other food	28	44	67	684	1,010	1,503	2,411
Tea and coffee	5	14	41	255	442	642	961
Other beverages	...	1	3	52	167	381	824
Subtotal	195	448	1,001	6,549	11,738	18,167	28,369
Textiles, clothes, and footwear	15	29	64	691	1,154	2,487	4,980
Housing, fuel, and light	80	121	307	1,580	3,034	4,348	7,082
Furniture and household services	6	19	39	253	457	773	1,400
Medical care and medicine	...	...	10	68	226	382	694
Transport and communications	...	...	4	99	200	388	915
Education	...	...	...	17	48	237	463
Culture and entertainment	...	...	...	3	14	63	130
Other	1	24	52	826	1,545	2,508	4,416
Total consumer expenditures	297	641	1,477	10,086	18,416	29,353	48,449
Gifts	...	...	1	4	40	205	204
Advance payments	...	...	...	2	...	61	108
TOTAL	297	641	1,478	10,092	18,456	29,619	48,761
Total families (number)	8	10	17	79	106	132	177
Total persons (number)	9	14	38	230	394	612	847
Persons/family	1.125	1.40	2.235	2.911	3.717	4.636	4.785

... Zero or negligible.
Source: Household Expenditure Survey, 1974-75.

			Expenditure intervals						
300-349	350-399	400-499	500-599	600-799	800-999	1,000-1,399	1,400-1,999	2,000 or more	Total
7,533	7,703	10,744	14,867	16,913	9,153	10,549	9,434	2,484	107,193
1,147	1,218	2,433	2,232	2,432	1,499	1,774	724	414	16,476
2,989	3,247	6,719	6,363	7,661	4,715	5,635	2,802	1,600	48,200
1,909	2,068	4,302	4,567	6,267	5,153	5,666	3,556	2,709	39,524
5,323	5,567	12,360	12,714	18,119	12,752	16,635	10,075	6,569	110,299
1,242	1,335	3,024	2,941	3,975	2,686	3,202	1,599	1,142	23,707
400	461	983	1,019	1,693	1,430	1,649	1,156	634	10,255
1,959	2,360	5,213	5,512	7,420	5,504	6,652	4,124	2,643	45,237
2,509	2,548	6,089	5,849	7,346	4,811	5,644	2,623	1,810	44,524
1,722	1,882	3,956	3,973	4,916	3,614	4,181	1,851	1;532	31,626
2,122	2,313	5,652	4,898	5,725	3,686	4,803	1,964	1,862	38,772
1,101	1,119	2,283	2,234	2,747	1,963	2,176	1,021	643	17,647
634	916	2,610	2,507	4,122	3,412	4,241	2,727	2,271	24,868
30,590	32,737	66,368	69,676	89,336	60,378	72,807	43,656	26,313	558,328
5,592	6,858	16,494	18,546	24,438	16,901	23,406	13,794	9,210	144,659
7,403	8,627	18,073	17,070	21,626	15,401	17,430	11,710	6,443	140,335
1,442	1,538	3,730	4,220	5,394	4,602	6,176	4,528	4,699	39,276
728	786	1,852	1,926	3,136	2,299	3,315	1,926	1,953	19,301
937	1,238	3,053	2,989	4,275	4,008	6,052	6,642	10,683	41,483
455	740	1,552	1,793	3,088	2,331	4,403	3,835	2,812	21,774
381	283	851	1,548	2,165	2,047	2,790	2,398	1,979	14,652
4,493	5,070	13,364	13,156	18,777	12,269	17,949	9,389	8,221	112,060
52,021	57,877	125,337	130,924	172,235	120,236	154,328	97,878	72,313	1,091,868
208	238	542	784	1,744	2,324	3,612	4,033	3,726	17,665
70	77	361	246	318	272	482	1,278	700	3,957
52,299	58,192	126,240	131,954	174,297	122,832	158,422	103,189	76,739	1,113,508
161	155	294	240	255	138	138	59	31	2,000
817	897	1,747	1,507	1,654	835	943	394	214	11,152
5.075	5.787	5.942	6.279	6.486	6.051	6.833	6.678	6.903	5.576

TABLE 4-6. ANNUAL FOOD CONSUMPTION PER PERSON, 1974-75
(kilograms)

Expenditure interval	Rural households					Urban households				
	Grain and starch	Dry beans	Meat, poultry, eggs	Milk and products	Vegetables	Grain and starch	Dry beans	Meat, poultry, eggs	Milk and products	Vegetables
Less than 50	223.7	9.4	3.3	6.0	34.5	191.1	6.8	3.5	7.6	43.1
50-74	203.3	7.7	5.8	5.2	39.6	243.9	9.9	7.5	10.3	65.6
75-99	202.6	8.0	5.4	5.8	38.1	213.0	12.6	6.7	6.7	48.3
100-149	231.6	8.5	5.7	6.0	39.7	198.9	11.8	6.9	9.3	56.0
150-199	231.6	9.6	6.5	7.4	43.8	210.9	9.2	7.8	9.6	60.4
200-249	255.4	9.5	7.1	8.4	41.1	206.5	10.0	7.4	11.0	57.5
250-299	261.0	9.6	7.8	9.3	44.6	214.9	11.2	8.7	12.9	67.3
300-349	258.3	11.2	9.1	9.3	50.3	233.2	12.2	10.7	15.0	74.7
350-399	290.3	11.0	9.5	9.4	51.0	217.2	11.8	10.3	16.4	73.9
400-499	298.7	12.3	11.6	12.9	57.6	155.5	12.1	11.7	18.6	78.5
500-599	312.4	14.5	12.3	13.4	56.2	249.5	12.9	13.8	22.9	86.2
600-799	350.5	15.2	13.8	18.5	69.8	258.6	12.8	18.0	28.0	94.5
800-999	420.6	20.7	16.2	21.2	77.4	277.2	15.6	25.3	41.2	115.2
1,000-1,399	400.3	27.2	25.6	31.9	105.0	282.9	16.4	28.5	44.1	122.0
1,400-1,999	468.1	16.8	24.9	40.1	102.5	605.6	16.0	40.7	65.4	145.1
2,000 or more	537.7	36.8	55.0	37.0	108.7	293.6	16.8	48.7	77.2	152.6
Total	292.3	12.4	10.8	12.5	55.0	243.1	12.8	16.2	25.4	88.2
Price (Egyptian pounds per metric ton)	39.54	115	800	160	49	39.54	115	800	160	49

Source: Household Expenditure Survey, 1974-75.

Using Ministry of Planning prices together with the consumer budget data yields per capita calorie intakes for low-income brackets of about 3,470 and 3,340 in rural and urban areas respectively. These numbers are close to those for North American food consumption and are obviously too high. Since most calories in the Egyptian diet come from grains, there is another reason to doubt the ministry's price of LE35 a ton, but the price of LE48 a ton appropriate to 2,500 calories a day is too high. Some overstatement of food consumption is suspected in the surveys — a not unusual occurrence. Both the Planning Ministry and the budget survey estimates for grain consumption exceed those of the Food and Agriculture Organization.[27] The FAO estimates are given in terms of flour, which may explain some of the difference. Another part may be explained by shifting mixes of high-quality and low-quality grain in consumption baskets as income changes. In any case, a rough average of 1,200 kilos per capita a year (1,860 calories per capita a day) is plausible.

27. Food and Agriculture Organization, Domestic Demand Projections for Agricultural Commodities, ESP/PS/EGY/73/4 (Rome, 1973).

5
Development Prospects

If the authorities do implement a package of policies on the lines
recommended in the preceding chapter, what are the prospects for
the economy over the next decade? To chart the prospective behavior of the Egyptian economy, simulation exercises were conducted.
In this chapter we merely point out some of the main elements in the
base run and comment on some alternative strategies. The results
of the simulation exercise must be regarded essentially as convey-
ing trends and orders of magnitude rather than precise predictions
because not all the implications of the policies discussed earlier
can be modeled. Furthermore, the data base is fairly weak, and
additional econometric and quantitative investigation is needed for
a fuller understanding of the relationships in the Egyptian economy.

BASE-RUN PROJECTION

The balance of payments turns out to be a major element in future prospects. The chief assumptions regarding the external sector for the base run of the projections can be summarized as follows:

- The aggregate growth rate is about 6.6 percent a year. The
  ratio of imports (payments for goods and services) to GDP
  is expected to remain virtually unaltered, although the import
  composition is expected to alter substantially.
- Export receipts for goods and services are expected to grow
  at a slightly higher rate (about 7.2 percent a year) largely
  because of the services sector (for example, workers' remittances, tourism, and the Suez Canal). A very conserva-
  tive view of the earnings from the petroleum sector is implicit in this projection.
- Gross capital inflow is expected to decline slightly in real
  terms. As a ratio of GDP, however, the decline is considerably more.

The simulation exercises indicate four issues of particular importance for policy purposes in the external sector. First, the projections assume that 37 million tons of crude oil will be produced in 1982; thereafter production is expected to go down steadily unless new sources of petroleum are discovered. Second, earnings from the Suez Canal will have to be at least maintained in real terms. Third, an additional export effort must be made to stimulate the growth of non-oil earnings. Fourth, sufficient incentives must be provided (through the exchange rate, for example) to maintain a rapid inflow of remittances from Egyptians working abroad.

Table 5-1 shows that in the base run the GDP at market prices is expected to increase in real terms at 6.5 percent a year in the coming decade. The rural component of GDP will be growing at only a little over 4 percent; given an estimated rural population of more than 21 million in 1986, this implies an annual per capita income in the rural areas of about LE116 in 1975 prices. For urban areas, the per capita income in 1986 works out to about LE280. A fairly generous rate of consumption of 6.4 percent annually over the entire period is projected by the model.

The model projects investment as the sum of national and foreign saving. Gross national saving, which is a better concept to use in projections for Egypt than domestic saving because of the increasing influence of factor income movements in the future, are projected to increase from about 15 to almost 20 percent of GNP between 1977 and 1986. This growth will imply a fairly sharp increase in the marginal rate of saving in the earlier years, but since much of the increase in income will come from petroleum and an expanded Suez Canal it will accrue directly to the government, making it amenable to direct policy action. The marginal savings rate over the period as a whole works out to 25 percent. Investment is projected to grow by 8.4 percent a year, which will make the ratio of investment to GDP in 1986 about 29 percent compared with 26 percent in 1977.

Given the foregoing assumptions and the measures proposed in this report for managing the economy, the balance of payments gap should remain manageable during the coming decade (see table 5-2). In order to strengthen the country's creditworthiness, the bulk of the payments deficit should be financed on concessional terms. The terms assumed for the simulation exercises are a mixture of grants and concessional loans, together with some financing through suppliers credits, that maintain the grant element in the total flows at around 60 percent. The debt service ratio, that is, the ratio of interest and principal repayments on medium- and long-term loans to total foreign exchange earnings, is then expected to fall from about 25 percent in 1977 to around 19 percent in 1986.

TABLE 5-1. STRUCTURE AND GROWTH, 1977-86

(constant 1975 prices)

Item	Millions of Egyptian pounds				Annual growth rates 1977-86 (percent)			Percentage share			
			1986							1986	
			Alternative			Alternative				Alternative	
	1977	Base	I	II	Base	I	II	1977	Base	I	II
GNP (market prices)	5,750	10,460	9,370	13,770	7.0	5.5	10.3	100	100	100	100
GNP (market prices)	5,520	9,720	8,580	13,030	6.5	5.1	10.0	97	93	92	95
GDP (rural)	1,660	2,430	2,020	2,820	4.3	2.4	6.1	29	23	22	20
GDP (urban)	3,860	7,290	6,560	10,210	7.3	6.1	11.4	67	70	70	75
Consumption	5,310	9,250	8,560	10,970	6.4	5.7	8.4	92	88	91	80
Investment	1,480	3,060	2,700	4,820	8.4	6.9	14.0	26	29	28	35
National saving	860	2,040	2,040	2,800	10.1	10.1	14.0	15	20	21	20
Domestic saving	630	1,300	1,280	2,060	8.4	8.2	14.1	11	12	14	15
Foreign saving	620	1,020	660	2,020	5.7	7.0	14.1	11	10	7	15

Source: World Bank projections.

98

TABLE 5-2. BALANCE OF PAYMENTS PROJECTIONS
IN THE BASE RUN, 1977-86
(millions of Egyptian pounds in 1975 prices)

Item	1977	Base	1986 Alternative I	1986 Alternative II
Merchandise exports	660	960	900	1,020
Merchandise imports	-1,700	-3,240	-2,840	-4,300
Trade balance	-1,040	-2,280	-1,940	-3,280
Nonfactor services (net)	190	520	520	520
Factor services (net)	230	740	760	740
Deficit on goods and services	-620	-1,020	-660	-2,020
Debt service				
Interest	-100	-140	-125	-180
Amortization	-280	-400	-315	-480
Debt service ratio[a] (percent)	25	19	16	23

a. Ratio of interest and amortization on medium- and long-term debt
to total foreign exchange earnings.
Source: World Bank projections.

ALTERNATIVE SCENARIOS

An alternative scenario is presented in table 5-1 for comparison
with the base run. It differs from the base run in essentially two
ways: the inflow of foreign capital is assumed to be about one-third
lower than in the base run, and the investment in agriculture reflects
the percentage allocation in the Egyptian 1978-82 plan. The lower
capital inflow operates through a lower growth of investment and
thus leads to a lower growth of GDP, namely, about 5 percent compared with the 6.5 percent in the base run. As a result of the lower investment in agriculture, the growth of the rural GDP is also,
of course, substantially lower and implies a per capita income in
1986 of LE96 compared with about LE252 for urban areas. Not surprisingly, the income distribution is likely to be more skewed than
in the base-run strategy — rural per capita income under this alternative amounts to about 38 percent of urban, compared with 41 percent in the base run — and shows further indication of the urban bias
in Egypt's investment allocations. The growth of both consumption
and saving is lower than in the base run. At the end of the period,
however, foreign saving comprises only 7 percent of GNP at market prices compared with 10 percent under the base run. On balance, a somewhat higher growth strategy (on the lines of the base
run) appears preferable because it offers higher levels of income,
consumption, and investment and is consistent with a manageable
situation in the external accounts.

So far we have been considering the effects on GNP and some other variables of the availability of financing for a certain level of investment. But we can turn the question around and ask: What would be the likely macroeconomic implications of Egypt's aiming for a significantly higher growth rate — say, 10 percent a year in real terms sustained over the next decade? The major implications that can be simulated in our model are shown as alternative II in the table.

The per capita income is 30 percent higher than in the base run, but the distribution of income between the rural and urban areas is of greater interest. Although the rural per capita income is higher in alternative II (at LE134 compared with LE116 in the base run), it amounts to only about 34 percent of the urban, as against 41 percent in the base run. The relative distribution is worse because the possibilities for income growth are limited in rural areas and the bulk of the targeted growth comes from the urban areas. This also explains the steep rise in the investment required to obtain the higher growth rate; the economy has increasingly to move into sectors with relatively higher capital-output ratios (as compared with those possible in agriculture) in order to obtain the planned growth rate. The investment ratio consequently rises to 35 percent of GNP (about 37 percent of GDP). Because of the level of aid flows that can reasonably be expected, domestic saving has to rise sharply, to 15 percent of GNP, implying a marginal rate of saving of 20 percent and a growth rate of over 14 percent a year over the period. Despite this, the inflow of external saving is considerably higher than under the other two alternatives. The servicing of this capital inflow also imposes a higher burden — the debt service ratio in 1986 works out to 23 percent, compared with 19 percent in the base run. In sum, aiming for a sustained growth rate of 10 percent or more in real terms over a decade could throw up a number of serious problems, unless they were provided for by conscious policy actions. These policies would have to focus on the deterioration of the urban-rural income distribution, the much larger savings effort that would be required, the size and nature of the external debt, and the burden of servicing it.

This recital of likely macroeconomic effects leaves out some important factors. As pointed out earlier, our rather aggregative model does not pretend to capture all the richness and complexity of the Egyptian economy and cannot model the effects of all policy alternatives (except in some crude way, such as by modifying the capital-output ratios in response to the adoption or rejection of a particular measure). Nor does the model address questions of institutional or administrative reform, but no one should underestimate their importance. Most of the policy reforms discussed in this report will have to be introduced during the period under review if the Egyptian economy is to attain the higher growth path, and failure to do so would probably reduce the long-run growth rate (from that of the base-run projections) by two to three percentage points; otherwise, the amount of external assistance needed will be substantially higher and will be required for a longer period.

PART TWO
Human Resources

6

Population Growth and Family Planning

The most striking feature of Egypt's urban and rural areas is that both are crowded. Not only do cities and towns have high population densities, but the countryside is dotted with closely spaced villages, many large enough to count as small towns in other countries. Furthermore, the congestion is intensifying rapidly. Egypt's population, currently more than 40 million, is growing at nearly 2.3 percent a year, nearly one million additional people annually. The costs of this population growth — of high birthrates, in particular — may be difficult to quantify but they are nonetheless real. Demands mount on already inadequate educational facilities and other infrastructure; the quality of health, education, and general living conditions declines; resources devoted to consumption and to social investment are denied to productive investment; the serious balance of payments situation is aggravated by additional food imports; the employment situation, already marked by chronic unemployment, is made worse; and pressure is intensified on Egypt's scarcest resource, fertile land. This chapter summarizes Egypt's salient demographic characteristics and the possible reasons for its fast population growth; describes the government's population policy and relevant institutions; discusses the social and economic effects of population growth; and finally projects a population of nearly 60 million by the year 2000 on the basis of relatively optimistic assumptions.

The first reasonably reliable census of Egypt took place in 1897, and thereafter censuses were conducted every ten years until 1947. The 1957 census was postponed until 1960 because of the Suez hostilities and there was a sample enumeration in 1966, but the next complete census was not taken until November 1976 (see table 6-1).

105

TABLE 6-1. POPULATION OF EGYPT
IN CENSUS YEARS, 1897-1976

Census years	Population (thousands)	Average annual growth rate (percent)
1897	9,715	—
1907	11,287	1.51
1917	12,751	1.23
1927	14,218	1.12
1937	15,933	1.14
1947	19,022	1.78
1960	26,085	2.38
1966	30,076	2.54
1976[a]	38,228	2.31

a. Preliminary.
Source: Central Agency for Public Mobilization and
Statistics (CAPMAS), Statistical Yearbook (Cairo,
October 1976); CAPMAS, Preliminary Results of 1976
Population and Housing Census (Cairo, March 1977).

The 1976 census figure of 38.2 million population is still preliminary. The overall growth rate of the population remains high, but
has slowed somewhat during the past ten years after accelerating
for several decades.

Trends in population growth over the past twenty-five years are
shown in table 6-2. Most estimates of birth- and deathrates are
based on a civil registration system that, by the standards of most
developing countries, appears to be very effective. The quality of
local registration figures varies somewhat, depending on whether
a health officer was stationed in the area. Because recording vital
statistics is an important part of his duties, the registration of
births and deaths is more complete in rural districts served by such
an officer. Where no health bureau exists, tax officials do the recording, generally as a subsidiary duty.[1] The censensus is that
since 1965 a fairly high degree of confidence can be placed in the
registration of births because a validated birth certificate is required in order to obtain the obligatory identity card, a ration card,
or admission into the school system. The Egyptian Population and
Family Planning Board estimates that the registered birthrate understates the true birthrate by only one or two points. Because of
the rationing system, however, some deaths may not be declared
promptly, and the crude deathrate may be somewhat higher than the
registration figures show.[2]

1. See Donald C. Mead, Growth and Structural Change in the Egyptian Economy (Homewood, Ill.: Richard D. Irwin, 1967), pp. 21-23.
2. John Waterbury, Manpower and Population Planning in the Arab Republic
of Egypt, Part I: Population Review, 1971, American Universities Field Staff
Reports, vol. 17, no. 2 (Hanover, N.H., 1972), p. 5.

TABLE 6-2. BIRTHS, DEATHS, AND RATES
OF NATURAL INCREASE OF POPULATION,
1950–54 TO 1975
(rate per thousand)

Period[a]	Birthrate	Deathrate	Natural Increase
1950–54	44.9	21.6	23.3
1955–59	44.0	19.9	24.1
1960–64	43.1	18.0	25.1
1965–69	41.1	15.8	25.3
1970–74	37.8	13.7	24.1
1972	36.9 (34.4)	13.2 (14.5)	23.7 (19.9)
1973	38.1 (35.1)	13.8 (12.9)	24.3 (22.2)
1974	36.8 (35.9)	13.0 (12.4)	23.8 (23.5)
1975	39.4 (37.7)	13.0 (12.2)	26.4 (25.5)

Note: The figures in parentheses are registered rates.
a. The figures are five-year averages from 1950 to 1974.
Source: Five-year averages: UN Population Division;
single years: Population and Family Planning Board, Egypt.

COMPONENTS OF POPULATION GROWTH

Deathrates, which have been substantially lower since World
War II, have declined only gradually since the early 1950s, though
they may have fallen more steeply in the mid-1970s. The rate of
natural increase from the early 1950s to the mid-1960s rose as a
consequence of virtually unchanging birthrates combined with slowly falling deathrates. After 1960 the picture changed slightly, and
birthrates fell steadily to reach a level of 37 per thousand in 1972;
the rate of natural increase was then about 2.4 percent. Subsequently birthrates have risen, and this, combined with falling deathrates,
accounts for the sudden jump in the rate of natural increase.

Mortality

The decline in mortality rates has been a universal feature of the
developing world. In Egypt life expectancy at birth is now about
fifty-five years, and mortality rates are similar to those of other
North African countries — well above those of East Asia and most
of Latin America, slightly below those of South Asia, and substantially below most of Africa. This might be expected in view of
Egypt's degree of development as measured by its per capita
income (US$280 in 1976). Infant mortality is estimated to be about
116 per thousand live births — again not unusual for a country of
Egypt's income level. Egypt is unusual, however, in having an extensive network of health services that should theoretically be capable of providing physician-based services, both curative and preventive, free of charge to the majority of the people. There are

fewer than 2,000 inhabitants per physician, and although most physicians are in urban areas, new medical graduates are obliged to serve in rural areas. On paper at least, the rural health system is well staffed compared with many developing countries.

Why then are mortality levels still so high? Among the causes are poor water supplies and a lack of environmental sanitation, which contribute to high rates of schistosomiasis, gastrointestinal infections, and other diseases of childhood and infancy. Most maternal deliveries are unattended by trained personnel. Rural medical personnel are limited in their ability to deal with these problems, particularly since the system has tended to be clinic-centered rather than community-oriented. Doctors in rural areas are not adequately trained in community medicine, and health personnel move from one assignment to another too frequently to develop a relationship with their communities. Other difficulties of the large public health system are related to supervision and staff motivation.

Much has been done to improve the supply of drinking water. It was estimated in 1976, for example, that 80 percent of the villages were served by government pumping and water treatment stations. But the water is too far from individual households to be used regularly. Meanwhile, environmental sanitation measures have lagged far behind.

Fertility

By the standards of many developing countries, especially Islamic ones, fertility levels in Egypt are not particularly high, and they are significantly lower than in the 1960s. One of the reasons for this is a trend toward later marriage, which began about 1964 and contributed to the decline in the birthrate beginning in 1967. The legal age for marriage is sixteen for females and eighteen for males, and the number of those who had never married increased from about 18 percent of the total population of legal age in 1960 to 25 percent in 1976. For males the increase was from 24 to 31 percent, and for females, from 12 to 20 percent. The number of those currently married declined from 70 percent in 1960 to 66 percent in 1976 — from 67 to 62 percent for males and from 68 to 65 percent for females. The decline in marriages is a reflection of increased urbanization, rising educational levels (especially among females), extended military service, and the difficulties of finding separate lodgings, especially in urban areas.

The apparent reversal of the decline in fertility in 1973 is extremely unusual in a developing country. Until data from the 1974-75 fertility survey are analyzed, this shift is impossible to explain. A plausible hypothesis is that at least part of the 1967-73 decline was a result of military mobilization, which entailed compulsory

military service and displaced the civilian population from the war
zones.   It is entirely possible that Egypt has been experiencing
something of a postwar baby boom since that time.

Along with the 1976 census, the fertility survey should provide
information about fertility differences between urban and rural
groups, between social classes, and between those with different
levels of education. With this background, it should be possible to
design research to explore more fully the reasons fertility fell in
1967-73 and then increased, remaining at a level so far above replacement. Almost all that can be said now is extrapolated from
research results elsewhere.

Among other factors likely to keep fertility high are the high levels of infant and child mortality. Biologically, the death of a nurs-
ing infant may reduce a mother's period of postpartum amenorrhea
and hence increase the period of exposure to pregnancy. A behav-
ioral factor in fertility is a desire of parents to replace children
who have died; when parents perceive the risk of losing children to
be high, they are likely to try to insure against it by having many
children. Another motive is the wish for several surviving children
as security against disability and old age. Moreover, the productive role of children is still so important in rural areas that it can
be a major reason for high fertility among rural families. The evidence for a proper assessment of these factors is unfortunately
not available.[3]

High fertility is also associated with the lower social status and
limited education of women, who have few options other than raising a family. The problem is one of social custom rather than legal
status. Islam, in its more liberal interpretation, has always granted Muslim women certain recognition — such as independent legal
and property rights — only recently acquired by women in Western
societies. Under Islamic law, a woman can keep her family name
after marriage; she can dispose of her property freely without a
husband or guardian as intermediary; she can be a guardian over
minors; and she can bring legal suit without having to secure her
husband's approval. The problem lies in the translation of many
of the legal rights into actual practice, and undoubtedly a lack of
education and awareness, particularly among the women themselves,
has contributed to the difficulties. Some observers believe social
conservatism has grown throughout Egyptian society as a consequence of increasing contact with the oil-exporting Arab states.

"Of all aspects of social development the education level appears
most consistently associated with lower fertility. And it is significant that an increase in the education of women tends to lower fertility to a greater extent than a similar increase in the education

3. According to a Population and Planning Board study published in 1977, birthrates were as high as 43.8 per thousand in rural areas compared with 34.0 in urban areas in 1975. Infant mortality was also higher in rural areas.

of men."[4] For these reasons if for no other, it is clear that efforts to improve Egyptian education, though in the right direction, are far from sufficient. Illiteracy rates decreased from 70 percent to about 57 percent among persons aged ten and over between 1960 and 1976. This decrease was more marked among the male population, with illiteracy falling by one-quarter, from 57 to 43 percent; for females the rate declined from 84 to 71 percent. But because of the natural rate of increase in the population as a whole, the actual number of female illiterates increased from 8.1 million to 9.4 million, or by about 17 percent, during this period. The number of male illiterates also increased but only by about 8 percent, from 5.7 million to 6.2 million.

Since 1962 women in Egypt have had equal rights with men in the education field, at least in theory. But the traditional image of women as mothers is still dominant. One of the main obstacles to female emancipation is the lack of employment opportunities in urban areas. Although the government recognizes that urban working women tend to have fewer children than their rural, agriculturally based counterparts, it has not encouraged them to compete for scarce jobs because this would only exacerbate male unemployment.

Policies and Institutions

As yet the antinatalist population policies of the Egyptian government have not had much impact on fertility levels.[5] These policies were formally initiated in 1962 but actually originated in 1939 when the newly created Ministry of Social Affairs was given the task of studying population problems. After the 1952 revolution President Nasser formed a National Population Commission to study the issue, and the first family planning clinics were opened in 1955. In 1957 the Egyptian Association for Population Studies — a voluntary family planning association — was founded. By 1965 there was widespread popular support for a national population program. In November of that year a presidential decree established a Supreme Council for Family Planning, headed by the prime minister and including ten other ministers, along with an Executive Family Planning Board to implement the council's decisions. The Ministry of Health's rural and urban health units were designated as the main channels for providing family planning services, and beginning in 1966 about 2,000 of these units (under the direct supervision of the board), provided contraceptives in rural and urban areas. That same year all voluntary family planning efforts were officially recognized and a General Family Planning Association was set up to

4. Robert S. McNamara, "Address to the Massachusetts Institute of Technology" (Washington, D.C.: World Bank, April 1977).

5. This section benefits from information provided in W. A. Hassouna and others, Proposal for a Community-based Integrated Family Planning and Maternal and Child Health Project (Cairo: Ministry of Health, December 1977).

coordinate their efforts.

The 1967 war severely curtailed the resources available for population planning, and it was some time before a fresh effort was made.
Various ministries supported a Family Planning Week in March 1968
to revive the people's interest. National and international agencies
contributed advice and encouragement as well as funds for the implementation of population programs. A plan was adopted to reduce the
birthrate by one per thousand annually, starting in 1970. In 1971
President Anwar el-Sadat called for the extensive involvement of
the Arab Socialist Union in combating illiteracy and promoting family
planning. In addition, the prime minister stated repeatedly that the
population problem was second in importance only to the problems
of defense.

In 1973 the Executive Family Planning Board was reorganized
as the Population and Family Planning Board, with responsibility
for planning and monitoring the program as well as for population
research. The Ministry of Health was then assigned the main responsibility for administration of family planning services, and a
Department of Family Planning was established within the ministry
at the central level. Because of inadequate staffing, resources,
and support, the new department had little impact on family planning efforts for several years. In 1977, however, the program was
given a new impetus. A director-general for family planning within
the ministry was given authority to plan, develop, and implement
an intensified family planning program in all governorates, and a
population project is now being developed with the World Bank.

Although coverage is still far from complete, the network of facilities is far more extensive than in most developing countries.
There are now about 3,675 family planning clinics, with approximately 64 percent of them serving rural areas. The supply of medical and paramedical personnel is generally good, with a physician,
nurse, and midwife (in principle) attached to each government health
unit. The extremely high population density in the habitable area of
the country greatly facilitates delivery and supervision of services.

In spite of this extensive network, family planning is not widely
practiced, especially in rural areas, where, according to most estimates, only 5 to 8 percent of couples at risk of pregnancy use some
form of birth control. Recent studies show higher rates, but they
are still too low to have much impact on fertility. The underlying
causes of this resistance to family planning have never been adequately studied, and research in this area demands the highest priority. Some critics ascribe the failures of the family planning program to a lack of demand for its services. But this is implausible;
in circumstances no more favorable to fertility reduction, the Indi-
an program has obtained much greater acceptance rates with a much
less dense network of services, and the program in Java and Bali
appears to have been even more successful. A pilot project in a
village in Menufia, under the auspices of the American University

in Cairo, has also had encouraging results: more than 30 percent of the women at risk in this community of 14,000 are said to be practicing family planning.[6]

Another argument is that personnel in the Egyptian program remain rooted to their clinics and do not attempt to make contact in peoples' homes. In rural areas especially, it is said, health units are staffed with people who have little, if any, training in contraception, and many of them have no motivation to encourage family planning.

Oral contraceptives are favored in the program and are used by about 70 percent of the participants. There are occasional interruptions in the supply, however, and the same brands are not always available. The IUD is promoted much less than "the pill" and sterilization not at all. Little use has been made of commercial channels, which have proved effective in other countries. A sociocultural barrier is that many married women believe (incorrectly) that family planning is contrary to the Muslim religion. But none of this provides a really convincing explanation of why the program has performed so poorly, or why the official target for an annual reduction of the birth rate by one per thousand seems so far from being achieved.

External Migration

Apart from births and deaths, external migration is another factor in the rate of population growth. The preliminary 1976 census estimated 1.4 million Egyptians temporarily residing abroad — nearly 4 percent of the population — but this figure is much higher than other estimates and is controversial. Most of the recent migration has been to neighboring oil-exporting countries, where an estimated 300,000 to 400,000 Egyptians were working in 1975. There are, of course, limits to the absorptive capacity of these countries, which generally have small populations and indigenous labor forces and are somewhat reluctant to increase further their dependence on foreign labor. The Ministry of Planning estimated that the number of Egyptians working abroad would taper off to about 1 million workers by 1980.

The Geographical Distribution of Population

The Egyptian population has always been concentrated in less than 4 percent of the total area. In the Nile Valley and the Delta, one of the most densely populated areas in the world, there are 1,030 people per square kilometer. The proportion of people living in towns and cities is higher in Egypt than in most countries at a

6. John Rowley, "Lessons for All to See," People, vol. 4 (November 1, 1977), p. 11.

comparable stage of development. In 1976 almost 44 percent of
the population was urban, compared with 37.8 percent in 1960 and
40.0 percent in 1966.[7]

Between 1966 and 1976 the number of urban dwellers increased
at an annual rate of 3.0 percent, a slight deceleration from the annual rate of 3.4 percent between 1960 and 1966. Since immigration
into Egypt is insignificant, urban growth is almost wholly a result
of migration from rural areas and natural increase. Greater Cairo,
already large, is growing slightly faster than the urban sector as a
whole. Between 1960 and 1976 the population of Greater Cairo increased by almost 70 percent, from 4.8 million to 8 million. Alexandria grew from 1.5 to 2.3 million, an increase of 53 percent.
The urban sector grew from 9.8 million to 16.1 million, an increase
of 64 percent, while the country as a whole grew from 26.1 million
to 38.2 million, an increase of 46 percent. Greater Cairo, which
received the lion's share of the rural-urban migration, had an annual growth rate of 4.1 percent and an average population density
of almost 24,000 people per square kilometer, ranging from a low
of 6,600 per square kilometer in Kasr el-Nil, one of the wealthiest
areas and the commercial and administrative heart of Cairo, to a
high of 101,000 in el-Faraz, one of the poorest. This represents
one person per ten square meters, which makes it extremely expensive to provide infrastructure.

Another manifestation of internal migration is the variation in
growth rates among governorates, as shown in table 6-3. Although
differences in the rate of natural increase could account for part of
this, most of the variation is caused by migration between governorates (figure 6-1).

As table 6-3 indicates, the pattern of internal migration has
changed in recent years. Before 1966 the urban governorates grew
at a relatively faster rate than the others. For example, in 1960-
66 the growth rate of urban governorates was 3.5 percent a year
while that of others in Lower Egypt was 2.2 percent and in Upper
Egypt 1.8 percent. In 1966-76, however, the rate of growth of urban governorates decreased to 1.7 percent, substantially below the
rate in Lower Egypt (2.2 percent) and that in Upper Egypt (1.8 percent). The rate of urban governorates was 1.1 percentage points
above the national rate in 1960-66 and dropped to 0.3 percentage
points below the national rate in 1966-76. Part of this decrease is
owing to war-related migration from Sinai, Suez, and Port Said,
but a significant part is owing to changes in the overall pattern of
internal migration. For the first time since 1927, population in
Lower Egypt grew faster than the national population: 2.2 percent
compared with the 2.0 percent national rate.

7. Central Agency for Public Mobilization and Statistics (CAPMAS), Preliminary Results of 1976 Population and Housing Census (Cairo, March 1977).

TABLE 6-3. ANNUAL INTERCENSAL RATES
OF POPULATION GROWTH (EXPONENTIAL)
BY REGION AND GOVERNORATE,
1927-37 TO 1966-76
(percent)

Region	1927-37	1937-47	1947-60	1960-66	1966-76
Urban governorates					
Cairo	1.99	4.61	3.55	3.9	1.9
Alexandria	1.66	2.91	3.47	2.9	2.5
Port Said	1.61	3.25	2.96	2.4	-0.7
Ismailia	3.25	6.69	3.51	5.2	0.2
Suez	2.01	7.69	4.76	4.3	-3.1
All urban governorates	1.91	4.22	3.54	3.5	1.7
Lower Egypt governorates					
Damietta	1.85	2.30	3.00	1.8	2.6
Dakahlia	1.21	1.70	2.40	2.1	1.8
Sharkia	0.89	1.50	2.20	2.4	2.2
Kalyubia	0.90	1.16	2.38	3.4	3.2
Kafr el-Sheikh	1.27	2.15	2.63	2.3	2.3
Gharbia	0.57	1.16	2.07	1.7	1.9
Menufia	0.47	0.09	1.34	1.3	1.6
Beheira	0.87	1.57	2.43	2.7	2.5
All Lower Egypt governorates	0.88	1.33	2.22	2.2	2.2
Upper Egypt governorates					
Giza	1.59	1.94	3.40	3.5	3.8
Beni Suef	0.98	0.89	1.24	1.3	1.8
Fayoum	0.82	1.06	1.67	1.8	2.0
Minya	0.98	1.12	1.54	1.4	1.9
Assiut	1.15	1.44	1.85	1.1	1.8
Souhag	1.42	1.38	1.54	1.1	1.3
Kena	1.19	0.84	1.48	1.4	1.5
Aswan	1.30	-0.48	2.09	5.0	1.8
All Upper Egypt governorates	1.18	1.16	1.82	1.8	1.8
Border area	-1.00	5.75	2.77	1.0	0.4
All Egypt	2.12	1.77	2.34	2.4	2.0

Source: Rates for 1927-37 through 1947-60 from A. R. Omran, ed.,
Egypt: Population Problems and Prospects (Chapel Hill: University of
North Carolina, Carolina Population Center, 1973), chap. 1, table 9.
Rates for 1960-66 and 1966-76 calculated from CAPMAS, Preliminary
Results of 1976 Population and Housing Census.

Figure 6–1. Rates of Internal Migration by Age and Sex,
1917-27 to 1947-60

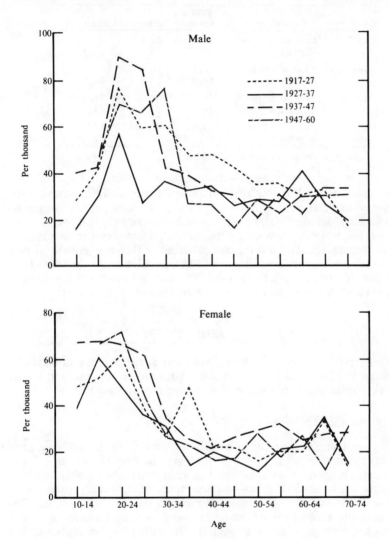

Source: K. C. Zachariah, "Sex-Age Pattern of Population Mobility in the UAR," paper presented to the International Union for the Scientific Study of Population, London, 1969.

TABLE 6-4. COMPONENTS OF URBAN GROWTH,
1937-47 TO 1966-76
(percent)

Period	Component	Total urban	Greater Cairo	Alexandria
1937-47	Natural increase	50.4	36.8	52.5
	Migration	49.6	63.8	47.5
1947-60	Natural increase	73.1	56.0	79.6
	Migration	26.9	44.0	20.4
1960-66	Natural increase	61.4	60.3	81.1
	Migration	38.6	39.7	18.9
1966-76	Natural increase	59.3	80.4	77.8
	Migration	40.7	19.6	22.2

Source: Derived from census data.

The principal governorates receiving an inflow from 1966 to
1976 were Giza on the southern border of Cairo and Kalyubia on its
northern border. Although net migration to Cairo proper decreased
substantially during this period, its suburbs remain the major attraction for migrants within Egypt. Natural increase rather than
migration has accounted for most of Greater Cairo's growth in recent years, however, and this trend has accelerated. In 1966-76
more than 80 percent of the growth was owing to natural increase
compared with more than 36 percent in 1937-47 (table 6-4).

THE CONSEQUENCES

Whether large families actually benefit rural parents is debatable,
but there is little doubt that they have adverse effects on land availability, social development, and employment prospects.

Population Pressure on Land

The most striking effect of population growth is the growing pressure on cultivable land. Table 6-5 shows the growth in both cultivated and cropped areas (that is, the area cultivated multiplied by
the cropping intensity) since the late nineteenth century, and the
decline in the number of feddans per capita during this period. The
growth in the size of the areas has slowed in recent years, and no
significant increase can be expected. In spite of the massive exodus
from the villages, the absolute number of inhabitants classified as
rural continues to grow. It was about 18 million in 1966; ten years
later it was 20.6 million. Agriculture is, of course, already very
labor intensive and yields are high by international standards. In
recent years, however, the growth of aggregate agricultural output
has been somewhat less than the rate of population growth (chapter 9).

TABLE 6-5. GROWTH OF POPULATION AND OF
CULTIVATED AND CROPPED AREAS, 1897-1975
(thousands)

Year	Population	Cultivated area		Cropped area	
		Feddans	Per capita	Feddans	Per capita
1987	9,715	4,943	0.53	6,725	0.71
1907	11,190	5,374	0.48	7,595	0.67
1917	12,715	5,309	0.41	7,729	0.60
1927	14,178	5,544	0.39	8,522	0.61
1937	15,921	5,312	0.33	8,302	0.53
1947	18,967	5,761	0.31	9,133	0.48
1960	26,085	5,900	0.23	10,200	0.39
1966	30,076	6,000	0.20	10,400	0.34
1970	33,200	6,000[a]	0.18	10,900	0.33
1975	37,772	6,500[a]	0.17	10,800	0.29

Note: Some figures differ from census data because they do
not include Bedouins.
    a. Approximate.
Source: Updated from CAPMAS publications.

The exact degree of labor surplus in Egyptian agriculture has
been a matter of controversy for at least two decades. Nevertheless, in spite of some changes in cropping patterns and perennial
irrigation, which require a high labor input, there is little doubt
that the demand for labor has not grown as fast as the population.
The old concern about the relation of population growth to fixed supplies of land would seem as important as ever, and there are few
reasons to expect the situation to change. Although the government
plans to expand the cultivated area, desert reclamation is necessarily slow and costly. Because the new lands tend to be far less productive than the old, such horizontal expansion is unlikely to have
a significant impact for many years.

Population and Social Development

Population growth has also been a brake on the rate of social
development, though many of the obstacles it has created have not
been insuperable. Health services, for example, are available to
a comparatively large number of people. In education, however,
enrollment in primary education, after rising at an average rate of
6.3 percent between 1952 and 1965, has since then not matched the
growth of the population of school-age children (table 6-6). Between
1965 and 1975 the population aged six to eleven years increased
at an annual rate of 2.4 percent. The growth rate of primary
enrollments over this period was only 1.8 percent; from 1971-
72 to 1975-76 it was only 1.6 percent. Consequently, enrollment in
primary schools, which rose from 46 percent of school-age children

TABLE 6-6.   ENROLLMENT IN PRIMARY
EDUCATION, 1952-53 TO 1975-76
(thousands)

School year	Population aged 6-11	Enrollment in primary school[a]	Enrollment rate (percent)
1952-53	3,328	1,540	46
1965-66	4,635	3,418	74
1975-76	5,883	4,075	70

a. At beginning of school year.
Source: Ministry of Education and interpolation
of census data.

in 1952 to 74 percent in 1965, fell to 70 percent in 1975-76.
   During the 1952-65 period enrollment of girls rose more rapidly
than that of boys (7.2 percent a year compared with 5.8 percent).
Female enrollment rose from 35 to 39 percent of total enrollment.
In 1965-75, however, female enrollment rose more slowly than male
enrollment, and its share dropped to 38 percent. During this same
period, the enrollment ratio for boys dropped from about 89 percent
to about 85 percent, and for girls from about 58 percent to 55
percent.
   It would, of course, be a mistake to attribute all the difficulties
in achieving 100 percent primary school enrollment to population
growth. Many parents do not believe that education is valuable for
their daughters, but this does not explain why enrollment rates fell.
At least some of the fall must be owing to the limited capacity of the
primary system.   There are still about forty pupils per teacher,
and about 60 percent of the primary schools operate more than one
daily shift. (For a fuller discussion of the educational situation see
chapter 7.)
   Whatever the reasons, the present downward trend has disturbing implications for the future. The continuing low level of female
education may inhibit a decline in fertility, particularly when it reduces the opportunities for outside employment. Because of the
poor prospects for labor absorption in agriculture, Egypt's future
development is going to depend on its ability to absorb more labor
in urban areas. The developing countries that have been most successful in this respect — principally those in East Asia — have had
labor forces with a much higher level of basic education than that
of Egypt.

Labor Force Growth

   Among the most serious of Egypt's population problems in the
long run is the rapid growth of the labor force. The population aged

TABLE 6-7. CRUDE
ACTIVITY RATES, 1937-76
(percent)

Year	Females	Males	Total
1937	7.9	65.1	37
1947	7.8	62.8	37
1960	4.8	55.2	30
1966	4.2	50.8	28
1976	9.2	52.9	32

Note: The crude activity rate is
the percentage of the population six
years of age and over that is economically active.
Source: CAPMAS, Population Census, 1937, 1947, 1960, 1966, and
1976.

twelve to sixty-four has grown at an average rate of about 2.5
percent a year since 1950 and is currently growing at 2.7 percent.
Because the Egyptian census includes children six to twelve years
of age among the "economically active" population (which no doubt
accords with reality in rural areas) it is difficult to interpret apparent changes in crude activity rates (table 6-7).

While female activity rates have risen significantly in the past
ten years, female labor force participation is still low.[8] Only
about 14 percent of the total labor force is female. This might
seem fairly typical of the Middle East, but the figure for Latin
America is 23 percent, for Asia 30, percent, and for sub-Saharan
Africa 32 percent.[9] The low participation rates of Egyptian females
are compared with international standards in figure 6-2. They reflect the fact that Egyptian society has emphasized the seclusion of
women and their domestic roles. Improved educational opportunities have increased their social and occupational mobility in recent
years, but job openings remain severely restricted by custom and
by the prevailing attitude that the widespread underemployment of
men makes it unrealistic to prepare women to compete with them.

More than 50 percent of those in the labor force are unable to
read or write, and a further 25 percent have no more than primary
education; only 2 percent have a university degree (see table 6-8).
This low level of education is a formidable obstacle to raising the
level of skills.

8. The labor force participation rate is defined as that proportion of the working-
age population holding or seeking employment.
9. James L. McCabe and Mark R. Rosenzweig, "Female Labor Force Participation, Occupational Choice, and Fertility in Developing Countries," Journal of
Development Economics, vol. 3, no. 2 (July 1976), pp. 141-60.

Figure 6–2. Female Participation Rates by Age in Egypt
and Agricultural and Industrialized Countries

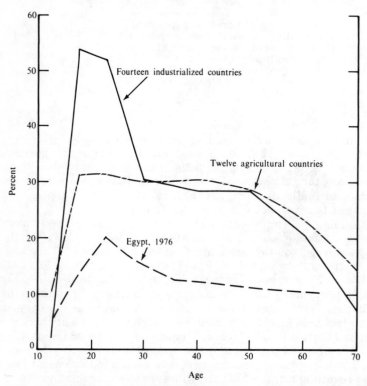

Note: Fourteen industrialized countries having less than 35 percent of active males engaged in agriculture and related activities are: Argentina, Australia, Belgium, Canada, Denmark, England and Wales, France, Israel, Netherlands, New Zealand, Norway, Sweden, Switzerland, and the United States.

Twelve agricultural countries having 60 percent or more of active males engaged in agriculture and related activities are: Algeria (Muslims), Brazil, Colombia, Costa Rica, Ecuador, El Salvador, Guatemala, India, Morocco, Paraguay, Philippines, and Tunisia.

Sources: United Nations, *Demographic Aspects of Manpower,* Report no. 1 (New York, 1962); and World Bank estimates based on 1976 census and 1972 labor force survey in Egypt.

TABLE 6-8. DISTRIBUTION OF POPULATION (AGED
TEN AND OVER) BY SEX AND EDUCATIONAL STATUS,
1960 AND 1976
(percent)

| Educational | 1960 census | | | 1976 census | | |
status	Male	Female	Total	Male	Female	Total
Illiterate	56.9	84.0	70.5	43.2	71.0	56.5
Literate	32.6	12.4	22.5	33.2	16.2	25.1
Qualified below university degree	9.0	3.4	6.2	20.4	11.6	16.2
University degree or equivalent	1.5	0.2	0.8	3.2	1.2	2.2

Source: CAPMAS, Population Census, 1960, and Preliminary Results of
1976 Population and Housing Census.

THE OUTLOOK

Table 6-9 summarizes a demographic projection based on the
plausible, but nevertheless optimistic, view that the recent upturn
in the birthrate is a temporary phenomenon reflecting demobilization, and that the downward trend in birthrates in 1967-73 was the
start of a long-term trend. The projected decline in the birthrate
is not likely to be achieved, however, without vast changes in Egyptian society, such as raising the level of female education, expanding modern sector jobs for women, reducing infant and child mortality, and mechanizing agriculture so that children will be less economically valuable in rural areas. These changes all move toward
the modernization of the country and its economy and will inevitably
entail high public and private expenditures to expand educational
facilities, improve levels of public health, and promote industrial
growth. Another prerequisite for a drop in the birthrate is the increased effectiveness of family planning programs. Reform of the
management and organization of the programs is needed as well as
a concerted and sustained drive by the government and additional
special funds.

The projection anticipates a steady decline in fertility until it is
only a little above replacement levels in the year 2000. Even under
this optimistic assumption, the population at that time would be approaching 60 million. It would still be youthful — about 30 percent
would be under the age of fifteen, compared with about 40 percent
now — and would probably continue to grow, if at a steadily dimin-
ishing rate. The population is projected to increase at an average
annual rate of 2.2 percent in 1975-80 and 1.4 percent in 1995-2000,
and an average of 1.8 percent for the whole period. The population

TABLE 6-9. POPULATION PROJECTIONS AND INDIRECT
GROWTH RATES TO THE YEAR 2000

Category	1975	1980	1985	1990	1995	2000
Total population						
(thousands)	37,772	42,069	46,472	50,908	55,251	59,374
Aged 6-11	5,883	6,348	6,644	6,877	7,085	7,169
Aged 12-64	23,843	27,229	30,852	34,575	38,302	42,000
Aged 65 and over	1,282	1,516	1,793	2,123	2,512	2,981
Population growth						
rate (percent)						
Aged 6-11	—	1.5	0.9	0.7	0.6	0.2
Aged 12-64	—	2.7	2.5	2.3	2.0	1.8
Aged 65 and over	—	3.4	3.4	3.4	3.4	3.4
Fertility rate		4.6	4.1	3.6	3.2	2.9
Net reproduction rate		1.7	1.6	1.4	1.3	1.2
Birthrate						
(per thousand)	—	34.2	31.4	28.7	26.0	23.3
Deathrate						
(per thousand)	—	12.7	11.4	10.4	9.6	8.9
Natural rate of						
increase						
(per thousand)	—	21.5	20.0	18.3	16.4	14.4

Source: World Bank projections.

of primary school age would grow relatively slowly — its rate of
growth declining from 1.5 percent in 1975-80 to 0.2 percent in 1995-
2000. But the population of working age (defined as twelve to sixty-
four years of age) would grow rapidly in the next decade — 2.7 percent in 1975-80 and 2.5 percent in 1980-85 — and would still be
growing at 1.8 percent in the last five years of this century.

The population would also be increasingly urban (table 6-10),
since the urban growth rate is likely to fall below 3 percent only after 1990. About that time, if the decline in population growth follows the projection in table 6-9, the rural population as a whole
would remain stable.

Inasmuch as Egypt is dependent on food imports with little potential for agricultural expansion, it is possible that balance of payments
difficulties would lead to belt-tightening and nutritional deficiencies.
Under these conditions deathrates would fall more slowly than projected here, and the population would be somewhat smaller in 2000.
But most alternative projections show a slower decline in fertility
and a larger, younger population in 2000, adding to the burdens of
social development, job creation, and urban crowding.

TABLE 6-10. TOTAL URBAN AND RURAL POPULATION, 1975-2000

(thousands)

Population	1975	1980	1985	1990	1995	2000
Urban	18,013	21,485	25,299	29,420	33,747	38,171
		(3.5)	(3.3)	(3.0)	(2.7)	(2.5)
Rural	19,759	20,584	21,273	21,488	21,504	21,203
		(0.8)	(0.6)	(0.3)	(0.0)	(-0.3)
Total	37,772	42,069	46,472	50,908	55,251	59,374

Note: The figures in parentheses are the percentage changes in the rate of growth over the previous period.
Source: World Bank estimates based on United Nations methodology.

Even with a fairly optimistic view about a decline in fertility and population growth, the growing urban labor force and other problems associated with urbanization are going to create serious difficulties for Egypt throughout this century and well into the next. Productive employment for urban workers will be essential not only as a source of income for families but also to provide manufactured exports to pay for the imports of agricultural products and raw materials that will be required. The policies that serve these ends are strongly linked to those that promote social development. Their successful implementation should help to ensure that the objectives of the next century are no longer mainly those of reducing growth rates of the population and coping with the consequences of its rapid growth.

7

Education and Manpower

Universal education, a prominent objective in government policy, is a relatively new idea in Egypt. Until the 1952 revolution the education system was geared to the social and economic elite of the country and barely touched the masses. In the twenty-five years since the revolution much has been accomplished, although literacy and enrollment rates remain low. With the open-door policy, the need for more vigorous efforts in the fields of education and manpower planning has become even more acute.

Egypt has an oversupply of people with an academic education but appears to be short of many needed skills, especially since the migration of labor to other Middle Eastern countries. The government's educational policy now emphasizes technical rather than academic skills, but it will take time for this to be reflected in output, and shortages continue in certain sectors, notably construction and industry. The modernization of the economy and the promotion of the industrial sector require a pool of well-trained industrial technicians and skilled workers. Bottlenecks are likely to continue at least into the early 1980s and will persist even beyond that unless more attention is given to manpower planning. A major problem is the lack of comprehensive data on which to base this planning.

Recent government policies have not succeeded in changing enrollment patterns. Egyptians retain a strong bias toward an academic education, which is strengthened by the government guarantee of employment to all graduates of institutions of higher education. This education-employment policy encourages entry into secure jobs in unproductive fields. Resource investment in this kind of job means lower rates of growth of labor productivity in agriculture and industry and fewer opportunities for productive employment. And it is the less privileged that suffer the most.

The government is aware of the national and sectoral imbalance in the demand for and supply of labor and is taking steps to correct it. It is seeking a better understanding of present and future manpower requirements in order to reorient the education system to actual manpower needs. Some of the main issues and government priorities that have emerged will be discussed toward the end of this chapter.

THE EDUCATION SYSTEM

After the 1952 revolution the new government accorded high priority to strengthening the education system and making it accessible to all social strata. As a result, school enrollment and the scale of government spending for education increased greatly. For example, enrollment in primary school increased from 46 percent of the children of primary school age in 1953-54 to 74 percent in 1965-66; since then it has dropped back to about 70 percent.[1] Current government expenditure for education has grown from about LE23 million in 1952-53 (less than 3 percent of GDP) to about LE280.3 million in 1976 (about 5 percent of GDP). Capital expenditure has also shown remarkable growth — from LE2.5 million in the first year of the revolution to LE25.7 million in 1976, a tenfold increase.[2] In 1976 recurrent educational expenditure amounted to 26.4 percent of central government recurrent expenditure, having grown from 21.1 percent in 1970-71. Capital expenditure in education was 2.1 percent of total central government capital expenditure, averaging 4.1 percent annually over the 1970-75 period (see table 7-1).

The Structure of the System

Most Egyptian children attend school, if only for a relatively short time. In the mid-1970s more than 4 million students were on the rolls of primary schools, and about 1.9 million were intermediate and secondary students. The compulsory education law requires all children to whom facilities are available to attend six years of elementary school beginning at age six. It is estimated, however, that about 20 percent of six-year-olds fail to enter primary school, and among those nominally enrolled, a number fail to attend classes with any regularity. The attrition rate from one grade to the next is high, especially among girls, many of whom complete no more than a year or two of school. Even among boys, authorities note that many fail to achieve permanent literacy. Most parents, however, have come to recognize the desirability of modern education, at least for their sons. The kuttub, a religious school attached to a mosque, has been replaced by the public primary school as the institution of mass instruction, but in many villages it continues to provide supplementary courses in religious studies.

After gaining an elementary knowledge of reading, writing, arithmetic, history, geography, science, and other subjects in six years

1. Robert Mabro, The Egyptian Economy, 1952-1972 (Oxford: Clarendon Press, 1974); CAPMAS, Statistical Yearbook for the Arab Republic of Egypt (Cairo, 1977; in Arabic); Ministry of Education estimates.

2. World Bank, Appraisal of an Education Project in the Arab Republic of Egypt, Report no. 1285-EGT (Washington, D.C., January 28, 1977).

TABLE 7-1. GOVERNMENT EXPENDITURE ON EDUCATION,
1970-71 TO 1976
(thousands of Egyptian pounds)

Agency	1970-71	1971-72	1973	1974	1975[a]	1976[a]
Recurrent expenditure						
Ministry of Education	101,781	106,156	130,263	143,965	158,704	204,804
Ministry of Higher Education	5,764	6,232	7,174	7,864	8,638	4,786
Universities	21,335	24,122	31,457	36,367	49,688	66,489
Ministry of Industries	958	1,080	1,267	1,304	1,193	1,393
Ministry of Housing	n.a.	n.a.	245	467	1,829	2,791
Ministry of Health	n.a.	n.a.	889	1,042	1,050	n.a.
Ministry of Agriculture	n.a.	64	309	241	207	n.a.
Subtotal	129,838	137,654	171,604	191,259	221,309	380,263
Percentage of central government recurrent expenditure	21.1	20.0	24.0	26.1	25.8	26.4
Capital expenditure						
Ministry of Education	5,434	5,782	15,609	6,603	18,923	8,869
Ministry of Higher Education	1,429	1,556	2,757	3,759	4,666	4,380
Universities	2,702	8,907	7,066	7,272	10,072	6,391
Ministry of Industries	300	205	98	90	309	569
Ministry of Housing	n.a.	n.a.	18	23	22	5,475
Ministry of Health	n.a.	n.a.	150	310	259	n.a.
Ministry of Agriculture	n.a.	50	40	26	40	n.a.
Subtotal	9,865	16,500	25,738	18,083	34,291	25,684
Percentage of central government capital expenditure	2.7	4.0	5.7	3.1	5.0	2.1
Total expenditure						
All agencies	139,703	154,154	197,342	209,342	255,600	305,947
Percentage of GDP	4.4	4.5	5.4	5.3	5.5	5.9

n.a. Not available.
a. Budget estimates.
Source: Ministry of Finance.

of primary education, the student sits for the Primary Certificate
Examination administered by the Ministry of Education. The number of students passing this examination has risen steadily from a-
bout 150,000 in 1967 to over 320,000 in 1972. (In 1976, 73 percent
of those taking the exam passed it.) They are then admitted to the
three-year preparatory program that culminates in the General Preparatory Certificate Examination. This intermediate stage of
education is intended to allow students to explore their tastes and

aptitudes so that they can make appropriate choices at the more specialized secondary level. Observers note, however, that because students are assigned to secondary programs on the basis of examination grades, they tend to avoid experimentation with unfamiliar subjects and to concentrate on rote learning.

About 10 percent of those who begin school reach the secondary grades; in 1975 about 310,000 students (67 percent of those participating) passed the preparatory examinations. Secondary schools offer a number of curricular options in two broad categories, the general or academic and the vocational or technical. The academic student may choose either a scientific or a literary program in the second and third years. Vocational and technical secondary programs are offered in a variety of trades, including commerce, and about 51 percent of the students enrolled in them in 1974-75.

About 100,000 students a year pass the examinations that complete the academic secondary program, and another 90,000 do so in vocational subjects. In both cases, this was about 70 percent of the students participating in 1974-75. In the late 1960s about two-thirds of those finishing academic secondary school continued their education. By the mid-1970s, largely because of the government's employment policy, this had grown to three in four.

The major responsibility for formal education and training lies with the Ministry of Education (MOE) and the Ministry of Higher Education (MOHE), both of which are headed by the same minister. MOE is responsible for primary, preparatory, general, and technical secondary schools and for primary teacher training. MOHE administered the higher institutions in the past but is now responsible only for postsecondary technical training. The ten universities are autonomous in their internal administration, subject only to the supervision of a Supreme Council for Universities, an advisory body chaired by the minister of higher education.

The technical institutes are more or less autonomous, forming part of the university system. They offer specialized instruction in a number of fields including commerce, industrial subjects (such as electronics), home economics, teaching (including art education, music education, and physical education), social work, physical therapy, and tourism. Their curriculums and physical facilities are in the process of being upgraded to university standards. A private university (the American University of Cairo) and several private institutes also exist.

Vocational training is also provided by various ministries: Industry and Mineral Resources; Housing and Reconstruction; Agriculture; Health; and Social Affairs. The Ministries of Health and of Tourism also offer postsecondary technical training. In 1976 the output of people with vocational skills in the industrial and construction trades was only about 2,600 and 1,800, respectively, much less than the average annual demand projected for the 1976-86 period.

Most nonformal, on-the-job training is under the Ministry of Industry and the Ministry of Housing and Reconstruction, but it has not been very successful in Egypt. Not enough money and time has been invested in on-the-job training programs, most factories are not geared to students, and the students are often inadequately prepared for practical work.

Academic Standards

The rapid expansion of the education system has frequently been at the expense of academic standards, particularly at the primary level. A serious shortage of trained teachers exists, and school facilities have not kept pace with the demand for them. As a result, about 60 percent of the primary schools operate more than one shift, with insufficient textbooks and materials. A shortage of qualified teachers persists in some parts of the system, a surplus in others, and there is no suitable planning mechanism to correct these imbalances.

All attempts to forecast teacher requirements by level and subject area have been hampered by a lack of data. The shortage of teachers, particularly at the primary level, stems in part from the low prestige of the profession and the low pay. Enrollment in primary teacher training is increasing at only 2.6 percent a year, while the average annual increase in primary students is forecast to be over 4 percent annually between 1975 and 1980 (see table 7-2). This is expected to lead to a shortfall of almost 8,000 primary teachers by 1980 unless immediate steps are taken to increase the number trained.

Severe overcrowding and overemphasis on formal examinations also have depressed academic standards, particularly at the university level. Universities enroll about four times their intended student capacity, with the highest ratios in the arts, law, and commerce. In addition, graduates of both academic and technical secondary schools are allowed to become external students without obtaining formal admission to the university. Although they are not permitted to attend classes, they may sit for degree examinations. These students support a thriving market in lecture notes and course work, which they memorize in an attempt to pass the examinations; they also markedly increase the burden on teachers, who must read all the test papers.

In an attempt to open the universities to talent rather than privilege, the government has instituted an admissions policy based entirely on grades received in the secondary school examination. Those with the highest grades have the first choice of the faculty in which they will enroll. Because medicine, science, and engineering schools are most in demand, they generally have the highest standards of admission.

TABLE 7-2.   ENROLLMENT IN FORMAL EDUCATION, 1974-75,
AND PROJECTED ENROLLMENT, 1980-81

| | | Enrollment | | Annual growth rate 1975-80 |
Stage	Grades	1974-75	1980-81	(percent)
Primary	1-6	4,074,893	5,029,000	4.1
Preparatory (including comprehensive)	7-9	1,199,554	1,874,000	6.9
Secondary general (including comprehensive)	10-12	340,326	395,000	1.9
Secondary technical	10-12	95,811	201,330	
Industrial[a]	10-14	2,825	13,500	10.2
Agricultural		38,429	78,120	
Commercial		213,209	319,960	
Primary teacher training	10-14	33,275	45,400	7.0
Technical training (industrial and commercial)		29,625	60,000	15.0
Higher technical institutes		49,687	50,000	0.0
Universities (and other higher education)		301,170	320,000	1.1

a. Includes five-year courses (grades 10-14).
Source: Ministry of Education and World Bank data.

An academic education, rather than a technical one, remains the
goal of many parents for their children. Government attempts to
limit the number admitted to academic secondary programs have
not been successful, and numerous higher institutions and universities have been founded in the provinces to absorb excess secondary
graduates as students and excess university graduates as teachers.
This widespread desire for a degree leading to a white-collar job
has repeatedly sabotaged efforts to train the middle level technicians
and skilled workers needed by industry. The content of many technical training courses has even been altered in response to student
pressure for a more academic curriculum like that of universities.
In addition, many graduates of engineering and other technically
oriented programs have found it difficult to get jobs in their field,
in part because much of their training is overly theoretical. Quality
training in most secondary technical schools and postsecondary technical institutes has been hindered by the inadequacy of accommodations and equipment and the shortage of qualified instructors.

Education of Females

Enrollment of females has grown at an even faster rate than
that of males, but boys still outnumber girls in primary schools

by about two to one, a ratio that persists into the higher levels.[3]
Until 1922 there was only one secondary school for girls and it had
only a handful of pupils. Now women account for more than one-
quarter of all Egyptians with higher degrees.[4] The illiteracy level
among females (71 percent) is still extremely high compared with
43 percent among males. According to the 1976 census about 25 percent of the total population (aged ten and over) is able to read and
write; in 1960 the corresponding figure was 22.5 percent. This increase was almost wholly because the number of literate females
rose from 12.4 percent in 1960 to 16.2 percent in 1976, a result of
compulsory schooling for girls. The corresponding proportion of
males able to read and write remained practically unchanged during
this period, growing only from 32.6 to 33.2 percent. The number
of females with primary and secondary qualifications has more than
tripled in the last sixteen years, increasing from 3.4 to 11.6 percent, while among males the percentage about doubled, from 9 to
20.4 percent.

Education of females has grown most rapidly at the university
level, increasing sixfold from 0.2 to 1.2 percent in the intercensal
period. Currently about 154,000 women have a university degree
or its equivalent in Egypt and have begun to move into employment
spheres, such as engineering, aeronautics, agriculture, animal
husbandry, and medicine, previously the preserves of men. The
recent gains only serve to underline the very narrow base of educated women that existed as recently as 1960. In the field of education as in other areas of Egyptian society, female emancipation
is still in its early stages. Despite recent gains, female students
are still less likely than males to finish school and to major in
career-oriented subjects.

Future Plans for Education

As outlined in the 1978-82 five-year plan, the government's education policy is predicated on three principles: (1) education is a
basic right; (2) it is a major duty of society to provide it; and (3)
education tends to democratize society. Because of the large number of agencies responsible for decisionmaking in education, it is
important to coordinate activities in the field. For this purpose and
to plan the country's overall education strategy, a National Council
for Education, Scientific Research, and Technology was established
in 1974. It is composed of the various institutions concerned with
educational matters and is directly responsible to the president, to
whom it acts as an advisory body. Effective coordination by this

3. Women constitute about 27 percent of the total enrollment in higher technical institutes and about 30 percent in the universities.
4. CAPMAS, Preliminary Results of 1976 Population and Housing Census.

council is essential to ensure a more rational approach to both education and manpower planning. Since one of the main problems the council faces is the lack of information, a High Committee headed by the prime minister himself was established in 1976, with a subcommittee consisting of seven undersecretaries, to collect basic data on manpower needs and to plan training projects. The subcommittee has initiated surveys of existing educational and training facilities and of the number and type of student teachers required and is planning to accelerate training with new and existing facilities.

The 1978-82 plan calls for coordinating the work of all ministries involved in educational planning. The High Committee could do this if it had a permanent technical secretariat. The plan also calls for improving vocational training so that students receive the **practical** experience required by industry. This task requires upgrading the quality and pay of teachers and improving the physical facilities. Other urgent needs are for nonformal youth and adult education, basic education and skills training for the urban poor, and qualitative improvements, particularly in basic education.

The 1978-82 plan allocates LE418 million for investment expenditures in education, research, and training. The bulk (98.6 percent) would come from the public sector (see table 7-3). Of total public investment expenditures during the plan period (around LE10 thousand million), 4 percent is allocated for education, which is in line with the 3.8 percent of actual expenditures during the 1970-76 period.

About three-quarters of the expected capital expenditures under the plan will support the formal education system, and another 12.5 percent is designated for scientific research. This leaves about 11 percent for technical education and training. While annual expenditures on technical education will almost double over the plan period, those on training are expected to be effectively constant. Given the recognized need for more and better trained skilled labor, these allocations represent a misplacement of priorities.

MANPOWER AND EMPLOYMENT

Apart from the population census, there are two sources of data on manpower and employment in Egypt. The first is the labor force sample survey conducted by CAPMAS, which is based on conventional sampling techniques of households. The second is from estimates derived by the sectoral ministries, such as industry, agriculture, and tourism, which are collated by the Ministry of Planning. This method of computation varies according to the sector but seems to be based more on estimated manpower requirements than on actual employment levels. Thus, for the agricultural sector, labor requirements are calculated in man-days per feddan per year for each crop.

TABLE 7-3. INVESTMENT IN EDUCATION, RESEARCH, AND TRAINING UNDER THE FIVE-YEAR PLAN, 1978–82
(thousands of Egyptian pounds)

Item	1978	1979	1980	1981	1982	Plan period	Percentage during plan period
Public sector							
Primary, preparatory, and secondary	23,420	25,920	31,985	33,985	36,985	152,295	36.3
Technical	4,500	5,074	7,000	7,500	8,000	32,074	7.6
University and higher education	32,880	36,280	40,015	42,015	43,015	194,205	46.4
Scientific research	7,700	9,900	11,000	12,000	12,000	52,600	12.6
Training	2,750	2,750	2,750	2,780	2,780	13,820	3.3
Subtotal	66,750	74,860	85,750	90,780	94,780	412,920	98.6
Private sector	1,100	1,100	1,000	1,100	1,200	5,500	1.1
Total	67,850	75,960	86,750	91,880	95,980	418,420	99.7[a]

a. Because of rounding the sum does not add up to 100.
Source: Five–Year Development Plan, 1978–82 (in Arabic), pp. 2/170–2/171.

These are applied to data on the cropping patterns and total area under cultivation to reach an aggregate labor requirement expressed in man-days. A standard working year of 190 days is used to arrive at the number of people required in agriculture.

Both approaches have their weaknesses. The CAPMAS survey does not disclose seasonal variations in the demand for labor or the intensity of work. The sectoral estimate suffers from averaging out wide variations in the level of technology, individual work effort, scale of operations, skill and know-how of the worker, and the characteristics of other inputs, particularly land. The reliability of the overall estimates depends on the quality and comprehensiveness of the technical measurements, the weighting system used, and the assiduity with which changes taking place in the principal parameters are monitored. In this book the data are derived from the population census and the labor force survey because they are more comparable with other national series published in the International Labour Office Yearbook of Labour Statistics.

Employment by Economic Sector

Table 7-4 shows the employment structure by major divisions of economic activity. Total employment went up by only 38 percent from 1947 to 1976, while the population more than doubled. This divergence between the two series is explained in part because the labor force data cover civilian employment only and omit the armed forces. In addition, the introduction of compulsory schooling, even though largely unenforced, has probably caused a decline in the number of children engaged in economic activity. In any event, the labor force participation rate, unusually low by world standards, was actually on the decline in Egypt between 1947 and 1972, from 37 to 27 percent. In the four years before 1976 it staged a recovery, but at 31.5 percent it is still below participation rates for countries at a similar stage of development.

Particularly significant are the changes in the agricultural sector. The number of persons engaged in agriculture continued to rise until 1971, but the rate of increase slowed. In the five years after the peak was reached, agriculture provided jobs for relatively fewer people, its share of total employment having dropped from 46 to 43 percent.

The most rapid expansion of employment has occurred in the construction industry; its share of total employment has grown from 1.6 percent in 1947 to 4.5 percent in 1976. Most of this growth took place in the five years from 1971 to 1976 when the number of people employed in construction more than doubled as a result of the rebuilding and housing program after the 1973 war. Employment in manufacturing has also grown rapidly, from 8.2 percent of total employment in 1947 to 12.6 percent in 1976. Not all of this growth can

TABLE 7-4. CIVILIAN EMPLOYMENT
BY ECONOMIC ACTIVITY, 1947-76
(number in thousands)

| | | Primary (agriculture) | | Secondary | | | |
| | | | | Mining,[a] quarrying, manufacturing | | Construction | |
Date	Total	Number	Per-cent	Number	Per-cent	Number	Per-cent
1947	6,994	4,086	58.4	574	8.2	113	1.6
1960	7,727	4,406	57.0	734	9.5	159	2.0
1966	8,334	4,447	53.4	1,089	13.1	206	2.5
1971	8,409	4,471	53.2	1,045	12.4	195	2.3
1974	9,030	4,212	46.6	1,150	12.7	315	3.5
1976	9,629	4,224	43.9	1,210	12.6	434	4.5

a. Includes petroleum.
Sources: CAPMAS, population Census, 1947, 1960, 1966, and 1976;
Labor Force Sample Survey, 1971 and 1974; and Ministry of Planning,
"Egypt: 1976-80 Five-Year Plan."

be considered productive, however. In Egypt, as in many developing countries, industry has a dual structure. On one side are the large-scale modern enterprises equipped with fairly up-to-date technology; the other includes small-scale establishments of the informal sector. Since the nationalizations of 1962, almost all large industrial enterprises (that is, those with more than fifty workers) have been in the public sector, which has received 90 percent of investment allocations and licenses. Since much of this investment has been capital intensive, the rate of labor absorption in the public sector has not been high. In 1947 manufacturing establishments employing more than fifty workers had a total labor force of 213,000.[5] By 1960 these establishments provided 270,000 jobs, an increase of 27 percent over the 1947 level.[6]

Despite the emphasis given to the state-controlled manufacturing sector in the first two Egyptian five-year plans (1960-70), manufacturing employment in the public sector (which more or less corresponds to the state-controlled group) had reached just 445,000 in 1966 and 526,000 in 1974, less than half the total manufacturing employment in those years and only two and a half times the 1947 figures.[7] The remainder was in private small-scale and handicraft establishments, with generally much lower levels of technology and productivity. Some industries in the informal sector with low-entry

5. Institute of National Planning, The Structure and Organization of the Egyptian Manufacturing Industry since 1945 (Cairo, 1974), table 1.5.

6. CAPMAS, Survey of Industrial Production, 1960 (Cairo, 1973).

7. M. A. Mongi and M. N. Hanafi, Labor Absorption in the Egyptian Economy (Cairo: Institute of National Planning, 1972), table 57; and National Bank of Egypt Economic Bulletin, vol. 28, no. 4 (1974), table 6.

Secondary		Tertiary					
Electricity, gas, and water		Commerce		Transport, storage, communications		Other services and unspecified	
Number	Per-cent	Number	Per-cent	Number	Per-cent	Number	Per-cent
23	0.3	590	8.4	203	2.9	1,405	20.1
37	0.5	641	8.3	260	3.4	1,489	19.3
51	0.6	599	7.2	340	4.1	1,602	19.2
26	0.3	807	9.6	324	3.9	1,541	18.3
38	0.4	883	9.8	396	4.4	2,036	22.5
47	0.5	1,016	10.6	422	4.4	2,276	23.6

thresholds (that is, low capital requirements), such as pottery, shoemaking, metal products, and handwoven textiles, have become overcrowded and wages are therefore low. Thus a significant part of the so-called industrial labor force is underemployed, though it is difficult to ascertain how much because there are no regular statistical returns from small-scale establishments.

Since 1966 a third growth sector has been commerce. (The decline in the six preceding years can probably be attributed to the severe import restrictions, the disruptions caused by the nationalization of the major trading organizations and department stores, and the scarcity of domestic products during the initial import-substitution phase.) After the liberalization of trade and general opening-up of the economy, the increasing volume of goods passing through wholesale and retail distribution channels brought a greater demand for labor in this sector. But here again part of the expansion disguises underemployment (for example, among street vendors) because some activity, requiring little skill or capital, provides a temporary haven for those forced out of agriculture and waiting in the cities for a better job to turn up.

Employment in finance, insurance, education, health, government administration, and other social and personal services has grown modestly in the aggregate. Its share of total employment rose from 20.1 percent in 1947 to 23.6 percent in 1976. Even when the unspecified activities grouped under this heading are excluded, service employment has grown unusually slowly over the past thirty years compared with most other countries. It may possibly be explained by the fact that employment in the army and paramilitary forces is not included. In addition, the expansion of public sector employment in education, health, and administrative services seems to have been offset by a relative decline in private and personal services.

The actual number employed in the tertiary sector as a whole has risen from 2.2 million people in 1947 to 3.7 million in 1976. Most of this growth has taken place in the past five years, however, during which employment increased by more than one-third. Officials estimate that one in three of these people are employed either directly or indirectly by the government.

Public Sector Employment

The rapid growth of public sector employment can be largely attributed to three factors. The first is the adoption in 1960 of a centrally planned economic system, followed by the nationalization of large enterprises in all sectors of the economy in 1962. Instead of market forces, administrative decision determined resource allocation, and this required a large bureaucracy. The elimination of competition between domestic enterprises and with foreign producers removed a constraint on administrative overhead in public sector enterprises, although admittedly costs would have grown with the volume of transactions in any event. Second, the expansion of free education, health, and other social services to the community at large became a major political objective, limited only by overall budgetary constraints rather than by effective demand. Third, productivity and efficiency took second place to social and political pressures to provide employment opportunities for the rapidly growing population, and the public sector was used as a depository for surplus labor.

Public sector employment today constitutes a form of unemployment benefit for those who might otherwise be out of a job. The beneficiaries come from all educational and occupational groups, ranging from unskilled laborers to messengers and clerks, technicians, university graduates, and high-level administrators. But graduates of higher institutions of learning have been the most privileged because they have been guaranteed jobs, and these were more often than not in government service. A combination of free university education and guaranteed employment accounts in large part for the sevenfold increase in university-level enrollment, from 54,000 in 1953-54 to 400,000 in 1976-77.[8] The government's objectives in guaranteeing employment may elicit sympathy, but the system has now reached such proportions that it is imperative to compare its

8. Mostafa H. Nagi, Labor Force and Employment in Egypt: A Demographic and Socioeconomic Analysis, Special Studies in International Economics and Development (New York: Praeger, 1971), table 17; and Ministry of Education estimates.

TABLE 7-5.   RATE OF UNEMPLOY-
MENT BY ECONOMIC ACTIVITY,
1957-72
(percent)

Activity	1957	1960	1968	1972
Agriculture	2.1	2.2	0.6	0.1
Manufacturing	4.4	6.0	4.7	0.5
Construction	10.7	15.3	7.4	0.5
Commerce	1.9	2.5	1.6	0.3
Services	n.a.	3.1	1.5	0.2
Unclassified	77.0	87.0	66.0	2.8
Average rate	5.1	4.8	2.8	1.4

n.a. Not available.
Source: CAPMAS, Labor Force Sample
Surveys.

costs and benefits objectively with those of alternative employment strategies.

Unemployment

Not all unemployment in Egypt is disguised as surplus manpower
attached to productive enterprises and organizations. The labor
force sample surveys have disclosed a small proportion of the labor
force without work and actively seeking it (see table 7-5). From
1957 to 1972 the rate of unemployment has fluctuated between 1.4
and 5.1 percent of the labor force, with a tendency to diminish in
recent years. Apart from unclassified activities, construction was
the most seriously affected sector until migration depleted its labor
supply. As one would expect, open unemployment tends to be higher
in urban than in rural areas. In Alexandria the rate was 9.2 percent in 1961 and 7.6 percent in 1970, while the figures for Cairo
were 7.5 and 3.5 percent, respectively.[9]

These employment figures cannot be compared with similar series
for industrialized countries, however, for they represent only the
tip of the iceberg. The underutilization of labor is manifested more
seriously in low-productivity employment and low rates of participation in the labor force, particularly among women.

Although female employment has increased more rapidly than that
of males, it accounted for only 9 percent of total employment in 1976.
Almost half the women workers are in community, social, and personal services and a fifth in agriculture.[10] With an increasing

9. Amr Mohie-Eldin, Employment Problems and Policies in Egypt (Geneva:
International Labour Organisation, 1975), table 19.
10. This may be understated because much of the female's economic activity
in the agricultural sector is seasonal and is supplementary to her role as housewife.

proportion of females receiving education up to the highest levels
(29 percent of university enrollment in 1976-77), ways need to be
found to ease their entry into economic activities where their skills
can be used more productively.

Although the legal age for leaving school is twelve and children
are obliged to attend school from the age of six, child employment
is still prevalent, especially in agriculture and informal urban activities not subject to labor legislation or inspection. About 265,000
of 5.5 million children between the ages of six and eleven were classified as members of the labor force in 1974; 85 percent of those
children actively employed were in rural areas.[11] An undisclosed
number of children work part-time on family farms. Child labor is
likely to continue as long as family enterprises remain the predominant organizational unit. Self-employed and unpaid family workers
contributed 51 percent of total employment in the whole economy in
1974, almost the same proportion as in 1960.[12]

Occupational Structure

In addition to the mobility between rural and urban areas and
among different economic sectors, there has been some change in
the occupational structure. Table 7-6 shows that the proportion of
higher professional, technical, and scientific personnel in the labor
force grew from 2.7 percent in 1947 to 5.7 percent in 1974. Increases occurred in the administrative, executive, managerial, and
clerical categories as well, while the share of farmers and related
workers declined from 60.5 percent to 45.6 percent. Egypt has a
higher proportion of professional and managerial workers than countries such as India (3.4 percent) and Nigeria (2.6 percent), but it
has a long way to go to reach the level of developed countries, such
as the United States (22.4 percent) and Sweden (22.9 percent).

LABOR MIGRATION

The relaxation of Egyptian policies governing the exit of nationals
and the increasing demand for expatriate labor by Arab oil-exporting
countries have caused many Egyptians to seek jobs in Libya and the
Persian Gulf States, a movement that began to accelerate in 1974.
Although exact information on the number of migrant Egyptian workers is not available, estimates range from a quarter to half a million, and one estimate puts it as high as one million, that is, between 2.5 and 10 percent of the labor force.[13] The controversial

11. CAPMAS, Labor Force Sample Survey, 1974.
12. Ibid., and CAPMAS, Population Census 1960 (Cairo, 1963), vol. 2.
13. Nazli Choukri, "The New Migration in the Middle East: A Problem for
Whom?" The Economist (November 13, 1976).

TABLE 7-6.   OCCUPATIONAL STRUCTURE OF THE LABOR
FORCE, 1947-74
(percent)

Occupation	1947	1960	1972	1974	1974 (thousands)
Professional, technical, scientific	2.7	3.7	5.5	5.7	522
Administrative, executive, and managerial	0.9	1.1	1.5	1.0	91
Clerical	2.0	3.7	5.1	5.5	507
Sales	6.8	8.1	6.9	8.4	769
Transport	2.4	3.1	18.4	22.2	1,999
Crafts, production, and processing	13.3	16.2			
Agricultural	60.5	53.1	51.6	45.6	4,126
Service	9.0	8.9	8.3	9.1	826
Not classified	2.5	2.2	2.7	2.5	235
Total	100.0	100.0	100.0	100.0	9,075

Source: CAPMAS, Population Census, 1947 and 1960; Labor Force Sample Survey, 1972 and 1974.

census estimate of 1.4 million represents about 14 percent of the labor force.

Whether this outflow represents a net drain on the economy cannot be conclusively discerned from available information. Not only is the total number of emigrants in doubt, but so are breakdowns by occupation, level of education, and duration of stay. Even if the figures were definitive, it would be difficult to know whether on balance it is to Egypt's advantage to have such a large proportion of its labor force working outside the country. Such a judgment would depend on a complex mix of economic and social criteria. Aside from such considerations as workers' remittances, unemployment, social overhead expended on human capital formation, and the brain drain, there are difficult questions about the interaction of these factors. The magnitude of the problem may be indicated by a World Bank estimate of workers' remittances of somewhat over US$1,000 million for 1977, which makes it likely that on average labor migration generates net benefits to the economy.

A better understanding of the factors influencing labor migration, the magnitudes involved, and the net effect on the economy are clearly needed. And without some idea of the likely extent of future migration accurate manpower planning would be impossible. For example, a technical training project might be designed to meet domestic demand for vocational skills, but if neighboring countries offer higher wages they might siphon off the graduates and inhibit domestic demand. Thus, proper manpower planning should extend beyond the boundaries of Egypt and take account of labor flows into and out of the country.

MAIN ISSUES AND PRIORITIES

While the overall open unemployment rate is relatively low and
has not reached the level normally associated with frictional unemployment, disguised unemployment and underemployment are believed
to be extensive, especially in the public sector. The government's
policy of guaranteeing employment to graduates of universities and
institutes of higher education would not be so harmful to the economy
if it simply led to the employment of excess workers that the economy was unable to absorb. But it seems likely that the policy encourages the diversion of labor from areas where it could be productively employed, for example, as technical and vocational workers
in industry or as skilled workers outside Egypt. The exact nature
and magnitude of this labor substitution has not yet been studied.
It may well be that discontinuing the government's employment policy would not by itself channel the excess labor in the bureaucracy
to areas where it is needed. Unless the "push" out of government
employment were accompanied by an effective "pull" toward the la-
bor-deficient areas, open unemployment would rise, accompanied by
social and economic problems.

Related to the imbalance of labor supply and demand is the overemphasis placed on formal education by government policy. The
high proportion of government expenditures directed to formal education stimulates the supply of graduates from higher institutes of
learning, who are subsequently absorbed by an artificially induced
demand for government bureaucrats. The government recognizes
this vicious circle and the corresponding need to encourage students
to enter vocational and technical fields, but the problem may be too
large for isolated projects to affect appreciably. It is therefore urgent that the government address the broad questions of education
and manpower planning on a national, and possibly a regional, level.

Manpower planning must rest on a data base that is sufficiently
comprehensive and detailed to allow for an understanding of what
manpower is available, how it is distributed, what is needed now and
in the future, what kinds of substitution practices exist in various
occupations and sectors, what the output of the education system is,
and how it can be geared to future manpower requirements, domestic
and possibly foreign. None of these questions has complete answers
at present. The government is aware of this shortcoming and is now
cooperating with international agencies on a manpower study to obtain detailed data on present and projected needs and translate them
into educational targets.

Policy in the past has been preoccupied with education as an investment in human capital that affects the supply of labor. But the
government also recognizes that education is desirable for its own
sake as a final consumption good that establishes a level of literacy
and awareness among the populace. The relatively high illiteracy

and early dropout rates from the education system offer a continuing
challenge to the government in its desire to attain this objective.

The government's education policy, as stated in the five-year
plan, is to equalize economic and social opportunity — and, in time,
income — by extending education to as wide a base of the society as
possible. It also aims at meeting the manpower requirements of the
economy, especially the industrial sector. Stated as such, these
goals are too broad to give much insight into the government's priorities in the field. A proper evaluation of priorities must rest on
decisions about competing options in a constrained system.

Investment allocations under the 1978-82 plan point to the continued dominance of formal education. This is to some extent understandable because of the momentum of the past and the absence of
an appropriate education-manpower planning study. Now that the
government has commissioned such a study, however, it should be
able to prepare an operational education-manpower strategy that
sets more precise priorities among the many options available.

8
Urbanization

Egypt is highly urbanized for a country with its economic structure and per capita income. The 1976 census estimated that about 16.1 million people, or about 44 percent of those present in the country, lived in urban areas, that is, centers with more than 20,000 inhabitants. The growth of the urban population has been rapid and sustained. Between 1947 and 1976 when the total population doubled, the urban population almost tripled (see table 8-1). The figure in the table for the total population in 1976 excludes the estimated 1.4 million Egyptians living abroad, the bulk of whom were likely to have come from urban areas. If they were added to both the total and the urbanized population, the proportion of the latter would be raised to 46 percent and its growth rate to 3.8 percent in the intercensal years.

The urban population is concentrated mainly in four governorates in Lower Egypt, which are considered wholly urban; these are Cairo, Alexandria, Port Said, and Suez. Another, Ismailia, is also highly urbanized and sometimes regarded as an urban governorate. The cities of Port Said, Suez, and Ismailia were virtually depopulated

TABLE 8-1. DEVELOPMENT OF NATIONAL AND URBAN POPULATION, 1947-76

	Total population		Urban population		
Year	Number (thousands)	Rate of growth (percent)	Number (thousands)	Rate of growth (percent)	Proportion of total (percent)
1947	19,022	—	6,200	—	32.6
1960	26,085	2.3	9,864	3.6	37.8
1966	30,076	2.5	12,037	3.4	40.0
1976	36,656[a]	2.1	16,086	3.0	43.9

Note: The rate of growth is the annual average for the intercensal years.
a. This figure excludes the estimated 1.4 million Egyptians living abroad.
Source: CAPMAS, Statistical Yearbook (Cairo, 1977).

142

between 1967 and 1974 when their inhabitants moved into the eastern Delta and Cairo. These cities are now being rapidly reestablished and are reported to have attained their 1966 population levels. The remaining provincial governorates have both rural and urban components. The contemporary demographic trend is for steady increases in the population of the governorates of Cairo, Alexandria, Giza, and Kalyubia (parts of the last two are included in Greater Cairo) and a general decline in the proportion of population living in Upper Egypt governorates.

The geographical distribution of population can change because of different natural rates of increase or domestic and international migration. So far, the decisive element in the pattern of urban growth has been migration within Egypt. Emigration has been a factor only in the 1970s, and evidence of different natural growth rates and, more particularly, different fertility rates is inconclusive. While lower fertility rates have been associated with urban parents having higher educational levels or better occupations, the extent of this difference and its impact on population growth is unknown. The country's high population density and the adequacy of communications are good grounds for assuming a relatively even natural population growth throughout the country; regional differences would tend to be dampened by migration or the pervasiveness of fertility habits.

The long-term trends in population redistribution are indicated in table 8-2, which compares annual regional growth rates. Until recently, the urban governorates have been the main recipients of migration, and population growth in Lower Egypt and the frontier governorates has lagged behind that in the rest of the country. Long-term trends identified from both census and residential records are: (1) regional redistribution of people from the densely populated, basin-irrigated plains of Upper Egypt to the irrigated Delta of Lower Egypt; (2) movement from rural areas to densely populated urban areas throughout the country; (3) migration from both urban and rural areas to the country's major cities, namely Cairo, Giza, Alexandria, and Aswan.

TABLE 8-2. ANNUAL REGIONAL POPULATION GROWTH RATES, 1927-70

(percent)

Region	1927-37	1937-47	1947-60	1960-66	1966-70
Urban governorates	1.9	4.2	3.5	3.7	3.6
Lower Egypt	0.9	1.3	2.2	2.4	2.3
Upper Egypt	1.2	1.2	1.8	1.9	2.0
Frontier governorates	1.0	5.8	2.8	2.0	1.6
All Egypt	1.1	1.8	2.3	2.5	2.5

Source: CAPMAS, census data.

TABLE 8-3. ESTIMATED ANNUAL RATE OF MIGRATION,
1947-60 AND 1960-66

Place	1947-60 Urban	1947-60 Rural	1947-60 Total	1960-66 Urban	1960-66 Rural	1960-66 Total
Urban governorates						
Cairo	1.2	...	1.2	1.5	...	1.5
Alexandria	1.1	...	1.1	0.5	...	0.5
Port Said	0.6	...	0.6	...	...	...
Ismailia	1.1	...	1.1	0.9	...	0.9
Suez	2.3	...	2.3	2.0	...	2.0
Total	1.2	...	1.2	1.2	...	1.2
Lower Egypt	0.6	-0.3	-0.1	1.9	-0.7	-0.2
Upper Egypt	0.6	-0.8	-0.5	2.4	-1.4	-0.6
All Egypt	0.9	-0.5	...	1.1	-0.7	...

... Negligible.
Source: Sandra K. Burden, "Population Movements and Distribution over
Time and Space," in A. R. Omran, ed., Egypt: Population, Problems and
Prospects (Chapel Hill: University of North Carolina, Carolina Population
Center, 1973), chap. 4, table 3.

As shown in table 8-3, from 1947 to 1966 the rate of net migration from rural to urban areas in both Upper and Lower Egypt accelerated. The average annual migration to urban governorates was
of the order of 1.2 percent over the entire period, varying from a
high rate of more than 2.0 percent in the city of Suez to virtually
no migration to Port Said. Despite high rates of migration to urban
areas of Upper and Lower Egypt, these areas were also net donors
of migrants to the other urban governorates.

Egypt's pattern of urbanization has been dominated by the growth
of the country's prime city, Cairo. One of the world's oldest cities
and the largest in the Middle East, it has been continuously inhabi-
ted for more than a thousand years. The relative importance of
Cairo and its immediate surroundings — Greater Cairo — can be
gauged from a comparison of the national, urban, and Cairene populations between 1947 and 1976. During that period, the urban population increased from 38 to 44 percent of the total, while the population of Greater Cairo increased from 11 to nearly 22 percent of
the total, to account for almost half the total urbanized population.

Cairo's growth is associated with a wide range of policy and non-
policy considerations. First, there is a predilection in Egypt for
the centralized location of the ministries and other national authorities — even those with responsibilities for services outside Cairo are
based in Cairo. Second, as the seat of government, Cairo has an
employment structure dominated by the services and public sectors.
Since the government is the employer of last resort, there is an inherent bias toward Cairo. Third, three of the country's major

universities are in Cairo and have provided free education since the mid-1950s.   Enrollment in Cairo's universities has grown from about 100,000 in 1968-69 to nearly twice that figure in 1975.   Many of these students have arrived from provincial cities and towns and are often accompanied by supporting family members and job seekers.

URBAN EMPLOYMENT AND STRUCTURAL CHANGE

Data on the structure, distribution, and development of the work force and employment situation for Egypt are scarce and often contradictory.   Until further details from the 1976 census are issued, the most recent comprehensive data available on the labor force were collected in the 1960 census.   They indicate a shift in employment opportunities from rural to urban areas and from agricultural to nonagricultural sectors.   The growth of nonagricultural opportunities has in turn given positive encouragement to the expansion of the urban economy.

About 42 percent of the country's total employment is found in urban areas, of which more than 90 percent is engaged in nonagricultural pursuits; in contrast, less than 30 percent of those employed in rural areas are in nonagricultural jobs.   The dominant elements of urban employment are: manufacturing, 26 percent; government and personal services, 28.2 percent; and trade and finance, 18.4 percent.   Together these sectors account for nearly three-quarters of the total.   The proportion of the total work force in agriculture declined from 55.3 percent in 1960-61 to 46.6 percent in 1974, with a corresponding increase in employment in government and personal services from 18.3 to 22.5 percent.   Other nonagricultural employment appears to have increased more modestly, and industrialization has not offered an immediate solution to employment problems.[1]

The capacity of services to absorb labor may at first appear a solution to the problems posed by the population expansion.   But the relocation of underemployed agricultural labor in services is not akin to the reallocation of resources in industry.   Growth of services is unlikely to contribute to development through external economics or technical progress.   The reallocation that has occurred is to a large extent a transfer of poverty, underemployment, and low productivity from one economic sector and geographical area to another.

Between 1947 and 1970 the government created a large proportion of all the new jobs.   The number of government employees is estimated to have increased from less than 310,000 in 1947 to nearly 770,000 in 1960 and 1,035,000 in 1966-67.   It is doubtful that this

1. Military mobilization, particularly since 1967, has affected civil employment to a degree that cannot be determined from available data.

rapid expansion was entirely warranted by the needs of public administration or that it led to a corresponding increase in the real output of government services. Open unemployment is avoided or contained by creating a large mass of underemployed public employees and officials. Again, the effect on economic development is likely to be negative because of the macroeconomic repercussions of budget deficits on aggregate demand, prices, the balance of payments, and the diversion of resources from investment to consumption.

The distribution of employment according to governorate or region is not available. Some idea of the spatial distribution of the work force can be gained from the 1960 census, however (see table 8-4). The governorates of Cairo, Giza, and Kalyubia, which make up Greater Cairo, contained 23.3 percent of the total labor force and no less than 48 percent of the total nonagricultural workers.

TABLE 8-4. STRUCTURE AND DISTRIBUTION OF THE AGRICULTURAL AND NONAGRICULTURAL LABOR FORCE, 1960

	Labor force (thousands)			Percentage share of cities		Ratio of nonagricultural to total
Governorate	Nonagricultural	Agricultural	Total	Nonagricultural	Total	
Cairo	1,115.7	26.8	1,142.6	28.4	13.6	2.09
Alexandria	458.4	25.0	483.4	11.7	5.8	2.03
Ismailia	46.2	37.8	84.0	1.2	1.0	1.20
Port Said	67.2	4.9	72.0	1.7	0.9	1.98
Suez	55.9	6.0	61.9	1.4	0.7	1.89
Kalyubia	132.3	202.2	334.5	3.4	4.0	0.85
Menufia	128.6	255.3	383.9	3.2	4.6	0.70
Dakahlia	197.4	461.6	659.0	5.0	7.9	0.64
Beheira	180.8	427.0	607.8	4.6	7.2	0.64
Sharkia	212.2	370.0	582.1	5.4	6.9	0.78
Gharbia	243.3	271.4	514.7	6.2	6.1	1.01
Kafr el-Sheik	77.6	261.5	339.1	2.0	4.0	0.50
Damietta	53.2	62.4	115.6	1.4	1.4	1.01
Giza	244.8	236.4	481.2	6.2	5.7	1.08
Fayoum	84.9	187.7	272.6	2.2	3.3	0.68
Beni Suef	71.1	206.8	277.9	1.8	3.3	0.54
Minya	137.7	381.2	518.8	3.5	6.2	0.57
Assiut	95.8	309.4	405.3	2.4	4.8	0.50
Souhag	130.3	353.2	483.5	3.3	5.8	0.57
Kena	110.6	304.2	414.8	2.8	4.9	0.57
Aswan	64.0	69.9	133.9	1.6	1.6	1.00
Red Sea	4.4	0.2	4.6	0.1	0.05	2.00
New Valley	2.2	3.2	5.4	0.1	0.06	1.67
Matruh	4.1	2.4	6.5	0.1	0.07	1.43
Sinai	9.6	2.0	11.6	0.2	0.14	1.43
Total	3,927.9	4,468.5	8,396.4	100.0	100.0	1.00

Source: CAPMAS, Population Census, 1960.

The corresponding proportions for Alexandria are 5.8 percent and 11.7 percent. In the government and personal services sector, above average concentrations are formed in metropolitan Cairo, Ismailia, and Upper Egypt. Lower concentrations are found in Alexandria, Port Said, Suez, and Lower Egypt.

URBAN HOUSING

The rapid and sustained growth of the urban population, the public commitment to the promotion of equity, and the low level of resources available for housing and urban utilities have all contributed to poor conditions in the cities, particularly in Cairo. Urban housing in particular seems to have steadily deteriorated since the early 1960s.

The Housing Gap

Neither investment in housing nor the number of units produced followed any discernible trend from 1960 to 1975. They fluctuated considerably owing to a shortage of raw materials, changes in housing policy priorities, initiation of special programs, and the war and defense effort. In no year did the number of units built keep pace with the formation of new households — about 90,000 per year. Only in 1975, when the housing sector received a high priority in public programs, was production close to the rate of new household formation, and then only if illegal building (without construction permit) is counted. The Ministry of Housing and Reconstruction (MOHR) estimates that illegal housing construction constitutes between a third and a half of total housing in the private sector. It is usually substandard and low cost, but it serves the very real needs of low-income households and must be taken into account.

Until the final results of the 1976 census are available, an analysis of the quality of the existing housing stock must rest on the preliminary results of the census and on extrapolations of 1960 data. There are about 1.9 million urban housing units, of which more than 15 percent can be said to be substandard. An estimated 0.5 million urban households live in these substandard units, with about 1.7 households per unit. The existing shortage is of the order of 1.5 million (see table 8-5). Even if building activity is double the official annual rate of 28,000 given in table 8-5, the total number of housing units lags so far behind the rate of household formation that the gap is widening every year. By 1985 it is expected to have reached 3 million units, and by the year 2000 population growth alone will create the demand for an additional 1.6 million units.

TABLE 8-5.   URBAN HOUSING STOCK AND ESTIMATED
SHORTAGE, 1975

Item	Number (thousands)
Total housing units, 1960	1,675
Demolitions, 1960-75	- 225
Subtotal	1,450
New construction, 1960-75	471
Total housing units, 1975	1,921
Substandard units (15 percent)	300
Total standard units	1,621
Total urban population, 1975	16,211
Total number of urban households[a]	3,329
Estimated shortage of standard units	1,456
Estimated shortage, including replacement[b]	1,756
Estimated shortage excluding one-person and two-person households	
Including replacement[b]	1,392
Without replacement[b]	1,092
Average annual household formation	90
Average annual demolition	10
Total shortage	1,492

a. Assumes average urban household size of 4.87 persons.
b. "Replacement" refers to dwellings that have been rendered completely
uninhabitable and need to be replaced.
Source: World Bank estimates.

Housing Conditions

Housing conditions are on the whole better in urban than in rural
areas of Egypt, but even in Cairo and Alexandria, which are probably the best served, conditions are very poor. In 1970 only 44
percent of the buildings in Greater Cairo were connected to public
or private systems of sewerage. Water was piped to 50 percent of
the buildings in the area,[2] while more than a quarter were not connected to any source. More than a third of the buildings were not
connected to electricity. Although the figures for 1970 and 1976 are
not strictly comparable, because they are for Greater Cairo and the
Cairo governorate respectively, they indicate that by 1976 the services had improved somewhat. Later figures on sewerage are not
available, but 70 percent of the dwellings were served with water in
1976, and another 11 percent had water inside the building. In 1976

2. This may be an overestimate because of the composition of the sample.

TABLE 8-6. HOUSEHOLDS IN DWELLING UNITS WITH ELECTRICITY, 1976

Governorate	Percentage of households with electricity			Total number of households (thousands)		
	Urban	Rural	Total	Urban	Rural	Total
Cairo	82.1	...	82.1	1,065	...	1,065
Alexandria	89.6	...	89.6	466	...	466
Minya	60.0	9.2	19.8	87	329	416
Kena	52.7	10.7	20.2	76	264	340
Egypt	77.0	18.6	45.7	3,248	3,738	6,986

... Negligible.

Source: CAPMAS, Preliminary Results of the 1976 Population and Housing Census (Cairo, March 1977).

some 82 percent of households in Cairo governorate were lit by electricity compared with less than 66 percent in 1970 in Greater Cairo (see table 8-6).

The average household size in Egypt rose from 5.0 persons in 1960 to 5.2 in 1976, each household occupying an average of 2.8 rooms or about 1.8 persons per room. Average household size in urban governorates declined from 4.9 to 4.8, however. Here the average number of rooms was 2.5 in 1976, while the degree of crowding was 1.9 persons per room.

The reasons for the poor quality of housing in Egypt include the government housing policies, the overlapping of administrative responsibilities among various public agencies, rising construction costs, the low priority given to public investment in housing during the war periods, and the absence of mortgage funds. The main inadequacies of the existing housing policy are: (1) Government policy, which is now being reconsidered, has been to rent rather than sell housing, leaving the full burden of maintenance and collection on the public sector. (2) Rent control on new buildings has been a great deterrent to investment in housing. The assessment sets rent at 5 percent of the land value, plus 8 percent of the building cost. Assessing committees generally estimate building cost in accordance with official standards, however, rather than actual costs. The government has recently abolished rent control on certain types of housing, which should encourage new private investment in this sector, and the methods of assessment and rent calculation are being changed. (3) Since 1973 the government has allocated public housing by assigning 20 percent to each of five categories: administrative action, households with young children, households with employees assigned to new locations, households returning from abroad, and members of the armed services. Some of these categories obviously bear no relation to income levels of the household, while the last three actually discriminate against the lower-income groups. If the objective is to make the majority of public housing available to lower-income groups, then the criteria for allocation should reflect this priority. (4) Financial assistance is unavailable to lower-income groups for the purchase of homes.

Other factors affecting the quality and quantity of housing have been the shortage of land, labor, and materials in both the public and private sectors. These shortages have caused a relatively sharp increase in prices; since 1973, for example, prices of construction materials have increased about threefold. The government is attempting to overcome the shortage of labor by sponsoring training programs in the construction industry, and to remove the constraints on building materials by encouraging local production and reducing delays in the granting of import licenses for them.

Another increasingly costly constraint on housebuilding derives from government regulatory measures, especially building permits that often take up to six months to obtain. The process includes approval of design, location, and site, allocation of building materials, and approval by municipal authorities. Most of the time consumed in this way could be eliminated by restructuring the application process. The continued use of official prices for housing construction in the budget allocation is particularly unrealistic.

Housing Production

The lengthy bureaucratic procedures affecting the quantity and quality of housing reflect the serious administrative overlapping in the housing sector. Housing is currently produced by public, semi-public, and private entities under the overall policy supervision of the Ministry of Housing and Reconstruction in an extremely complicated system.

Public sector. In the public sector production is controlled by MOHR working with the housing and reconstruction administrations in the governorates. MOHR controls the budget allocations and sets overall production levels. The governorates are responsible for the design and construction, which is normally done by private contractors selected through public bidding. Financing for MOHR housing programs is from the national budget. In addition, since 1976 a fund has been created within MOHR to finance low-cost housing with funds from government, banks, and insurance companies. The fund began operations by participating in the financing of middle-income housing in 1977 and in 1978 was involved in financing lower-middle-income housing in a number of governorates. MOHR production during 1976 was about 70,000 new and rehabilitated units.

Ten publicly owned companies also produce housing under the supervision of MOHR. Most of these companies were once private, profit-motivated developers and builders. They were nationalized in the mid-1960s and have since operated under the limited control of MOHR. Their financing comes from private banks and insurance companies, from land sales, and from repayments on old projects. Some are also starting savings programs for prospective home buyers, and the savings are used to help finance construction. Housing produced by these companies has been mostly for upper-income families. Current projects include five-room apartments of about 200 square meters, with two baths, and a maid's room. One company estimated that the average unit cost of this housing would be LE7,000 to LE15,000. Almost all housing produced by these companies is sold as condominiums, and the companies are responsible for collecting the monthly payments. Estimates on collections vary from 10 to 40 percent delinquency.

Semipublic sector. Housing cooperatives were first permitted in 1944; in 1954 a new law granted an annual budget of LE2.5 million for cooperatives under the direction of the Ministry of Social Affairs. In 1961 responsibility was transferred to the Ministry of Municipal and Social Affairs, which later became MOHR. In 1971 the General Organization for Housing Cooperatives (GOHC) was established to promote and supervise the development of cooperatives and to serve as the link between them and MOHR. In developing a typical housing cooperative GOHC reviews its application and checks land ownership, checks architectural drawings and building permits, executes loan agreements, assists in contracting and inspection, registers the cooperative and reviews its bylaws, and issues permits for building materials. In 1975 the program was shifted from upper-income projects to the middle-income level. At the same time, government financing was increased to LE10 million a year. A new proposal is now under discussion to increase government financing to LE20 million a year. From 1967 to 1976 housing cooperatives have helped to finance and produce approximately 26,000 units at a cost of about LE41.5 million. The 1976 budget provided for about 10,000 units.

The major sources of financing for housing cooperatives are savings from cooperatives and their members, government budget allocations, and income from completed projects. GOHC is looking for new ways to encourage saving for housing cooperatives. Until 1970 financing was provided for fifteen years at 5 percent interest to cooperative groups and 6 percent interest to individuals. Home improvement loans were granted at 3 percent interest for twenty years. In 1975 terms were extended to thirty years at 3 percent interest.

In the past, GOHC has made loans for cooperative apartment buildings with one apartment for each member, for cooperative land subdivisions where each member purchased a lot and then built a small apartment building for sale or rent on a speculative basis to nonmembers, and to individuals who are not members of a cooperative. After the 1975 redirection of the housing cooperative program, loans were limited to dwelling units costing less than LE5,000. Most

loans were for units costing between LE3,000 and LE1,500 per unit.
The average 1976 loan was about LE2,000. The size of the dwelling
unit was reduced, and new projects were "complete developments"
with community facilities.

A recent law makes public sector enterprises earmark 15 percent of their profits for the provision of services, including housing,
to their employees. The earmarked amounts are deposited in a special fund in the Finance Ministry and drawn upon in accordance with
national budget allocations for each service sector in any given year.
Two-thirds of this fund is for facilities such as schools and hospitals, and one-third is for housing. The industrial housing funds are
channeled through the local services councils. The program has so
far been very limited in scope because of the low profits of public
sector enterprises and the low priority national investment policies
have given services, including housing, until recently. Nevertheless, the program is expected to gain new momentum in the near
future as a result of the government's commitment to relieve the
severity of the housing shortage.

Private sector. Some housing is produced by private, profit-
oriented companies for higher-income families. In addition, an
estimated 50 percent of all housing constructed in urban areas is
done by private individuals through self-help or by small contractors. This unorganized construction often takes place illegally,
without building permits and on land to which the occupant does not
have clear title, and often to expand or rebuild existing structures.
In the past, mud, brick, and wood were the major materials, but new
construction uses mostly fired "red brick" and concrete. There are
no firm figures on the number of new or rehabilitated dwelling units
constructed by private individuals in this way.

Housing Investment

During the 1974-77 period, investment in housing can be divided
into Canal Zone reconstruction and other investment. Since reconstruction in the Canal Zone is, to a large extent, influenced by criteria other than supply alone, it cannot be assumed that once the
immediate needs for reconstruction are met an equivalent sum of
money will be made available for new housing. An estimated LE80
million of expenditures was financed by Arab states specifically for
reconstruction in the Canal Zone and must be deducted from the total investment figure of LE160 million. The remaining LE80 million can be further divided into public and private investment in
housing. In 1975 the private sector accounted for about LE50
million (63 percent of expenditure) and the government for about
LE30 million.

The Ministry of Planning estimated tentatively that Egypt would
spend about LE1,200 million on housing and attendant public utilities

during the 1976-80 period. Some LE350 million (28 percent) was allocated for the provision of public utilities, LE200 million (17 percent) for local government units, a further LE200 million for industry, and LE450 million (38 percent) for the private sector. Actual housing expenditures were understated, however, because of the government's practice of monitoring private sector housing based on a construction cost of LE16 to LE20 per square meter. Actual construction costs may often be as much as twice the government figures.

The Ministry of Housing and Reconstruction developed a program for 1976-80 which suggested the building of 741,000 housing units, composed of 295,000 public and 446,000 private housing units. Total expenditure was calculated to be LE1.3 billion, not including Canal Zone housing reconstruction, which works out to an average cost per unit of LE1,695 for public and LE1,838 for private units. But in 1975 public housing cost on average between LE2,500 and LE3,000 per unit, and the Suez master plan indicated a cost of LE2,225 for a four-room house of 65 square meters. The Joint Housing Team of MOHR and U.S. Agency for International Development (USAID) recommended in its 1976 report a mix of private and public-assisted housing, which would result in an average weighted cost of approximately LE2,000 a unit.[3] Production of this standard of housing could have amounted to about 425,000 units if LE850 million were made available as indicated by the Ministry of Planning, or about 600,000 units if there were LE1,320 million as suggested by MOHR. Either level is ambitious and represents a greater annual production than occurred during the 1970-76 period. Meeting even the lower target would require substantial changes in the housing delivery system.

At a cost of LE2,500 per unit and an annual public housing investment of LE30 million (assuming a constant real commitment and no change in real prices), the present program of nearly complete subsidy could produce about 12,000 units a year, or 120,000 units over a ten-year period. If the housing commitment increases at a rate of 6.5 percent a year, 172,000 units could be produced. These levels of production fall far short of the need. Moreover, 80 percent of the urban population could not afford the units unless the cost were subsidized, which makes the program very costly to the government.

Solutions to the Housing Problem

The Egyptian government has come to recognize that its conventional housing policy is inadequate to meet the existing deficit, not to mention the anticipated demand in the immediate future. As a

3. Joint Housing Team of MOHR and USAID, Immediate Action Proposals for Housing in Egypt (Cairo, June 1976).

result, the Ministry of Housing has been studying ways to optimize housing investment and reduce costs through improved design, site planning, lower standards, smaller unit sizes, mobilization of private savings for housing, increased cost recovery, stimulation of the private housing industry, a training program for the construction industry, and assurance of an adequate supply of construction materials. Following these changes, the ministry proposes to introduce a comprehensive package of measures and policy changes.

The starting point for improving the housing program is to reduce the average cost per unit. The most immediate way to do this is to cut the size of the units. The present average of 60-70 square meters is larger than international standards for public housing, and a reduction to around two-thirds of this area would not make for undue crowding. Egyptian residential architecture is characterized by multistory structures tightly clustered around small courtyards and laced together with narrow streets. This high density development, a result of the scarcity of land, is in marked contrast to the five-story apartment buildings laid out in rows that the government now builds. Recent technical opinion has suggested that costs could be reduced by 15 to 20 percent by improving the site planning, altering the present building configuration to create central utility cores, and reducing the standard of finish to leave some of the interior detailing to the prospective owners. Lower costs for infrastructure and an adequate supply of labor and raw materials would also help reduce unit costs.

In Egypt, as in other countries, the housing program has been based on the design of a standard dwelling unit with a fixed number of rooms and room size, specified plumbing fixtures, and so on. These standard units are usually built at the lowest cost possible and made available to low-income families with the government providing high subsidies. Of course the problem is that few governments have the resources to subsidize a sufficient number of units to meet the tremendous demand. A lucky small proportion of low-income families receive such houses while the vast majority continue to expand the squatter areas or increase the density of central city slums.

Several countries have tried to tackle the housing problem by segmenting the population to be served on the basis of income and setting a house price that is affordable without subsidies for each target group. The MOHR and USAID study applied this approach to Egypt, using the data from table 8-7 on income distribution. Those in group A (not shown) earn the highest income — more than LE1,500 a year — and it is generally agreed that they can and should obtain housing through the private sector. Target groups B through E (those with an income between LE150 and LE1,500) can be served with housing by the government on a sliding scale of subsidies. Units for these groups are considered by the Joint Housing Team to be first targets for the cost-reduction program.

TABLE 8-7.   ESTIMATING THE UNIT COST AFFORDABLE
BY INCOME GROUPS WITHOUT SUBSIDY
(Egyptian pounds)

Target group	Annual income		Annual payment	Total loan (30 years at 6.5 percent)	Down payment		Total affordable house
	Amount	Percentage for housing			Percentage of total cost	Amount	
B	1,500	17	255	3,330	17	682	4,012
	1,400		238	3,107		636	3,743
	1,300		221	2,886		591	3,477
	1,200		204	2,664		545	3,209
	1,100		187	2,442		500	2,942
	1,000		170	2,220		455	2,675
C	900	15	135	1,763	15	311	2,074
	800		120	1,567		276	1,843
	700		105	1,371		242	1,613
	600		90	1,175		207	1,382
D	500	13	65	849	10	94	943
	400		52	679		75	754
E	300	7	21	274	10	30	304
	200		14	182		20	202
	150		10.50	137		15	152
F	100	Special Program					

Source: Joint Housing Team of MOHR and USAID, Immediate Action Program for Housing in Egypt.

If present standards for housing units were followed, all households in group B could afford public housing without subsidy, but
those in lower-income groups would require major subsidies from
the government. The preliminary proposals by the Joint Housing
Team are a considerable improvement over existing plans because
they relate the standards of housing to income groups and ability to
pay. The proposals do not go far enough, however, because they
still leave a large subsidy element for many income groups. Consideration should be given to an entirely new housing program that
would focus on the needs of the lower income groups by providing
a "core" house with a lower standard of utilities and a smaller land
area. Core housing programs have been used by many countries
to resolve the dilemma of too heavy a subsidy for standard housing.
There are grounds for believing that the direct provision of housing
in the current program ignores a useful source of private saving
from the poorer members of urban society, that is, those who build
informally, outside the law and without any form of assistance. The
Joint Housing Team offers evidence that self-help schemes would
be successful with the 40 percent of the urban households that cannot afford government-built housing. Such schemes might include

the provision of sites and services — cleared house lots with paved roads, utilities, and the like — and upgrading programs.

Increasing the returns to the government from its housing investment should be another important objective of the housing program. It would not only increase the number of units built but also reduce net consumption. At present, government ownership of housing units increases consumption directly with the net additions to its stock each year because recoveries from government housing do not even cover the cost of maintenance. Those with access to government housing thus sometimes receive more than 100 percent subsidies, which are regressive in their effect. To increase recoveries the government is beginning to sell instead of lease the units it constructs. This reduces losses from rent default and eliminates the problem of maintenance since owners tend to keep buildings in better repair than do tenants.

Conclusions

The critical condition of urban housing in Egypt, especially in Greater Cairo, and the relative underdevelopment of secondary cities have no simple or immediate solution. More efficient utilization of resources can lead to immediate and often substantial increases in the quantity of housing and basic infrastructure. And more specific use of the housing subsidy in government-built housing programs and a more consistent approach to cost recoveries based on affordability would increase the cost effectiveness of the present delivery system. Since housing investment in the past has accounted for about one-third of total investment, both public and private, an improvement in the efficiency of the current delivery system could make a substantial inroad on the housing deficit.

Public saving at present amounts to less than 12 percent of GDP and, while steps are being taken to expand saving, it is needed for many purposes with higher priority. Even if the basic shortage of investment resources were overcome, a variety of administrative and technical constraints would still hinder the urban sector's absorptive capacity. Although there is a wide range of potentially productive projects in utilities and transportation that could be undertaken more or less immediately to alleviate the present critical situation, uncertainty over the timing and availability of investment funds has vitiated serious attempts at planning for this sector in the past.

URBAN SERVICES

In addition to the poor housing conditions, Egypt's urban population suffers from poor urban services, such as public trans-

port (particularly in Cairo), filtered water, sewerage, refuse
collection, health, and education. At the moment, delivery mechanisms for water, sewerage, and urban transport are heavily constrained by economic and institutional inefficiency. There has been
a lack of capital for investment and maintenance over the years and
a failure to ration services through the price mechanism. For instance, actual receipts collected for water are only 10 to 20 percent
of the cost of the water supply. Sewer services are provided free.
Electricity charges are increasingly out of line with costs. Fares
for public transport in Greater Cairo were last set in 1952, and the
revenues of Cairo Transport Authority now cover only one-third of
the operating cost. Until a new approach is taken toward pricing,
and until the institutions are freed from some of the constraints of
labor, management, and investment, there would be little benefit
in committing additional resources to the production of services.

Sewerage

The lack of adequate sanitary sewers is one of the largest — if
not the largest — technical obstacle to new housing development in
most areas of the country, especially in Greater Cairo. The first
sanitary sewer project for the city of Cairo was completed in 1914.
At that time, the system was designed for a projected population of
960,000 persons by the year 1932, and an average discharge of 50
liters per person a day, which would create a maximum discharge
of approximately 48,000 cubic meters a day. By 1932 the actual
discharge was about 91,000 cubic meters a day; in the 1940s it was
about 150,000 and by 1960, 500,000 cubic meters a day. Despite
this increase in discharge the sewerage system was not enlarged.
Instead, to postpone the danger of excess discharge and overflow,
temporary measures were taken, such as the Nile siphon project,
which served the southern and western areas of the city. In addition, new connections were prohibited from time to time, which
kept an increasingly large percentage of the population from access
to sanitary sewers.
    By 1964, when the daily discharge was up to 780,000 cubic me-
ters, some streets and buildings were flooded with raw sewage.
The capacity of several pumping stations and treatment plant reser-
voirs was increased, and a study was prepared to modify the system
to accommodate discharges projected to 1985. The modifications
were limited by the lack of funds, and even after implementation
the danger of overflow remained. By 1974 wastewater was up to
1,250,000 cubic meters a day, reflecting a per capita daily discharge
of 156 liters.
    The Cairo system collects sewage at detention areas or major
interceptors and pumps it to plants for treatment, after which it is
discharged into reclaimed desert land for agricultural purposes.

The system has continued to expand, particularly since 1965, to increase the capacity of pumping stations and of primary and secondary treatment plants. The expansions have not been enough to meet the demands of a rapidly growing area, however, and the system is dangerously overtaxed, while many districts remain without service.

The Cairo region is also serviced by two networks in the Helwan area south of Cairo and the Giza area to the west. The Giza system, established in 1945 to receive a maximum discharge of 5,000 cubic meters a day, was already receiving a discharge of 110,000 cubic meters a day by 1969.

The Helwan system is adequate for the town of Helwan, but the area is growing fast because of industrial development. The inefficiency of the treatment plant causes frequent back-ups at the site, and many semirural settlements around Helwan are not connected to the system. A new system is now being designed for this area.

The Alexandria sewerage system is also overtaxed and in need of expansion, particularly in light of the planned expansion of the industrial areas of the city. The problem is exacerbated by the discharge of untreated industrial sewage into Lake Mariut and the Mediterranean, creating a threat to health as well as to tourism — one of the city's most important industries.

Water Distribution System

The extensive irrigation system developed over the centuries attests both to Egypt's dependence on the Nile as a source of water and to Egyptian ingenuity in maximizing the yield from this important resource. The construction of the Aswan High Dam has substantially increased this yield by regulating the water flow and eliminating floods. The rapid growth of both Cairo and Alexandria, however, has increased the demand for potable water beyond the capacity of the existing system.

The government has been increasing the capacity of filtration plants despite unexpected difficulties with treatment apparently caused by the regulation of the Nile. The government has also been developing groundwater sources to supplement the surface water supplies. In some parts of Cairo and Alexandria a nonpotable water supply system furnishes water for private and public lawns and gardens. In areas not served by the system, however, residents use potable water for gardening purposes, thus placing an additional burden on the potable water system. MOHR has conducted several studies to quantify the problem, make projections to the year 2000, and design new wastewater and water supply systems.

The preliminary results of the 1976 census give an idea of the general availability of filtered water in Egypt. Among the urban population 69.2 percent have access to filtered water either in the dwelling unit or in the communal structure; 12.3 percent do not have a supply close by. Only 5.5 percent of the rural population have filtered water either in the house or in the structure; 58.2 percent have access to a common supply near their house, and 36.3 percent have no supply near the house. The services vary considerably from area to area even in the same governorate. In the Cairo governorate, for example, 77 percent of the units in the el-Gamalia area have an individual water supply, 25 percent have supplies within the structure, and only 8 percent have their water supply outside the structure. By comparison, in the Helwan district only 44 percent of the units have domestic potable water, 36 percent have to use a common supply outside the building, and 5 percent have no supply nearby.

Refuse Collection

The collection and disposal of refuse presents a major problem in Egyptian cities. In each city the governorate or the city council accepts responsibility only for cleaning streets, and refuse collection from houses is left to pig farmers (zabaline) in Cairo and Alexandria and to contractors in other cities. Unfortunately, both the zabaline and the contractors collect refuse only from wealthy neighborhoods where the pickings are good, since the refuse is usually sorted out and recycled. The concept of regular refuse collection from all buildings does not appear to have taken root in Egypt. Most people dispose of their refuse by dumping it on sidewalks, in sewer manholes, and other places where it breeds insects carrying diseases and constitutes a serious health hazard. Again the governorates and city councils lack funds to remedy the situation, and the contractors lack supervision. No global solution for this problem has so far been worked out.

Electricity

In contrast to the short supply of other urban services, electricity generation in Egypt is adequate to meet demands in the short term. The concentration of population in Egypt has considerably eased distribution, but at the same time problems of distribution have limited the growth of consumption. Better organized than other urban utilities, the distribution of electricity will improve with the expansion of the role of national distribution zones and the centralization and rationalization of generation (see chapter 17). Tariffs appear to need immediate restructuring, however, to remove some arbitrary and discriminatory advantages to some classes of users, particularly industry. A sector survey is currently being prepared by consultants for the World Bank, and bilateral assistance on electricity distribution is planned by USAID.

Urban Transport

Transport within cities in Egypt is generally the responsibility of the local governorate under the broad direction of the Ministry of Transport. Cairo has had a long tradition of privately owned transport systems, commencing in modern times with the tramways installed as part of the Belgian development of Heliopolis. All forms of transportation except taxis are now under public authorities following nationalization in the early 1960s. The Cairo Transport Authority currently operates a fleet of some 1,700 vehicles comprising 1,300 buses, 220 trams, and 110 trolley buses. At least 25 percent of the fleet is out of service, however, because of age, overloading, inadequate maintenance, and lack of spare parts. The authority operates twelve garages and four regional workshops and employs some 25,000 workers — 10,000 drivers and conductors; 8,000 mechanics, electricians, and engineers; and the remainder in management, administration, stores, and employees for the authority's staff hospital. The cost of operating the authority was about LE35.0 million in 1976. Fares, last set in 1953, yielded about LE15.0 million in revenue, and the resulting deficit of LE20.0 million was financed by central government. The deficit, which was nonexistent in 1964, has mounted because the authority is prevented from increasing fares, and the terms and conditions (and in some cases the number) of its employees are exogenously determined.

The authority's investment budget is funded through the ministry, and major items are voted in the People's Assembly. It has been depressed by the growing operating deficit and the increasing world prices for imported inputs. For example, prices of vehicle parts in 1975 in many cases exceeded 1973 prices by 100 percent. The Cairo Transport Authority serves approximately 3.5 million passengers daily. According to the 1966 sample census, 37 percent of the labor force work outside Greater Cairo, but even within that area many districts are so large that some people need public transport to cross them. The estimated demand is based on fare collection, but many fares are not collected because passengers ride on the roof of the bus or avoid payment in the crowd inside. On some routes vehicles have two conductors to reduce the loss of potential revenue.

Public transport is complemented by an estimated 18,000 taxis. The number appears to have grown by 300 percent in the last fifteen years because of rising incomes and the progressive deterioration of the public transport system. More and more of the capital's vast pool of office workers prefer to share a taxi with other people and avoid two separate crowded bus trips.

The number of private cars registered in Cairo has increased rapidly from 33,000 in 1962 to 104,000 in 1973, and is mounting at an annual rate of 15,000 to 20,000. When the vehicles registered in the adjoining governorates of Giza and Kalyubia are added, the streets of Greater Cairo are used by nearly a quarter of a million motor vehicles daily. To this number must be added 80,000 animal-drawn vehicles and a similar number of bicycles, hand carts, and movable vendors' stalls.

The condition and width of Cairo's roads reflect their age. In the old quarters and the business district near the center, roads are narrow and irregular; the modern areas on the outskirts are served with broad avenues. The use of sidewalks for parking, the influx of slow-moving animal- and human-powered vehicles, and pedestrians on the carriageways all contribute to habitual congestion. The greatest single improvement to the public transport system would be stricter enforcement of traffic regulations and simple traffic management as recommended by the Cairo Transportation Study of 1973. The first stage of recommendations, which would cost only a few thousand Egyptian pounds, has only recently been introduced because of conflicting and overlapping jurisdictions for traffic control. Synchronized traffic lights at sixty city intersections, operated by twelve television monitors, have also been recommended but are delayed by lack of funding.

An answer to Cairo's public transport system has been sought for twenty years. The possibility of an underground system was first explored in 1954, and the cost was estimated at LE1.0 million per kilometer. As the transportation crisis has worsened, cost estimates have grown proportionately. In 1968 the cost of twenty kilometers running along the north-south axis of the city was estimated to be LE3.5 million per kilometer. The eight kilometers of track proposed to join the southern railway system with the northern metro, thus by-passing the highly congested central area, would cost LE8 million per kilometer.

Health

Hospitals, clinics, and other health facilities and personnel are adequate for the population demand. At present there are one doctor and two nurses for every 5,000 to 8,000 people, which is high in comparison with other developing countries. Nevertheless, neither health nor family planning services are reaching the majority of the population, particularly the poor. This, however, is because of poor management rather than population pressure as is the case with other social services, such as education (for details of the quality of education, see chapter 7). Although health facilities are available, doctors and nurses are not usually there to provide the needed service. Attempts are being made by the authorities, particularly in Cairo, to improve management and supervision and to provide incentives for the doctors and other personnel.

Initiatives in Urban Services

The poor quality of urban services (public transport, water, sewerage, refuse collection, health, and schooling) is caused by almost the same factors responsible for poor housing conditions: the shortage of funds, weak local administration, overlapping administrative responsibilities, and the virtual absence of urban planning. The government recognizes the dimension and severity of the growing urban problems and is developing a set of policies within the overall framework of its new economic development strategy and liberalization process. Many of these urban policy initiatives are still at an exploratory stage and fragmented, and a coherent analysis of these initiatives, their interrelationships, and their potential impact remains to be done. It is nevertheless apparent that major improvements can be achieved only over the long term because of such severe constraints as the political difficulty of an immediate move to eliminate built-in subsidies for urban services; institutional weaknesses in the sector, including a serious and growing shortage of qualified administrators and technicians; and the high cost of rehabilitating and expanding neglected infrastructure.

Spatially, the government intends to redirect growth away from Greater Cairo to other areas with nonagricultural land. In November 1973 the minister for housing and reconstruction appointed a four-man Advisory Committee for Reconstruction (ACR) to develop and guide the political commitment for reconstructing the cities and major settlements damaged during the conflicts of 1967 and 1973. In 1975 the responsibility of the ACR was broadened to include large-scale rehabilitation of Cairo's urban services and housing, further strained by a stream of evacuees from the Canal Zone. Projections that the present Egyptian population would double to around 70 million by the year 2000 and become increasingly urban raised questions about traditional patterns of land settlement that threatened to conflict with the use of the land for agricultural purposes. The task of the ACR was accordingly broadened to develop a strategy to accommodate the country's growing urban population. The strategy put forward by the ACR is threefold: the reconstruction of the Canal Zone cities of Port Said, Suez, and Ismailia; the establishment of new cities in the desert; and the rehabilitation of Cairo and Alexandria.

As a first step, detailed master plans for the Canal Zone cities, together with their potential agricultural hinterlands, were presented to the government in March 1976. These studies, and a comprehensive regional plan for the Suez Canal Zone completed in June 1976, were supported by the United Nations Development Programme (UNDP). The terms of reference for the studies called for planning urban facilities to accommodate target populations by the end of the century of between 750,000 and 1 million in the cases of Suez and Port Said and 1.5 million in Ismailia and the surrounding agricultural settlements in the Canal Zone. Already much of the reconstruction work has been carried out, and these cities have regained their pre-1967 size.

The continuous growth of Cairo and the conflict of land use for urban and agricultural purposes led ACR to explore the idea of establishing new cities in desert areas, although it was recognized that they would not necessarily solve the growing problems of congestion and pollution in central Cairo itself. The establishment of three self-sufficient, economically viable cities has been contemplated: Ramadan Ten City, sixty kilometers from Cairo on the road to Ismailia, to accommodate a population of 500,000; Sadat City, eighty kilometers away on the Cairo-Alexandria Desert Road, for an initial population of 500,000; and King Khalid City, on the Cairo-Fayoum Desert Road, to accommodate a population of 500,000. Initial studies have identified a number of formidable obstacles to this policy option: the socioeconomic feasibility of the public investment programs to create the necessary basic infrastructure; the economic and commercial feasibility of the cities as a base for industrial establishments; the capacity of the construction sector to build a completely new city in the time envisaged; and the organizational capacity of public utilities to provide services to the desert sites, which now are some fifteen kilometers from a permanent water source and not yet served by transport facilities.

The most serious problems relate to the expected cost of building a new desert city. Some very preliminary estimates suggest that an average discounted cost of LE40.0 million a year would be required over the life of the project. Furthermore, a very long payoff period is expected because accumulated front-end costs will be very heavy before benefits begin to accrue. A comparison of the incremental costs of providing urban infrastructure, housing, and services suggests that in the Egyptian context these are minimized for existing cities of at least 250,000 inhabitants. Given the current acute constraints on financial and managerial resources, the magnitude of the task, the uncertainty of popular acceptance of the strategy, and the existence of more cost-effective solutions to deal with growing urban populations, it seems unlikely that the government can afford to concentrate exclusively on the option of desert cities.

A number of master planning and project preparation studies are under way for water supply, sewerage, and electricity, with financing already committed for several projects. For instance, a World Bank loan for a US$122 million water supply project in Alexandria was approved in early 1977. In mid-1977 the Bank also approved a loan for a US$70.6 million regional electrification project serving thirteen cities and nineteen rural zones. USAID in late 1977 approved financing for a sewerage project in Alexandria and a water supply project in Cairo, and studies of institutional and financial issues in these sectors have been initiated. In this regard, the International Development Association (IDA) is providing assistance through a technical assistance credit for a water supply project approved in December 1977, and USAID is helping finance a management and tariff study of water supply and sewerage in the six largest cities.

Implementation of these new policies will be facilitated by steps taken by the government in 1975 to devolve powers and responsibilities from the central government to the governorates. In 1977 eight economic regions and regional planning councils were established, the main purpose of which is to help set priorities for allocation of central and local government resources and to develop social and economic development policies at the regional level. In January 1978, as part of the devolution process, the governorates took full control over all local technical and administrative staff, including those appointed by the ministries.

FUTURE URBAN GROWTH

Although Egypt is already a highly urbanized country, the degree of urbanism varies widely. Indeed some so-called urban areas are more like overgrown villages, with little of the infrastructure or economic activity usually associated with cities. The direction of future urban growth is of the greatest importance for Egypt's economic development. Greater Cairo and the twenty next largest Egyptian cities have geen growing at rates between 3 and 4.5 percent a year, averaging a little less than 4 percent. By 1980 the population of Cairo and the twenty other cities was expected to grow by 2.8 million, and by a further 3.1 million between 1980 and 1985. On the basis of past trends, well over half of this will be located in Greater Cairo, which may have to accommodate 3.8 million more inhabitants by 1985 and Alexandria a further 1.3 million.[4]

The importance of the growth of Greater Cairo and Egypt's urban areas in general can be appreciated from the following illustration. A reduction of Cairo's population growth rate from 4 to 3 percent a year would reduce the absolute number to be housed by 1985 by nearly 0.9 million. If these 0.9 million people were redirected to Egypt's ten major provincial cities (excluding Alexandria), the additional population would effectively double their expected rates of

---

4. Estimates of the present population of these cities have been made by extrapolating past trends. The projections are merely indicative of the order of magnitude involved. The actual outcome will depend to a considerable degree on emigration trends from Egypt.

growth, from 3.5 to around 7.0 percent a year, which is an extremely high rate of urban agglomeration.   If Alexandria were included, the rate of growth for all eleven cities (excluding Greater Cairo) would average 5.5 percent a year, still a high rate over such a period.

PART THREE
Productive Sectors

9
Agriculture: Structure and Performance

Despite a twenty-five-year development strategy that heavily favors industry, agriculture remains the largest sector in the Egyptian economy. It employs 44 percent of the work force, provides 29 percent of GDP, and about 30 percent of exports. In addition, the vital textile industry as well as most of the service sector — transport, commerce, finance, and government — are directly connected to agriculture. Because of the close linkages between farm and nonfarm sectors, changes in aggregate agricultural output or its composition are generally reflected quickly throughout the entire economy. In 1952, following the revolution, farming contributed about 28 percent of GDP. In 1975 the figure was still of the same magnitude at 30 percent. The major structural change was the increase in the share of GDP by the nonfarm commodity sectors at the expense of distribution and services.

Egypt has a total surface area of 238 million feddans.[1] Farming is limited to about 6.5 million feddans along the Nile River and its Delta; the other 232 million feddans are mostly unproductive desert. Almost all the cropland is irrigated because the country is virtually rainless. The major crops are cotton, rice, and maize in the summer, and berseem (Egyptian clover), wheat, and beans in the winter. Vegetables are increasing in importance with three crop seasons a year.

It is not surprising that Egypt is still so dependent on the farm sector. The soils are mostly riparian silts and clays of great depth, fertility, and uniformity. The topography is such that erosion is not a problem and land is well suited to irrigation. Abundant water of good quality flows down the Nile and is distributed to farms through a well-developed storage and distribution system. Egypt is spared the vagaries of rainfall, it enjoys maximum sunlight and growth rates, and the warm subtropical temperatures permit year-round plant growth. Such a mixture allows cropping intensities of 190 percent, with higher yields than many other countries, in a complex

---

1. A feddan equals 1.038 acres or 0.42 hectares.

rotation of crops developed over many generations. These resources (soil, water, and climate) and the system of dual-purpose cropping are ideally suited to interproduct substitution.

Within the agricultural sector, production is characterized by technological dualism. About 85 percent of the farmers, using bullock and human labor, work their three feddans or less for both the market and their own consumption. The other 15 percent use varying amounts of machine technology to produce single-purpose crops specifically for off-farm sale. Except for some scattered Bedouin sheep flocks, there is no rangeland grazing, and animal production is part of a complex multipurpose farm system. Although the gross value of animal production is only one-third that of crop production, most farm operations depend on animal draft power. Farmland must therefore be allocated to both fodder and food crops, and the choice among crops is influenced by whether they permit the joint production of by-products suitable for animal feed, such as straw. The allocation process is further complicated by the traditional two- or three-year rotational cycle and the crop quotas imposed by the government. Purchased inputs such as inorganic fertilizer, certified seed, improved varieties — especially for cotton — and pesticides are common, but machinery is usually limited to community-operated threshers, sprayers, and plows.

Over 90 percent of the land titles are for lots of less than five feddans. Leasing is common on about 40 percent of the farms so that the average farmed unit is 3.5 feddans. The distribution of ownership is still skewed. Since 1952 the government has tried to overcome the problems of smallness and poverty by a series of land reforms, cooperative management of pooled farms, public sector investment, and a program to maintain farmers' incomes through price intervention.

Direct government intervention began with land reform after the revolution in 1952. At that time 4,000 landlords owned the same amount of land as 2.6 million peasants, while another 1.2 million laborers were landless. A series of reforms eventually limited ownership to 50 feddans a person, and land was distributed to those owning little or none. Changes in land rents, tenancy conditions, and farm wages affected a great many people. Although the average holding rose from 0.8 to 1.2 feddans after the reform, the combination of a fixed land area and a rising population, inheritance laws, and lack of opportunities elsewhere aggravated the problems of smallness, fragmentation, and rural poverty.

Cooperative membership was made compulsory so that land could be farmed in large contiguous areas, with machinery and extension services offered to groups of farmers. Cooperatives and the associated credit banks displaced the private entrepreneur in supplying inputs and credit and became the major marketing channel for the most important crops. The intent was to direct the decisions of the many small independent farmers by allocating production quotas that were tied to the supply of inputs. The resulting pattern of agriculture was to be consistent with the government's production targets for food and exports without reference to prices.

Public sector investment in agriculture has been considerable, with such notable projects as the Aswan High Dam and the partial reclamation of almost a million feddans of fringe land for irrigation development. Construction of the High Dam, together with completion of a system of dams and barrages along the Nile, allowed perennial irrigation through a vast network of canals and considerably intensified farming in the "old land." Unfortunately, the plentiful supply of water and the absence of any user charge led farmers to overirrigate, causing a serious drainage problem. Measures to correct the unusually high water tables and salt damage are hampered by inadequate budgetary allocations.

Investment in extending irrigation and service infrastructure into marginal soils on the desert fringes had by mid-1976 added 0.9 million feddans of "new land" to the existing 5.6 million feddans of old land. The new lands should make a positive contribution to sectoral development after technical and economic problems have been solved. So far, however, the program has done little to solve the problems of the small farmer or to add to food production and foreign exchange earnings. Huge cost overruns, long gestation periods, poor physical performance, and management problems have made the program a burden to the sector and added to the difficulty of maintaining productivity in the Delta and the Nile Valley.

In the mid-1950s agriculture's share of the total investment budget was 9 percent. This rose to over 25 percent by the mid-1960s during construction of the High Dam but then dropped to 7 percent by 1975. Concomitant with the rise in public investment, the private sector's share of gross fixed investment in agriculture fell to 4 percent.[2] Large investments in capital-intensive industry over the last two decades generated only 20 percent of the total increase in employment, so that most of the increase in the work force went into agriculture and the bureaucracy.

The pattern of employment generation has changed little, and the economy still depends on farm work to support about 50 percent of the population as owners, tenants, and laborers. With the labor force in agriculture growing faster than output, labor productivity has fallen. Wages in agriculture have remained about one-third the average wage in all sectors, with growth of 5 percent a year in money terms, lagging behind the 8 percent a year average growth for all sectors.

2. It is not clear what items are included in private investment, particularly whether on-farm investment by smallholders in plant and animals is considered, and what allowances are made for depreciation of capital stock. Subsequent sections contain more detailed analysis.

The net budgetary burden of the consumer subsidy program rose from LE11 million in 1972 to LE491 million in 1975 under pressure from two major forces. On the one hand, population grew faster than production, and consumption patterns shifted toward subsidized items, largely because of increasing urbanization and the fact that subsidies went mostly to urban residents. On the other hand, the structure of farm production moved in a different direction from changes in consumption patterns, necessitating large increases in food imports at a time when international prices were at record high levels. Egypt's capacity to pay for these imports declined as farmers planted record low levels of cotton, the economy's major export earner. Although the initial aims of the system of production quotas and price controls in agriculture were to equalize farm incomes and provide basic food at low, stable prices, the existence of parallel markets began to pull resources away from regulated crops as their relative profitability fell.

Since the 1952 revolution the population has almost doubled. In spite of increases in irrigated land area, improved cropping intensity, and gains from research, the pressure of population on a relatively fixed area of land already intensively farmed has resulted in declining per capita performance. Total sectoral production has increased at less than 2 percent a year compared with a population growth rate of 2.3 percent a year. Egypt no longer exports wheat but instead imports twice as much as is produced domestically; the quantities of cotton and rice available for export have declined. The contribution of agriculture to the general growth of the economy has varied, but it has generally been below the average growth rate for the economy as a whole, exerting a strong downward pressure.

GROWTH

Aggregate agricultural output in real terms has risen slowly and unevenly since the 1950s.[3] The estimates in table 9-1 are from el-Tobgy's excellent study, based on Ministry of Agriculture data for growth measured in terms of value added at constant prices. From 1952 to 1971 the overall growth rate was 2.2 percent a year; from 1971 to 1974 estimates of total production by both the U.S. Department of Agriculture and the Food and Agriculture Organization (FAO), using Ministry of Agriculture data, show an annual growth rate of 1.7 percent and a negligible increase or a decline in per capita food production because increases in productivity and area lagged behind population increases. The National Bank of Egypt also calculated

3. All growth rates in this chapter are derived by computing the first three values in a series and averaging them. This figure is V_0. The average of the last three values is V_1. These are substituted in the compound growth rate formula, $i = (V_i/V_0)^{1/n} - 1$, where n = number of years -2.

TABLE 9-1.   VALUE ADDED IN AGRICUL-
TURAL PRODUCTION, AT CURRENT AND
CONSTANT 1952 PRICES
(millions of Egyptian pounds)

| Period | Value added | | Index (constant 1952 prices) |
	Current prices	Constant 1952 prices	
1952	252	252	100
1952-54	279	254	101
1955-59	364	275	109
1960-64	459	311	123
1965-69	675	349	138
1970-72	839	393	156
Growth rate (percent)	6.1	2.2	2.2

Source: H. A. el-Tobgy, Contemporary Egyptian
Agriculture (Beirut: Ford Foundation, 1974), p. 210,
based on Ministry of Agriculture data.

1.7 percent as the average annual growth rate of value added in the
sector for the second half of the 1960s. [4] Hansen and Marzouk give
a growth rate of 1.5 percent for the sector for the first three years
of the 1960-65 plan. [5] The Ministry of Planning in its Follow-up Report estimates a real rate of growth in 1975 over 1974 of about 1.7
percent (instead of the planned 3.5 percent). [6] Because of the importance of agriculture, the average commodity growth rate for the
whole economy in that year was dragged down to 8.1 percent instead
of the planned 12.8 percent.   Despite the difficulties of precise estimation, this general picture of a slow growth of production in relation to the needs of a rapidly increasing population is verified by
escalating food imports and declining exports.
    Disaggregation of the data shows interesting differences in the
behavior of individual crops.   Although the aggregate value at constant 1950 prices of wheat, maize, rice, and cotton grew at around
1.2 percent a year for the twenty-five years between 1950 and 1975,
this was biased downward because of the heavy weighting of cotton
and the absence of values for berseem.   Wheat grew at 2.3 percent
a year, maize 2.6 percent, rice 4.5 percent, and cotton fell 0.1
percent.   Because cotton values accounted for between 20 and 25
percent of the value of field crop production, the overall average

4. National Bank of Egypt, Economic Bulletin (1972), no. 1, p. 57.
    5. Bent Hansen and Girgis A. Marzouk, Development and Economic Policy in
the UAR, Egypt (Amsterdam: North-Holland, 1965), p. 296.
    6. Ministry of Planning, Follow-up Report for the 1975 Plan (Cairo, 1976).

fell. The addition of long-season berseem values to the series would push the average up again to at least 2.5 percent, because it is now about as important as cotton. The food grains as a group grew at 2.9 percent, long-season berseem at 2 to 3 percent, and vegetables at 3.3 percent a year. Because of the absence of detailed production data for berseem, a reasonable guess would put the average rate of growth at about 2.5 to 2.7 percent a year.

Table 9-2 indicates changes in growth rates by crops in production, yield, and area. Wheat output from 1965 to 1975 has shown strong growth at 3.4 percent a year since the poor performance of the mid-1960s, despite decreases in areas planted. Maize has not displayed a strong growth trend but was affected most by the one-shot change in growing season made possible by the new dam, which increased yields considerably. Rice benefited more from an increase in area planted than from yield increases, which were not sustained after the 3.6 percent increase of the 1950s. Cotton output has been affected most by the decline in area under cultivation, and the yield improvements of the early 1960s have not been maintained.

TABLE 9-2. ANNUAL GROWTH
IN PRODUCTION OF SELECTED
CROPS, 1950-75
(percent)

Crop	1950-60	1960-70	1965-75	1950-75
Wheat				
Production	2.7	0.3	3.4	2.3
Yield	2.7	1.3	3.6	2.6
Area	0.1	-1.0	0.8	-0.2
Maize				
Production	1.2	3.9	2.3	2.6
Yield	0.3	5.5	1.0	2.3
Area	0.9	-1.6	1.2	0.3
Rice				
Production	5.7	6.3	2.6	4.5
Yield	3.6	0.5	0.8	1.7
Area	2.3	5.8	1.7	2.9
Cotton				
Production	0.4	0.8	-1.6	-0.1
Yield	0.4	3.1	0.4	1.1
Area	-0.5	-1.6	-2.2	-1.2

Source: Computed from Ministry of Agriculture data.

STRUCTURAL CHANGE

Despite government-imposed limitations, the structure of output continued to change from 1952 to 1978, moving away from cotton and cereals toward meat, fruit, and vegetables. Substitution of products with a high income elasticity of demand for those with a low income elasticity of demand is normally a sign of economic development, but when this shift occurs without a significant change in aggregate production, it indicates that effective demand has been modified by a change in income distribution. In Egypt's case, resources are being bid away from items of high mass consumption, with the government filling the gap through its import subsidy program of food grains. The changes in relative plantings are illustrated in figure 9-1.

Area under cultivation is chosen as the numeraire because sowings rather than yield better reflect production decisions of farmers. The cotton area index has declined and production has fallen to the level of the 1950s, despite increases in farm-gate prices. The maize area index has returned to its former level with yields and production increasing slowly. Rice plantings and production have peaked, being limited by the distribution of water. Recent rises in producer prices have begun to increase wheat supplies. The production of fruit, vegetables, and berseem has continued to dominate the growth in output. A closer look at cotton indicates that the decline is not a cyclical downswing, but a change in the long-run trend, particularly over the last ten years. As cotton has become less profitable for farmers, they have increased plantings of more profitable crops, particularly those not subject to marketing controls.[7]

PRODUCTION, CROPPING PATTERN, AND ROTATIONS

In 1974 field crops accounted for 56 percent of the value of agricultural output; vegetables, 14 percent; fruits, 5 percent; meat, 11 percent; dairy products, 8 percent; poultry, meat, and eggs, 4 percent; and wool and honey, less than 1 percent. Among field crops, berseem is the most important in area and value. A part of the berseem crop is complementary to cotton, that is, it is grown in a different season on the same land. The so-called long-season berseem, however, directly competes with cotton since it is grown at the same time. While the long-season variety accounted for less than half as many feddans as were planted in cotton before the revolution, it now occupies about 300,000 more feddans than cotton. (In 1975 cotton was planted in 1,346 million feddans, long-season berseem in 1,688 million feddans, with total berseem plantings of about 2.8 million

---

7. An analysis of farmers' response to relative profitabilities is summarized in Appendix A to this chapter.

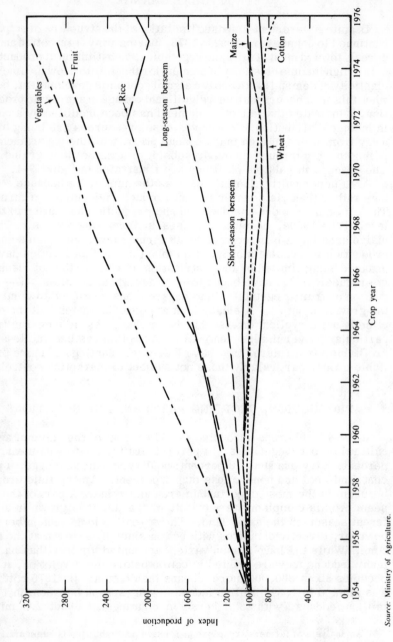

Figure 9–1. Index of Area for Major Crops, 1954-76

Source: Ministry of Agriculture.

176

feddáns.) Statistical Appendix table 14 shows the distribution of crops by season for the 1950-78 period.

Wheat and berseem, which provide food for the farmer and his animals, are the leading winter crops. In the summer, cotton and rice are the most important cash crops, and maize and sorghum are the major subsistence crops. Although summer crops are more important, such crops as berseem and wheat overlap seasons. During the past two decades there has been a shift toward horticulture, away from field crops, and a relative decline in the production of plants compared with animals. There has also been a shift toward the production of higher value items, as determined by relative prices.

Egypt's cropping pattern is determined more by what the farmer needs, his degree of commercialization, and government quotas than by the limitations of soil or climate. Cotton became a major crop in the system when fertility was not generally maintained by purchased inputs. Because of cotton's heavy demands on the soil, monoculture was inappropriate, and cotton was usually planted in rotation with a mixture of multipurpose crops in two- or three-year cycles. In a basic three-year system cotton is balanced by a legume (generally berseem and beans) in the first year; berseem in winter followed by maize or rice in summer in the second; with wheat followed by maize or rice the most common choice for the third year. In the hotter areas sorghum or millet may be substituted for maize, and barley has proved more successful than wheat when grown under the scanty rainfall of the Mediterranean coast or the poor soils beyond the reach of the irrigation network. Where the network supplies sufficient water, rice displaces maize because of its higher profitability. Vegetables usually fill small patches between crops but are rapidly becoming main crops where there is access to a market.

It is usual to divide a farm into as many portions as there are crops in sequence. The cropping calendar shows the major interactions — for example, winter wheat (seven months) cannot be grown in sequence with summer cotton (seven months). Only short-season summer crops, such as rice and vegetables, fit the rotation. In 1975 areas planted in cotton fell to 24 percent of all summer plantings, maize remained unaffected at 41 percent, rice rose to 19 percent from 13 percent, and vegetables rose to 16 percent. As would be expected from such relative shifts, exports of cotton decreased, consumption and exports of rice and vegetables increased, imports of wheat increased, and production and consumption of meat increased.

Irrigation water is distributed to farms in a rotation system that both influences, and is influenced by, cropping patterns. Canals are left dry during January for clearing by farmers. During the rest of the year water is turned on for seven days and then off for seven days.

In rice areas a four-day cycle is followed. No water is officially allowed for berseem after May in order to break the life cycle of cotton pests that live in berseem during the winter.

Crops

   Coarse grains: Maize, sorghum, millet. Staple food grains of the farm family lead all other cereals in area and production. Three-quarters of the annual production of 2.5 million tons[8] of maize is grown in the Delta; production tapers off toward the south and becomes negligible near Aswan, where it is replaced by more heat-tolerant sorghums and millets. About 0.8 million tons of sorghum and millet (mostly sorghum) are grown annually, equal to about one-third of the maize production. In the northern part of the Delta where the soil is heavier and less well drained, maize is replaced by rice. Sorghum and maize are competitive crops in the transitional zone in the south as are rice and maize in the north.

As shown in figure 9-2, larger yields rather than increases in area have been responsible for the higher production of maize. The lower curves in the figure show the percentage of the total maize area grown in the traditional flood season (Nili) and the percentage grown in the summer. Yields in the summer season are about 70 percent higher than in the Nili season, but water availability formerly limited summer plantings to less than 5 percent of the total maize area. The figure shows the dramatic technological change that took place in the 1964-65 season when water became available in the summer from the Aswan High Dam. Summer plantings quickly rose on average from 16 to 72 percent of total acreage, with a consequent decline in the Nili season crop. Average maize yields are now very good, but there is strong evidence that the factors of production are used below capacity and that the domestic food-grain gap can be met without either imports or increased plantings at the expense of other crops. The Ford Foundation reports that although high-yielding maize hybrid seed is available to farmers, less than one-third of the maize area is planted with it. The prevailing farm system requires a dual purpose, lower-yielding type to provide food grain for on-farm breadmaking and summer fodder for the farmer's animals. Furthermore, hybrid maize seems more susceptible to certain diseases than local varieties. For the small farmer operating close to the margin, with perhaps some bad experience with the government-controlled marketing system and only intermittent exposure to a weak extension service, the primary concern is with survival and self-sufficiency in the traditional manner.

Another major restriction on maize yields is drainage; see table 9-3, which shows the three-year average of yields before and

8. All references to tons in this book are to metric tons.

Figure 9-2. Indexes of Maize: Area, Yield, and Production and Percentage of Total Maize Area Devoted to Summer and Nili Maize, 1954-76

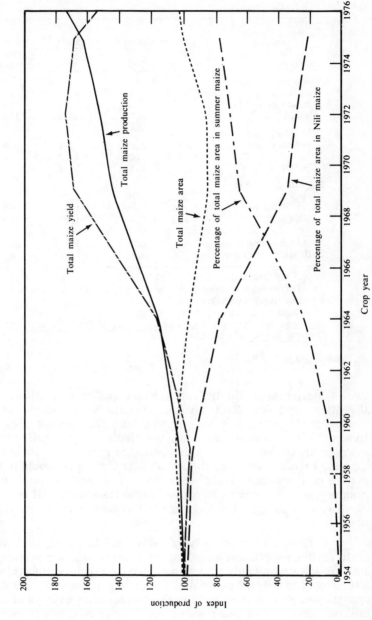

Source: Ministry of Agriculture.

179

TABLE 9-3.   EFFECT OF DRAINAGE ON MAIZE YIELDS

Locality	Area (feddans)	Yield[a] (tons[b] per feddan) Before	After	Increase in yield (percent)
Minya governorate				
Maghagha	700	1.40	1.54	10
Mayana el-Wakf	2,005	0.98	1.12	14
Malatin	2,300	0.56	1.12	100
Beni Suef governorate				
El-Wasta	13,000	0.890	1.12	26
Nasir	19,500	1.000	1.33	33
Ehnasia	14,500	0.812	1.02	26
Fayoum governorate				
Toutoon	n.a.	1.07	1.53	43
Kasr el-Basel	n.a.	0.99	1.19	20
El-Hamidia	n.a.	0.99	1.28	30
Weighted average yield		0.90	1.18	n.a.
National average yield		n.a.	1.50	n.a.

n.a. Not available.
a. Three-year average before and after installation of drainage system, which was begun in 1970.
b. Tons in all tables are metric.
Source: Ministry of Irrigation, Upper Egypt Drainage Project, General Report (Cairo, 1971).

after installation of tile drainage, which was begun in 1970. For the Minya and Beni Suef governorates the weighted average increase is 31 percent, which agrees with the Fayoum figures. Even with the drainage installed, the yields are generally below the average for the country. On the available evidence, with wide margins for estimate errors, it seems clear that Egypt could produce enough maize without using more land. It is just as clear that no simple solution, such as improved varieties alone, will be sufficient without an associated change in the farm system and market conditions.

Rice. Rice is an extremely valuable crop to Egypt, both as a food grain for the people and as an export earner. Among primary products rice is second only to cotton in export earnings, but these usually amount to only 12 percent of cotton export income; in 1975 rice exports were LE24 million compared with cotton exports of LE201 million. Because of heavy water requirements, about 96 percent of the rice is produced in the northern part of the Delta where irrigation canals guarantee four days wet to four days dry.

During the 1950-76 period the area planted in rice doubled, yields rose by almost half, and production almost tripled (see figure 9-3). The three major factors influencing production were the provision of water from the Aswan High Dam, government imposition of area requirements, and the introduction and acceptance of a new high-yielding variety of rice. Before water became available from the High Dam, the rice area was contingent upon the Nile flow during summer and therefore generally fluctuated below 700,000 feddans. After 1965 the area expanded to over a million feddans and stayed at that level. Government quotas at this time required a substitution of rice for maize in the northern Delta where the soil was better suited for rice because drainage was impaired. Furthermore, since rice was produced for export, it had different fiscal implications from those of maize, which was produced for domestic consumption. The development of the Nahda variety of rice further increased production. During the five years from 1955 to 1959 when its use spread to 85 percent of plantings, rice yields rose 33 percent.

In addition to its importance as a domestic food grain and as an export earner, rice is valuable as a reclamation crop in the new lands during the salt-leaching phase of development. The overall average yield of 2.3 tons per feddan is quite high in light of the salinity of some areas. Future increases in output should come from a decline in salinity, from the development of salt-tolerant rice and of varieties resistant to blast disease and skin borers, and from an increase in planted area.

In the long run, rice production can be increased substantially by double cropping and by extending areas under cultivation into Upper Egypt. Double cropping would be a major departure from traditional rotation practices and would require considerable research into suitable varieties. In the northern Delta where there is a high water table, technical factors favor rice over other grains and cotton. Cool season varieties of rice exist for double cropping, notably in Japan, and could be adapted for Egypt. In other parts of the world, rice is continually double cropped without deleterious effects, although it does put greater strain on technical services. Expanding the production of rice would curtail production of other crops, and it would be necessary to improve the canal networks. Substitution of winter rice for some winter wheat would lead to a net increase in food grain without a loss of cotton production.

Cotton. Egypt is a minor cotton producer, growing only about 4 percent of world production, but it is a major cotton exporter, second only to the United States. Production is concentrated in the long-staple varieties. Egypt contributes about 40 percent of the world trade in long-staple cotton, and its share of extralong-staple is about 60 percent. Its influence in the long-staple market is strengthened because the other major producer, Sudan, follows

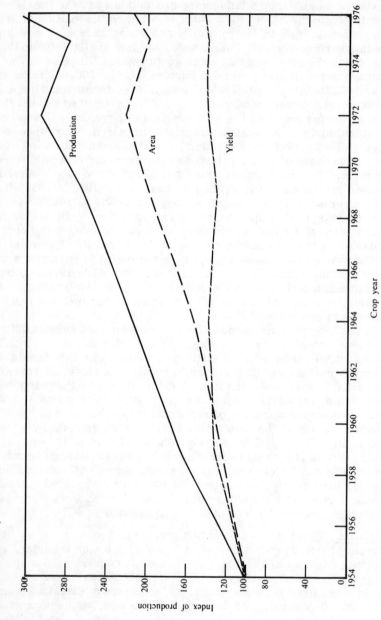

Figure 9-3. Indexes of Rice (Paddy): Area, Yield, and Production, 1954-76

Production

Area

Yield

Index of production

Crop year

1954 1956 1958 1960 1962 1964 1966 1968 1970 1972 1974 1976

0 40 80 100 120 160 200 240 280 300

Source: Ministry of Agriculture.

Egypt's lead. For the country as a whole cotton has been the nexus around which economic activity has revolved for over a hundred years. Gross national product, economic development, consumption, foreign relations, and village activities have been, and still are, reflections of the cotton harvest. For the farmer, cotton has been the major source of cash. The basic rotation and allocation of farm inputs always began with the cotton-production decision. In recent years, however, this influence has been weakening steadily. From a high of nearly 2 million feddans in cotton during the late 1950s to mid-1960s, planting dropped to an estimated 1.24 million feddans in 1976, the lowest since World War II disrupted international cotton trading. Production fell from 1.5 million tons of seed cotton in 1965 to 1.06 million tons in 1975. Farmers are wary of government controls and declining profitability and are turning to more rewarding crops within the limitations of the compulsory delivery system. Cotton producers receive less than 60 percent of the value of their crop (adjusted for transport and processing). Yet even in 1975 cotton and cotton products still accounted for about 53 percent of total commodity exports.

Trends in cotton planting from 1910 to 1976 are shown in figure 9-4. Over the entire period there has been about 1.7 million feddans planted in cotton, with 82 percent of the observations lying within the range 1.5-1.9 million. With the obvious effects of World War II removed, 95 percent of the observations lie within this range. This is to be expected since in a three-year rotation cotton appears once in six seasons, and 1.7 million feddans is approximately one-sixth (16 percent) of the total cropped area. Until the nationalization of the textile industry in 1961, the only significant departures from the trend of plantings were downward. Since 1965 a new long-term direction is indicated, rather than a cyclical or shock movement, because of the decline in the relative profitability of cotton at the farm level. The short-term cyclical fluctuations around the trend line probably represent a lagged response to previous prices and stocks with some seasonal effect.

The indicators for area, yield, and production of cotton for 1954-76 are shown in figure 9-5. During this period the gross cropped area expanded through changes in intensity of land use and extension of farmed areas, resulting in an even more serious decline in cotton plantings as a proportion of the total than shown by the simple time series. Although government control over land allocations was expanded considerably, the response of farmers to declining profitability was so immediate that the government's quota decisions amounted to little more than recognition of what farmers had already done. Counteracting the decline in area planted was a strong increase in yield owing to an excellent breeding program. As with other crops, cotton land is producing below capacity. With installation of drainage since 1970, production was increased as much as

Figure 9–4. Changes in Cotton Area, 1910-76

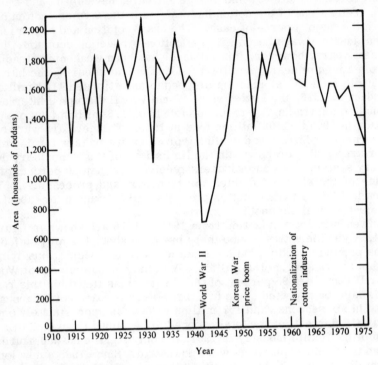

Source: Ministry of Agriculture.

Figure 9–5. Indexes of Cotton: Area, Yield, and Production, 1954-76

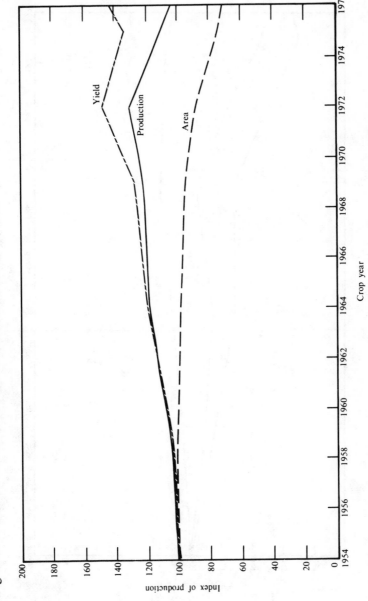

Index of production

Crop year

Yield

Production

Area

Source: Ministry of Agriculture.

Figure 9–6. Indexes of Wheat: Area, Yield, and Production, 1954-76

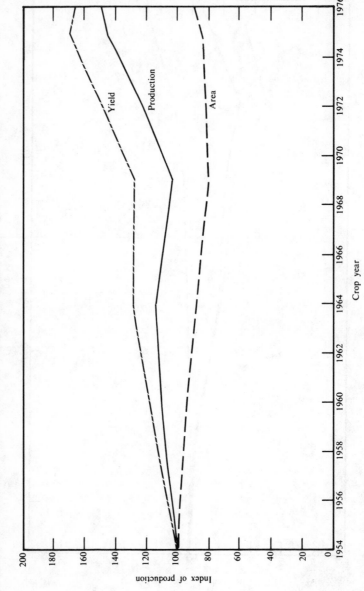

Source: Ministry of Agriculture.

TABLE 9-4. EFFECT OF DRAINAGE ON COTTON YIELDS

Locality	Area (feddans)	Yield[a] (qintars[b] per feddan) Before	Yield[a] (qintars[b] per feddan) After	Increase in yield (percent)
Minya governorate				
Maghagha	700	5.0	6.5	30
Mayana el-Wakf	2,005	5.0	6.0	20
Malatin	2,300	2.0	4.0	100
Beni Suef governorate				
El-Wasta	13,000	3.33	5.0	50
Nasir	19,000	4.15	5.8	40
Ehnasia	14,500	4.8	6.3	31
Fayoum governorate				
Toutoon	n.a.	3.36	4.57	36
Kasr el-Basel	n.a.	3.3	3.75	13
El-Hamidia	n.a.	3.0	3.47	15
Weighted average yield		4.07	5.67	39
National average yield		6.51	n.a.	n.a.

n.a. Not available.
a. Three-year average before and after installation of drainage system, which was begun in 1970.
b. One qintar equals 157.5 kilograms of seed cotton.
Source: Ministry of Irrigation, Upper Egypt Drainage Project, General Report (Cairo, 1971).

100 percent in some areas (see table 9-4). The weighted average yield was increased 40 percent when three-year average yields before and after drainage installation are compared.

Winter Crops

Wheat. Wheat is the major food crop, with per capita consumption of about 145 kilograms a year for urban dwellers and 88 kilograms for those in rural areas. Because of the increase in the population and migration from rural to urban areas where real income is higher, effective demand for wheat has been pushed up strongly at a time when wheat acreage has generally been falling. The average area of wheat was 1.571 million feddans in the early 1950s and slipped to 1.297 million feddans in the early 1970s. Trends for the twenty-year period are illustrated in figure 9-6. The area planted in wheat has risen again to about 1.3 million feddans, concurrent with increases in farm-gate prices, but because of the increase in the total crop area, its relative decline has been greater than these raw figures show.

As a proportion of the total cropped area, wheat fell from 16 to 12 percent from 1950 to 1975, about the same as for cotton. Production continued to rise, however, because the effect of yield outweighed that of area planted. By 1975 production was at a record level of more than 2 million tons, mainly as a result of better varieties and use of inputs. During this period population rose 90 percent (from 20 million to 38 million) while wheat production increased only 45 percent. Changes in consumption patterns have worsened the situation, and the import bill for wheat is a major hard-currency burden on the balance of payments. Egypt now imports about 60 percent of its wheat (3 million tons) and is vulnerable to price fluctuations on the international grain market. For instance, in 1972 the average import price was LE30 a ton including cost, insurance, and freight (c.i.f.); by 1973 it was LE73 a ton, rising to LE100 a ton in 1974; in 1976 it had fallen back to less than LE70 a ton. Wheat import statistics for 1974 and 1975 are shown in table 9-5. In 1974 wheat imports accounted for 68 percent of consumer commodity imports and 28 percent of total imports. The comparable figures in 1975 were 52 percent and 20 percent.

This situation is serious only if the resources diverted to other products earn less in convertible foreign exchange. This would appear to be the case because relative world price movements have been in favor of wheat in the short run. Several studies have examined whether Egypt should produce high-value crops in which it may have a comparative advantage (for example, long-staple cotton) and import some food grains, or whether it should diversify and be reasonably self-sufficient. There is no simple answer to this question. Much depends on the mean and variance of supplies, domestic and

TABLE 9-5. IMPORTS OF WHEAT BY VOLUME, VALUE, AND PRICE, 1974-75

Item	1974		
	Quantity (millions of tons)	Value (millions of Egyptian pounds)	Price (Egyptian pounds per ton)
Wheat grain	3.206	301.6	94.1
Wheat flour	0.418	41.5	99.2
Total grain equivalent	3.760	343.0	n.a.
Total consumer commodities imported	n.a.	500.0	n.a.
Total commodity imports	n.a.	1,247.0	n.a.

n.a.   Not available.

Source: Ministry of Planning, 1976.

foreign, and the related mean and variance of relative prices, as well as the different distributional consequences of domestic production as opposed to imports. Policy goals need to be specified and a methodology adopted to measure the tradeoffs over the planning period. Recent wheat imports may be viewed in the long run as a temporary shock not requiring resource adjustment. If this degree of variance is unacceptable, however, the reallocation of resources may be desirable. Questions of equity should also be considered since cotton production puts foreign exchange into the hands of the government, berseem production puts meat on the table of those who can afford it, and grain production reaches the masses.

Apart from allocating a larger area to wheat, output may be increased by improving the factor productivity of the land. To cite again the Upper Egypt drainage project, the three-year average for wheat yields with drainage were 20 to 100 percent more than the three-year average without drainage. Of course, drainage alone did not account for the entire increase because the project drew attention to the overall problem of productivity. A great deal can be achieved by expanding credit and by changes in technology, such as the application of correct fertilizers and the use of high-yielding varieties (HYVs) of seed.

The experience with high-yielding Mexican wheat is shown in table 9-6. The spectacular rate of acceptance of this variety, from 0.3 percent of total area planted in 1972 to 37 percent in 1974, is

| Item | 1975 | | |
	Quantity (millions of tons)	Value (millions of Egyptian pounds)	Price (Egyptian pounds per ton)
Wheat grain	2.939	252.2	85.8
Wheat flour	0.705	58.3	97.3
Total grain equivalent	3.870	320.0	n.a.
Total consumer commodities imported	n.a.	612.5	n.a.
Total commodity imports	n.a.	1,610.0	n.a.

TABLE 9-6. WHEAT: AREA AND YIELD OF DIFFERENT
VARIETIES, 1972-76

	Area (thousands of feddans)		HYV area as percentage of total	Yield (ardebs[b] per feddan)		
Year	All varieties	HYVs[a]		All varieties	HYV[a]	Other varieties
1972	1,239	4	0.3	8.69	11.45	8.68
1973	1,248	67	5.4	9.82	13.68	9.60
1974	1,369	507	37.0	9.17	10.26	8.52
1975	1,394	187	13.4	9.72	11.34	9.47
1976	1,387	180	12.9	n.a.	n.a.	n.a.

n.a. Not available.
a. High-yielding varieties of wheat of the Mexican short-straw group.
b. An ardeb equals 198 liters.
Source: Ministry of Agriculture.

almost matched by the rate of its rejection; the drop was from 37
percent in 1974 to 12.9 percent in 1976. The immediate cause of
the drop in 1974 was the high temperature during the immature stage
of the grain. The effect was a decrease in yield, which, while still
above that for other varieties, was insufficient return to the extra
factors involved. For the HYVs gross returns are higher, but net
returns are less.

In general, the complaints about the HYVs are that they require
higher labor inputs and cash, the value of the straw is less, the
darker wheat is less acceptable, the rate of flour extraction is less,
and the lower water absorption of the flour causes problems in baking. Of particular importance is the staggered ripening of the multiple tillers, or stalks, in combination with the problem of grain
shedding. The harvest time is more critical with greater relative
losses. Furthermore, the harvest coincides with corn cultivation,
whereas other wheat varieties can wait. Perhaps the most serious
drawback of the HYVs is their lack of resistance to rust under local
conditions. In 1977 a government campaign led to another expansion
of these wheats with results as unfortunate as in 1974.

Once more there is an urgent need to intensify applied research
and extension services and to develop complementary pricing and
investment policies. Demand for wheat will rise faster than the
projected population increase of 2.3 percent a year as incomes rise
and more of the population moves to urban centers. The derived
demand for convertible foreign exchange for wheat imports will go
up accordingly, fluctuating with world grain supply. Egypt has to
make two decisions: (1) how much wheat to produce and how much
to import in exchange for exports of other crops, and (2) what
manipulations in sectoral conditions are required to realize the

TABLE 9-7. BERSEEM PRODUCTION, 1972

Type	Cuttings Number	Weight (tons)	Area (millions of feddans)	Production of green fodder (millions of tons)
Short-season	1	6.5	0.848	5.512
Short-season	2	13.0	0.385	5.005
Full-season	3	19.5	0.188a	3.666
Full-season	4	26.0	1.398	36.348
Total			2.819	50.000

a. Area of seed production.
Source: El-Tobgy, Contemporary Egyptian Agriculture.

quantities desired. This entails detailed economic and financial consideration of public and private profitability, measured in terms that include the average and the likely variance of the outcome.

Berseem (Egyptian clover). Berseem covers 26 percent of all of Egypt's cropped areas, a total of 2.8 million feddans. This is more than the combined area of its two major competitors, cotton and wheat, which is 2.6 million feddans. Berseem is an intermediate product, grown for either winter fodder or as a soil conditioner before and after cotton (or rice and maize in rotation), and is planted from mid-September to November. It is cut and fed to stock as green feed from December to May. If one or two cuts are taken, the residue is turned in and the land prepared for spring planting of cotton. If more cuts are taken, as is becoming common, cotton planting is delayed, reducing its yield. If the berseem is kept for four cuts, no cotton crop follows. This type is called full-season berseem; berseem plowed after one or two cuts is called short-season berseem. About 10 to 15 percent of full-season berseem is left after the third cutting for seed setting, and this is usually harvested in June.

Berseem yields are high; the first cutting is taken about fifty to seventy-five days after planting, the second after fifty more days, and the others after thirty to forty days. Four cuttings are usually taken from the full-season berseem with from four to more than six tons per feddan per cut (see table 9-7). Silage and hay are not commonly made. Although yields are high, it should be possible to get more fodder with less land because little breeding work has been done and, as elsewhere, drainage is limiting yields. In some areas, yields have increased up to 97 percent after installation of drainage systems.[9] By substituting improved factor productivity for area

9. H. K. Bakhati, A. I. el-Shabassy, and others, Evaluation of Tile Drainage at Mehallet Mousa (Cairo: Ministry of Agriculture, 1974).

TABLE 9-8. SUGARCANE: AVERAGE AREA,
PRODUCTION, AND YIELD, 1950-54 TO 1975

Period	Area (thousands of feddans)	Production (thousands of tons)	Yield (tons per feddan)	Index of yield
1950-54	96	3,306	34.5	100
1955-59	111	4,186	37.7	109
1960-64	122	4,726	38.7	112
1965-69	145	5,635	38.9	113
1970-72	194	7,475	38.6	112
1973	198	7,349	37.1	107
1974	208	7,018	33.7	97

Source: Ministry of Agriculture.

expansion, more animal fodder can be grown without losing foreign exchange earnings from cotton or foreign exchange savings from food-grain production.

Perennials. Sugarcane is a major industrial crop and the main field crop of southern Egypt. Domestic supply has been unable to keep up with the demands of a rapidly growing population for an item with a high income elasticity of demand. Consumption of sugar is around 20 kilograms per person a year, and imports of refined sugar are currently about 100,000 tons a year. The sugarcane area has expanded rapidly from 96,000 feddans during the early 1950s to 220,000 feddans in 1975. It is generally grown for three annual harvests and is thus outside the usual rotation. Most of the cane is grown under contract to sugar mills, and production is limited to milling capacity (see table 9-8).

The recent decline in yields to the levels of the 1950s is the result of poor drainage. Because sugarcane is in the ground for three years, there is a long period for the buildup of pests and diseases, such as those that stunt the growth of ratoons, or sprouts. The joint effort by the farmer and the mill requires a high level of technical efficiency and supporting services since sugar production depends not only on the tons of cane produced but also on the content of sugar in the cane. The Egyptian sugar industry can increase output by restoring soil fertility and reorganizing the interaction of miller and grower.

Horticulture

Vegetables. Vegetable plantings have expanded from about 259,000 feddans in the early 1950s to 900,000 feddans in 1976. Tomatoes, potatoes, and melons account for about two-thirds of both the total planting and value of vegetables. Crops are grown during all three

seasons, with summer vegetables predominating. Most of the vegetables are grown for urban consumption, but an increasing amount
is exported. Tomatoes dominate in terms of area planted and cash
value while potatoes are the leading export vegetable.

Vegetable crops are advantageous to the producer because: (1)
they are labor intensive — tomatoes, for example, require 192 man-
days a year compared with 99 for cotton and short-season berseem,
and 65 for wheat and maize; (2) they can be grown at various times
of year, and thus plantings can be adjusted to periods when labor is
available; (3) they give high returns to labor; and (4) they are not
subject to farm-gate price controls, and payments go directly to the
grower without passing through the cooperative. (Controls do not
exist on retail margins.) Because of these advantages the production of vegetables would seem to make economic sense except that
marketing is hampered on both the domestic and export side. Export
outlets are good in the short run, but because other North African
producers are also expanding output, vigorous efforts in quality control and cost efficiency are needed. Vegetable prices fluctuate widely,
and high wastage of the crop occurs in times of surplus. Domestic
sales are mainly in the urban areas, and production has been limited
to the capacity of the storage and transport systems to deliver an acceptable product. In rural areas vegetables are not traditionally consumed in large amounts. This situation is gradually changing, however, and the best long-run prospects seem to be in the domestic
market if accompanied by investment in marketing infrastructure and
in processing seasonal surplus. The most promising external markets are in Saudi Arabia and the Persian Gulf States, where market
prices for good quality items are high.

Fruits. In recent years the area planted with fruit has greatly
expanded. Freedom of prices and marketing has served as an inducement to the farmer as has the opportunity to intercrop during the gestation period. Once a field is registered as an orchard, all cropping
requirements are removed. Fruit and vegetables are commonly
grown together around cities. The most important fruits are citrus,
dates, mangoes, grapes, and bananas, representing about 85 percent
of the total value of production. Citrus fruits predominate, and oranges are now third in importance among agricultural exports, after
cotton and rice. Almost all dates are locally consumed, while some
special varieties of mango are exported. The total area planted with
fruit crops expanded from 94,000 feddans in 1950-54 to about 285,000
feddans in 1975.

Animal Production

Cattle. In the Egyptian system, animals compete with people as
well as complement them in the production and consumption of scarce

food supplies. Virtually no rangeland is available for livestock, and all fodder must come from arable land; this raises the fundamental question of how to allocate a limited area between food for animals and for humans. The spectacular long-run increase in the berseem area and decrease in wheat and cotton areas are responses to relative price signals. Meat prices are not controlled and production is heavily subsidized. (Prices of imported beef are of the order of 50 piastres a kilogram c.i.f., whereas the actual domestic selling price is about 160 piastres a kilogram for somewhat the same grades. Because of an unevenly applied price policy that favors berseem and meat production and lowers the profitability of traditional crops, cattle holding is often the best investment for the small farmer. For the fellahin, or peasants, the animal is not only a source of food, providing meat and milk as well as draft power for food crops; it is also a status symbol, a store of wealth and insurance. A simple technical or economic analysis may partly explain Egypt's livestock industry but leaves many of the complex interrelationships untouched. Traditionally, the raising of livestock has been intertwined with crop production, with crops as the final output and meat and milk as residuals. As population builds up, so does demand for food and hence demand for animal draft power and meat.

Animal feed is in chronic short supply, especially in the summer. Winter feed is mainly berseem and summer feed is straw and concentrates, such as cereal grains and cottonseed cake. The substitution of berseem production for wheat and cotton aggravates the summer feed shortage and has necessitated feed imports. An excellent study of feed balance by the Ministry of Agriculture, which is discussed by el-Tobgy, shows that animals merely survive on a hunger ration during summer and autumn, whereas the surplus winter protein is a wasteful and expensive source of energy. [10]

Although meat production rose from 238,000 tons in 1960 to 302,000 tons in 1974 and imports increased to 21,000 tons, per capita consumption of beef and poultry fell from 12.2 kilograms a year to 11.6 kilograms in the same period. Since animal products have a high income elasticity of demand, this indicates either an overall slight decline in per capita real income or a redistribution of income in favor of a smaller group. It seems likely that it has been the latter because meat consumption has shifted to urban areas where there is more purchasing power. With prices of meat uncontrolled and its production enjoying considerable protection, the price of the limited supply has been pulled upward at a faster rate than the overall price rise.

Poultry. Poultry production makes eminent economic sense under Egyptian conditions. The principal reasons are: (1) the

10. Muhammad Kotb and others, Nutritional Status of Livestock in Egypt (Cairo: Ministry of Agriculture, 1973).

conversion ratio of grain per kilogram of poultry is up to 3:1 as a-
gainst the 10:1 ratio for beef; (2) commercial poultry production
is capital intensive whereas beef is more land intensive because of
its feed requirements; (3) poultry production can be organized with
relatively few highly skilled operators, whereas beef is produced by
many small farmers who have multiple objectives, many of which
are other than economic; and (4) the short breeding cycle of poultry makes it amenable to rapid improvement in breeding for specific traits.

Egypt has begun to invest heavily in this activity. From previously negligible levels, public sector investment in poultry in 1972 rose
to LE6 million out of a total Ministry of Agriculture investment budget of LE9.8 million. This sort of investment is economic only if
the net social benefits are greater than the costs — that is, the investment must be productive, and the scarce funds must find their
best use in this subsector. A joint study by the Ministry of Agriculture and the U.S. Department of Agriculture and USAID concludes
that many public sector broiler houses are either overdesigned, operating under capacity, or needlessly delayed in completion.[11] The
public sector units, the cooperative units, and specialized private
sector producers are all hampered by shortages of feed and birds.
Foreign exchange allocations for feed, antibiotics, and materials
are restrictive. Despite the heavy direct investment, about 90 percent of the chickens and eggs are still produced on traditional small
farms. The report recommends that the present units be completed
and that the operation and expansion of intensive broiler production
be tailored to the availability of foreign exchange and management
capacity. It must be acknowledged that public funds for investment
in agriculture are extremely limited. This makes a strong case for
encouraging production by small farmers — a case strengthened on
grounds of equity.

APPENDIX A: FARMER RESPONSE TO PRICE CHANGES

Because sectoral performance is the sum of each farmer's activity, it is useful to gain an understanding of the factors influencing
farmers' decisions and their behavior. Obviously, incentive is difficult to define in a multipurpose cropping system, but some feel for
the relative attractiveness of alternatives may be gleaned from table
9-9. The incentives are of two types, cash and noncash. Cash objectives are to minimize cash costs, maximize cash returns,
and to maximize the difference between the two. The noncash

11. U.S. Department of Agriculture, Egypt: Major Constraints to Increasing
Agricultural Productivity, Foreign Agricultural Economic Report no. 120 (Washington, D.C., 1976), pp. 133-37.

TABLE 9-9. INCENTIVES PER FEDDAN FOR SELECTED CROPS IN 1976 PRICES
(Egyptian pounds)

Crop	Cash costs[a]	Cash return[b]	Cash surplus[c]	Surplus per man-day[d]	Gross marginal value[e]	Free retention ratio[f] (percent)	Land occupancy period (months)[g]	Amount marketed[h]
Wheat	12	75	63	2.3	73	70	7	part
Rice	19	92	72	1.5	44	33	5	part
Short-season berseem	5	n.a.	n.a.	n.a.	21	100	4	none
Long-season berseem	7	105	98	6.1	85	100	7	all
Cotton	27	146	119	1.2	66	0	8	all
Maize	12	82	70	5.0	47	100	5	part
Tomatoes	48	240	192	2.9	159	100	4	all
Oranges	60	245	185	1.5	122	100	12	all

n. a. Not applicable since short-season berseem was being fed to livestock and not marketed.
a. Off-farm payments, labor not costed.
b. Gross value of primary and secondary product.
c. Cash return minus cash costs.
d. Returns per man-day.
e. Gross value of output minus variable costs.
f. Amount available for free-market sale.
g. Time from planting until sale.
h. A commercial crop would be expected to be influenced more by cash considerations.
Source: Ministry of Agriculture data.

196

objectives are to maximize the total value of production, whether sold or not, to minimize the time from planting to the sale of the crop, and to maximize the amount marketed free of cooperative control, after providing enough food and fodder for on-farm consumption.

Table 9-9 shows the gross marginal value for each crop, that is, the total value of output less variable costs of production. In the short run, at least, fixed costs have to be repaid regardless of how much of which crop is planted, and these costs are not quite so important in the Egyptian small-farm system as in highly capitalized systems.

Labor-intensive vegetables have the highest gross margins but are limited by markets. Plantings are, however, expanding rapidly. Fruit crops have a high gross margin but are restricted by the long period to reach maturity and the small-farmer's need for food grain and animal fodder. These crops are very popular near cities and are often tied to land speculation and capital gains. Of the field crops, long-season berseem has the highest margin, followed recently by wheat, which has displaced cotton. Maize now has a higher margin than rice and short-season berseem, which is difficult to value because much of its contribution is in the maintenance of cotton yields. When the length of time each crop occupies the land is considered, the order of gross margins stays essentially the same, except for cotton, which then falls below rice to become the least attractive field crop on the basis of gross margins per feddan per unit of time. On a rotational basis for a fully commercial farm, the most profitable mix would be a combination of those crops having the highest gross margins per feddan per unit of time subject to technical constraints, such as the need to follow cotton by berseem. This would lead to expansion of areas of long-season berseem, wheat, and maize, and a contraction of areas under cotton, rice, and short-season berseem. This is what was happening in the 1970s (see figure 9-1).

The typical Egyptian small farmer is only partly commercialized, and his decision variables are not strictly those of the large farmers. The small farmer first allocates land to his own food crops, maize, and some minor crops, and then to his animals, berseem, and straw. He then has to satisfy to some extent area and quota requirements before the cooperatives will supply the desired inputs, mostly for cotton, wheat, and rice, and tries to minimize the effect of these requirements. Any land left over can be freely allocated to long-season berseem, over-quota amounts of cotton, and wheat, rice, fruit, and vegetables to maximize profits where market opportunities exist. Planting of long-season berseem or wheat during winter precludes a crop of cotton the following summer because there is not enough time for a full growing season for both. This would favor a longer-term expansion of shorter-season summer crops, such as rice and vegetables. The small-farmer's attitude toward this may lead him to choose minimum exposure to certain markets for inputs and outputs.

Cotton has by far the highest cash costs for inputs and is sold entirely through the cooperative market system. It also has the longest period between selling and cash payments. There is some doubt whether announced prices are relevant because the cooperatives' control over the disposal of surplus on each farmer's account often reduces the effective price received. Finally, as can be seen by dividing the operating surplus by labor requirements, cotton returns the lowest profit per man-day worked. It is not difficult to understand the changes in Egypt's cropping pattern when these farm-level relationships are considered.

Studies of the effect of price changes on supply have been hampered by the complexity of these relationships. The evidence shows, however, that farmers are neither unresponsive to price changes nor perverse in their reaction. The major determinants of price response are the high degree of product substitution technically possible, the farmers' attitude toward market exposure, the compulsory delivery quotas and their enforceability, and the dual-purpose crops. The major limitations on the measurement of response to current and projected prices are the large number of competing crops in a complex rotation and the multiple grades with price differentiation within a crop, for example, cotton.

APPENDIX B: ORGANIZATION OF THE SECTOR

The administration of the sector is the responsibility of the Ministry of Agriculture, in cooperation with the Ministry of Irrigation. Other ministries are involved in the supply and disposal of inputs and outputs, policy, and planning. For instance, the Ministry of Trade and Supply is responsible for the trade of sectoral inputs and outputs as well as the subsidy program for basic foods. The Ministry of Industry is involved in setting the procurement price for domestically processed products, and the Ministry of Planning is concerned with sectoral investment plans and economywide priorities. The High Committee of Planning, composed of ministers from the departments concerned, initiates policy changes, allocates inputs, and sets targets for output. The High Committee also coordinates the views of the various ministries on the issues presented by the Ministry of Agriculture. A combined position is then forwarded to the Council of Ministers, which submits recommendations to the Farmers' Committee and the People's Assembly for ratification. The draft proposal is then returned to the full Assembly and eventually becomes a presidential decree. The line ministries implement these decisions through their agencies. Among these are the Principal Bank for Development and Agricultural Credit, an autonomous authority under the jurisdiction of the Ministry of Agriculture, the General Organization for Cooperatives in the Ministry of Agriculture (changed to the Department of Cooperatives in 1976), and the General Organization for Cotton within the Ministry of Supply.

At the regional level there are twenty-five governorates, of which seventeen are of major agricultural significance (nine in Lower Egypt, four in middle Egypt, and four in Upper Egypt). In each governorate there is a village level organization. The Agricultural Support Services and the Cooperative Network closely parallel this pattern of general administration.

Agricultural research has a long tradition in Egypt, particularly in cotton breeding. Research is conducted not only by the Ministry of Agriculture, but also by the Ministry of Irrigation, the National Research Center, and the universities. Many problems of pricing and farmer response may be traced back to a weak sectoral data base at the farm level, which makes it difficult to forecast likely responses. Although various international agencies are also involved in major research efforts, the fundamental problems remain unaddressed. These relate to the basic concepts of a research system, what its form and function should be, what its linkages to the farm and extension system should be, how to test its performance against international standards, how to equip the system properly, and what is an appropriate level of staffing.

Agricultural extension services spread the use of modern inputs, such as improved varieties and inorganic fertilizers, significantly increasing yields in the 1960s. In recent years, however, extension work seems to have declined in effectiveness, and the network needs to be strengthened. Budgetary allocations for the work have decreased, while urban-based staff have increased in number, resulting in weak farmer linkages. Extension is organized through the Department of Agricultural Extension and a High Advisory Council, with participation by research institutes and agricultural universities. Regional representation is through the governorate director of agriculture along with provincial supervisors and district agents. Until recently there has been an inadequate ratio of one agent for 1,500 to 2,000 farmers, with a concentration of agents in Cairo, most of whom are without field experience.

The cooperative system in Egypt is parastatal and falls under the jurisdiction of the Ministry of Agriculture. In 1976 the Department of Cooperatives, with an undersecretary, was formed to supersede the Egyptian General Cooperative Organization. There are four national groupings of cooperative societies: the General Society for Land Reclamation, the General Society for Agrarian Reform, multipurpose societies within the General Agricultural Cooperative Society, and specialized societies within the Cooperative Society for special crops. Independent lines of command flow from the national level through the governorates to joint cooperatives at district levels down to village cooperatives. As of November 1975 there were 133 land reclamation societies, 654 agrarian reform societies, and 4,200 multipurpose agricultural cooperatives at the village level. The complex structure gives rise to overlapping functions, conflicting lines of authority, and duplication of staff. In 1976 the problems had become so great that the Egyptian General Cooperative Organization was dissolved, and many of its functions were transferred to the Agricultural Credit System. Another bill to alter the functional responsibilities of the cooperative societies and the credit banks was proposed in 1977, but by early 1978 the roles of the two agencies still had not been defined. Enforced membership in farm cooperatives has been a key tool of sectoral management in the postrevolutionary era. Theoretically it provides a two-way delivery system of goods and services as well as a communications network. Plans for the aggregate output of the sector, together with the required inputs of fertilizer, seed, and credit, filter through the cooperative system and eventually are expressed as farm-level allocations. All the cotton and parts of various other crops are requisitioned by the cooperatives as the government agent. The cooperatives directly intervene in the conditions of production through the pooling of fragmented holdings and by performing various agricultural tasks, such as protecting cotton plants. Cooperatives often provide tractor services for draft power and stationary threshers at harvest. Goods and services are entered against the farmer's account, and payment is deducted from the imputed value of the requisitioned output. Through these means the cooperative affects production, consumption, and investment. In general, the cooperatives have performed important functions, but they have grown somewhat unresponsive to farmer perceptions, and their power has often been resented and evaded.

At the village level each cooperative is managed by an agricultural graduate from the Ministry of Agriculture, assisted by an accountant from the Agricultural Bank and sundry other employees. Complementing this line of authority is an elected board, 80 percent of whose members must be small farmers. Their contribution to effective decisionmaking is necessarily weak because they have no say on policy matters or daily management of the society. The system has been affected by shortages, inefficiency, and loss of faith on the part of the farmers. By 1973 about 65 percent of the village societies were running at a loss, as were 45 percent of the reform societies.

Credit is provided exclusively by government banks and agencies. Following the enactment of the agrarian reform laws and the reorganization of local administration, the government reviewed the outmoded lines of credit and established a new system. At the apex was a General Organization of Agriculture and Cooperative Credit responsible to the Minister of Agriculture, under which were seventeen governorate-level agricultural credit and cooperative banks. These banks continued to operate outside the jurisdiction of the banking laws and of the Central Bank. In 1976 the Egyptian General Organization for Agricultural and Cooperative Credit was replaced by the Principal Bank for Development and Agriculture Credit (PBDAC). Expanded functions, responsibilities, and privileges were laid down in a new charter that became law in 1976. Some small contribution to credit supplies is made by Egypt's four commercial banks, which are also state-owned.

The major functions of the credit system are provision of short- and medium-term loans to farmers and cooperatives, procurement and supply of agricultural inputs, and the marketing of crops. Non-credit activities are undertaken through agencies. Previously all farm credit had to go through the cooperatives, but now the credit banks can loan directly to farmers. The loans are predominantly short term, generally for crop production. The technical staff of the Ministry of Agriculture anticipates production costs for each area at the start of each agricultural year. Each farmer is entitled to credit for the full crop production cost, according to a production plan prepared by the village cooperative. All inputs are provided in kind, and cash loans are given only for machinery service charges and hired labor. No tangible security is obtained, but the farmers undertake to sell their output through designated marketing agencies. Medium-term loans make up about 1 percent of the total and are used mostly to establish orchards and purchase farm machinery and cattle. The low level of use of this facility indicates a low on-farm investment rate, and the restrictions on development are probably related both to low expectations of profit and effective credit rationing. The interest rate to farmers in 1976 was 3 percent on short-term and 6 percent on long-term loans. In 1977 this was changed to 4 percent on short-term and 9 percent on long-term loans. The on-lending rate is lower than the average borrowing rate of the credit system by some 2 percent. A substantial part of the loan portfolio remains overdue. The basic problem with the performance of the credit system seems to be that it is used as an agency for policies other than provision of credit. For example, the system has been used as a source of income transfer (by writing off debts) and for the distribution of feed and pesticides.

The marketing of farm products is one of the major spheres of influence of the government in the sector. Provision of inputs and credit is tied to compulsory sales of output to the cooperatives. Both the quantities and the procurement prices are set beforehand. The over-quota amounts are freely sold at local market prices. Generally, the requisitioned commodities are either urban foods (such as wheat, sesame, sugar, broad beans, lentils, and rice) or export crops (such as cotton, rice, onions, and groundnuts). Most of the compulsory minimum delivery quotas were enforced throughout the

1960s and the early 1970s. Some changes introduced in 1976 and 1977 allow more freedom for disposal of the crops by the farmers. There are considerable price differences for the same commodity in different markets, ranging from 27 percent more than the cooperative price for wheat in the free market to 100 percent more for rice. The marketing and pricing system is in effect a transfer mechanism to extract a certain surplus from the sector. From the cooperatives the products pass to government processing, exporting, and retailing companies. The banks are the purchasing agencies on behalf of the state and maintain regular storage facilities. Private processing organizations usually offer higher prices than public companies although they are often penalized by various administrative controls.

Within the Ministry of Agriculture and Land Reclamation there are many autonomous or semi-autonomous authorities, whose activities range from overseeing cooperative activities to directly producing goods for consumption. As public sector organizations, they compete directly with the ministries for funds and skilled manpower; as producers, they compete directly with the cooperatives and private individuals for sales without having to stand the test of profitability. The major enterprises affecting the sector in this way are the General Organizations for Cotton, Land Reclamation, Cooperatives, and Poultry Production. The Cotton Organization is the monopoly purchaser of the cotton crop and is responsible for administering policy affecting cotton. The Land Reclamation Organization implements that program and retains control over reclaimed lands. The Cooperative Organization administered the cooperative's activities until recently, and the Poultry Organization constructs and operates large-scale capital-intensive broiler production units.

10
Agriculture: Policies, Issues, and Recommendations

The government's basic strategy and policy objectives for the agricultural sector can be traced back to the 1952 revolution, which had as one of its major goals the alleviation of rural poverty. The first moves were to transfer assets and incomes within the sector and to improve the legal position of tenant farmers. Transfers of assets were effected by the land reforms of September 1952, income transfers by fixing taxes and rents, and legislation was passed against tenant displacement. It was clear that redistributive measures alone would be insufficient, however, and that an increase in the productive base would be necessary. With only 3 percent of the land area under cultivation and much of the Nile's waters unused, the obvious solution was to enlarge the resource base by increasing irrigation supplies and extending the farmed area. This led to the decision to build the Aswan High Dam and to institute land reclamation.

This program placed a heavy burden on the public finances at a time when the largest economic sector and thus the most significant source of funds was agriculture itself. The effort to extract the required resources from the agricultural sector led the government to intervene directly on an increasingly wider scale — from the nationalization of the cotton trade in 1961, to a system of government monopolies, exchange controls, price differentials, and compulsory delivery quotas on the export crops to maintain supplies. A second land reform was introduced in 1961. Beginning in 1963 the government also reorganized the cooperative system. Its objectives were, first, to promote efficiency through land consolidation, pest control, and modernization while retaining private ownership of small farms; second, to make the cooperative a government agency for collection and distribution. This market intervention was designed to maintain rural incomes by guaranteed minimum prices and at the same time to extract a surplus to pay for a consumer subsidy program to maintain urban incomes. The intervention further provided investment funds for nationalized industry as well as captive markets for its output at protected prices. The domestic fertilizer industry, for example, was protected by the establishment of a fund, and fertilizers were distributed through the cooperatives. The government's subsidy program for urban consumers mainly affected wheat and cotton, leading to compulsory wheat deliveries and the purchase of cotton at prices below those in the free market.

This system of government controls represented a formalization and intensification of activities that had loosely existed long before the revolution. Public investment in irrigation infrastructure was an ancient tradition, and cooperatives had existed for some fifty years, as had production controls to manage supplies. Price interventions through export taxes were introduced in 1948; stock interventions to protect domestic income from foreign shocks dated back to World War II when international trade was disrupted; and subsidies have been in force, either directly or through foreign exchange premiums, at least since 1952.[1] The policy package introduced in the 1960s was basically unaltered, with marginal changes resulting from the open-door policy in 1973. What was new were the land reforms and the pervasive circumscription of the private sector. Government interventions have become so widespread that they have led one observer to comment, "while ... statistically, the agricultural world is included within the private sector, the regulatory powers of the government are so intensive as to deprive the categorization of much meaning."[2]

POLICY PERFORMANCE

Initially the system promised sectoral, industrial, and consumer gains in a reasonable time. Shortfalls in growth soon manifested themselves, however. Although the first five-year plan achieved a 35 percent rise in GDP, which was close to the 40 percent target, agriculture's growth rate was only about 1.5 percent a year as against the planned 5 percent a year. Sector targets were "obviously out of touch with realities."[3] Continuing poor performance after twenty years of systematic planning points to the need for serious reconsideration. It is not easy to evaluate the performance of individual instruments given the problems of the data base, the multiplicity of instruments, and the complexity of Egyptian farming. Vital information on employment, land tenure, and physical input-output relationships is either too old or unreliable.   Many

1. Bent Hansen and Girgis A. Marzouk, Development and Economic Policy in the UAR, Egypt (Amsterdam: North-Holland, 1965), p. 242.

2. John Waterbury, Public versus Private in the Egyptian Economy, American University Field Staff Reports, vol. 21, no. 5 (Hanover, N.H., 1976), p. 5.

3. Hansen and Marzouk, Development and Economic Policy in the UAR, Egypt, p. 296.

instruments, such as exchange rate manipulations, are implicit in their effect and difficult to trace. Targets are not separated from goals and often not tied to particular instruments. Overall, however, evidence suggests that agricultural growth rates are low, real incomes per capita in agriculture are static or falling, and the small farmers often manage to circumvent the system. Furthermore, a serious problem of management arises because agricultural production is primarily a private venture, carried out by some 2.6 million smallholders, with a wide variety of capacities, activities, and techniques, and all the holdings are dispersed and small.

The major problems of Egyptian agriculture stem from: (1) a system of inflexible and frequently conflicting price controls that neither efficiently allocates resources nor adequately supports the profitability of enterprises; (2) the heavy implicit taxation of agriculture, which depresses rural incomes to perhaps half the level of those in the urban sector; (3) the inability of heavy public investment in the new lands to add substantially to output; (4) the acceleration of drainage problems; (5) rapid urbanization and population growth, which increases consumer demands for resources and decreases the exportable surplus; (6) overestimation of the surplus available from the agricultural sector; and (7) uneven incidence of taxation on different activities in the sector. The following sections describe in more detail the policy instruments and raise the main issues to be dealt with at present.

PRICES AND MARKETS

Prices of inputs and outputs are set in two parallel markets. These are the free village market, subject to demand and supply considerations, and the cooperative marketing system through which the state bank purchases crops on behalf of the government. Each market is distinct in price and other characteristics, but some cross-influence occurs. Cotton and a percentage of major export or import-substitution crops are sold only through the cooperative systems, while amounts that are over the quota and other crops may be sold in either market. To illustrate the system, table 10-1 gives quota requirements during the 1965-70 period. All the cotton, 27 percent of the wheat, 66 percent of the rice, and 57 percent of the onion crop on average were requisitioned at prices determined by the state agency as the monopoly buyer. Since then the list has grown to include other crops such as sesame, groundnuts, broad beans, and lentils. In 1977 wheat quotas were dropped as farmers increased acreages in response to price rises.

Compulsory prices in the cooperative system were well below the average of those on the free market in the 1960s, ranging from 50 percent to 20 percent lower (see table 10-2). Furthermore,

TABLE 10-1. MINIMUM COMPULSORY DELIVERIES
FOR REQUISITIONED CROPS, 1965-70

Crop	Minimum compulsory deliveries per feddan (absolute numbers)	Average yield per feddan (1965-70)	Compulsory deliveries as percentage of average yields per feddan	Free retention ratio (percent)
Cotton	—	—	100.0	0.0
Wheat (in ardebs)[a]	2.0	7.25	27.6	72.4
Rice (in daribas)[b]	1.5	2.25	66.0	33.0
Onions (in tons)	4.0	7.00	57.0	43.0

— Not applicable.
a. An ardeb equals 198 liters.
b. A dariba of rice (in husk) equals 945 kilograms.
Source: Abdel Fadil, Development, Income Distribution, and Social Change in Rural Egypt (1952-70) (Cambridge: Cambridge University Press, 1975), p. 89.

free-market prices have risen much faster over time. Producer prices for cotton, for example, have risen at an average of only 1.7 percent a year since 1950. From 1965 to 1975 the rise accelerated to 3.7 percent a year, but as the prices of purchased inputs rose 5.8 percent a year, a 2.1 percent net shortfall resulted, even with subsidies. This contrasts with long-season berseem, cotton's main competitor, which had an estimated increase of output prices of 11 percent a year and an increase in input prices of 5 percent, leaving a net increase in return of 6 percent. Like cotton, rice and maize had price increases for their output that were less than the increases in the prices of their inputs (see table 10-3).

TABLE 10-2. AVERAGE GOVERNMENT PROCUREMENT
PRICES AND AVERAGE FREE-MARKET PRICES,
SELECTED CROPS, 1967-68

Crop	Egyptian pounds		Price differential (percent)
	Average price for compulsory purchases	Average price for free retentions	
Wheat (per ardeb)	4	5.1	27.5
Rice (per dariba)	20	40.0	100.0
Onions (per ton)	11	16.5	50.0

Source: Abdel Fadil, Development, Income Distribution and Social Change in Rural Egypt, p. 89.

TABLE 10-3. ANNUAL PERCENTAGE CHANGES
IN OUTPUT AND INPUT PRICES,
SELECTED CROPS, 1965-75

Commodity	Output	Input	Difference
Berseem[a]	11.0	5.0[b]	6.0[b]
Rice	5.4	7.1	-1.7
Wheat	6.8	5.2	1.6
Maize	6.0	6.3	-0.3
Cotton	3.7	5.8	-2.1

a. Actual prices (per cut per feddan) are available for some years
only. Missing data were approximated by using meat price indexes.
b. Estimated.
Source: Computed from Ministry of Agriculture data.

Taxes and Subsidies on Input Prices

Direct subsidies are now paid by the authorities on pest control,
fertilizer, gypsum, improved seeds, fodders, fuel oil and diesel,
and many minor items. In 1972 and 1976 incentive payments were
made to expand cotton plantings, and in 1973 such payments were
made for early cotton plantings. As shown in table 10-4, most of
the payments have gone to pest control on cotton, while fertilizer
subsidies have become important only since 1975. Domestic prices
of fertilizer have remained relatively fixed since 1960. During the
1960-73 period imported fertilizers were taxed in order to protect
local production. Since 1974 when world prices began to rise sharply, all fertilizer production has been heavily subsidized. Domestic
production now accounts for 40 percent of fertilizer requirements.

Indirect subsidies are far more important and consist mainly of
the unrecovered portion of public sector costs, including investment
in agriculture and irrigation infrastructure, operation of the irrigation system, and provision of agricultural services. The total cost

TABLE 10-4. DIRECT SUBSIDY PAYMENTS
FOR AGRICULTURAL INPUTS, 1972-77

(percentages of total)

Subsidy	1972	1973	1974	1975	1976	1977[a]
Pest control on cotton	84.7	79.5	90.5	27.2	35.2	58.3
Imported fertilizer	...	...	2.4	68.7	52.7	14.0

... Negligible.
a. Allocated.
Source: General Authority for Agricultural Crops Stabilization Fund.

of these indirect subsidies has averaged about LE75 million a year (after deduction of LE15 million a year in land taxes) compared with about LE12 million a year for direct subsidies. The subsidies are made through nonrevision of land tax schedules, exemptions from payments of land and income taxes, absence of water prices, and direct public sector investments. Wages are supported through consumer subsidies and taxed through lower producer prices.

Taxes and Subsidies on Output Prices

Two major types of implicit taxes predominate. One is an export tax of 40 to 50 percent, which is derived from the higher valued exchange rate for agricultural transactions. The second is the difference in local currency between the fixed buying price of the government agency and its selling price.[4] For rice, the price differential has resulted in an average tax of 25 percent at the nominal rate of protection. The net effect of input subsidies, output price differentials, and the exchange rate tax was a net tax rate on value added of about 30 percent on average, but this rate rose to 87 percent in 1974. For cotton, the net tax rate has been around 55 percent, rising to 79 percent in 1974. For wheat and maize, the import-substituting crops, taxes through price differentials have generally been near zero, with a small degree of taxation in some years and subsidization in others. When the adjusted world price equivalent is used as the numeraire, however, it is clear that the usual outcome is net taxation on value added, which has risen to 50 percent in both the export-earning and import-substituting groups. Meat production has been heavily protected through exchange controls, and the effective subsidy rate is currently over 100 percent. Berseem production derives some protection as a meat input, but its price is also influenced through derived demand for draft animal power for crops that are taxed.

Effects of Price and Market Policies

Under these policies, prices lost much of their function in resource allocation, and farmers became isolated from domestic and international market forces. But the complex system of direct controls in lieu of prices proved too slow for changing circumstances. Conflicting signals were sent to producers, and it became impossible to predict the net effect.

Cotton policy is a clear example of massive policy confusion. The simultaneous use of many policy instruments does not necessarily imply confusion, but a net effect directly opposite to stated

---

4. All prices in these analyses are adjusted for equivalence of grade, location, stage of processing, marketing costs, and so on.

aims certainly does. The farmer might be subject to such diverse government measures as a heavy export tax and domestic tax on output prices, a price support, a subsidy on pest control, either a tax or subsidy on fertilizer, a subsidy on water supplies, a seed subsidy, physical controls over input use and minimum area planted, and incentive payments to expand his planted area and to plant the crop earlier. Although the number of instruments may well equal the number of targets, it seems clear that the measures are not operating independently. If nonprice variables are to substitute for prices and incomes, serious difficulties in estimation and implementation arise that are not being dealt with satisfactorily. The net effect has been that cotton plantings have fallen to record lows, quota evasion is widespread, efficiency is suffering, and relations between planners and farmers have deteriorated. A similar situation prevails with other crops. The underlying causes are that farms are nonspecialized and can produce a wide combination of competing crops at various input levels; the tax incidence affects profitability of different crops unevenly; the output tax swamps the input subsidies; and the ability and willingness of the government to police regulations has been deficient.

The changes in sown areas shown in table 10-5 indicate that more profitable crops have expanded at the expense of less profitable ones. During the period of controls, the total cotton and wheat area declined in absolute terms by 0.697 million feddans. In relative terms the decline was even greater as extra land became available. Berseem, fruit, rice, and vegetables expanded to take up the difference. A reasonable explanation is that farmers, like everyone else, invest in the expectation that the crops they grow will yield maximum profit.

TABLE 10-5. GROSS CHANGES IN SOWN CROP AREAS BETWEEN THE MID-1950s AND 1970s

Land availability	Millions of feddans	Increased plantings	Millions of feddans
Wheat area reduction	0.234	Full-season clover	0.700
Cropped-extension area	0.700	Rice	0.300
Other crop adjustments	0.100	Fruit	0.140
Total	1.497		1.490

Source: Calculated from Ministry of Agriculture data.

INCOME AND EMPLOYMENT

The two components of agricultural income are wages and profits, and from 1965 to 1975 these rose at about the same rate (when
rents are included in profits) for most controlled crops. A farmer's net income depends to a great extent on his ability to minimize
his plantings of price-controlled crops. Vegetable growers with access to urban markets have had larger increases in incomes than
cotton growers, whose real incomes seem to have fallen. This profit is capitalized into rents, so that cotton land rent per year is currently about LE20 to LE30 per feddan compared with LE120 per
feddan for vegetable land, although the only difference is the quota
allocation for cotton. The income of wage earners in agriculture
has been eroded because the number of those nominally employed in
the sector has grown faster than the sectoral income. Agricultural
wages have declined faster than the overall decline in real wages and
are now about one-third the average real wage for all sectors (see
table 10-6). Real wages in the whole economy peaked in 1974 and
began to decline thereafter. The trend has not changed substantially
since then. Actual wage rates in agriculture in 1974-75 varied from
30 to 70 piastres per man-day, depending on region and season. At
a weighted average of 50 piastres per day, the annual wage in agriculture for 1974 shown in table 10-6 represents 130 days worked per
year per worker. This suggests the possibility of serious underemployment in the agricultural sector. In 1977 adult wage rates for unskilled farm labor ranged from 40 piastres per man-day to 120 piastres per man-day. The higher wages are earned during the wheat
harvesting season in May and June with higher rates near cities.
There are also regional differences in income distribution, depending on the degree of industrialization and type of crop grown. The
Institute of National Planning estimated that by 1970 the weighted
average per capita income for the border areas was less than one-
third that for urban areas; it concluded that regional incomes are
a function of the distance from these urban areas.

Intersectoral transfers of income have been considerable, especially the transfers out of the agricultural sector. The average
subsidy rate on full costs of agricultural production has been about
18 percent, whereas the average tax rate on output of major crops
has been about 30 to 40 percent. Because of the greater weighting
of the value of outputs, the net resource transfer out of agriculture
has been large. In 1975 if cotton growers had received no subsidy
on fertilizer and pest control and if no taxes were levied on output,
their cost of production per feddan would have risen by LE15 whereas their income per feddan would have risen by LE175. The transfers to the Treasury from the cotton crop alone more than cover the
full cost of all subsidies, direct and indirect, as shown in table 10-7.

TABLE 10-6.   AVERAGE ANNUAL WAGES AND SALARIES
BY ECONOMIC SECTOR, 1969-70 TO 1975
(Egyptian pounds at current prices)

Sector	1969-70	1970-71	1972	1973	1974	1975[a]
Agriculture	53.0	55.6	57.3	60.5	65.1	87.0
Industry and mining	191.8	248.2	257.1	287.1	297.0	311.0
Construction	184.6	190.5	198.6	222.6	233.2	340.0
Transport and communications	245.6	260.3	266.7	279.7	291.4	315.0
Trade and finance	158.0	162.7	182.0	190.1	195.5	219.7
Other	283.1	299.4	305.9	320.0	366.9	n.a.
Overall average	142.6	157.3	167.5	179.7	195.2	244.0
Real wages[b]	142.6	153.6	158.5	156.5	153.9	n.a.
Annual change (percent)	—	7.7	3.2	-1.3	-1.6	n.a.

n.a.   Not available.
a.   Provisional.
b.   Deflated by consumer price index, 1969-70 = 100.
Source: Ministry of Planning.

To the net outflow from cotton crops should be added the large contribution of rice and other crops because "total transfers in" includes all crops; cotton is the only one for which the national accounts list explicit Treasury transfers.

It seems valid to consider much of the current expenditure budget of the Ministries of Agriculture and Irrigation as an income transfer to surplus employees hired under the full-employment program for graduates. Some public sector investment may well be excluded from the transfers in because much of the expense on new land is nonproductive. Various analyses of intersectoral resource flows point to different conclusions, depending on the exchange rates applied and the items considered as inflows. Within the sector, the burden of the transfers out has fallen heaviest on those producing the traditional crops. Those using more purchased inputs usually gain the most from subsidies.

The most important transfer of assets occurred as part of the land reform of 1952 when landholdings in excess of 200 feddans were requisitioned by the government for distribution to tenants in plots of at least two, and not more than five, feddans per family.[5] Excess holdings could also be sold at fixed prices before the requisition. In 1961 the upper limit was reduced to 100 feddans per person,

5. On the land reforms, see Gabriel Saab, The Egyptian Agrarian Reform, 1952-1962 (London: Oxford University Press, 1967); and Saad M. Gadalla, Land Reform in Relation to Social Development, Egypt (Columbia: University of Missouri Press, 1962). On landownership, see Gabriel Baer, A History of Landownership in Modern Egypt, 1800-1950 (London: Oxford University Press, 1962).

TABLE 10-7. NET EFFECT OF AGRICULTURAL
PRICE TRANSFERS, 1973-76
(millions of Egyptian pounds)

Item	1973	1974	1975	1976
Transfers to Treasury of Cotton Organization	64.8	136.8	54.0	92.4
Exchange rate gains	114.0	177.0	129.0	100.0
Total transfers out	178.8	313.8	183.0	192.4
Direct subsidies	15.8	12.7	101.5	56.8
All public sector investments in agriculture	51.0	54.0	84.0	49.0
Current expenditure of Ministry of Agriculture	16.4	19.8	21.3	26.0
Current expenditure of Ministry of Irrigation	18.4	19.9	26.0	28.8
Total transfers in	101.6	106.4	232.8	160.6
Net flow	-77.2	-207.4	49.8	-31.8

Source: World Bank calculations from official data.

and it was again reduced to 50 feddans per person or 100 feddans
per family unit by a reform law in 1969. By 1970 about 940,000
feddans had been distributed to more than 362,000 tenants and
small farmers. In addition, the government laid down strict conditions of tenure and payment for leasing and initiated the multipurpose cooperative system, which enabled groups of small farmers
to pool their work on fragmented parcels of land and provided a reliable channel of credit from the banks.

But the greatest effect of the land reform has been to improve
conditions of tenant farmers. Although 362,000 farmers received
land titles, more than a million tenant farmers benefited from tenure reform. Even after the reforms, about 40 percent of the total
area continues to be rented. Before the revolution, sharecroppers
paid exorbitant rents for the use of land with no certainty of continued use. Agents collected the rent, received a commission, and
passed on a share to absentee landowners or other intermediaries.
Little credit was available. Under the new laws, land can be directly leased only to tenants who farm the land themselves; the rent may
not exceed seven times the basic land tax (this condition often seems
to be evaded in practice, however); sharecropping rents must not
exceed half the income from the crop after expenses are deducted;
and leases must be in writing and apply for at least three years.

Despite its success in breaking the political power of large landowners and improving conditions for small farmers and tenants,
land reform has fallen short of some of its major objectives. For

small-scale farmers — by far the largest group — the reform only
temporarily slowed the long-run increase in the smallness and poverty of farms. This was inevitable, given the inheritance customs
and a farm population that was growing faster than the farmed area.
At the turn of the century the average small farm plot was 1.5 feddans, and by prerevolutionary 1952 it was 1.2 feddans per farmer
for the same 95 percent of families. After 1952 it fell again, presumably because the size of the allocated plots had been calculated
to be just sufficient for the subsistence needs of one family. Surprisingly, the reform has not greatly affected the skewed distribution,
although it altered the absolute number of feddans owned by those
in the "large farm" class. Before the reforms 6 percent of the owners held 65 percent of the land, whereas after the reform this same
6 percent held 43 percent of the land but in smaller average-size
holdings. The other 94 percent gained only an extra 22 percent of
the land; moreover, the absolute number of farmers in each group
rose rapidly.

A further limitation of the reform is that it did little to resolve
the problem of landless laborers.[6] Although the absolute number
declined after the reforms, there are now more landless laborers
than before the revolution. Farmers are almost exclusively smallholders, though their holdings are not as small as the pattern of
legal ownership indicates because many registered owners do not
work their land but lease it to other small owners. The difference
between the farmed units and registered farm titles is illustrated
in table 10-8, which shows that while 94.5 percent of the registered
titles were less than five feddans in size, only 83.4 percent of farmed
units were below this size.[7] These figures are somewhat dated but
are reliable enough to give a reasonable picture. For all practical
purposes the overwhelming proportion of the 2 million Egyptian farmers work units of less than three feddans. This pattern of ownership
is fairly constant throughout the country, with no great regional
differences.

It is difficult to estimate total employment in the sector as well
as the utilization rate. Controversies abound, with analyses based
on obsolete and statistically inadequate data. It is starkly clear,
however, that there is, in the aggregate, a surplus of labor within
the sector. Even if all of Egypt's 6 million feddans of farmland were
planted in vegetables — the most labor intensive of all crops — at
full cropping intensity, excess manpower would exist. With 4
million farmers and laborers, each able to give 300 man-days a year,
a total of 1,200 million man-days would be available. With 6 million

6. Landless laborers are here defined as those farming either no land at all or
small plots from which only a minor fraction of their income is derived.

7. A farm title is a legal document of ownership. A farm unit or holding is the
decisionmaking entity regardless of type of ownership.

TABLE 10-8. DISTRIBUTION OF FARMED HOLDINGS, 1961, AND REGISTERED FARM TITLES, 1965

Size of holding	Farmers or owners Thousands	Percent	Total area Thousands of feddans	Percent	Average holding size (feddans)
Farmed holdings					
Less than 5 feddans	1,411.5	83.4	2,429.2	40.6	1.72
5.1-10	175.6	10.4	1,088.1	18.2	6.2
10.1-20	57.8	3.5	720.1	12.0	12.5
20.1-50	35.9	2.1	673.3	11.3	18.8[a]
50.1-100	7.5	0.4	319.7	5.3	42.6
More than 100	3.8	0.2	751.8	12.8	198.0
Total	1,692.1	100.0	5,982.2	100.0	3.54
Registered farm titles					
Less than 5 feddans	3,033	94.5	3,693	57.1	1.22
5.1-10	78	2.4	614	9.5	7.87
10.1-20	61[b]	1.9	527	8.2	8.64[b]
20.1-50	29	0.9	815	12.6	28.1
50.1-100	6	0.2	392	6.1	65.3
More than 100	4	0.1	421	6.5	105.3
Total	3,211	100.0	6,462	100.0	2.01

a. An average size of 18.8 in the 20-50 group is obviously wrong and may be a translation error.
b. Robert Mabro considers that the number of owners in this class should be about 42,000 and the average size of holding should be about 12.55 feddans (The Egyptian Economy, 1952-1972 [Oxford: Clarendon Press, 1972]).
Source: Central Agency for Mobilization and Statistics.

feddans, all under labor-intensive vegetable production requiring 60 man-days per feddan for each of three crops a year, no more than 1,080 million man-days would be required. This does not include women and children, and most of the crops actually planted require considerably fewer man-days per feddan.[8] Admittedly, much of this surplus labor is engaged in public sector works, and many registered landowners lease out their land and do not work in the sector. In addition, the labor requirements at peak periods may be up to six times greater than they are at slack periods in the crop cycle. The limited evidence suggests a pattern of temporary labor shortages in some regions rather than an overall labor shortage throughout the year. Farm budgets support this view.

8. Some additional labor required to look after livestock and the like would be more than covered by women and children.

Data from the Ministry of Planning also support the view that the reported labor shortage in agriculture may be a function of its real wage rather than the number technically available. As shown below, the percentage of the work force in agriculture fell during the 1968-76 period while the absolute numbers rose:

	1968	1969	1970	1971	1972	1973	1974	1975	1976
Percentage of total work force in agriculture	50	49	48	46	46	46	45	44	43
Number of adult workers (thousands)	3,867	3,964	4,048	4,056	4,094	4,163	4,153	4,217	4,223

Within the limitations of these data, there seems not to have been a mass exodus of workers from the sector as a whole. Those leaving the countryside for industry, education, military service, and work in other lands seem to have done little more than ease the pressure on farm jobs aggravated by natural increases in rural populations. Changes in cropping intensity and land area have also been of marginal help. Pockets of labor shortage are to be expected, however, since wages in the sector are, on average, one-third those in other sectors. These shortages are seen in areas closest to alternative job opportunities or to sources of income transfers, that is, in cities or the poorest farm districts. The Ministry of Planning estimates that the average annual wage in 1976 for the farm sector was LE107. At LE0.5 per man-day, this could represent 214 days worked a year or 107 days a year at LE1 a day plus off-farm income. This suggests that while labor may be tight in particular areas, there is not a serious shortage in agriculture or in the economy as a whole. Other sectors might provide labor to agriculture if conditions were different.

Two approaches are possible. One is to adjust wages to encourage labor mobility among regions and sectors in accordance with its marginal productivity. This would need to be done in the context of output price adjustments. The other is simply to use labor-substituting inputs in districts of labor shortages. Such mechanization is occurring rapidly. With serious distortions in the relative price ratios of labor and capital, however, a policy of rapid mechanization could lead to an economically and socially undesirable mix of labor and capital. Pressure for rapid mechanization in what is essentially a labor surplus economy is now apparent. But the labor surplus is not readily observable because the policy of guaranteed jobs and consumption subsidies decreases the incentive to work at low-paid, low-status farm work. In either case, the wage bears no relation to the social value of the marginal product.

These considerations are far from simple academic exercises. When surplus labor is rapidly moving out of agriculture, causing a labor constraint at harvest time, a conventional approach to the goal of reasonably full employment throughout the year would be rapid mechanization. With considerable structural unemployment, however, indiscriminate mechanization would have serious consequences, and alternative ways of spreading the peak period for labor or improving supply mobility are needed. The employment situation, with its seasonal patterns, needs to be studied carefully in order to develop an appropriate mechanization policy.

A study of wage data for cotton in 1975, by governorate, indicates that the closer the region is to Cairo, the higher the wages. It is reasonable to expect a temporary labor shortage during the peak harvest period when the farm is close to a city in which highly subsidized urban wage rates and relatively effective income transfer mechanisms exist. In such cases the wage rate may well reflect the marginal product of labor; in other areas the wage rate might be higher than the marginal product as a result of institutional forces or minimum wage laws.

As should be clear from this discussion, the effects of government incomes policies have not been consistent and are often conflicting. The heavy implicit net rate of taxation on agricultural incomes has kept them substantially below the level of urban incomes. The burden of resource transfers out of agriculture has fallen heaviest on farmers growing traditional crops, such as cotton. Regional imbalances in incomes have also occurred as a result of the effects of controlled area allocations on cropping patterns. Real wage rates in agriculture have fallen faster than the average; in 1974 they were about one-third the overall rates. The size of large farms was reduced by the land reform and conditions of tenancy were improved, but the average farm size also became smaller owing to population growth, and the skew in the distribution remained. All of this points to the need for a carefully developed and coherent mechanization policy that takes account of employment.

INVESTMENT

Investment policy and its repercussions can be traced back to two major decisions in the late 1950s and early 1960s: development strategy would be based on public investment, largely directed toward industry, particularly heavy industry; and massive investment would be undertaken in the Aswan High Dam.

As a consequence of the stress on the industrial sector, investment in agriculture has declined as a proportion of total investment — the share of agriculture, irrigation, and drainage in total public sector investment fell from about 25 percent in the mid-1960s to an estimated 7 percent in 1975.[9] When the figures are adjusted for inflation, it is evident that the drop was also substantial in real terms. Of the amounts invested in agriculture, the share of the private sector was small — some estimates place it at only LE2 million to LE3 million in the mid-1970s, or about 4 percent of gross fixed investment.[10] If this estimate is even remotely correct, it has disturbing implications because an investment of that size would hardly be sufficient to maintain the private capital stock. Most of it would have to come from large farmers who were able to expand production through more flexible combinations of crops.[11]

There appear to be strong reasons for the unwillingness of the private sector to invest heavily in general agriculture. The private sector currently produces about 97 percent of gross agricultural income.[12] Most of the private investment is going into fruit, vegetable, and animal production where the returns are higher, while most of the value of production is in field crops, which are taxed more heavily. Thus another unfortunate result of the price policy appears to have been a weakening of private incentive to invest in agriculture.

The decline in private investment has not been made up by public investment. Moreover, public investment has been directed largely toward land reclamation, irrigation, and drainage projects, leaving little for general agriculture (table 10-9). The new lands have been receiving the largest, if decreasing, share of the funds — averaging about 40 to 60 percent of the total until 1972 — although they contribute only about 2 percent of production. Investment is now necessary for drainage of the old lands, about 70 percent of which are waterlogged and saline, conditions aggravated by the changeover from basin to perennial irrigation.[13] The drainage program is for restoration and deferred maintenance to prevent further declines in production and to restore capacity to previous levels rather than to provide net increments to productivity. Despite the assistance provided by the World Bank, USAID, and other donors, and the stated high priority assigned by the government to the drainage

9. Ministry of Planning, Follow-up Report for the 1975 Plan (Cairo, 1976).

10. National Bank of Egypt, Economic Bulletin.

11. No estimate is available of on-farm investment by the small farmer, which in the case of buffalo and cattle could be considerable. Studies elsewhere on voluntary saving by small farmers show that their savings rate can be considerable. Marcia L. Ong, Dale W. Adams, and I. J. Singh calculate an average propensity to save of 0.12-0.28 and a marginal propensity to save of 0.35-0.69 for Taiwan between 1960 and 1970 ("Voluntary Rural Savings Capacities in Taiwan, 1960-70," American Journal of Agricultural Economics, vol. 58, no. 3 [August 1976], pp. 578-82).

12. National Bank of Egypt, Economic Bulletin.

13. United Nations Food and Agriculture Organization (FAO), Perspective on Egyptian Agriculture (Rome, 1973).

TABLE 10-9. PERCENTAGE OF TOTAL
AGRICULTURAL SECTOR INVESTMENTS
BY MAJOR CATEGORY, 1968-75
(percent)

Category	1968	1969	1971	1972	1975
Agricultural services	5.8	8.0	11.7	3.2	2.7
Land reclamation and associated activities	72.0	69.7	61.1	46.0	36.6
Drainage	8.8	9.0	11.3	23.9	29.2
Public sector poultry	0.7	0.8	5.0	11.3	21.2

Source: Ministry of Planning data.

program, investment has been inadequate to meet urgent needs.
Drainage projects have been seriously delayed by administrative constraints (especially a shortage of engineering staff), the capability
of the local civil works-contracting industry, and by lack of local
funds, although such funds were available for projects in the new
lands.

An important share of agricultural investment went to the Aswan
High Dam, which brought perennial irrigation to an additional 0.7
million feddans of the old lands (4.8 million of the 5.5 million feddans were already under perennial irrigation before construction).
The planners estimated that the dam could bring another 1.2 million feddans under cultivation, and by 1970 about 805,000 feddans
of new lands (desert, swamps, and saline soils) had been treated.
Production effects were to include shifts from flood-season maize
to higher-yielding summer maize, from cotton to higher-value sugarcane in Upper Egypt, and from wheat to rice in the Delta (see table 10-10). Crop and property damage from floods was eliminated.
With the quantum increase in the capacity of the irrigation system
and with no means to control usage, however, the outmoded drainage
system was unable to handle the amount of water farmers put on
their land. Another adverse consequence is that the high cost of
the dam fixed the pattern of public investment and closed major development options. Choices of strategy were, and to a considerable
extent still are, limited by the need to reap the full benefits of the
original investment in the High Dam and to invest heavily in drainage
works. This need explains much of the pattern of public investment in the sector and the shortage of funds for other agricultural purposes.

One of the major justifications for this loss of alternative development opportunities was the dam's ability to bring extra land into
production. About 900,000 feddans of extra land are being reclaimed.
Of this, 700,000 feddans are allocated for cultivation and are expected to produce 5 percent of total agricultural output by 1980. The
costs have turned out to be higher, the potential lower, and gestation periods longer than expected. In 1960 the full cost of bringing

TABLE 10-10.   CROPPING CHANGES
SINCE COMPLETION OF THE
ASWAN HIGH DAM
(thousands of feddans)

Crop	1952	1971
Summer maize	27	1,171
Nili maize	1,677	351
Sugarcane	92	193
Rice	545	1,140

Source: Ministry of Agriculture.

land into production was estimated at LE190 per feddan; it is now
LE600 to LE1,000 per feddan. Moreover, much of the reclaimed
land is of poor quality. One report describes 76 percent of the new
lands as "shallow to rock; others covered with windblown sand having a high water table in an unirrigated state; some are coarse tex-
tured, gravelly and loamy sands that will not use irrigation water
efficiently. These soils are not good and cannot be expected to give
returns on inputs comparable to those from old lands."[14]   Instead
of the three to five years initially planned, it took about fifteen years
of capital absorption before enough was earned to cover even operating expenses.

Egypt's current agricultural strategy seems in need of serious
modification, especially its emphasis on, and investment in, new
lands. The new lands can make a contribution once the needs of the
old lands are adequately met. Otherwise the rate of increase in total production will drop as the smaller net increments from the new
lands displace the actual and potentially larger ones from the old.
Many of the problems with the new lands have arisen because there
has been no well-structured basic agronomic research program.
Experiments with pilot farms would have provided the basis for proper technical, economic, and financial analyses and led to potentially
viable operations. Even the heavy government investment has not
been enough to permit full implementation of the projects that were
started. In retrospect, it is easy to understand the dilemma of the
Egyptian planners. Faced with the urgent problem of land shortages,
they chose the high-risk high-payoff option of trying to develop
900,000 feddans in a short period rather than the time-consuming,
safer strategy of gradual expansion. Population growth and the
attendant political compulsions are such that the 1978-82 five-
year plan intends to continue large-scale expansion despite this
experience.

14. FAO, Perspective Report, Land and Water Development and Use (Rome,
1973), p. 6.

FOOD PRODUCTION AND CONSUMPTION

Egypt is a net importer of wheat, flour, cooking oil, sugar, frozen beef, and mutton. With a population growth rate of up to 2.5 percent a year, changing patterns of consumption, and a lagging growth rate of food production, food supplies have deteriorated. Since the early 1950s, wheat production has grown at 2.3 percent a year, maize at 2.6 percent, and rice at 4.5 percent. From 1965 to 1975 fruit, vegetable, and meat production rose rapidly, generally going to the urban areas where effective demand is stronger. The government's revenues from implicit taxes on agriculture and export duties were used partly to raise standards of living through food subsidies, and these have affected consumption patterns. The gap between food demand and supply began to widen, particularly for those items with a high income elasticity of demand — for example, fruits, vegetables, and meat — and since price and production policies discouraged field crops, supplies of highly income-elastic crops expanded at the expense of others.

Corn, wheat, barley, rice, sorghum, and millet are the principal cereals grown (see chapter 9). Corn, the staple food of the fellahin, is the most important. Domestic wheat supplies only slightly more than half of local demand. Rice is particularly popular in urban areas but is mainly a profitable export item. Sorghum and millet substitute for corn in Upper Egypt rural diets while barley often substitutes for wheat. Grain legumes are second in importance to cereals, and broad beans, lentils, chickpeas, lima beans, haricot, and cowpeas are the most common. Fenugreek is used in baking corn bread,. the main component of the rural diet, and peanuts and sesame are used for cooking oil. Vegetables are traditionally a small item of consumption in rural areas while poultry, meat, and eggs serve mainly as cash products to meet debt payments and operating expenses of farmers. Butter and cheese are consumed locally. The tenant farmer often uses his wheat crop in payment of rent and grows maize for his family's needs and berseem for his animals, buying back enough wheat for special feast days.

The major determinants of consumer demand are increased population, changes in consumption patterns, and income changes. Egypt's population is expected to grow, at least in the short run, at not less than 2 to 3 percent a year, with urban areas experiencing a 3 to 4 percent average annual increase, leaving a net increase in rural population of at least 1 percent a year. The United Nations Food and Agriculture Organization (FAO) calculates that the calorie supply for urban areas of Egypt met 98 percent of requirements in 1970, while the figure for rural areas was 90 percent.[15] Data from the Ministry of Agriculture show that the national per capita supply

15. FAO, Perspective Report on Food Supplies and Nutrition (Rome, 1973).

TABLE 10-11. CONSUMPTION OF STAPLE
FOODS
(thousands of tons)

Item	Actual 1976	Forecast 1980	Absolute increase
Wheat	4,808	5,843	1,035
Flour	738	897	159
Maize	3,996	4,438	442
Rice	1,404	1,643	239
Meat and chicken	520	628	108

Source: Ministry of Planning.

of calories has declined from 2,701 a day in 1965-66 to 2,552 a day
in 1972-73. This reflects food shortages, especially among the poor,
and at least in rural areas these shortages become more acute at
certain seasons of the year. Similarly, the low income levels, the
skewed income distribution, and the high cost of plant and animal
protein prevent adequate supplies of protein from reaching the majority of people. The FAO report estimates, however, that dietary
deficiencies in calories are more serious than those in proteins.
This underlines the need for a policy that stimulates grain production even if it were at the expense of berseem and meat.

It is difficult to project food demands with any real accuracy,
but certain magnitudes and directions can be gauged. At the projected growth rate, the population would reach 47 million by 1985,
about 26 million of which is likely to live in urban areas. As the
population becomes more urbanized, demand will increase for all
food, especially wheat and meat. With a relatively fixed area of
arable land and structural problems limiting technological progress,
the bulk of the deficit will have to be met by imports. The International Food Policy Research Institute projected a 2.4 percent growth
rate for food-crop production in the long run, on the basis of past
performance.[16] But it estimated that a 5 percent growth rate in
production would be needed to satisfy demand.

The Ministry of Planning estimated that more than a million
extra tons of wheat and over half a million extra tons of rice and
maize would be needed in 1980 as well as another 108,000 tons of
meat (see table 10-11). This was expected to increase demand for
imports not only of food but also of inputs, thus taxing Egypt's productive resources to the full. During the 1970s per capita grain production fell about 4 percent while per capita consumption as a whole
rose by almost 9 percent. This has resulted in a widening food-
grain gap from 61.9 kilograms per capita in 1970-71 to 97.2 kilograms per capita by 1975-76 (see table 10-12). Unless this trend

16. Food and Investment Requirements of Food Deficit Developing Countries: A
Progress Report (FPI/77/1, Washington, D.C., July 8, 1977), p. 8.

TABLE 10-12.   FOOD-GRAIN DEFICIT, 1969-72 TO 1976-77
(kilograms)

Food grain per capita	1969- 72[a]	1970- 71	1971- 72	1972- 73	1973- 74	1974- 75	1975- 76	1976- 77
Production	194.7	196.2	196.8	188.0	190.1	187.3	184.0	188.0
Consumption	253.6	258.1	262.2	269.2	285.7	286.4	281.2	n.a.
Deficit	58.9	61.9	69.4	81.2	95.6	99.1	97.2	n.a.

n.a.   Not available.
a.   Figures are a two-year average.
Source: International Food Policy Research Institute, Recent and Prospective Development in Food Consumption: Some Policy Issues (Washington, D.C., July 1977), tables 2 and 4.

can be contained, this too will increase pressure on the balance of payments.

BALANCE OF AGRICULTURAL TRADE

The early postrevolutionary industrailization drive and the accompanying program of import substitution were attempts to minimize the domestic effects of external factors over which Egypt had little control, particularly foreign exchange flows of trade balances and capital movements. Economic policy for agriculture has also been directed toward these foreign exchange objectives. In 1965 and 1970 agriculture accounted for about 87 percent of the value of total commodity exports, but a decline began in 1972 and the share slipped to 75 percent by 1975. In current prices, the value of agricultural exports rose 105 percent during these ten years whereas the value of other exports rose 270 percent.

Of greater interest are the price and quantity effects for the dominant agricultural exports, seed cotton, rice, and cotton yarn. All of these showed strong growth in current prices. In constant prices, however, the value of cotton exports declined 12 percent by 1970, then a further 19.5 percent by 1974 because of the difference in quantity owing to declining production, rising domestic consumption, and increasing processing before exporting. The value of rice exports in constant prices rose about 95 percent by 1970, then declined 79 percent by 1974 as domestic consumption rose. Similarly, the value of cotton yarn exports in constant prices declined between 1970 and 1974 even though it rose during the 1965-70 period. The important point is that over the ten-year period the price of these exports rose significantly, but Egypt was unable to take advantage of it because the growth in domestic consumption outpaced that in production and reduced the exportable surplus.

Imports

Increases in the quantity and value of agricultural imports far outstripped the increases in quantity and value of exports. Imports

were mainly basic foodstuffs, which supplemented domestic shortfalls in production, especially of wheat and flour. Imports of wheat
grain-equivalent (wheat and flour) rose from about 1.977 million
tons in 1964-65 to nearly 4 million tons in 1976-77. Wheat import
quantities and values differ among sources of data primarily because under "temporary admissions" procedures customs data seriously underrecord imports.

It appears that between 1973 and 1974 imports of wheat grain-
equivalent rose 4.6 percent and a further 24 percent between 1974
and 1975. Because of a fall in the average price from LE112 a ton
in 1974 to LE88 a ton in 1975, however, the value of grain-equivalent
imports was reduced from the high of LE330 million in 1974 to LE320
million in 1975 (table 10-13). Both the value of wheat imports and that
of all food imports as a percentage of total imports fell over the period.
Table 10-14 shows that between 1973 and 1974 about 4.5 percent of the
50 percent increase in the value of wheat imports was owing to changes
in quantity and the other 45.5 percent to price change. Between
1974 and 1975 the 3 percent decline in the total value of wheat imports reflected a 24 percent increase in the quantity.

Exports

At the same time, Egypt's ability to use its own exports to finance
wheat imports was being eroded because the rise in the price of its

TABLE 10-13. WHEAT IMPORTS, 1973-76

Item	1973	1974	1975	1976[a]
Wheat grain (millions of tons)	2.23	2.63	2.81	2.90
Flour (millions of tons)	0.43	0.28	0.62	0.62
Grain-equivalent[b] (millions of tons)	2.80	2.93	3.63	3.72
Value of grain-equivalent (millions of Egyptian pounds c.i.f.)	220.00	330.00	320.00	256.10
Total value of all imports (millions of Egyptian pounds)	658.00	1,364.00	1,761.00	1,646.00
Grain-equivalent imports as a percentage of all imports[c]	33.00	24.10	18.10	15.51
Average price per ton (Egyptian pounds)	78.60	112.00	88.00	69.00
Domestic production (millions of tons)	1.83	1.88	2.03	1.96
Total consumption (millions of tons)	4.64	4.81	5.66	5.68

a. Budgeted quotas.
b. The conversion factor for wheat grain to flour is 75 percent. Grain-
equivalent is the sum of grain imported as grain plus the amount of grain
from which the flour imported was obtained.
c. "All imports" refers to all food and nonfood commodities.
Source: Ministry of Supply.

TABLE 10-14. PRICE AND QUANTITY
EFFECT ON IMPORT VALUE
OF WHEAT, 1973-76

(value in millions of Egyptian pounds)

Item	1973	1974	1975	1976
Value (current price)	220	330	320	256
Total difference	—	110	-10	-64
Percent change	5	50	-3	-20
Value (1973 price)	220	230	285	272
Difference owing to quantity	—	10	55	7
Percent change	—	4.5	24.0	2.4
Price effect[a]	—	100	-65	-71
Percent change	—	45.5	-27.0	-22.0

a. Price effect is the total difference minus the quantity difference.
Source: Computed from table 10-13.

main export, raw cotton, was not keeping pace with the increase in
wheat prices. Table 10-15 shows the change in terms of trade between cotton and wheat. The capability of cotton exports to finance
wheat imports has fallen dramatically — from 21 tons of wheat per
ton of Menoufi extralong-staple cotton in 1969 to 9.4 tons of wheat
in 1975, and from 16.4 tons of wheat per ton of Giza 67 long-staple
cotton in 1969 to 7.7 tons of wheat in 1975.

In summary, although agricultural production (primarily cotton)
has provided Egypt with most of its foreign exchange in the past,
the lagging growth of the sector has resulted in an increasing burden of food-grain imports. This has occurred at a time when the
terms of trade of cotton exports to wheat imports have been deteriorating with the steady fall of both cotton and wheat production.

TABLE 10-15. TERMS OF TRADE FOR COTTON
AND WHEAT, 1969-70 TO 1975-76

(Egyptian pounds)

Item	1969-70	1973-74	1974-75	1975-76
Wheat price (c.i.f. a ton)	25	79	112	88
Cotton price (f.o.b. a ton)				
Menoufi (extralong)	530	1,200	1,068	829
Giza 67 (long)	410	1,100	844	677
Menoufi/Wheat	21.0	15.0	9.5	9.4
Giza 67/Wheat	16.4	14.0	7.5	7.7

Source: Ministry of Supply and Technical Secretariat for Cotton Sector.

TECHNOLOGICAL CHANGE

The major changes in <u>technique</u> have used more inputs to gain additional output without affecting the input-output relation. These changes include increased cropping intensity as a result of the shift from basin to perennial irrigation; the switch from Nili-season maize to summer season, which yielded 50 percent increases as water became available from the Aswan High Dam in 1964-65; the rapid expansion in the use of inorganic fertilizers; and the extension of the irrigation network into the marginal soils of the new lands. In contrast, the major changes in <u>technology</u> have involved shifts in the production function to get more output from the same combination of factors. These changes include the development and adoption of Nadha rice, which yielded a 33 percent increase; the release of new cotton varieties in the early 1960s; the rapid acceptance and subsequent rejection of HYV wheat;[17] and the pooling of fragmented holdings within the cooperative system, while individual smallholder ownership was maintained.

The gains have been impressive, but many of the present problems in agriculture are manifested in the rate of technological change. Because technological changes will be adopted only when the profit inducement is strong and the sociological environment is suitable, change may not occur for many reasons. Farmers may not know about the possibilities of change; profit expectations may not be worth the investment effort; incomes may be so low that no surplus is left for investment; extrasectoral constraints — such as the ability to absorb displaced farm labor — may make the social consequences of change unacceptable; or suitable technologies may not be developed. However appealing the technology, forcing it into a system where technological changes are not evolving does not seem to have been successful. For example, family settlements in the new lands failed because the technology developed was not suitable for small farmers, and HYV wheat has been rejected because it was developed without the ability to resist rust or grain shredding. In the case of hybrid maize, the varieties did not yield their potential because farmers continued stripping leaves from the growing plants to feed livestock, a failure coupled with the issue of mechanization.

The basic problem is to increase the absorptive capacity of farmers and their willingness to change. The profit opportunities must be sufficiently enticing and the farmers must have some investable savings or credit. Equally important is the necessity for applied research to find and adapt the appropriate technology and for an extension system capable of delivering the message coherently. This will require a major strengthening of research facilities as well as substantial improvements in the extension services.

17. A high-yielding variety (HYV) of Mexican short-straw wheat (see table 9-6).

PROSPECTS FOR AGRICULTURE

Total agricultural production needs to grow at around 4 percent a year initially to feed a population growing at 2.3 percent, to close the food supply deficit, and to contribute resources for the development of other sectors. Because of the shortage of arable land, most of the production growth will have to come from yield increases, but a yield increase of about 2 percent a year seems the maximum that can be expected for long-run sustained growth (see chapter 9). The inescapable conclusion is that steady technological advances are necessary but that they are not sufficient in themselves to permit the planned rate of growth of 4.5 percent a year. Major institutional and policy changes are also needed for this purpose (see below). Unfortunately, the 1978-82 five-year plan proposes no more than marginal adjustment of the present system and continues to force partial technological changes. Whether the plan targets will actually be achieved will depend on basic policy changes and developments outside the sector that have not been adequately treated in the plan. Most of the sector's current problems are almost identical to those discussed in Egypt's official yearbooks in 1959 and 1960, however, and the solutions currently proposed in the plan are also almost the same.[18]

International Specialization and Comparative Advantage

Egypt has had a long history of international specialization and still accounts for 60 percent of world trade in extralong-staple cotton and 40 percent of trade in long-staple cotton. The quantity available for export is declining, however, as producers do not see sufficient private profit in the farm-gate prices. In the past, policy has tended to widen the divergence between social and private profit. Whether marginal changes in production should be directed toward import substitution or increased exports, and how to give farmers the incentive to follow the policy, are difficult matters to settle, particularly when faced with the recent volatile behavior of world markets and the need to satisfy multiple objectives other than maximizing economic growth. The broader question is whether to pursue economic development through agriculture or industry. One way to approach the problem is to calculate the economic cost of producing goods that compete for resources both within and between sectors. Those sectors or subsectors with the lowest economic cost per unit of revenue should be encouraged by means of the producer price, taxation, and exchange rate system. It must be stressed, however, that such analyses of comparative advantage give only partial guidance for resource allocation.

18. United Arab Republic (UAR) Yearbook, 1959 and 1960 (Cairo: Information Department).

Egypt has a clear comparative advantage in the production of cotton and rice, its major export crops. Their value added at world prices is about twice their domestic resource cost, measured as an opportunity cost. For both wheat and maize, the domestic resource cost is slightly higher than the value added, and higher still for meat production using prime crop land. These findings agree with those of other analysts. Hansen and Nashashibi have calculated the economic cost of agricultural production and find it generally competitive.[19] For cotton production it took 29 piastres worth of resources valued at international prices in 1964 to earn 39.1 piastres (US$1.00) worth of output. By 1975 the cost had risen to 36 piastres at this exchange rate. The official exchange rate discriminates against cotton since at the parallel market rate it would earn 70 piastres at a cost of 43 piastres. In 1964 wheat cost more than it earned, and this is still the case at the higher exchange rate; at the lower exchange rate, while less competitive than cotton, wheat is economically worthwhile. Such an approach is partial and static, however, and is suitable as a first approximation only. Clearly, the inelastic demand for long-staple cotton affects the price and hence the domestic resource cost at every level of production.

The next question is whether the pricing and taxation system has encouraged production of those crops with the most potential for contributing to overall growth. Long-run protection has discriminated against agriculture in general and the most competitive crops in particular. Cotton and rice have been taxed at a 40 percent rate whereas noncompetitive meat has been protected at 50 to 100 percent. Wheat and maize fall midway between these groups. Fruits and vegetables are untaxed. As would be expected, resources are going into meat, berseem, and horticulture and out of cotton and rice. Although it seems that the optimal tax rate has been passed, there is an urgent need for a complete reorganization of the farm tax structure. Many of the current fiscal arrangements were made under circumstances quite different from the present. This is not to deny the government's obligation to raise taxes in the sector but rather to reinforce the Ministry of Agriculture's position that tax reform is overdue.

A change in the structure of protection as well as the unification of exchange rates to favor those crops (and sectors) with a comparative advantage would induce farmers to select a cropping pattern that maximized both social and private profitability.[20] Calculating

19. Bent Hansen and Karim Nashashibi, Egypt: Foreign Trade Regimes and Economic Development (New York: National Bureau of Economic Research, 1975).

20. This topic is discussed in further detail by Kamil Hindy, "Short Note on Agricultural Prices and Subsidies in the Arab Republic of Egypt" (Cairo: Ministry of Agriculture, 1976). It is again stressed that comparative advantage should not be the only criterion for resource allocation, but it is a major consideration that should be identified explicitly.

the effects on government revenue is a complex matter, but on balance it should increase. For instance, a decrease in taxation revenue per unit of cotton should be less than the increase in revenue from greater production induced by higher farm-gate prices. Evidence of a significant supply response to relative price changes is the decline in cotton acreage. Fixed costs in agriculture should be taxed so as not to affect allocation of inputs and outputs. One example would be the land taxes, which no longer reflect current market rents. Clearly, a case exists for taxing some inputs to increase efficiency — such as charging for water to reduce usage in the presence of considerable drainage problems. Under the present structure of protection farmers are heavily subsidizing both government and consumers because they are receiving less than the economic value of their factors of production, which is mostly labor. The penalties have been highest in the export crops — cotton, rice, and onions — because they are the easiest to control.

Regional Specialization

Egypt's system of rotation, which is based on cotton, maintains the quality of the soil under conditions of limited agricultural development. As such, the system is effective. It provides food for humans and animals as well as cash to individual producers, no matter how small. Farmers are able to operate independently and do not have to rely on such supports as marketing and extension services and subsidies for purchased inputs. Their level of production, however, remains far below optimum. As agricultural systems develop, there is usually a move to regional specialization with a view to developing international trade. This leads to some dependence, but the gains from specialization increase profitability, provided more sophisticated support services are available.

Technically, there seems no reason why Egypt cannot begin to move from a fairly general system of rotation to a supervised system of regional monoculture, at least to the extent its technical services can support it. Rice is double-cropped continuously in other countries without adverse effects, and cotton is grown every year without deterioration of soil structure or fertility. Egypt's bottlenecks are institutional. The greatest potential for increased production lies in regional specialization, provided the price system is responsive and a modified monoculture can be successfully supported. Before this happens subsistence production must diminish, and this may increase the pressure for land consolidation and mechanization, thus aggravating the problem of rural unemployment. Ultimately, industry's inability to absorb labor from agriculture is a major constraint on agricultural production.

For the time being, it seems advisable to introduce regional specialization gradually, with continuous monitoring of soil conditions and plant growth as well as the effects on the welfare of the people. Already some regional specialization exists but only to the extent that different crops are rotated as one moves from south to north. The question comes down to the relative gains — both technical and social — from rotation in modern agriculture. In the short run, there is much to gain by having each farm grow only one crop in a given year of the rotation rather than the present system of growing some of everything each year.

RECOMMENDATIONS

To reduce the crippling burden of high food imports, a growth rate considerably above the current level of 1.6 percent a year is required if the situation is not to deteriorate further. Even more is needed if agriculture is to contribute capital transfers to other sectors. At the minimum, an annual growth rate of about 4 percent, at constant composition and prices, will need to be sustained in the 1980s, with the overall index of production increasing 50 percent during this period and per capita consumption held at constant levels.

To attain these growth rates, the sector will need major changes in technology, institutions, and policies, accompanied by complementary changes in related sectors. Not all these changes are likely in the near future, and there will be a lag between implementation and effect. It is possible, though, to group the problems according to their anticipated solutions — those with probable short- or medium-term solutions and those requiring a longer time or heavily constrained by the performance of the rest of the economy. Priorities, courses, and timetables can be set accordingly.

The major but by no means exhaustive groups of problems are listed in table 10-16. For short-term technical problems it is recommended that drainage, soil, and water management programs be accelerated. Regional specialization should be introduced on a trial basis and closely monitored in a single-crop system of rotation (for example, rice followed by rice rather than multicrop rotations and multipurpose crops). Land-use planning should be implemented to prevent urban encroachment. Longer-term recommendations for technical change include seeking ways to provide more animal feed in the summer, improve disease control, and reduce postharvest losses.

Institutional recommendations in the short term include the establishment of a field-oriented farm-management and economic service bureau within the Ministry of Agriculture to provide an unambiguous and relevant data base for planning at both the farm and sectoral levels. The technical extension services need to be upgraded, decentralized, and better equipped. The cooperative network should be reestablished as a genuine self-help system sensitive to farmers'

TABLE 10-16. MAJOR PROBLEMS IN THE AGRICULTURAL
SECTOR

Area	Short term	Long term
Technical	Drainage and irrigation Rotation Regional specialization Inputs Land-use planning	Food gap Disease control Postharvest losses
Institutional	Farm management services Extension services Cooperatives Decentralization	Farm size Farm fragmentation Land tenure Research Technological changes
Economic	Pricing, equity, and efficiency Investment Production Marketing	International specialization and comparative advantage
Intersectoral	Subsidies and consumption Taxation Statistical measurement	Labor productivity Linkage

needs as well as to national priorities. Solutions for most of the
longer-term problems (farm size, fragmentation of holdings, land
tenure and absentee ownership, and so forth) depend on factors outside the sector. All that can be recommended at this stage is that
these be realistically incorporated as constraints in planning.

A complete review of economic problems is needed to attain an
internally consistent set of measures directed toward a mutually
compatible set of objectives. This will require planners to specify
policy goals in detail, resolve policy conflicts, identify policy tradeoffs, and examine alternative policy instruments to see which achieve
most in relation to cost. Some recommendations are:

● Establish a consistent and explicit methodology to determine
which pattern of agriculture is socially worthwhile and to adjust
private profit incentives accordingly. Studies by the Department
of Agricultural Economics of the Ministry of Agriculture show that
at current prices social and private profit are widely divergent.
The methodology suggested for policy planning, programs, and projects is to estimate the social marginal value of inputs and outputs
(which generally means starting with international prices and making adjustments for policy purposes); to calculate the domestic resource costs of producing each crop and compare these costs with
the world price to indicate the direction of comparative advantage;
and to change effective rates of protection so that they pull resources

in that direction. Economic development can then proceed as rapidly as possible by consistently choosing policies and projects that contribute most to growth, stability, and equity at the least social cost.

● Make the decision whether the system of regulated prices for agricultural output should continue. Although price administration has achieved some first-round equity effects, it has been at the cost of serious resource misallocation. If major changes in price regulation are considered, special attention should be given to transitional problems.

● If administered prices are to continue, even in the short term, a major improvement is needed in the information base on which prices are set. Specifically required is a set of disaggregated, farm-level input-output data for all crops in all areas under various rotational schemes.

● Any regulation of output prices should deal with sets of prices rather than with single prices in isolation. For a farmer the output price is not so important as the profitability of a crop (or combination of crops) in relation to that of other crops (or combinations) that could be grown. The choice of crop is also determined by the consumption needs of the farm family and livestock. If price adjustments are envisaged, usually more than one price will need to be adjusted.

● Cost-plus pricing should not be adopted for small farmers because it can be an extremely arbitrary process. There are wide margins for unmeasurable errors that arise from the difficulties of imputing cash costs to uncosted factors (particularly in placing a cash value on family labor) and of realistically weighing cash inputs, which may vary greatly from farm to farm.

● Except in special cases, input subsidies in the form of low land taxes, low interest rates, free water, and the like should be abolished, and output prices should be set at levels and in ratios with one another that have some connection with the long-run moving average of world prices.

● If the sector is capable of generating a surplus for taxation, alternative means of appropriating this surplus (instead of price manipulation) should be examined. One method would be through fixed levies, which do not distort production in the way that unbalanced price manipulation does. The land tax might be increased and output prices allowed to rise.

● Investment policies should be reexamined, particularly with respect to the relative shares of public and private investment, which are at least partly determined by the effects of price policies on

rural incomes and savings. Past and proposed new land investments and their potential should be closely studied. Most of the
flexibility of sectoral development strategy is lost because of the
continuation of projects with very long gestation periods. In some
cases, it might be better simply to drop an uncompleted project if
further expenditures cannot reasonably be expected to be recovered.

• Production policy should consider three major questions: (1)
whether complex rotations need to be maintained countrywide if regional crop specialization can be supported by technical and economic services; (2) whether quota allocations through the cooperative
run counter to price policy; and (3) whether current price controls
over food crops, but not over meat and berseem, conflict with the
aims of production policy by encouraging berseem and meat at the
expense of food crops.

• As an alternative to the cooperative monopoly for marketing
inputs and outputs at the farm level, a system, such as supervised
private traders, should be considered to induce some competition.

In the area of intersectoral problems it is recommended, first,
that the package of consumer subsidies be reexamined. Although
they are currently financed in part by low producer prices, the two
need not be connected in this manner. Second, effective ways of
stimulating other sectors should be sought to absorb labor from
agriculture in order to raise productivity levels within the sector.
Third, industry should develop strong backward and forward linkages with agriculture, which means that farm incomes must be
raised to increase purchasing power.

Simplistic suggestions about what to produce at what prices are
clearly inappropriate. The overriding need is to develop an effective three-way communication among the farmers, technical and
economic analysts, and national decisionmakers in order to make
reliable judgments about what is happening and why, and what to do
about explicit social needs. Since past controls have not prevented
farmers from responding to price signals, it would seem that prices
still have an integral role in a long-term development program in
agriculture.

The basic problems of Egyptian agriculture stem from shortcomings in sectoral management and macroeconomic policies. An irres-
olute approach to correcting these deficiencies could vitiate the recommendations given here. For instance, reequipping the extension
service would have limited success if the service were to continue
as a depository of surplus university graduates who were guaranteed
jobs under the full-employment policy. More fundamentally, as long
as the multitude of controls continues, agriculture will remain unattractive to investors. For many years to come, the foundation of
Egypt's economy will be the soil of the old lands. If ways are found
to make the best use of this vital resource, much else — and not only
in the agricultural sector — would follow.

11
Industrial Development

Industry has become a large and significant sector of the Egyptian economy. The share in GDP of manufacturing and mining has increased from an estimated 9 percent in 1946 to about 24 percent in 1976. Industry currently employs more than a million persons, that is, some 13 percent of the civilian labor force. The share of industry in total exports has also rapidly increased from 6-8 percent in 1952-54 to 40 percent in 1978. Because of its weight in the economic structure, the contribution of industry to GDP growth has become substantial. From 1965 to 1978 industry may have contributed more than 25 percent of the increment in real GDP. Because of Egypt's population density and limits on agricultural growth, industrial growth is and must be a priority goal of national development policy.

Although industry has been growing, and upturns and downturns in industrial output have tended to correspond to similar, though less sharp, fluctuations in GDP, it is not yet a leading sector. Linkage between Egyptian industry and other sectors of the economy are not particularly strong yet. Industry buys cotton and food products but does not seem to induce much growth in the agricultural sector by demands for increased quantities, qualitative improvements, and product diversification. Nor does domestic industry supply agriculture with new inputs adapted to Egyptian conditions. To qualify as a "leading sector," industry must induce or transmit growth elsewhere in the economy, develop new and strong backward and forward linkages, generate technical progress, and thus benefit sectors that purchase manufactured inputs. There has been some transmission of growth to mining and certain services and some trade creation with these sectors, but not very much.

Egyptian industrialization has tended to be inward-looking. Since 1930 the dominant feature of industrialization has been import substitution, a characteristic shared with most developing countries. This pattern has prevailed in Egypt under a variety of economic systems: free private enterprise between 1930 and the early 1950s, the mixed system of the 1950s, and the planned socialist economy

233

of the 1960s and early 1970s. It is too soon to judge whether the liberalization measures of 1973 and the opening up of the economy to foreign investors will succeed in changing the industrial pattern from import substitution to export orientation because the transition between these patterns is likely to take years.

Import substitution is generally characterized by the rapid emergence of a sector producing consumer durables. In Egypt the production of consumer durables was introduced in the late 1950s and, though growing, has not yet become significant. Instead, the industrial structure is dominated by the production of basic consumer goods (textiles, shoes, food, beverages, and cigarettes) and essential intermediates (building materials, fertilizer, chemicals, paper, petroleum products, and some metals) for the domestic market. The capital goods industry — machinery, tools, implements — is small. The middle stage of an import-substitution process is usually characterized by a declining but still dominant share of consumer goods, an expanding share of intermediates, and a very small share of capital goods.

An appraisal of industrialization in Egypt must consider that industry, despite its long but interrupted history, is still young. It must allow for external circumstances — the defense burden, for example — which have been responsible for the deterioration of performance. For a balanced appraisal of performance, factors other than allocative efficiency must be considered. Output and productivity growth, externalities in the form of skill formation, development of new institutions, and contributions to employment are other important elements. Egyptian industrialization may have been inefficient, but there were also periods of significant productivity growth. Not surprisingly, these periods were free from the interference of wars or of too heavy a military burden. Industrialization in Egypt as elsewhere has yielded external benefits, contributing to incomes, jobs, and skills.

HISTORICAL BACKGROUND

Egyptian industrialization began at the time of Muhammad Ali (1820-40). Several lessons relevant to present issues of industrialization may be drawn from this distant but important episode. The first lesson is that industrialization presupposes a certain degree of prior development: some skills and resources must be available and some institutional, administrative, and transport infrastructure must be present. It is possible to argue that some of the projects implemented in the past — for example, the iron and steel plant, the military aircraft factory, the car assembly lines — were undertaken prematurely. In the earlier era, failure led to closure; in modern times, failure is less conspicuous but more costly.

Because governments are reluctant to close down factories, they continue producing at high costs and with severe underutilization of capacity.

The second lesson is that because tariffs can be used to close the domestic market to competing imports, they remain a powerful instrument for implanting infant industry, despite the well-known costs and the theoretical superiority of subsidies. The third lesson relates to repetitions in the pattern of industrialization. Textile mills dominated the manufacturing sector under Muhammad Ali as they dominate it today. Food processing was important then as now. Great attention was also given to foundries, wood and metal workshops, and arsenals — the equivalent of the intermediate goods sector in modern industry.

Attempts were indeed made in the late 1890s and early 1900s to set up a modern textile industry, but by and large they failed. The British imposed an 8 percent duty on domestic textiles to countervail the 8 percent uniform ad valorem tariff. The policy was designed to shield British textiles from potential Egyptian competition in the export market, and it wholly ignored the case for moderate protection of infant industries. In practice, the textile industry was subjected to negative effective protection because some of its inputs were necessarily imported (or were domestic tradables) and hence affected directly or indirectly by the 8 percent tariff.

It would seem that Egypt earlier had no immediate comparative advantages in industries other than building materials, beverages, tobacco, a few food products, soap, two or three chemical products, and perhaps petroleum refining.[1] The question is, Have things changed much in the intervening years and, if so, in which direction? It would also seem that Egypt did not have a clear advantage in textiles, which became the dominant industry in the manufacturing structure only when afforded protection. The moot questions are whether the textile industry was merely in need of temporary protection during a relatively short stage of infancy, or whether it suffers from a fundamental lack of comparative advantages.

One disadvantage is that the high-quality Egyptian cotton is an expensive input for the production of cheap and low-grade products such as coarse yarn and grey or thick fabrics. But Egypt does have the advantages of low labor costs, the availability of medium- and long-staple cotton, and an established textile industry. Because of the deterioration in the physical facilities since nationalization, however, the overemployment in the textile mills, and, more important, the failure to develop efficient management and a skilled labor supply, Egypt may have jeopardized this comparative advantage. At any rate, high-quality production of textiles from high-

1. In the early days of the petroleum industry, it was economically advantageous to refine at the oil fields.

quality cotton has not been achieved. Underspinning of the long-staple cotton, prevalent before 1970, was probably not as uneconomical as often alleged because of its high international price elasticity. At present, when exports may be constrained by increased local demand, underspinning may be a problem, however. This would be minimized by introducing the capacity for cotton-polyester blends in new projects and importing short-staple cotton.

It is difficult to quantify industrial growth in the 1930s, and the judgment that development was rapid is based on indirect evidence. Import-substituting industrialization had proceeded for barely ten years when World War II broke out. The disruption of foreign trade closed domestic markets to competition, but it also prevented Egyptian industry from importing equipment and spare parts necessary for new investment and the replacement of worn-out machinery. Thus the development of industry during the war was uneven: some sectors benefited, others were retarded, and yet others struggled with varying degrees of success to meet new demands with little means.

The war created conditions for the resumption of industrialization in 1945. Many firms had made significant profits and had retained large liquid balances, which they were able to use after the war for financing new investments. The Allied armies employed and trained a work force of 100,000 to 200,000 men in various plants and workshops. Thus, a large pool of skilled workers and foremen became available to industry. Entrepreneurial talent also emerged in response to import shortages. There was significant human capital accumulation and financial resources were built up, but the physical stocks of machinery and goods were run down. The experience of the war, following so closely the Great Depression, reinforced the case for import-substituting industrialization. During the war entrepreneurs and capitalists acquired a better knowledge about the demands of the market; they learned from direct experience that certain goods could be produced by domestic industry; they discovered which domestic goods, in which quantity and quality, could be absorbed by a market closed to imports. For all intents and purposes, it can be said that modern industrialization in Egypt had a new and significant beginning soon after the end of World War II.

GROWTH OF INDUSTRIAL OUTPUT

Much industrialization has taken place in Egypt since 1945, though at an uneven pace. This is observable in the increased share of industry in GDP at the expense of that of agriculture (table 11-1). These structural changes took place throughout 1945-75, despite the different economic systems that divide this period into two distinct phases.

TABLE 11-1.   CONTRIBUTION OF INDUSTRY
TO GDP AT CONSTANT PRICES
(millions of Egyptian pounds)

Year	Industry in GDP	Index	Annual increase (percent)
At constant 1954 prices			
1945	91	100.0	—
1946	92	101.1	1.1
1947	101	111.0	9.8
1948	113	124.2	11.9
1949	126	138.5	11.5
1950	133	146.1	5.6
1951	132	145.0	-0.8
1952	132	145.0	0
1953	134	147.2	1.5
1954	146	160.4	8.9
1952-53	140	100.0	—
1953-54	143	102.1	2.1
1954-55	152	108.6	6.3
1955-56	163	116.4	7.2
1956-57	174	124.3	6.7
1957-58	190	135.7	9.2
1958-59	202	144.3	6.3
1959-60	213	152.1	5.4
At constant 1959-60 factor costs			
1959-60	256.3	100.0	—
1960-61	285.6	111.4	11.4
1961-62	309.9	120.9	8.5
1962-63	329.2	128.4	6.2
1963-64	369.6	144.2	12.3
1964-65	385.0	150.2	4.1
1965-66	394.3	153.8	2.4
1966-67	397.1	154.9	0.7
1967-68	378.4	147.6	-4.8
1968-69	415.6	162.1	9.8
1969-70	442.4	172.6	6.4
At constant 1969-70 factor costs			
1969-70	542.0	100.0	—
1970-71	600.2	110.7	10.7
1971-72	615.9	113.6	2.6
1972	615.4	113.5	—

(Table continues on the following page.)

Movements in industrial output from 1945 to 1975 may be assessed from different sets of data.[2]   First, various national income estimates at constant prices may be used to suggest the growth of industry's contribution to real GDP.   The problems with national income estimates for developing countries are familiar: the weakness

2. For a discussion of the behavior of industrial investment, which is relevant to an appraisal of output growth, see the appendix to this chapter.

TABLE 11-1 (continued)

Year	Industry in GDP	Index	Annual increase (percent)
	At constant 1972 factor costs		
1972	589.3	100.0	—
1973	602.6	102.2	2.2
1974	638.3	108.3	5.9
1975	n.a.	n.a.	11.9[a]

n.a. Not available.
a. Estimated.
Notes: From 1945 to 1954 industry includes manufacturing, mining, and electricity. In the other series, electricity is excluded.
Source: Data for 1945-54 and 1952-53 to 1959-60 from Bent Hansen and Donald C. Mead, Growth and Structural Change in the Egyptian Economy (Homewood, Ill.: Richard D. Irwin, 1967); data for 1959-60 to 1975 from the Ministry of Planning.

of the data on which they are based, the difficulty of making comparisons over a long period because of the inconsistent procedures used to arrive at estimates, the changing concepts and definitions, unexplained revisions of older estimates, and the like. Second, there are a number of industrial production indexes. Most official indexes cover only the past three decades. A UN index suffers from certain inconsistencies, and an index constructed by Mabro and Radwan covers a long period starting in 1939 but unfortunately does not go beyond 1969-70.[3] Estimates of movements in the volume of industrial production for 1973, 1974, and 1975 have been made for this book.

Some broad movements in the volume of industrial production for 1945-75 may be depicted with a fair amount of confidence if all these various elements of information are pieced together. The national accounts data presented in table 11-1 reveal a short but sharp boom in industrial production soon after World War II, that is, between 1947 and 1950, and a period of sustained growth at a fairly high rate stretching between 1954 and 1964. The data further reveal a downturn in performance after 1964, which is evidenced in several sources. The rates of growth of industrial output then begin to decline, reaching negative values in 1967-68. There was a short recovery between 1968-69 and 1970-71, followed again by stagnation

3. Robert Mabro and Samir Radwan, The Industrialization of Egypt, 1939-1973 (Oxford: Clarendon Press, 1976).

until 1974. The national accounts suggest a high rate of increase in industrial output in 1975.

The Mabro-Radwan index of physical production reveals the same broad features, although the rates of increase for individual years and average rates for subperiods are obviously different from the figures obtained from the constant price estimates of national accounts (see table 11-2). The postwar boom of 1947-50 and the period of high growth between 1954-55 and 1964-66 are picked up by this index. The downturn after 1963-64 is also visible here, although the methods of estimation are entirely different. Mabro and Radwan have much lower rates of growth of industrial output in 1968-69 and 1969-70 than do the national accounts. If their estimates were to be treated as the more reliable, the years from 1968-69 to 1974 would be characterized as a time of relative stagnation with fairly low rates of growth.

If the various constant-price estimates in table 11-1 are spliced together — a rather crude procedure because of changes in definition, coverage, base for the constant-price estimate, and so on — the index of production would stand at 527.4 in 1975 (1945 = 100). This implies an average compound rate of growth of 5.69 percent

TABLE 11-2. INDEXES OF INDUSTRIAL PRODUCTION,
1945 TO 1954 AND 1952-53 TO 1969-70

Year	Index	Annual increase (percent)	Year	Index	Annual increase (percent)
1945	100.0	—	1952-53	100.0	—
1946	103.5	3.5	1953-54	108.2	8.2
1947	110.6	6.8	1954-55	120.7	11.5
1948	130.7	18.1	1955-56	129.6	7.4
1949	148.5	12.1	1956-57	140.2	8.1
1950	153.9	3.6	1957-58	152.9	9.0
1951	168.6	9.5	1958-59	162.5	6.3
1952	173.0	2.5	1959-60	175.9	8.2
1953	176.5	2.0	1960-61	203.2	15.5
1954	195.3	10.5	1961-62	224.7	10.6
			1962-63	250.5	11.5
			1963-64	280.2	11.8
			1964-65	292.8	4.5
			1965-66	299.3	2.2
			1966-67	297.2	-0.7
			1967-68	291.0	-2.1
			1968-69	301.2	3.5
			1969-70	315.4	4.7

Note: The 1945-54 index is constructed using a small number of commodities. The 1952-53 to 1969-70 index involved 159 commodities.
Source: Robert Mabro and Samir Radwan, The Industrialization of Egypt, 1939-1973 (Oxford: Clarendon Press, 1976), tables 5.2 and 5.3.

a year. The average compound rate for 1945 to 1969-70 is 5.64 percent a year, while the Mabro-Radwan index, again spliced together, suggests a higher rate of 7.2 percent for the same period. The discrepancy is explained in part by the fact that the national accounts index is of the Paasche type and the Mabro-Radwan is of the Laspeyres type. A second, more important reason is that the national accounts reflect the whole of the industrial sector, that is, both the slow-growing small manufacturing sector and the fast-growing modern, large-scale industry; Mabro-Radwan's index mainly reflects the growth of output of establishments in which at least ten persons are engaged.

The important conclusions for the 1945-70 period are, first, that the average rate of manufacturing growth was substantial, though not extremely high. Second, output performance was uneven, and much of the growth achieved after World War II is attributable to the short postwar boom and to the high rates sustained between 1954 and 1964. Third, output performance was unsatisfactory after 1964 not only because of the sharp dip from high rates of growth to negative values in 1967-68 but also because the subsequent recovery was short and followed by three or four years of stagnation.

Between 1969-70 and 1975 the value added (at constant 1970 prices) in the industrial sector increased at an annual rate of 5.5 percent. This has to be interpreted with some caution, however. The growth between 1969-70 and 1973 was very small — less than 1 percent annually — while in the 1973-76 period it rose to 11.6 percent a year. The post-1973 figures reflect the rapid increase in the utilization of installed capacity made possible by more external assistance in this period, but the figures are inflated by the inclusion of crude petroleum production, which became especially important in the most recent years. Consistent data are not available to separate the share of petroleum from that of manufacturing, but a rough estimate suggests that perhaps 4 percentage points of the post-1973 growth of the composite manufacturing, mining, and petroleum sector could be attributed to the petroleum subsector.

INDUSTRIAL STRUCTURE

Many aspects of the industrial structure must be considered, notably the industrial composition of output, its division between domestic absorption and exports, the distribution of employment and of the capital stock by branch of activity, the composition of establishments by size, and the location of plants and firms. Linkages between various sectors are also important, and input-output tables would reveal, among other things, the cost structure of every industry and the degree of dependence on inputs of a given origin (particularly imports). Import-substitution strategies also result in typical patterns of structural change. The moot question is whether the pattern of industrialization associated with import substitution involves structural weaknesses that, in the end, defeat the purposes of the development strategy. The issues of interest that arise in this context are: How much structural change has taken place? What stage of industrialization has been attained? Have all the possibilities of significant import substitution been exhausted? Is the industrial structure sufficiently flexible to accommodate a change of strategy, say, from import substitution to export promotion?

Composition of Output

The industrial structure of Egypt can be analyzed by looking at the gross value added by the various manufacturing sectors to the Egyptian economy. Individual sector data are shown in table 11-3. The individual sectors are then grouped in three categories in table 11-4. Basic consumer goods include food, beverages, tobacco, ginning and pressing, spinning and weaving, and wearing apparel. Intermediate goods include wood, paper, printing, leather, rubber, chemicals, coal, petroleum products, and miscellaneous. Though some of these are consumer goods, the output in this category includes important intermediates used by industry and other sectors, for example, fertilizers for agriculture and building materials for the construction sector. The last category includes nonelectric and electric machinery and transport equipment. This sector relates mainly to capital equipment, consumer durables, and transport vehicles. Since at present there is little production of machinery in Egypt, consumer durables and machinery repair dominate this category.

Basic consumer goods. Throughout the 1969-70 to 1978 period textiles occupied the dominant position among manufacturing sectors. Textiles, defined as spinning and weaving and clothing and wearing apparel, accounted for 27 percent of total value added in 1969-70 and 30 percent in 1978. The importance of textiles in Egyptian industry is confirmed by other indicators, such as employment and exports. In 1966-67 there were 246,500 persons employed in the so-called modern textile industry (establishments employing ten or more workers). This figure represented some 43 percent of the manufacturing labor force in establishments of this size. The employment share of textiles in all manufacturing establishments in 1966-67 was 32.3 percent. The growing importance of textiles in Egypt's manufacturing exports can be gauged from table 11-5, which shows that yarn and fabrics accounted for some 20 percent of all merchandise export earnings and for two-thirds of manufactured exports.

In the late 1950s and thereafter, planners devoted a large proportion of industrial investment to textiles, thus helping this industry to

TABLE 11-3. GROSS VALUE ADDED IN MANUFACTURING BY ACTIVITY, 1969-70 TO 1978

(millions of Egyptian pounds at current factor cost)

Activity	1969-70	1970-71	1971-72	1973	1974	1975	1978
Food industries	104.5	110.7	115.4	122.3	130.5	140.0	182.1
Beverages	4.9	5.7	6.6	7.1	9.6	12.0	21.4
Tobacco	14.2	15.8	17.8	20.2	23.8	27.6	37.2
Ginning and pressing	6.2	6.5	8.5	8.9	9.2	8.0	10.1
Spinning and weaving	114.7	129.7	133.1	123.6	137.5	160.0	283.8
Clothing and wearing apparel	22.9	28.3	29.9	44.8	55.4	50.7	131.0
Wood	15.8	17.4	17.5	17.0	18.6	18.7	44.4
Paper	9.8	11.4	12.4	13.2	17.5	22.0	21.9
Printing, publishing	14.5	15.0	15.5	16.5	17.5	18.0	21.7
Leather	4.9	5.4	5.8	8.3	10.5	9.8	9.5
Rubber	5.4	6.3	5.8	5.7	7.0	9.2	10.7
Chemicals	54.9	59.7	64.1	58.1	73.9	96.3	131.5
Petroleum products	9.8	12.2	13.1	21.5	n.a.	48.1	90.3
Coal products	1.4	1.9	2.1	2.1	4.7	7.4	10.7
Nonmetallic	23.5	25.8	29.2	28.1	31.4	40.1	47.7
Basic metals	23.9	25.9	29.9	34.2	41.3	52.2	100.6
Metallic products	16.6	17.5	18.9	19.0	21.5	28.0	39.4
Nonelectrical machinery	6.4	8.8	8.2	7.8	8.1	10.1	12.9
Electrical machinery	16.9	19.0	19.1	19.2	25.1	33.2	57.4
Transport equipment	14.9	18.9	20.7	23.2	26.2	32.3	59.9
Miscellaneous	30.4	31.3	32.9	36.7	51.9	56.0	61.3
Total	516.5	573.2	606.5	637.5	721.2	879.6	1,385.5

n.a. Not available.
Source: Ministry of Planning.

maintain, and even enhance, its dominant place in the industrial structure. The planners were able to ignore tariffs because the government was prepared to use quantitative restrictions on imports to protect domestic production; the tariff could be superseded by the imposition of quotas or, in the extreme case, by the virtual prohibition of
competing imports. Egyptian planners maintained that they were thus
able to decide on the economic merits of a textile investment project
from the standpoint of society as a whole. In fact, it is not clear
whether planners found textiles to be profitable for the economy in
terms of social opportunity costs and benefits, or whether they merely
followed precedent and decided that the country ought to accord priority to the industrial processing of its local raw materials.

TABLE 11-4. PERCENTAGE COMPOSITION
OF GROSS VALUE ADDED BY INDUSTRIAL
CATEGORY, SELECTED YEARS

Category	1947	1966-67	1969-70	1975
Basic consumer goods	79.8	55.0	51.6	49.7
Intermediate industries	19.7	38.2	40.6	40.6
Consumer durables and equipment	0.5	6.8	7.4	9.3

Note: Columns may not add up to 100 because of rounding.
Source: Table 11-3.

There is evidence that the textile industry in Egypt does not yield
an economic return when measured by the social opportunity costs of
resources used. Hansen and Nashashibi estimated that the rates of
return at international prices for yarn were 0.9 percent in 1960 and
-10.2 percent in 1969-70; for cotton fabrics, the figure is -15 percent in 1965-66.[4] The main input into the textile industry, long-staple
cotton, is of very high quality (and hence high opportunity cost). Unless this raw material is used to produce a high-quality output (which
commands a high international price), the activity will show negative
value added at international prices, indicating an absence of comparative advantage.
      The consensus among students of the Egyptian economy has long
been that the economics of the textile industry are inherently wrong
because a high-quality input is used for manufacturing a coarse product. From this it is frequently argued that Egypt ought to import
short-staple cotton for domestic processing. Given the f.o.b. price
differential between short- and long-staple cotton, the results of
following this advice will depend on transport costs, on the elasticity
of world demand for Egyptian long-staple cotton, and on external
diseconomies that may arise from the import of cotton (such as con-
tamination of domestic Egyptian cotton). A second option might be
to reduce the land allocated to extralong-staple cotton in favor of
food or medium-staple cotton products. In addition, the quality of
manufactured cotton products could be improved by raising the average count of yarn and switching toward the production of high-quality
fabrics. Such a policy would be part of an export promotion strategy and might call for a radical change in the ideas about industrialization that have prevailed in Egypt since 1930.
      The second most important sector is food industries, although
the share of value added contributed by this sector has declined

4. Bent Hansen and Karim Nashashibi, Egypt: Foreign Trade Regimes and Economic Development (New York: National Bureau of Economic Research, 1975),
table 8.4.

TABLE 11-5. SHARE OF YARN AND FABRICS
IN EXPORT EARNINGS, SELECTED YEARS
(percent)

Year	Export share of textiles	Year	Export share of textiles
1946	0.3	1966-67	19.2
1952-53	3.3	1969-70	16.7
1956-57	8.3	1973	17.1
1959-60	9.7	1974	18.4
1964-65	14.0	1975	20.7

Source: Central Agency for Public Mobilization and Statistics and
Ministry of Planning.

from 20 percent in 1969-70 to 13 percent in 1978. In establishments
employing ten persons or more, the value added share of food declined
sharply between 1952 and 1966-67 from 18.2 percent to 10.7 percent.
    A large component of the food industry is made up of small estab-
lishments: canneries, grain mills, dairies, and the like. This sector may have been growing at about the rate of food consumption in
the country, and this trend will probably continue. The modern food
industry in Egypt has suffered from difficulties from the start. The
sugar industry, beset by bankruptcies and reorganization, has required subsidies and exceptional tariff support from the latter half
of the nineteenth century until World War II. The canning and dairy
product industries both suffer from an inadequate availability of inputs — the production of fruit, vegetables, and milk, though growing,
does not provide much opportunity for a rapid expansion of these industries. A food industry that would have to rely on imported food
inputs for rapid expansion may not, because of transport and storage costs, turn out to be competitive.

    Intermediate goods. Chemicals constitute the third most impor-
tant manufacturing sector, accounting for 11 percent in 1969-70 and
9 percent in 1978. The output of chemicals consists of (1) important
intermediates, such as fertilizers, alcohol, detergents, paints, caus-
tic soda, acids, which are essential inputs for both agricultural and
industrial production, as well as (2) some consumer goods, such as
soap, cosmetics, and pharmaceuticals. Chemicals benefited from
an import-substitution strategy because of a fairly large and expanding market. Fertilizer consumption, for example, increased at a
fast rate after World War II, and the demand for fertilizers will increase much further if growth in agricultural yields is to be sustained. Egypt is not yet self-sufficient in fertilizers, as table 11-6

TABLE 11-6. SUPPLY OF NITROGEN
FERTILIZERS, 1962-72
(thousands of tons of nitrogen)

Supply	1962	1965	1968	1970	1971	1972
Production	107	159	140	119	109	103
Imports	56	116	147	203	174	285
Total	163	275	287	322	283	388

Source: United Nations Food and Agriculture Organization.

shows, but projects near completion or under implementation will increase domestic output in the coming years beyond the point of self-sufficiency, thus creating an export potential.

Industrial chemicals benefited from the secondary effects of the import-substitution strategy. As domestic production of consumer goods displaced imports, an internal market for the industrial inputs required for such production began to expand and opened up further opportunities for import substitution. As income grew, the composition of consumer demand shifted toward manufactured goods with high income elasticities. Some parts of the chemical industries — such as pharmaceuticals, cosmetics, and paints — benefited from this demand pull.

Among intermediate goods, a significant increase in value added has occurred in the petroleum products sector. In 1969-70 petroleum products contributed 2 percent to gross value added. A ninefold increase in this sector increased its share to 6 percent by 1978.

Capital equipment and consumer durables. There was hardly any manufacture of capital equipment or consumer durables in Egypt in 1947, and the present share of these industries in gross value added, though increasing, is below 10 percent. It is misleading to treat this category as representing a capital goods sector, since most of the output is transport equipment, car repairs, and consumer durables. In richer developing countries, such as Iran or Brazil, this category commands a much higher share of value added. But it is typical of most import-substituting patterns that capital goods are discriminated against, in part because the cascading structure of tariff protection implies negative effective rates for this sector.

Summary. It may thus be concluded that changes in the gross value added shares of industries between 1947 and 1978 occurred according to well-defined patterns. Table 11-4 shows that the share of basic consumer goods industries fell from close to 80 percent in 1947 to 50 percent in 1978. At the early stage of industrialization, manufacturing is almost entirely confined to food, beverages, cigarettes, wearing apparel, and textiles; this was the case in Egypt in 1947, when there was hardly any production of consumer durables,

machinery, or transport equipment. The intermediate manufacturing sector accounted for only some 20 percent of value added in 1947.
In the late 1940s, however, private entrepreneurs began to show
some interest in industries such as plastics, nitrogenous fertilizers,
and rubber. Their investment decisions induced a process of structural transformation, which continued in later years when government planners took over. The structural transformation was not
initiated by planners, but they imparted a strong momentum to
changes that had begun before their era. By 1978 the gross value
added share of intermediate industries increased to 41 percent. Further rises can be expected. The value added share for capital equipment and consumer durables has also risen since 1947, but still remains at a fairly modest level.

Small-Scale Industry

In this section, establishments employing one to nine workers
will be referred to as the artisanal sector, and those employing
ten to fifty workers, as small-scale industry. (Different boundaries, such as ten to one hundred workers, would probably be equally
defensible for small-scale industry on grounds of low capital-labor
ratios.) Information on private sector industry, particularly on the
small-scale segment, is distressingly fragmentary and unreliable.
Tracing and assessing developments in the sector is thus extremely
difficult, and conclusions should be treated with caution.

In the wake of the nationalizations and punitive sequestrations in
the early 1960s, only relatively small manufacturing establishments,
mostly employing less than fifty workers, remained under private
ownership. The private sector has virtually been excluded from the
intermediate and capital goods industries, and its share tends to be
larger in consumer goods and generally in industries where scale
economies are not very important. Despite the uninviting climate,
small-scale industries have managed to hold their own and even
grow, accounting for about one-third of total value added generated
in industry and 54 percent of total industrial employment. The sectoral distribution of private ownership, given the narrow confines
of private initiative until the recent change in government attitude,
has not changed perceptibly since the late 1960s. Leather, woodworking and furniture, wearing apparel, and engineering (including
metallic products) remain the dominant industries of private activity and, by extension, of small-scale manufacturing. Among the
4,000 private establishments each employing ten or more workers,
90 percent of the total employ ten to fifty workers and account for
57 percent of total employment (some 122,000). There have been
no discernible changes in the size structure of enterprises. Greater Cairo presents the major concentration of private manufacturing

industries, accounting for 57 percent of the total number, 64 percent of employment, and 67 percent of the value added generated by the establishments employing ten or more in the private sector, a trend that remains virtually unchecked.

The artisanal sector is heavily oriented toward the production of a wide range of household goods for local markets. As a result of the inhospitable climate, this sector does not appear to have grown significantly, at least in the decade from 1965 to 1975. Nor does the structure of artisanal activities seem to have changed much. Though information is sketchy, the rank order for amount of employment and number of establishments has been roughly as follows: ready-made garments, woodworking and furniture, food processing, engineering and metallurgy, textiles, shoes and leather products, and repairs. About three-quarters of the artisanal establishments have fixed assets valued in 1974 at less than LE100 and 97 percent at less than LE1,000. This underscores the very low capital intensity of the small artisanal workshop. Over 72 percent of the establishments employ only one worker, while 98 percent employ five workers or less. The average number per establishment has been two workers from 1965 to 1975, indicating no structural change. Employment in the artisanal segment probably amounts to about 330,000.

About 50 percent of the artisanal enterprises are members of cooperative societies. The cooperative system provides virtually no credit facilities to its members; nor does it make it any easier for them to obtain credit from institutional sources. Some cooperatives do assist by purchasing materials in bulk and winning approval of foreign exchange requirements for imports. In the case of ready-made garments, shoes, and furniture, several cooperatives purchase and market all or part of the output of their members. The quality of technical assistance currently provided to the artisanal sector leaves much to be desired, however.

The performance of the private manufacturing sector in recent years has been impressive. Output, which stagnated during 1972-74, increased by a remarkable annual average of 15 percent in real terms between 1974 and 1976, reflecting the vitality and favorable response of the sector to the government's encouragement of private initiative. Leather, building materials, chemicals, woodworking and furniture, and engineering industries were the fastest growing. Only 6 percent of total private manufacturing output was exported in 1976, even though private sector exports almost doubled between 1973 and 1975; the leading industries were chemicals, leather, garments, and furniture. Eastern European countries, particularly the Soviet Union, account for 94 percent of total private exports. Such heavy reliance renders exports highly vulnerable to political developments and strongly suggests the need to redirect trade.

Employment in the private sector grew at an impressive annual rate of 6.7 percent during 1966-74, compared with 2.4 percent in the public sector, raising its share in total industrial employment from 47 to 54 percent. The record of the private sector is even more impressive in view of the overstaffing of public enterprises. Private sector employment reached an estimated 623,000 in 1974, of which about 70,000 were in establishments of ten to fifty workers and possibly about 330,000 in the artisanal sector. The share of the private sector in total industrial investment was exceedingly small during 1970-74, averaging about 4 percent a year in current prices. In 1975 private investment increased by sevenfold to LE108 million and accounted for 10 percent of the total; the percentage was slightly higher in 1976. On the basis of approvals by the Government Organization for Industry, engineering, textiles, chemicals, and food-processing projects accounted for 90 percent of total planned investment in 1974-76. Average planned investment per project for all industries in the private sector taken together has been rising since 1970 — more dramatically in 1975 and 1976 — reflecting a tendency toward larger-size projects and increased capital intensity. Nevertheless, capital-labor ratios (based on planned investment) in the order of LE2,600 (US$4,000) should still be viewed as relatively low.

INDUSTRIAL FINANCING

Financial Institutions

Institutional financing for industry has been provided in the past almost entirely by the banking sector. Of the nonbanking institutions, only insurance companies have recently shown interest in providing long-term financing to a few large industrial projects. The two stock exchanges, in Cairo and Alexandria, have not been contributing to the mobilization of industrial finance. No new securities have been issued since the mid-1950s. The exchanges have about forty-three listed securities with a total market value of about LE160 million, of which bonds represent 60 percent (mainly four government issues) and stocks 40 percent (mainly issues of mixed public and private sector companies). The annual turnover volume is about LE10 million in Cairo and LE3 million to LE4 million in Alexandria.

The banking sector continues to be dominated by the four public sector commercial banks — Bank Misr, Banque du Caire, National Bank, and Bank of Alexandria (BOA) — all fully owned by the Central Bank of Egypt. The sector specialization of each of these banks was removed in 1975 with the promulgation of the new banking law (Law 120). Other than some short-term financing, however, BOA continued for a while to be almost the sole source of institutional finance for industry.

The government's open-door policy in recent years has led to the establishment of many new financial institutions (joint venture banks, foreign bank branches, and offshore institutions), most of which are only gradually initiating operations.[5] Significant interest in development banking has also been shown by some of these joint venture banks.

Financing of Public and Private Sector Investment

Major industrial sectors. Public sector industrial investments continue to be financed primarily from the Treasury and from internally generated funds. The commercial banks generally finance only working capital, although some investments in fixed assets are financed with short-term loans that are rolled over, making them disguised term loans. Many private sector businessmen use the local resources so obtained for purchasing foreign exchange in the "parallel" or the "own-exchange" market to import capital or consumer goods. The Development Industrial Bank (DIB) provides long-term financing for public sector projects, as did BOA previously, but the amount is small in comparison with total investments and is generally for small reconstruction and expansion projects. When DIB does finance larger projects, it constitutes only a small portion of the total financing, supplementing insufficient budgetary allocations and internally generated funds.

For private sector investments, the main source of external long-term investment funds is DIB (and previously BOA), for both local currency and foreign exchange. Limited term lending for investment projects has also been undertaken by Chase National and Cairo Barclays. Among the local commercial banks only Bank Misr plans to finance a few large industrial investments (particularly in textiles), in an effort to regain a semblance of its prenationalization status as an important industrial financier and holding company. It also finances agroindustrial projects, for which it has received credit from the International Development Association (IDA). Other financial institutions have shown some interest in consortium financing (with DIB or other institutions) of large industrial and tourism projects; these institutions include insurance companies and the local joint venture and offshore banks. Aggregate data quantifying the sources of self-financing and external financing of industrial investment are not compiled in Egypt.

Small-scale industry. A small-loans scheme catering to the needs of artisans was instituted by the commercial banks in 1975, whereby loans up to LE2,000 (including working capital) and up to three years'

5. At the last count sixty-nine banks had operations in Cairo — thirty-three local and joint venture banks, twenty-five representative offices, and eleven finance and investment houses.

maturity were offered to small enterprises at the normal costs applicable to other loans. No special incentive was offered to the banks for such lending, and the scheme was a failure because bank branch managers perceived that such loans had low profitability and high risk. Only the National Bank has retained interest in small-scale industrial lending, and it provides mainly short-term and occasional medium-term local currency loans at the standard interest rates. At the end of 1975 the National Bank's outstanding loans to small-scale industry amounted to around LE0.5 million (compared with a total portfolio of LE1.4 billion) to some 3,500 clients. Although these are small loans, it could not be confirmed that the clients are all small enterprises; some medium-size enterprises may well be included.

The main financier of small-scale industry, as of private investment in general, is DIB. In the first six months of 1977 its medium- and long-term loans (approved) to small-scale industry amounted to LE3 million for about 240 projects, mostly in Cairo and Alexandria where a large majority of Egyptian small-scale industry is centered. Again, it could not be confirmed that the clients are all small enterprises.

A third institution catering to small-scale industry is the Nasser Social Fund, a public sector organization administering various social funds and programs. Only a small portion of its financing is for productive purposes, and the amount is reported to be small in comparison with that of the DIB. Its financing of small-scale industry has been limited to bulk purchasing from abroad and resale on an installment basis of machinery and equipment (confined so far to one operation involving lathes), taxis, and tourist buses. A small profit margin is added to the resale price. It also finances raw material for small-scale industry through the cooperative organizations.

APPENDIX: INDUSTRIAL INVESTMENT

In Egypt during the three decades considered in this study, the share of industry in total investment has generally tended to exceed its share of GDP. In the short but very significant postwar boom of 1945–50, the share of industrial investment was estimated at some 25 to 30 percent of total investment (compared with the combined share of industry and electricity of 10 to 15 percent of GDP in these years). The private sector, the sole industrial investor at that time, did not seem reluctant to invest in these years. It is impossible to say whether it would have continued to invest with the same momentum had the private economy retained its dominance after the revolution, but it is important to dispel the notion that little was happening on the industrial front in Egypt before 1952. The share of industrial investment seems to have fluctuated in the range of 24 to 27 percent between 1952 and 1967 with perhaps a very slight upward trend. It increased from 1967 until 1975 to levels close to 32 to 35 percent. This phenomenon was partly a result of a sudden drop in the shares of electricity and agriculture following the completion of the High Dam, and the increased expenditures on petroleum exploration and development (petroleum is included in the data under industry). The abrupt change in the investment share of industry does not reflect a significant growth of investment in manufacturing.

Estimates of investment in industry (mining and manufacturing) at current prices for the 1947-75 period are presented in table 11-7. They confirm the occurrence of an investment boom after World War II, a decline in investment activity between 1952 and 1954, followed by a new expansionary phase that reached its peak in 1963-64. Investment in industry between 1964-65 and the end of the 1960s tended to remain fairly constant at a slightly lower level than the peak, which suggests a decline in the volume of investment year after year during this period. Increases in the current value of industrial investment in later years may be largely due to expenditures

TABLE 11-7. INVESTMENT IN MANUFACTURING
AND MINING, 1946-47 TO 1976
(millions of Egyptian pounds at current prices)

Year	Investment	Year	Investment
1946-47	13.1	1961-62	50.3
1947-48	18.5	1962-63	80.5
1948-49	28.0	1963-64	105.4
1949-50	29.5	1964-65	99.9
1950-51	31.6	1965-66	100.6
1951-52	35.2	1966-67	98.4
1952-53	29.5	1967-68	80.8
1953-54	27.2	1968-69	101.1
1954-55	33.6	1969-70	123.1
1955-56	49.8	1970-71	125.7
1956-57	31.1	1971-72	140.0
1957-58	35.6	1972	119.7
1958-59	47.8	1973	154.3
1959-60	49.3	1974	234.0
1960-61	67.8	1975	394.1
		1976	560.8

Source: Ministry of Mining.

on petroleum (and not to increases in manufacturing investment) and
to high rates of price inflation. It may be tentatively inferred that
real investment in manufacturing tended to fall after 1964-65 until
1969-70.

To judge from these data and from Radwan's capital formation
series, it appears that the gross capital stock in industry grew at
a fairly fast, though declining, rate between 1945 and 1962 and
thereafter at a much slower rate. [6] The rate of net capital formation in industry may well have been negative at the end of the 1960s
and perhaps in the early 1970s. Of course, all these statements
refer to aggregates. What seems to have happened (broadly speak-
ing, since 1965 or at the latest 1967) is that industrial investment
was allocated mainly to the erection of a few new plants, [7] while replacement, maintenance, and modernization of existing equipment
were neglected. As significant additions to the capital stock had
taken place after World War II and throughout the 1950s, the need
for replacement must have been large by the end of the 1960s. Recent studies and inspection of Egyptian industrial plants strongly suggest that equipment and machinery in several sectors, including textiles, are due for replacement or overhaul.

There are no complete sets of data on the pattern of industrial
investment for the whole of 1945-76. Fragmentary evidence suggests that most industrial investment between the end of World War
II and 1954 — that is, under free private enterprise — was concentrated in textiles, food, building materials, and some metallurgi-
cal and chemical industries. Yet a few new products were introduced during this short period, notably calcium nitrate fertilizers,
plastics, and some consumer durables such as refrigerators and
metal furniture. The most significant changes in the pattern of investment took place between 1954 and the early 1960s. The investment structure became more diversified to include paper, metals,
chemicals, rubber tires, consumer durables, and other nontraditional industries. This period of transition brought about profound
changes in the structure of the economy and of industry. In the late
1950s intermediate goods claimed a larger share of investment than
in earlier years, a pattern that seems to have remained stable until
1967, after which there were significant increases in the investment
shares of metals and chemicals. The shift toward metals may well
have been premature. Egypt, responding to the opportunities of

6. According to Samir Radwan, Capital Formation in Egyptian Industry and
Agriculture, 1882-1967 (London: Ithaca Press, 1974), the average rate between
1946 and 1962 would have been 5.5 percent and between 1962 and 1967, 1.6 percent.

7. About 40 percent of investment in manufacturing since 1968 has been absorbed
by a single venture, the Helwan steel complex.

Soviet aid, the only significant form of foreign assistance available
to the country between 1964 and 1972, seems to have adopted a (possibly costly) strategy, which emphasized the role of heavy industry
in economic development.

There seems to be a close relation between the movements of
output indexes and of the capital formation series. In both cases it
is possible to discern phases of growth in the second half of the
1940s and in 1954-64. The stagnation in 1952-53 affected both output and investment, and the decline in performance between 1964
and the early 1970s is manifested by all these indicators. Several
explanations may account for this close relation. There is, of
course, a simple Keynesian explanation which proceeds from autonomous changes in investment to induced changes in output. If this
explanation were retained, it would be interesting to note the very
short time lags in Egypt between changes in investment and the response of industrial output. An alternative explanation stresses the
significance of imports in developing countries open to foreign trade.
Industrial investment has a large import content in the form of raw
material and semifinished inputs. In times of balance of payments
difficulties, especially when the government has recourse to severe
(and usually badly administered) quantitative restrictions on imports,
both industrial investment and industrial output will necessarily suffer. Conversely, the rates of investment and output growth will tend
to be high, and even to rise, when finance for imports happens to be
available. The critical role of import capability in industrial growth,
especially in developing countries that follow an import-substitution
strategy, has long been recognized. The high performance of 1954-
64 occurred when the foreign exchange constraint was not too important. Egypt had accumulated sterling balances during World War II,
which enabled it to finance with ease small balance of payments deficits in the 1950s; it then had access to both U.S. and Soviet aid. It
is perhaps no accident that the turning point in performance in 1964
happened just when the United States withdrew its aid; moreover, it
was when the import-export gap in Egypt was widening for a variety
of domestic and external reasons. The sensitivity of industrial
growth to imports was again manifested in 1975.

Although output indexes and capital formation series seem to
move together, the turning points do not coincide with the dates that
marked changes in the economic system. There was both a boom
and a downturn under free private enterprise between 1946 and 1954.
There was a strong expansion under the mixed economic system
of 1954-60 but also in the first three or four years of the plan
(1960-61 to 1964-65) just after the nationalizations. And there
was sluggish and unsatisfactory performance after 1964 for a
wide variety of reasons, not all related to the nature of the economic system.

12
Major Issues and Policies for Industry

The major issues for Egyptian industry from 1945 to the present were its productivity, managerial and technical efficiency, international competitiveness, and export performance. Each is the subject of a separate section below, and the economic policies developed in response to these issues are discussed in the second half of this chapter.

PRODUCTIVITY

The significance of industrialization for economic development is related in part to the higher productivity of manufacturing compared with other major economic sectors and in part to the role of total factor productivity in growth. Measurements of productivity growth in developing countries are particularly difficult because of data problems. Indicators of productivity growth in Egyptian industry suffer from the usual statistical and conceptual defects that characterize such measures, but they may provide some useful information.

Mabro and Radwan suggest that average rates of total factor productivity growth in Egyptian industry were not negligible between 1945 and 1962.[1] They were slightly higher than 3 percent a year between 1945 and 1954 and around 2.7 to 2.9 percent between 1954 and 1962. The rates of productivity growth seem to have been higher under free private enterprise than under the mixed economy of the 1950s. The difference is slight, however, and it would be unwise to draw strong conclusions from it.

Productivity growth in the period after 1962 is not comparable to that of earlier years because the government's 1962 employment drive forced thousands of redundant workers and employees on the public sector. In such a situation there is no meaningful way of measuring the true contribution to growth of labor inputs and hence

1. Robert Mabro and Samir Radwan, The Industrialization of Egypt, 1939-1973 (Oxford: Clarendon Press, 1976), pp. 185-86.

the contribution of other sources of output growth. All measures of growth in average output per man or man-hour employed and all measures of total factor productivity growth after 1962 show negative rates. This does not necessarily mean that technical progress, innovations, or organizational and management improvement suddenly ceased to take place, nor does it mean that labor ceased to acquire new skills and experience. It simply means that for obvious statistical reasons the exogenous growth of employment is associated with a fall in output per man and thus exaggerates the contribution of output increases to output growth.

Movements in the rates of productivity growth confirm the results suggested by an analysis of other indicators such as output growth and investment. Performance in Egyptian industry began to deteriorate very seriously around 1962-64. The main, but not sole, culprit in the decline of productivity was the employment policy. The mismanagement of foreign exchange budgets and import procedures, and to some extent the maladministration of the public sector by the growing bureaucracy, probably also affected productivity adversely. The need to improve productivity remains a key issue for any viable strategy of industrialization.

X-EFFICIENCY

Very little can be said about improvements or deterioration in managerial and technological efficiency, sometimes called X-efficiency, in the period before 1975. Data on capacity utilization for odd years were gathered by different agencies and researchers under a wide variety of circumstances and for different purposes, and they are not readily comparable. What is certain is that capacity underutilization has been a chronic ailment of Egyptian industry, irrespective of changes in the economic system. Different branches of manufacturing industry have been affected by underutilization of capacity at different times. The food industry seems to have suffered from serious problems in this respect, and excess capacity in plant and equipment has been regularly noted by successive observers for three decades. The seasonality of agriculture, which provides the main inputs, may be partly responsible for the phenomenon. Several food industries — canning, dairy products, and perhaps sugar — suffer from permanent as opposed to seasonal underutilization of capacity. Other sectors where X-efficiency leaves much to be desired are iron and steel, car assembly, and electrical equipment.

Although excess capacity has characterized industrial performance in Egypt for a long time, the problems became more acute in the second half of the 1960s and in the early 1970s. The government tended to blame the foreign exchange constraint, but this was only partially responsible. Public sector firms, which depended on government allocation of imported raw materials and intermediate goods, sometimes ordered larger quantities than required, piling up stocks of some items while running short of others. An examination of data on aggregate imports of intermediates suggests that the quantities made available were reasonably large in relation to total consumption of inputs, yet bottlenecks continually appeared, leading to underutilization of plants. One cannot but conclude that the composition of both stocks and imports tended to be unbalanced, and that better management of inventories could have helped prevent a number of bottlenecks. This does not mean that the foreign exchange constraint was not binding, but that defective management made it much tighter than it might have been.

Data on stocks of inputs, inputs purchased, and inputs used up in production by Ministry of Industry public enterprises in 1973 and 1974 illustrate the high level of stocks (see table 12-1). At the end of 1974 stocks were equivalent to 63 percent of the annual purchases of material inputs and 73 percent of the value of material inputs used up during the year. In 1973 the ratio of stocks of inputs to inputs purchased was 59 percent. On the face of it, these ratios do not suggest low levels of aggregate stocks. The considerable underutilization of capacity in these years, however, points to poor management of stocks and imports.

There is also evidence of much wastage of inputs and raw materials in Egyptian industries. In the cotton textile industry, for example, where the normal waste rate is between 10 and 20 percent (depending on the mix of carded and combed yarn), the additional wastage is of the order of 8 percent of consumption (4 percent owing to straight wastage and another 4 percent owing to the use of more

TABLE 12-1. VALUE OF STOCKS OF MATERIAL INPUTS AS PERCENTAGE OF MATERIAL INPUTS PURCHASED AND USED, 1973 AND 1974

Sector	Percentage of inputs purchased		Percentage of inputs used, 1974
	1973	1974	
Spinning and weaving	32.5	59.2	65.8
Wood	39.9	45.5	51.3
Chemicals	68.0	63.0	73.4
Engineering	99.6	100.6	120.2
Metals	66.0	65.0	79.9
Building materials	83.1	88.8	110.2
Average	59.1	63.4	73.3

Note: These data cover Ministry of Industry enterprises only.
Source: Ministry of Industry.

combed yarn than necessary). The equipment, which is often old and worn-out, suffers from lack of maintenance and contributes to wastage. Inadequate supervision, lack of incentives, ineffective management, and negligence on the part of labor have also been blamed.

A further problem of technological efficiency relates to the uneconomic use of long-staple cotton, an expensive, high-quality input, in the production of coarse yarn and fabric. The failure to take full advantage of the qualitative potential of an input may be treated as a problem of X-efficiency. Historically, the modern textile industry expanded very rapidly in Egypt, after tariffs were imposed, and acquired a dominant share of manufacturing employment and output. The local availability of a major input for a basic consumer goods industry seems to have, initially at least, helped rapid industrialization. Yet the local availability of a raw material does not necessarily imply comparative advantages in the manufacturing of derived products. To turn the apparent advantage into a real economic advantage, investment in the production of fine fabrics and innovative uses of cotton may be required.

COMPETITIVENESS

Considerable work has been done on the international competitiveness of Egyptian industries.[2] Hansen and Nashashibi show that, on the basis of an evaluation of domestic resource costs, sugar, cement, and superphosphates were competitive by the end of the 1950s. Mabro and Radwan, using a slightly different method, found that cement was definitely competitive, and sugar and alcohol fairly so, in 1960. Both sets of authors agree that phosphates remained very competitive in 1964-65 and that coarse yarn was not, largely because of the use of high-value Egyptian cotton. Mabro and Radwan feel that the production of fine yarn should have been encouraged because Egypt seems to be competitive in the production of that commodity.

Not surprisingly, Hansen and Nashashibi show that iron and steel, car assembly, and perhaps paper, are unsuccessful industries with domestic resource costs sometimes as high as ten times the official dollar rate in Egyptian pounds. There is some disagreement on nitrate fertilizers, which fared less well in calculations made for 1964-65 by Hansen and Nashashibi than in the Mabro-Radwan evaluations. Interestingly, cement and phosphates continued to do well in the 1960s, and there was no change in the relative compet-

2. Bent Hansen and Karim Nashashibi, Egypt: Foreign Trade Regimes and Economic Development (New York: National Bureau of Economic Research, 1975), especially pp. 309-16; and Mabro and Radwan, Industrialization of Egypt, pp. 191-236.

itiveness of nitrate fertilizers and rubber tires between the 1950s and 1960s despite the change in the economic system. The efficiency of textiles deteriorated markedly, however, as measured by a substantial increase in the domestic resource costs per dollar earned.

Egyptian industrialization has comprised both good and bad projects, so that different industries now display varying degrees of competitiveness. Industry rankings by one measure of competitiveness, effective protection, are discussed in the appendix to this chapter. Investment planning was responsible for costly errors when scarce resources were devoted to projects that were either ill-conceived (wrong scale, wrong technology, faulty linkages) or ill-suited to the economic condition of the country.

EXPORT PERFORMANCE

Egyptian industrialization has not been export oriented; import substitution has been its dominant characteristic since 1930. Exports of manufactured goods did not remain stagnant, however, and the initial concentration of the export basket was progressively reduced. The share of manufactured goods in total exports has indeed increased from some 6 to 8 percent in the early 1950s to 48 percent by 1975 (see table 12-2). Two-thirds of the value of manufactured exports is accounted for by cotton yarn and textiles. As a result of industrialization and export substitution Egypt has been transformed from an exporter of raw cotton to a secondary producer, increasingly exporting processed cotton in the form of yarn and textiles. Significantly, cotton continues to dominate the scene, either directly or indirectly, in spite of diversification.

Diversification in the commodity composition of Egypt's export basket over the 1952-75 period has consisted of three elements. The first, already mentioned, is the switch from raw cotton to textile products. In 1952-53 raw cotton accounted for about 83 percent of the total value of merchandise exports, textiles a mere 3.3 percent. In 1975 these proportions were 37 and 20 percent respectively. The second shift was away from cotton in favor of other agricultural products such as rice, fruit, and vegetables. The share of this category in 1952-53 was 8 percent, but it increased in 1975 to about 13 percent. The third shift was toward manufactured goods other than textiles. Their share increased from 2.5 percent to some 20 percent in the two end years considered. The average compound rate of growth of the value of manufactured exports was about 13.3 percent a year between 1952-53 and 1969-70, compared with an average rate of growth of 3 percent of total exports.

Since the mid-1950s Egyptian trade has been heavily directed toward the Eastern bloc. Egypt may have derived some advantages

TABLE 12-2. PERCENTAGE SHARE OF MANUFACTURED
GOODS IN TOTAL EXPORTS, 1952-53 TO 1975

Years	Share of industry in total exports	Years	Share of industry in total exports
1952-53	6.0	1964-65	24.5
1953-54	8.0	1965-66	26.5
1954-55	11.5	1966-67	30.0
1955-56	9.0	1967-68	31.0
1956-57	12.0	1968-69	34.0
1957-58	12.5	1969-70	29.5
1958-59	11.5	1971	34.0
1959-60	18.0	1972	36.5
1960-61	19.5	1973	32.0
1961-62	25.5	1974	35.5
1962-63	21.5	1975	48.0
1963-64	24.5		

Note: Manufactured goods include petroleum products.
Source: Ministry of Planning.

of market security, stability, and higher prices,[3] but bilateral
trade and concentration in the same geographical area also imposed
costs. Egypt missed the advantages of exposure to the demanding
requirements for quality and standardization of products in Western markets. Such an exposure might have spurred improvements
in methods of production and in efficiency. In addition, the period
of bilateral trade coincided with considerable expansion in the industrialized world, which would have offered Egypt many opportunities for growth and dynamic performance.

ECONOMIC POLICIES FOR INDUSTRIALIZATION

Since the introduction of tariff protection in 1930, industrialization has followed a typical import-substituting pattern. Radical
changes in the nature of Egypt's economic system, first toward
planning and then toward liberalization, have not deflected industrialization from that course. The policies most relevant to an

3. For example, average prices (in Egyptian pounds per kilogram) for exported
textiles in 1975, as provided in a World Bank survey of the Egyptian textile industry, were:

Product	All markets	Hard currency areas
Yarn	1.91	0.95
Fabric	1.66	1.09
Garments	6.44	3.00
Towels	2.50	2.00
Other items	2.36	1.67

understanding and an appraisal of Egyptian industrialization thus relate to foreign trade, especially import and foreign exchange policies.

Foreign Trade Regimes

Between 1930 and 1950 the government's major form of encouragement to industry was import tariffs. After the boom of the Korean War, industry was further encouraged by increased tariff protection, import licensing, and the imposition of other taxes and duties on imports (see the appendix to this chapter).

In 1953 the government introduced a comprehensive import entitlement scheme. The entitlements were transferable and commanded a premium, which in the 1950s ranged between 5 and 15 percent depending on the currency and the time. The effects were those of a partial — and, to judge from the size of the premium, small — depreciation of the currency. In September 1955, however, the entitlement scheme was dropped as part of an agreement with the United Kingdom. Egypt returned to a uniform exchange rate at the official parity. Instead of devaluing the currency, an import tax of 7 percent was introduced. Import controls were further tightened, and the trend that had begun after the Korean War continued to assert itself until the 1970s.

Between 1957 and 1962, when the government finally devalued the Egyptian pound, the authorities continually interfered with the exchange rate through indirect means and frequently changed their minds. Export premiums were introduced, but their level and commodity coverage varied; import surcharges were also used. At the end of 1961 the complex system of differentiated premiums and surcharges was replaced by two rates: in one case a 10 percent depreciation of the official rate was applied to imports of raw materials, foodstuffs, and capital equipment; and in the other a 20 percent depreciation was applied to almost all other imports and exports. This unification of implicit exchange rates prepared the way for the small devaluation of May 1962, which raised the value of a U.S. dollar from 35.2 to 43.5 piastres for all transactions except Suez Canal tolls and students' scholarships abroad.

In 1961 the government nationalized virtually all export-import enterprises and turned foreign trade into a public sector activity controlled by the state. When both industry and foreign trade are nationalized and investment decisions are centrally planned, import tariffs lose their significance as instruments for protection. Planners make the investment decisions, and the government then protects the industries it owns by quantitative restrictions on imports. In such a situation tariffs affect price and cost structures but not investment decisions.

The performance of industry since the nationalization of foreign trade has been extremely sensitive to the administration of the foreign exchange budget, and hence to import quotas and controls. Between 1961 and 1973 the foreign trade regime was most illiberal and extensively centralized. In 1963 the right of private industrial firms to import directly was abolished. Import licensing thus became superfluous and was abolished the following year. In the import administration system in operation since 1964, a central body decided the foreign exchange allocations to the forty-six administratively defined sectors, but the detailed allocation within each sector was left to individual ministries. According to Hansen and Nashashibi, the peculiarity of this system was that (at least at the beginning) the foreign exchange devoted each week to imports was linked to actual export earnings and payment obligations of the preceding and following weeks.[4] This rigid arithmetical link between weekly budgets and weekly receipts seems to have been relaxed in 1965, and it is doubtful that it was ever implemented with rigor. Yet the system, as devised, unnecessarily restricted allocation decisions. The important point, however, is that centralization, lack of flexibility, and the absence of a convincing procedure for appraising the relative needs of various sectors and individual enterprises led to considerable misallocations of foreign exchange to imports. The pattern of imbalances in the composition of import orders has already been described. Over time, many imported commodities appear to have displayed repeated cycles of surplus holdings and shortages. The important implication is that industry in the 1960s suffered perhaps more from the maladministration of imports than from the binding limitations of total foreign exchange availability.

Liberalization in the early 1970s did not abolish the system of foreign exchange budgeting and import administration. A parallel foreign exchange market was created and an own-exchange import scheme was introduced. By offering a more attractive rate than the official rate for certain transactions, the parallel market encourages remittances from Egyptians residing abroad, transfers by citizens of such countries, tourism, and exports of nontraditional items. These new foreign exchange resources are then made available to the private sector for industrial imports, tourism-related goods, and certain payments. The parallel market thus made foreign exchange available to economic agents who previously were denied access to it, but at a higher price than the official rate. The import procedures applied in this context to the private sector have been changed more than once since 1973. Though cumbersome, they are not unduly restrictive.

4. Egypt: Foreign Trade Regimes and Economic Development, p. 123.

Export Policies

The policy measures implemented under different economic systems in favor of industrial exports were not very effective for two reasons. First, Egyptian policymakers have been traditionally concerned with cotton exports and the maximization of foreign exchange earnings from that trade. Second, the industrialization strategy, which relied heavily on tariff protection and on planning for self-sufficiency, discriminated against exports.

The government often had recourse to measures that may be construed as partial or indirect devaluation — for example, export accounts, import entitlement, and multiple exchange rate systems were widely used in the late 1940s and 1950s. Egypt devalued only in 1962, but it is difficult to assess the relevance of such measures since a large proportion of the country's export was absorbed by the Eastern bloc and some developing countries under bilateral trade agreements.

Export subsidies, combined with tariffs, are akin to a devaluation. Egypt has often used subsidies to promote exports of selected manufactured goods such as textiles. In the 1950s and 1960s institutions were established that operated as equalization funds and, among other functions, levied taxes on inputs of domestic output and subsidized exports. The earliest of such foundations was the Cotton Spinning and Weaving Fund, established in 1953. Although funds were created later for leather, tobacco, rayon, fertilizers, and other products, the range of manufactured goods granted export subsidies has always been extremely limited; cotton yarn, fabric, and some food products constitute virtually the whole range. The subsidy given to textiles varied considerably from year to year. In the early 1960s it was as high as 30 percent of the unit value. In 1966-67 the subsidy was approximately 3 to 4 percent of the unit price. In the early 1970s public sector textile firms received a 12 percent subsidy for exports to convertible currency countries and a 3 percent subsidy for exports to bilateral trade agreement countries.

Price Administration

Price administration, which in Egypt is both complex and extensive, necessarily involves implicit taxes and subsidies, with varying effects on exports. In some instances prices are manipulated to produce a desired effect; for example, certain industrial inputs are supplied by the government at low, fixed prices in order to lower costs of production for the benefit of domestic consumers and for competitiveness in foreign markets. Often the effect of administered prices bears no relation to the stated objectives, but is the unpredictable outcome of interactions between a given input-output structure and autonomous price-fixation measures relating to many

commodities and services. Cotton textiles furnish an example. In
certain years cotton was sold to domestic spinners at prices higher
than the export price. Such an implicit tax on the input must be set
against the explicit export subsidy in working out the total net effect.
In other years, however, the domestic price to spinners was set at
a lower price than the export price. The direct subsidy was thus
compounded by an indirect price difference.

The government is now encouraging manufactured exports (indeed, all exports), especially from the private sector. The Foreign Investment Law can be seen in this context as an export promotion measure. Foreign investment in free-trade zones benefits
from incentives designed on the assumption that the entire output
of these areas will be exported. The incentives are: complete exemption from all taxes and tariff duties for an indefinite period, no
restrictions on repatriation of earnings and capital, and an implicit
subsidy on the infrastructure because public utility services are
grossly underpriced. The private sector generally is encouraged
to export through a set of incentives, including the favorable parallel market rate (applicable with limitations to certain goods only),
the right to retain a portion of their foreign exchange earnings for
own-imports, and a rebate on duties and certain taxes paid on inputs for the production of exported goods.

Cotton Policies

Textiles are a major branch of manufacturing in Egypt, and cotton is a main domestic industrial input. Policies relating to cotton
are thus of major significance to industrial development and performance. Of particular interest are the very old prohibition of raw
cotton imports in Egypt and the more recent policy that determines
prices to domestic spinners in relation to export prices. Before
the nationalization of the cotton trade in 1962, all measures, such
as export taxes and foreign exchange premiums, that were applied
to cotton sales abroad had some effect on the domestic textile
industry.

The prohibition of cotton imports was not initially a protectionist measure; when it was introduced in 1916 Egypt had no modern
textile industry and cotton producers were doing very well on foreign markets. The motive was to protect plants from diseases
originating abroad. The prohibition meant that the Egyptian textile
industry had access only to long-staple cotton though it produced
largely coarse yarn and fabrics.

The price policy is characterized mainly by constant prices to
domestic spinners. The selling price to the textile industry was
increased only once in a stepwise fashion. In the early 1960s the
export price was lower than the domestic price and the textile
industry was in a sense penalized. The effect of such price

differentials — in fact a tax on inputs — is to reduce the degree of protection granted otherwise to the industry. But from 1965-66 onward the export price was consistently higher — in some years considerably so — than the sale price to domestic spinners. The rationale of the policy, of course, was to prevent a sharp rise in the cost of living that would result from an increase in the price of textiles. The main burden is borne not by the government, but by farmers who receive much less than the export price for their cotton. More precisely, the policy has tended to stabilize both the selling price to spinners and the buying prices from farmers, while the government absorbs fluctuations in export prices. Yet some adjustments had to be made to both selling and buying prices. In the early 1960s farmers received more than the export prices and less than prices paid by domestic spinners (see table 12-3). In the second half of the 1960s they received less than the export price and almost as much as paid by the local industry. From 1971-72 on, though buying prices were slightly raised, they received much less than export prices and somewhat more than the domestic selling price. Such a policy may be justified in terms of income stabilization, but its allocative effects may be seriously distorted.

TABLE 12-3. PRICES OF MEDIUM-STAPLE
COTTON FOR DOMESTIC SPINNERS AND
EXPORT, 1961-62 TO 1975-76
(Egyptian pounds)

Year	Price for domestic spinners	Export price
1961-62	75.25	56.00
1962-63	75.50	63.50
1963-64	75.50	69.25
1964-65	75.50	76.50
1965-66	75.50	101.00
1966-67	75.50	94.00
1967-68	75.50	96.00
1968-69	75.50	96.00
1969-70	75.50	94.00
1970-71	80.50	91.00
1971-72	80.50	105.00
1972-73	80.50	171.00
1973-74	80.50	280.00
1974-75	80.50	205.00
1975-76	80.50	n.a.

n.a. Not available.
Note: The export price is the price ruling at the end of the marketing year. The medium-staple cottons considered are Ashmouui and Gizabb.
Source: General Organization for Cotton.

Policies for Industrial Goods

Price controls were introduced in Egypt at the beginning of World War II when the economic system was very liberal and almost completely dominated by private enterprise. A severe inflation resulted from the disruption of trade and the expansion in domestic demand fueled by military expenditure. The price controls affected a small range of commodities, such as bread, sugar, cooking oil, kerosene, and certain textiles for mass consumption. Rents of dwellings were also subjected to controls. The balance between supply and demand was achieved largely by quantitative rationing and subsidies. The black market, as usual in such circumstances, produced the final adjustments. The policy was justifiable during the war as a temporary corrective to a structural imbalance.

Since the emergence of the public sector in industry, prices of manufactured goods have been administered by the authorities on the principle of cost-plus pricing. Costs are defined in the accounting sense of actual outlays, not in the economic sense of the best marginal opportunity. The margin above costs is supposed to give a fair accounting profit to the public enterprise of 10 to 15 percent. Such a principle is far from satisfactory: the cost-plus price may not correspond to optimum output; the function of profits as an indicator of efficiency is vitiated; and the firm is under less pressure to seek cost-reducing improvements in its methods of organization and operation. Moreover, administered prices do not clear markets, while the unexpected buildup of unwanted stocks and regular shortages are common under such a price system.

The formal responsibility for industrial prices lies with the Industrial Control Board within the Ministry of Industry. In practice, several official agencies, commissions, and boards have responsibilities for determining prices, and though they are supposed to operate at different levels — national or regional; factory, wholesale, or retail — or are specific to different sets of products and commodities, conflicts often arise. The general cost-plus principle is not adhered to. Certain products are considered "essential" and their prices rigidly maintained at some low, unprofitable level. Usually there are either subsidies directly linked to the product and its main inputs or indirect compensation, such as a higher price allowed on a joint product of the firm. Thus, in textiles the heavy cotton fabrics are apparently subsidized while the finest varieties are subject to heavy indirect taxation. Commodities considered luxuries may have their prices administratively determined, but the markup is usually more generous. These more than other commodities tend to attract indirect taxes, sometimes referred to in Egypt as "price differences." If costs happen to rise, they will generally be passed on to the prices of luxuries, but not necessarily to those for necessities.

Frequent complaints about price determination in Egypt relate to the insufficient administrative resources, such as personnel, information, and the ability to monitor and verify, in the agencies responsible. Moreover, the list of products subject to price controls is imperfectly specified, the price review mechanism responds more readily to pressures to raise prices than to the need to lower them when costs are falling, and the numerous objectives of price administration — chiefly income distribution but also demand management, raising fiscal revenues, allocating foreign exchange and other resources — conflict in a chaotic manner.

The industrial price policy is in urgent need of a complete overhaul. It could be dangerous and self-defeating to dismantle the administered price system overnight. It is essential, however, to plan a transition over the medium term to a situation in which policy interference with the market mechanism is restricted to a few measures and controls for certain distributional objectives. The reform could begin with the removal of certain anomalies, say, the coexistence of an implicit tax on cotton sold to domestic spinners and a subsidy on yarn or fabrics. Another common anomaly is the imposition of tariffs on certain imports used for the production of a heavily protected good. It would be preferable to abolish the tariff on the input and to lower the protection given to the final good. Eventually industrial firms must be exposed to markets — first the domestic and later the world market. But this may not be possible unless the problems of technological efficiency are tackled in conjunction with the problems of poor administration. Price reforms should be part of a package of interdependent nonprice measures. Some industries need investment for the modernization of their plants; others, technical assistance on the shop floor, in the offices, or for quality control; still others need access to credit or to certain material or human inputs. To remove price distortions without supplying the "missing factor" may turn out to be ineffective.

Employment Policy

The efficiency of Egyptian industry may have been seriously impaired by the employment policy that since 1962 has caused large-scale overmanning of public sector enterprises. Its justification is social welfare, but a policy that forces firms to absorb workers in excess of their production requirements is costly. Moreover, the surplus labor in offices and on the shop floor has to be occupied in some way; this leads to more red tape, an excessive subdivision of labor, and redundant steps and movements in all processes.

The social welfare policy went beyond simple employment, it legally guaranteed tenure for workers and employees. It is virtually impossible to dismiss a worker in a public enterprise and extremely difficult to do so in the private sector. Although there is a need to protect employees against unfair dismissal, security of tenure is not conducive to industrial efficiency, especially in a system that does not generally use monetary incentives to improve performance. A reform of the labor law seems essential. The right to dismiss should be introduced with some important safeguards, and consideration might be given to a scheme for unemployment benefits. If this is not possible, public enterprises must be allowed to provide performance-related rewards to individual workers and employees. In any case, public enterprises should be allowed to adjust the size of their labor force to their requirements: in time, overmanning can be cured through simple attrition.

Small-scale Industries

Major problems adversely affecting productivity and the quality of output or services and, by extension, constraining the growth of small-scale industries include: out-of-date machinery, deficiencies in production and management (in product design and development, production planning and work methods, material selection, quality control, preventive maintenance, and so on), poor working conditions and housekeeping, and marketing problems.[5] Their relative importance varies with the industry and the size of the establishment. To correct the situation, extensive technical assistance is necessary. The introduction of more sophisticated techniques and specialized machines creates a need to upgrade skills, while increasing shortages of skills (mainly because of emigration to oil-rich Arab countries) suggest the need to accelerate training. Shortage of space is a vexing problem and calls for appropriate schemes — such as industrial complexes (flatted factories) or industrial estates — to accommodate small-scale industry, a task fraught with difficulties. The dilapidated infrastructure, particularly in telecommunications and transport, poses other problems, as does the timely procurement of raw and intermediate materials, despite recent improvements. The situation is compounded by lack of access to institutional finance, particularly for small-scale industries at the lower end of the size range, and by institutional restraints.

Administrative responsibility for small-scale industry is divided among half a dozen ministries. This dispersal hampers the development of consistent regulations and their uniform implementation, undermines the ability to focus on common problems, and impedes proper action and the coordination of effort. It would be highly desirable to assign responsibility for all activities in the sector, probably excluding handicrafts, to the Small Industries Department in the Ministry of Industry, when it is properly reorganized and revitalized. Administrative procedures as such do not seem particularly

5. Similar problems afflict the artisanal sector.

cumbersome. Rather it is the processing phase and manner of conduct that create inconvenience and delays, and efforts to improve efficiency in these areas should be beneficial.

So far the government's measures aim primarily at easing bureaucratic bottlenecks, particularly in the issue of licenses, and foreign exchange restraints on the importation of raw materials and equipment, a policy that is already yielding tangible results. The sector still appears to be discriminated against in areas such as taxation, duties on imports of capital goods, and the 10 percent price margin that favors the public sector in purchases of government stores. Remedial action is called for to place private industry on an equal footing with the public sector. Because of the massive problems of verification and policing, price controls cannot be monitored judiciously. In addition, though they affect a rather limited range of products, price controls tend to thwart the promotion of new projects or the modernization and expansion of the small-scale industries affected (shoemaking, textiles, food processing). Prices ought to be allowed to attain levels reflecting true opportunity costs.

Some industries that offer the most promise are engineering (including transport equipment), food processing, ready-made garments, footwear and leather products, woodworking and furniture, printing, and chemicals. The strength of these industries lies in the growing demand for and export potential of their products, their relatively insignificant scale economies, and their production of differentiated products for specialized markets. In addition, they complement larger industry through manufacturing operations in which the processes are readily separable (for example, the production of specialized machine products, components, and tools); craft or precision handwork; simple operations of assembly, mixing, or finishing; and the provision of services and repairs. These promising industries belong to the so-called modern small-scale industrial sector but have a relatively low capital intensity, and their expansion should enlarge employment for the urban poor. About 50 percent of the investment outlay in the next several years would probably be for the replacement of old equipment, which would have zero employment effect;[6] some 45 percent would be for expansion and 5 percent for new entries, both of which would have a positive employment effect. The investment for expansion would vary among subsectors, but is likely to hover around LE2,000 to LE4,000 per job created. Within these subsectors, the target group should include primarily enterprises with from ten to fifty workers and preferably those with some specialization in the management function, which would enhance their potential for continued viability and self-sustained growth.

Support need not necessarily be confined to these subsectors or to enterprises of this size. Larger enterprises (those employing

6. Replacement of obsolete equipment preserves existing jobs, however, which otherwise might be eliminated.

fifty to a hundred workers) may well have a low capital-labor ratio and thus a substantial employment effect, as in the manufacture of ready-made garments. Modern establishments employing nine or less workers should be catered to for similar reasons. Technical assistance should be extended to all interested enterprises employing a hundred workers or less, but any attempt to encompass a great many subsectors, though desirable, would be impractical at this initial stage. Technical assistance, while not unimportant, does not rate top priority in the case of ready-made garments, food processing, or printing.

POSSIBLE FURTHER ACTIONS

While progress has been made in creating an environment to encourage the expansion and growth of the industrial sector, much remains to be done. Broad objectives have been set in the five-year plan, and appropriate legislative actions have been taken. Foreign industrial investments remain below expectations, however, and Egypt's capacity for absorbing substantial additional industrial investment remains relatively limited.

In accordance with the foregoing list of issues, the following actions are recommended:

- Price controls need to be reduced further to allow incentives for increased efficiency.
- Management of public sector companies must be given more responsibility over marketing decisions and greater freedom over pricing decisions. Management should also be allowed to raise wages of some employees beyond the limits now imposed and to reduce excess staff. Responsibilities for investment need to be defined. Management must be given responsibility and incentives for proper maintenance.
- A policy package needs to be developed to encourage the import-substitution process as well as to provide incentives for exports, particularly to convertible currency areas.
- Egypt's construction industry needs to be strengthened and expanded by providing incentives and encouraging joint ventures.
- Steps that would benefit small-scale industries are:
  — Develop a workable information system and a reliable flow of data on small-scale industry and the private sector in general.
  — Undertake a census (or sample survey) of private manufacturing to establish the present status of the sector.
  — Work out a system whereby the ministry would monitor the implementation of the investment projects it approves.

— Assign responsibility for all small-scale industry activities, probably excluding traditional handicrafts, to the Ministry of Industry, ensuring proper coordination with other ministries and agencies.
— Eliminate existing biases against small-scale industry with respect to incentives, procurement, and taxation.
— Review the existing incentives to ascertain their effectiveness in redirecting exports.
— Eliminate controls on prices and profit margins.
— Encourage subcontracting arrangements.

APPENDIX: EFFECTIVE PROTECTION

The impact of tariffs, taxes, and import restrictions on the industrial structure of production (with allowance for deviations in the value of the exchange rate) may be assessed using the concept of effective protection. Effective protection is more relevant than nominal protection for such an analysis because it takes into account changes in the prices of both inputs and outputs owing to policy interferences with import trade. Effective protection is usually defined as a measure of the percentage increase in value added made possible by the protective structure. In other words, effective protection measures the excess of value added at domestic prices over value added at world prices as a percentage of either. Effective protection is sometimes taken as a broad indicator of efficiency. Industries that seem to enjoy high rates of effective protection are thought to be inefficient, the assumption being that they would not have survived without the help of a favorable tariff structure.

The concept of effective protection, however, should be applied with caution. There are problems both of measurement and interpretation. Though it is often assumed that tariffs raise the domestic price to the full value of the border price plus impost, this is not necessarily correct. Further, it is wrong to expect definite correlations between the pattern of protection and the pattern of investment, because protection is but one of the factors that influence the investment pattern. In Egypt since the late 1950s, planning decisions that were almost wholly independent of the tariff structure determined the allocation of investable resources.

The data provided in tables 12-4 and 12-5 on effective protection in Egyptian industry should be treated as a broad indication of the relative efficiency of different branches of manufacturing. The precise levels of protective rates do not mean much; the ranking by industry is of greater interest.

The data for 1959 suggest very heavy protection for some basic consumer goods industries, such as textiles, leather, and wearing

TABLE 12-4. RATES OF EFFEC-
TIVE PROTECTION (REP) FOR
SELECTED INDUSTRIES, 1959
(percent)

Industry	REP
Tobacco	100
Textiles	92
Leather and products	80
Wearing apparel	67
Electrical machinery	62
Rubber	59
Transport equipment	47
Metallic products	43
Basic metals	41
Nonmetallic products	34
Paper	33
Wood	32
Chemicals	32
Machinery (nonelastic)	23
Furniture	22
Food	21
Petroleum products	17
Beverages	210

Note: REP here is the difference
between value added at domestic and
world prices as a percentage of value
added at domestic prices. Nontraded
inputs are treated as part of value
added. An REP of 100 percent or over
means that value added at foreign
prices is negative. When REP is negative, value added at domestic prices
is smaller than value added at foreign
prices, which means that the tariff
structure discriminates against the
industry.
Source: Mabro and Radwan, Industrialization of Egypt, p. 61.

apparel. The high place of electrical machinery, rubber, and transport equipment in the ranking is not surprising. It is difficult to
compare the two sets of data because the first relates exclusively
to industry groupings, while the second relates mainly to commodities. The general impression derived about ranking is consistent,
however. Thus, as Mabro and Radwan show, yarn, the major textile product, appears to have been more protected in 1959-60 than
sugar, a main product of the food industry; and textiles enjoyed
more protection than food, rubber (tires in Hansen and Nashashibi),
and chemicals (represented by fertilizers in Hansen and Nashashibi).

TABLE 12-5. RATES OF EFFECTIVE PROTECTION IN TEN MANUFACTURING INDUSTRIES, SELECTED YEARS

(percent)

Industry	1954	1957	1960	1962-63 to 1963-64	1964-65 to 1965-66	1969-70
Cement	-31	-45	-35	n.a.	-28	n.a.
Phosphates	15	34	n.a.	n.a.	7	n.a.
Nitrates	25	48	n.a.	n.a.	12	n.a.
Sugar	n.a.	n.a.	-5	n.a.	n.a.	14
Tires	n.a.	n.a.	240	262	n.a.	n.a.
Cotton						
Fabric	n.a.	n.a.	n.a.	n.a.	68	n.a.
Yarn	n.a.	31	62	n.a.	n.a.	213
Automobiles	n.a.	n.a.	n.a.	305	n.a.	n.a.
Paper	n.a.	n.a.	n.a.	240	n.a.	n.a.
Iron and steel	n.a.	n.a.	n.a.	n.a.	599	n.a.

n.a. Not available.
Source: Hansen and Nashashibi, Egypt: Foreign Trade Regimes and Economic Development, p. 310.

or nonmetallic products (cement).[7] The considerable increase in the rate of effective protection for cotton yarn in 1969-70 is worth noting as well as the high rates for steel (1964-65). The high figures for rubber tires are a bit suspicious and may not be representative of the industry in later years.

7. Mabro and Radwan, Industrialization of Egypt; and Hansen and Nashashibi, Egypt: Foreign Trade Regimes and Economic Development.

13
Petroleum and Natural Gas

The planning and development of the petroleum and natural gas sector has proceeded effectively despite changes in the political setting and in the orientation of the economic system. Since the early 1950s the objective has been to exploit the country's hydrocarbon resources at the maximum rate possible, and this has been done in partnership with experienced Western international oil companies. In spite of the waxing and waning of Egypt's political relations with Western countries during this period, the domestic petroleum sector maintained a continuous and fruitful relation with Western oil companies. By offering attractive terms for exploration and production, Egypt has had no difficulty finding experienced foreign partners. Because of the capital and technological intensity of the sector, its development has been possible with a relatively small number of technically competent nationals and foreigners, unencumbered by excessive regulation.

As early as Roman times, oil seepages were noted near the mouth of the Gulf of Suez, but the first significant modern discoveries in Egypt were not made until 1909. In spite of early discovery and commercial exploitation in Gemza, 160 miles south of Suez, the rate of subsequent discovery and development of Egyptian oil fields lagged behind that in other Middle Eastern countries, making Egypt one of the relatively smaller producers in the area today.

In 1963 the government intensified the search by signing exploration and development agreements with several oil companies. Oil fields were discovered in and near the Gulf of Suez, but some of those in Sinai came under Israeli control following the 1967 war and were not returned to Egypt until the end of 1975. The loss of the Sinai fields was counterbalanced by the development of the relatively large el-Morgan field and by new discoveries in the Gulf of Suez (July and Ramadan) and the Western Desert (Abu Gharadeeq and Razak). Natural gas has been recently discovered and exploited near Alexandria and in the Western Desert.

274

OIL- AND GAS-BEARING STRUCTURES

More than 90 percent of Egypt's oil is produced from the Gulf
of Suez, an arm of the Red Sea, 320 kilometers long, between the
Eastern Desert and Sinai Peninsula. More than 300 exploratory
wells — including about eighty which are either offshore or on is-
lands — have been drilled in this area of about 20,000 square kilometers, resulting in the delineation of twenty-eight oil fields.

The Western Desert covers an area of 650,000 square kilometers
from the Mediterranean coast to latitude $25^{\circ}N$ and is bounded on the
east by the Nile Delta. More than 200 exploratory wells have been
drilled, but only seven commercial discoveries of oil or natural
gas have been made. Gas fields with cumulative reserves of more
than 1.6 trillion cubic feet have been discovered at Abu Gharadeeq
and Abu Qir. Hopes of making a major strike still persist as giant
fields have been discovered in similar structures in the neighboring
countries.

In the Nile Delta, an area of about 50,000 square kilometers,
fifty exploratory wells have been drilled. No oil has been discovered, though four gas fields have been found. Only one, Abu Maadi,
is considered commercially exploitable. Most commercially exploitable oil fields have been in production for a considerable time.
Of the estimated recoverable reserves of 530 million tons of oil,
about 350 million tons are now estimated to remain.

NATURAL GAS

The current production level of associated gas in Egypt is around
100 million cubic feet a day (Mmcf/d), which is flared, except for
a nominal amount used at the oil fields. Most of the associated gas
comes from the oil fields in the Gulf of Suez. Recent discoveries
have added to the availability of associated gas, and present estimates of recoverable reserves are in the order of 800,000 million
cubic feet.

Nonassociated gas on a commercially exploitable scale has been
discovered at several fields. The most important are described
here, and the recoverable reserves and projected levels of production are shown in table 13-1.

Abu Gharadeeq was discovered in 1971 and has an estimated recoverable reserve of 0.6 trillion cubic feet. Gulf Petroleum Company (GUPCO) has been producing gas from this field since 1977.
The gas is transported from Abu Gharadeeq through a 24-inch pipeline over 370 kilometers to Helwan, near Cairo.

Abu Maadi was discovered in the Nile Delta by Ente Nazionale
Idrocarburi (ENI), an Italian firm. After the renegotiation of the

TABLE 13-1. NATURAL GAS RESERVES
AND FORECAST OF PRODUCTION

Area	Recoverable reserves (trillion cubic feet)	Millions of cubic feet a day		
		Actual 1978	Projected	
			1980	1985
Abu Maadi	1.0	19	50	110
Abu Gharadeeq	0.6	55	100	100
Abu Qir	1.2	...	55	120
Abu Qir North	3.0	...	...	n.a.
Gulf of Suez	0.8	Flared	Flared	80
Amal[a]	0.5	...	...	...
Total	7.1	74	205	410

... Zero or negligible.
n.a. Not available.
a. Production planned only on the contingency that associated
gas for the Ras Shukeir project falls below 80 Mmcf/d.
Source: Egyptian General Petroleum Corporation (EGPC).

production-sharing agreement its ownership was transferred to the
Egyptian government, and the field is now being operated by Petro-
bel (Belayim Petroleum Company), a subsidiary of the Egyptian
General Petroleum Corporation (EGPC). The recoverable reserves
of this field are estimated at 1 trillion cubic feet, capable of supplying 100 Mmcf/d for about twenty-five years.

An offshore gas field on the periphery of the Western Desert and
the Nile Basin, Abu Qir was discovered in 1969. The field is estimated to have recoverable reserves of 1.2 trillion cubic feet which
would sustain a supply of 100 Mmcf/d for around thirty years. A
57-kilometer pipeline, with a capacity of 100 Mmcf/d, has been constructed from Abu Qir to Alexandria and from there to Damanhur
via Kafr el-Dawar.

A recently discovered offshore field, Abu Qir North is located
55 kilometers northeast of Alexandria and about 20 kilometers north
of the existing Abu Qir gas fields. So far, one exploratory well has
been drilled and tested. While further drilling will be required to
delineate the field, recoverable reserves are estimated from the
existing production data at 3 trillion cubic feet.

Offshore in the Gulf of Suez, the Amal field has recoverable reserves of 0.5 trillion cubic feet. It will be developed by EGPC, if
necessary, to supplement the associated gas supply to Suez and
Cairo.

EXPLORATION AGREEMENTS

Exploration agreements have changed from the concessions of the pre-1960s to participation agreements, which were subsequently converted into production-sharing agreements. Under the concession arrangements, the government imposed a royalty and tax on the oil companies that did not exceed the companies' net-of-cost realization (computed on the basis of a posted price) by more than 50 percent. In 1963 the government of Egypt for the first time entered into a participation agreement (with ENI) by which the costs of exploration and development were shared equally between the foreign contractor and the national oil company. The profit oil was also shared equally, with the government reserving the right to tax the foreign contractor to a maximum level of 50 percent on its share of profit oil. By this device, the government's "take" was increased significantly over the earlier concession arrangements.

In 1970 the government of Egypt entered into the first production-sharing contract. The cost of exploration and development was borne exclusively by the foreign contractor and amortized, interest-free, over the next four and eight years, respectively. After amortization and the operating costs were taken into account, the profit oil was shared between the foreign contractor and the government in the ratio of 40:60. In successive agreements, Egypt has improved upon these conditions, and in some Egypt's share in the profit oil has been negotiated at 87 percent. The minimal cost recovery factor is assumed at 20 percent, and if costs fall below this level the difference accrues to the state. The contractor's share of oil is free of all taxes.

PRODUCTION

The exploration policy was designed to maximize oil production without the government's having to bear the risks of exploration. The policy has been successful; of the 1978 production of about 500,000 barrels a day, almost 470,000 barrels are produced from fields discovered by foreign oil companies. Since 1973 even stronger efforts have been made to attract foreign oil companies. At present, foreign contractors share oil with the national company at an average ratio of 1:3. The remuneration to foreign oil companies is attractive, and in 1978 averaged about US$1.50 a barrel.

The forecast of petroleum production is shown in table 13-2. It should be stressed that the projections are predicated upon new discoveries being made which would not only double the current level of production but would also compensate for the decline in production from oil fields that have already peaked. A failure to make

TABLE 13-2.   FORECAST OF PETROLEUM PRODUCTION
(millions of tons)

Operating company	Actual 1978	Projected 1980	1985
General Petroleum Company (GPC)	1.3	1.1	0.4
Oriental Petroleum Company (COPE)	4.1	5.3	3.4
Gulf Petroleum Company (GUPCO)	17.9	19.5	12.0
GUPCO (Abu Gharadeeq)	0.5	0.4	...
Western Desert Company (WEPCO)	0.5	0.4	0.1
EGYPTCO (Moleha)	...	...	0.1
DEMINEX	...	0.2	7.5
New discoveries	...	...	23.0
Total	24.3	29.4	46.5

...   Zero or negligible.
Note: The table does not include oil produced in territories under Israeli occupation.
Source: EGPC.

new discoveries at the assumed rates could result in a significant shortfall in production. Of the 1978 production (around 500,000 barrels a day), about 20 percent was the share of foreign partners, 40 percent was consumed domestically, and the rest was available for export.

DOMESTIC DEMAND

Consumption of petroleum products has been rising rapidly and in 1978 was more than 10 million tons compared with 6.7 million tons in 1974. The overall annual growth rate has been in the order of 11.8 percent, with liquefied petroleum gas (LPG) recording the sharpest increase (16 percent). Consumption of LPG would have been higher except for the physical constraint of supply. EGPC projects that, in the absence of demand management or a significant increase in the price, a growth rate in consumption of 12.5 percent would be maintained until 1985. This relatively high growth rate is attributable in part to a quantum jump in thermal power generation, which is projected to rise from 17,000 million kilowatt hours (kWh) in 1980 to 28,000 million kWh in 1985. The growth rate beyond 1985 would depend, in part, on the induction of nuclear power; delays in commissioning the proposed plants would increase the reliance on fossil fuels for power generation. On the basis of past trends and the assumption that GNP grows at about 6.5 percent a year in real terms, the pattern of consumption is projected in table 13-3.

TABLE 13-3. PROJECTED CONSUMPTION
OF PETROLEUM PRODUCTS
(thousands of tons)

Product	Actual			Projected	
	1974	1977	1978	1980	1985
Butane and propane	159	247	297	350	630
Gasoline	556	833	958	1,200	2,200
Naphtha	24	18	23		
Kerosene	1,109	1,363	1,389	1,750	2,600
Turbine fuel	119	101	182	350	400
Gas oil	1,055	1,507	1,706	2,500	3,500
Diesel oil	168	150	154		
Fuel oil and natural gas					
Power	849	1,529 ⎱	5,192	3,600	7,700
Other	2,471	3,031 ⎰		3,700	5,400
Asphalt	64	142	...		
Lube oil	93	129	147	390	670
Total	6,667	9,050	10,048	13,840	23,100
Availability of natural gas (fuel-oil equivalent)				1,650	3,300
Demand for liquid hydrocarbons				12,190	19,800

... Zero or negligible.
Source: EGPC.

The projected demand for hydrocarbons by 1985 is around 23 million tons. A qualitative change in the pattern of consumption is, however, expected, with natural gas being increasingly used as a substitute for liquid hydrocarbons. Egypt is making conscious efforts to increase the absorptive capacity for natural gas. The current production potential is 300 Mmcf/d against a demand of 110 Mmcf/d. The situation will be reversed by 1985 when the peak demand of about 950 Mmcf/d (average demand of 700 Mmcf/d) is expected to outstrip the production potential of 400 Mmcf/d. The gap between the projected demand and the likely supply of gas will have to be covered by liquid hydrocarbons that would otherwise have been exported. To remain an exporter of oil, Egypt will have to increase its exploratory efforts for gas and accelerate the program of developing known gas fields.

PRICES AND FISCAL CONTRIBUTION OF THE SECTOR

The worldwide price increases and consequent fall in the growth of oil consumption has had no impact in Egypt. Domestic prices are

TABLE 13-4. PETROLEUM PRODUCT PRICES, ESTIMATED COSTS, AND SUBSIDIES, 1978

Product	Pump-head price	Average refining cost	Average transport cost	Market-ing cost	Price net of marketing cost	International price[a]	Quantity marketed (thousands of tons)	Subsidy (millions of U.S. dollars)[b]
	U.S. dollars a ton							
Liquefied petroleum gas	74.88	10.94		40.32	34.56	170.00	275	37
Gasoline								
Premium	160.70	9.07	0.29	13.10	147.60	150.00	530	1
Regular	124.56	7.92	0.29	12.10	112.46	140.00	330	9
Kerosene	16.51	6.05	0.58	8.21	38.30	130.00	1,400	128
Gas oil	43.49	5.62	0.14	3.91	37.58	120.00	1,457	120
Diesel oil	35.42	4.61	2.30	6.91	28.51	120.00	147	14
Fuel oil	10.80	1.30	0.29	1.73	9.07	75.00	3,998	264
Gas	—	—	—	—	11.50	75.00	635	40
Total							8,772	615

— Not applicable.
a. LE1 = US$1.44
b. Based on September 1978 prices; since then there has been an appreciable increase.
Source: EGPC and World Bank estimates.

still maintained essentially at 1956 levels, except for motor gasoline, the retail price of which has successively been increased and is now more or less at par with international prices. The pumphead prices are fixed through a governmental decree, and the revenue accruing to the government and EGPC is what is secured from the sale of products, net of refining, marketing, and transport costs. The 1978 product prices, the estimated costs of refining, transportation, and marketing, and the implicit subsidy in relation to international prices are indicated in table 13-4. At the existing level of consumption, the subsidy implicit in the current prices is around US$70 a ton. Since many subsidies are built into the downstream operation, however, especially in the transport sector, the costs indicated in the table are at best a rough approximation. The real cost to the economy is probably higher and likely to increase with the growing consumption of oil products.

In its accounts, EGPC values Egypt's share of the oil produced and refined locally in terms of the net-back it derives from the domestic sale of the manufactured products.[1] Its present net-back per ton of local crude averages around US$11 a ton, a figure net of about US$17 a ton paid to the government in excise fees and Treasury dues. Thus, the total revenue derived from the domestic sale of crude is around US$30 a ton or US$4 a barrel — which is about equal to what it costs Egypt to produce a barrel in terms of cost oil and profit oil. In relation to the level of petroleum production, the fiscal and budgetary contribution to the economy is minimal. For 1978 a production level of 25 million tons valued at around US$2,500 million was envisaged, but Egypt was expected to secure only about US$1,000 million from domestic sales and exports.

MAJOR ISSUES

Four major issues will have to be addressed if Egypt is to obtain the maximum benefits from its resources of oil and gas. These concerns are with pricing policy, energy planning, the optimal use of natural gas, and improved technical data.

The 1978 price of a barrel of crude for domestic consumption was about US$4 (including excise taxes and other charges), compared with an export price of US$33 a barrel. As a result of this price difference Egypt is losing the opportunity of using its finite petroleum wealth to mobilize domestic financial resources, the shortage of which is becoming the main constraint on investment. Moreover, the subsidy implicit in such a pricing policy encourages wasteful consumption. In the absence of major new discoveries, the peaking

1. The net-back is the weighted average sale price to distributors, less average refining and transportation costs, Treasury dues, and excise fees.

oil fields and the sharply rising internal demand could transform
Egypt from an exporter to a net importer by the mid-1980s. This
means that domestic prices for petroleum products will have to be
increased significantly.

Egypt's energy planning suffers from serious gaps and inconsistencies. Indeed, a national energy policy, in the sense of an explicit statement of objectives in the energy field and specific plans for
achieving them, does not exist. It will be important to develop the
capability to prepare and implement energy development plans that
take into account the possibility of substitution between different
sources of energy — hydro, thermal, and nuclear. This question
is discussed more fully in chapter 17.

At present the production potential of natural gas is greater than
the demand, but this is expected to be reversed over the next few
years. The real danger is that as a result of the imbalance liquid
hydrocarbons will be diverted from export to the domestic market.
Since foreign oil companies are likely to have little interest in developing gas resources for domestic consumption, Egypt will have
to take the initiative in gas exploration and in adding more production wells.

A related question is the optimal use of natural gas. Egypt must
upgrade this resource from a fuel-oil equivalent to higher value uses.
There are areas where gas may be used as a substitute for liquid
fuels, thereby increasing exports (fuel oil) and reducing imports
(LPG and kerosene). Government policy has encouraged such sub-
stitutions since, in recent years, it has become more and more difficult to meet domestic consumer demand in large urban areas at
a reasonable cost. The international prices for LPG and kerosene
(the two main fuels used) have increased rapidly, putting a heavy
burden on Egypt's balance of payments. In addition, the rapid change
in Cairo to modern high-rise buildings makes the regular use of
portable fuels extremely hazardous.

The energy needs of domestic consumers in urban areas could
be met by either electricity or piped gas. The government has reviewed these alternatives and concluded that electricity would not
be energy efficient and would be more costly than gas. It has therefore decided to create gas distribution networks in the major cities.
The first step is the construction of a network in four districts of
Cairo: Maadi, Helwan, Heliopolis, and Nasr City, which, because
of the nature of the housing and the income level of consumers, appear to be the most suitable. This project should be followed
by the expansion of gas distribution to other areas in Cairo and
Alexandria.

Egyptian policymakers assume that the country will produce 1
million barrels of oil a day (about 50 million tons a year) by 1983.
This rate of production depends heavily on new discoveries that would
not only double the current level of production, but also compensate

for the shortfall that will result from the peaking of the oil fields. New discoveries have not yet kept pace with the increased output, and the production-reserve ratio has been falling. A more vigorous involvement by foreign oil companies has been inhibited by the absence of proper data. It is important for Egypt to undertake studies that would reorganize, coalesce, reinterpret, and expand the existing geological, seismic, and drilling data. The primary focus should probably be on areas in the Western Desert and the Nile Delta.

14
Tourism

Egypt is richly endowed with resources for tourism. It has shel-
tered three of the world's greatest civilizations — Pharaonic, Christian, and Islamic — and the remnants of this past are among the
world's oldest and most spectacular tourist attractions. In addition to its archaeological sites it has many natural assets — the Nile,
the desert, and the beaches along the Mediterranean coast. As the
most important cultural, religious, and political center of the Arab
world, Egypt has a cosmopolitan character that appeals to both casu-
al visitors and those steeped in its history and culture.

TOURISM ASSETS

The oldest and most important historical attractions are the temples and tombs of the Pharaonic dynasties, which are scattered
throughout the Nile Valley. In fact, the valley constitutes a vast
museum where archaeological work expands the knowledge of man's
past. Fascination with Egypt's antiquities continues unabated, as
demonstrated by the success of Pharaonic museum exhibitions in
several countries and by the popular support given to Unesco's reconstruction projects at Abu Simbel and Philae. The dynastic temples and tombs of greatest interest to tourists are: (1) the Giza
pyramids of Cheops, Chefren, and Micerinos, the Sphinx, and the
Sakkara (ancient Memphis) step pyramid and temples, all in Lower
Egypt and the vicinity of Cairo; (2) the Minya temples, the Beni
Hassan tombs (including those of Pharoah Ikhnaton and Queen Nef-
ertiti), and the Tel el-Amarna temples in Middle Egypt, 250 to 300
kilometers south of Cairo; and (3) in Upper Egypt the temples of
Luxor (ancient Thebes) and Karnak and the Necropolis in the Valley
of the Kings and the Valley of the Queens, about 670 kilometers south
of Cairo; and still farther south the temples of Esna, Edfu, Aswan,
Philae, and Abu Simbel.

Later historical sites include buildings and artifacts from the
Roman and early Christian periods, the most important of which are
in Alexandria. Because other Mediterranean countries have remains

284

from these periods, these sites have not attracted the attention from
tourists they rightly deserve. Other attractions include numerous
mosques and churches, the most interesting of which are in Cairo.
Cairo also offers several excellent museums, notably the Egyptian
Museum,[1] the richest museum of antiquities in the world, covering a period of 5,000 years; the Coptic Museum, which has a rare
collection dating back to the Christian era; and the Islamic Art
Museum.

In most of Egypt the climate is conducive to year-round tourism.
In the greater part of the Nile Valley and along the coast it is mild
and rarely rains. The summer temperature is rather high, but
low humidity makes the heat bearable. The climate of the Mediterranean coast is less favorable but is capable of sustaining a six-
month tourist season. Average temperatures there compare favorably with those of beach resorts of most other Mediterranean countries. Along the Mediterranean in the winter and the Red Sea in the
summer, strong coastal winds may cause sand storms. Because
of high temperatures and wind conditions, the tourist season along
the Red Sea does not include summer, but it can probably extend as
long as nine months.

Beach-oriented tourism, which makes up the bulk of the world's
tourism market, has developed in Egypt, although it has reached
major proportions only in Alexandria, the most important tourist
destination after Cairo. Unfortunately, most of the beaches near
Alexandria are polluted with oil, debris, and seaweed, and the
beaches east of the city are generally unattractive owing to dark,
silted sand and unclear water. For 560 kilometers west of Alexandria, however, the beaches are generally endowed with fine white
sand and clear blue-green water. The best area lies between el-
Alamein and Aquiba (100 to 300 kilometers west of Alexandria).
The new terminal of the Suez-Mediterranean oil pipeline and the
planned industrial development at Sidi Krei will probably make the
first 100 kilometers west of Alexandria unsuitable for international
tourism. Domestic tourists should continue to be attracted, however, especially for day visits from Alexandria, where the beaches
are overcrowded in summer.

A paved highway and a railroad run along the coast from Alexandria to the Libyan border, and there is an airport at Marsa Matruh.
The coastal region west of Alexandria is sparsely populated, mostly by Bedouin nomads, and undeveloped. Sidi Abd el-Raman and
Marsa Matruh are the only beaches where any significant development has taken place.

The Red Sea coastline extends for hundreds of kilometers from
Suez to the Sudanese border. Along the shore are small sandy
beaches, rugged mountains, views of the desert, and a great wealth

---

1. Unfortunately, its maintenance does not do justice to its riches.

of coral reefs and fish. The two main beaches — and practically the
only developed ones — are Ein Sukha, 55 kilometers south of Suez,
and Ghardaga, 385 kilometers south of Suez. There are small hotels
in both places, but after years of military use, they would have to
be renovated for tourism. A coastal road from Suez gives access
to Ein Sukha, while Ghardaga can be reached by road from Luxor
and by air. Like the northwest Mediterranean coast, it is sparsely
populated, underdeveloped, and surrounded by vast deserts.

The Nile remains a major tourist attraction. Not only does it
greatly enhance the cities bordering it but in recent years week-long
cruises along the Upper Nile have become popular with foreign tourists. Prospects look promising for several other cruises, including
some on the Lower and Middle Nile, and the cruiser fleet is being
substantially expanded. The desert close to the Nile and to Egypt's
main cities is another significant, if still unexploited, natural tourism asset. Camel rides and tent accommodations have been offered
with some success among Western tourists.

Until 1952 Egypt was the most important banking and financial
center in the Arab world as well as its main political, cultural, and
religious center. As such, it attracted both Arab and Western tourists. With the decline of its banking and financial status in the 1950s
and 1960s Egypt lost some of its appeal for tourists, who turned instead to Lebanon. Recent events have reversed that trend, however,
and Egypt has practically recovered its original position as the most
cosmopolitan country of the Arab world. Cairo and Alexandria continue to offer attractions for tourists, with their active night life,
rich folklore, handicrafts, and modern markets as well as their history and antiquities. Arab visitors prefer these big cities to other
places and spend an estimated 95 percent or more of their time in
them.

COMPARATIVE ADVANTAGES AND LIMITATIONS

Two major tourist areas overlap in Egypt: one, the Mediterranean basin — the most important tourist destination in the world (almost 60 million visitors a year) and heavily beach-oriented; the
other, the Middle East — much smaller (a few million visitors a
year) and more oriented to religion and culture. Egypt's Mediterranean area is fairly far from the main generating countries of central and northern Europe, but it is one of the closest of the Middle
Eastern countries.[2] This fact has had, and will continue to have,

2. This disadvantage of distance was reinforced after the big increase in air
fares following the 1973 energy crisis. On a back-to-back charter operation
from, say, Paris or London, a typical tour to Egypt's Mediterranean coast would
cost about US$40 to US$80 more than one to Tunisia or Morocco. (On scheduled

some bearing on the type of tourist Egypt has been receiving and the particular assets that it has decided to develop.

Accessibility

Compared with many other tourist destinations, Egypt is quite favorably located at the crossroads of most air and sea routes to Europe. Cairo's recently expanded airport is serviced by almost forty commercial airlines from all continents, including most of the major international carriers, with about 250 incoming and outgoing flights a week. Because several airports have been closed or restricted since the 1967 war, the only other commercially operational airports are in Luxor and Aswan. With the development of the Suez Canal, sea traffic has become very heavy. Access by road, on the other hand, is virtually limited to Libyan tourists because of the great distances.

Prices

Prices of goods and services purchased by foreign visitors in Egypt are generally very low. Hotel rates, however, are higher than those of most other Mediterranean destinations, though competitive with those of the Middle East. The rates of apartments and villas, the favorite accommodation of Arab tourists, are also high.[3] For all other items, such as food, entertainment, taxis, handicrafts, entrance fees to museums, historical sites, and sound and light performances, prices are kept very low by price controls and preferential exchange rates for tourists. Since the items most purchased by foreign visitors are also consumed by Egyptians, the pricing policy applicable to tourism has remained inseparable from macroeconomic pricing policies. It should be possible to remove a number of these items from price control without any inflationary effect on the general price level.

Costs

Hotel construction costs were rather high by international standards until 1972, but after the introduction of the parallel market rate they were reduced by about one-third in U.S. dollars. In the last few years, costs have increased steeply (20 percent, 25 percent,

flights the difference would, of course, be much higher.) This figure is not insignificant compared with a one-week total package cost, including air transport, accommodation, food, and ground transport, of the order of US$250 to Spain, US$320 to Tunisia, and US$380 to Egypt. Comparisons are difficult to make owing to differences among hotel categories, quality of food, and services, but they indicate the relative importance of distance and air fare.

3. Rents of US$1,500 to US$2,000 a month for a furnished three-bedroom apartment were not rare in the summer of 1977.

and 35 percent, in 1974, 1975, and 1976, respectively).[4] In Cairo, without land, it was estimated to cost LE25,000 (or some US$38,750 at the parallel market rate of LE0.645 in May 1976) per room for a five-star hotel, LE17,000 (or US$26,350) per room for a three-star hotel, and LE10,000 (or US$15,500) per room for a one-star hotel.[5]   Although these costs are not out of line with other Middle Eastern countries (about US$40,000 per room for a five-star hotel in Jordan, for example), they are more than for most other Mediterranean areas (for example, roughly US$20,000 per room for a four-star hotel in Tunisia and Morocco). Moreover, costs are significantly higher outside Cairo — as much as 40 percent higher in Upper Egypt and up to 60 percent higher in the western part of the Mediterranean coast (for example, Marsa Matruh). The main reasons for the cost increases are the overload of Egyptian constructing companies and the lack of skilled labor, caused by reconstruction of the Suez Canal area and emigration.

Infrastructure development costs for the Nile Valley seem to be low by international standards because Egypt's main transport, power, and telecommunication lines run north from Aswan along the Nile, and soil conditions, water supply, and sewerage do not pose major problems. Infrastructure costs for mass tourism development along the northwest and Red Sea coasts are significantly higher than along the Nile and most of the competing destinations in the Mediterranean. The main problem in these coastal areas is the scarcity of water and the absence of international airports.

THE TOURISM MARKET

Early in the twentieth century Egypt became a popular winter resort for rich Europeans and an obligatory destination for archaeologists and scholars who were fascinated by its Pharaonic treasures. Later as Egypt established itself as a cultural, political, and financial center of the Arab world, Arab visitors began to arrive. They have continued to come in increasing numbers over the past twenty-five years;[6] the record of Western tourists, though also upward, has been somewhat different and far more irregular.

Tourist Arrivals

In the mid-1950s about 150,000 foreign tourists (about 1 percent of the Mediterranean market) arrived in Egypt each year, of whom

4. Estimated by Misr Grand Hotel Company, the government agency supervising the construction of hotels.
5. Hotel standards in Egypt are somewhat lower than those in the same category elsewhere.
6. With a slight dip in 1977.

TABLE 14-1. EGYPT'S SHARE OF MEDITERRANEAN TOURIST ARRIVALS FROM EUROPE AND NORTH AMERICA, 1965-75

Year	Total Egyptian arrivals from Europe and North America (thousands)	Total Mediterranean arrivals from Europe and North America (thousands)	Egypt's share of total (percent)
1965	196	26,521	0.7
1966	213	30,828	0.7
1967	112	31,247	0.4
1968	74	31,039	0.2
1969	86	35,525	0.2
1970	66	38,653	0.2
1971	90	42,913	0.2
1972	134	47,198	0.3
1973	128	50,367	0.3
1974	172	44,900	0.4
1975	242	47,789	0.5

Source: Calculated from Batelle Research Centre, "Prospective Study of Tourism in the Mediterranean Basin" (Geneva, 1976).

60 percent were European and American and 33 percent Arab. In 1978 the number had increased to about 1.05 million foreign tourists (48 percent European and American and 43 percent Arab). While the number of Arab tourists has increased with little interruption and at an average rate of 12 percent a year since the mid-1950s, the growth in tourism of Europeans and Americans has been irregular and slower (about 8 percent a year on the average). This was the result of significant reductions in the aftermath of the 1956 nationalization of the Suez Canal, the 1967 war, and, to a lesser extent, the 1973 war, which left Egypt with a share of about 0.5 percent of Mediterranean tourist arrivals from Europe and America (table 14-1).

TABLE 14-2. TOURIST ARRIVALS AND LENGTH OF STAY IN EGYPT, 1952-78

Item	1952	1966	1968	1972	1973	1974	1975	1976	1977	1978
Foreign tourist arrivals (thousands)	76	579	319	541	535	668	793	984	1,004	1,052
Nights spent (thousands)	n.a.	9,793	4,376	6,614	6,394	6,505	5,854	6,796	6,339	7,137
Average length of stay (days)	n.a.	16.9	13.4	12.2	12.0	9.8	7.4	6.9	6.3	6.8

n.a. Not available.
Source: Ministry of Tourism.

TABLE 14-3. LENGTH OF STAY AND NIGHTS SPENT IN EGYPT BY NATIONALITY, 1955-78

Year	Average length of stay (days)				Total nights spent (thousands)				
	Arab	European	American	Other	Arab	European	American	Other	Total
1955	41	31	11	16	1,773	2,198	298	127	4,396
1956	34	36	15	13	2,085	2,677	350	119	5,231
1957	32	78	14	45	2,155	3,183	154	405	5,097
1958	24	25	12	17	1,960	1,121	200	372	3,653
1959	21	21	14	18	2,771	1,453	262	438	4,924
1960	18	17	9	14	2,291	1,531	331	407	4,560
1961	21	16	8	13	2,257	1,668	358	362	4,645
1962	17	16	8	11	1,964	1,349	303	550	4,166
1963	12	10	7	10	1,869	1,311	434	603	4,023
1964	19	12	6	13	3,856	1,986	426	756	7,024
1965	29	13	6	11	7,068	2,388	395	610	10,401
1966	25	12	6	11	6,439	2,327	424	593	9,783
1967	24	14	12	12	3,960	1,597	396	417	6,370
1968	19	8	5	6	3,436	625	125	189	4,376
1969	17	8	4	7	3,341	687	148	220	4,396
1970	16	8	5	6	3,676	537	128	233	4,574
1971	18	9	6	8	4,619	827	189	344	5,979
1972	15	8	7	8	4,810	1,095	286	423	6,614
1973	9	7	5	6	2,874	777	186	255	6,394
1974	11	9	5	7	4,544	1,261	293	407	6,505
1975	8	7	6	6	3,621	1,411	425	347	5,854
1976	8	6	6	5	4,081	1,855	500	360	6,796
1977	7	5	5	5	3,529	1,748	593	469	6,339
1978	8	6	6	5	3,717	2,085	840	495	7,137

Source: Ministry of Tourism and Central Agency for Public Mobilization and Statistics.

The total number of foreign tourist arrivals grew from 76,000 in 1952 to 1.05 million in 1978, a rate of 10.7 percent a year (table 14.2). Two periods, separated by the 1967 war, are distinguishable. From 1952 through 1966 the growth was steady and at 15.6 percent a year on the average. With the 1967 war, about 40 percent of the market was lost, but from 1968 to 1975 recuperation was fast (at a 13.9 percent average yearly rate of arrivals).

Length of Stay and Nights Spent in Egypt

Although the number of tourist arrivals has surpassed the level reached before the 1967 war, the number of nights spent in Egypt by foreign tourists in 1978 was still 40 percent below that of 1966. This was because the average length of stay was cut more than 50 percent (see table 14-2). The decline was particularly dramatic in the case of Arab tourists, but for American and European tourists it was less marked, dropping from about ten to seven days (see table 14-3).

In the mid-1950s Arab tourists used to stay an average of more than a month in Egypt. They would typically rent a furnished apartment or villa for the entire summer. By the mid-1960s the average length of stay had gone down slightly, to three to four weeks, indicating no substantial change in the pattern of visits. After the 1967 war, however, there were two changes: a steep increase in visitors from border countries, especially Libya, who stayed shorter periods, and a further decline in the length of stay of all Arab tourists. Perhaps because of the high rents charged for apartments and villas some Arabs found it cheaper to spend part of the summer vacation in Europe. As a consequence, the average length of stay of Arab tourists declined from two to three weeks in 1968-69 to less than ten days in 1976-78.

In the mid-1950s European tourists, too, would stay more than a month in a hotel, usually in Upper Egypt. For them Egypt was predominantly a winter resort, although some would also stay for long periods in Alexandria during the summer. The decline in their length of stay to roughly one week in recent years was largely owing to the change in type of visitor — from rich, long-staying, and resort-oriented tourists to middle-class businessmen and culture-oriented tourists, whose stays were much shorter.[7] Because the American tourists have always been predominantly businessmen and culture-oriented, no significant change in their pattern of visits has occurred. The reasons for the reduction in the length of stay may be transitory in the case of Arab tourists (their visits will probably lengthen as the supply of furnished apartments expands and their price declines), but those affecting European visitors seem to be more permanent.

7. The reduction in the length of stay has been typical worldwide with the introduction of cheap air fares and mass tourism.

TABLE 14-4. VISITOR ARRIVALS FROM SELECTED
COUNTRIES, 1968-75
(thousands)

Country of origin	1968	1971	1973	1975	Average growth rate, 1968-75 (percent)
Libya	37.4	77.9	125.1	101.8	15.4
Sudan	21.3	33.2	32.9	61.4	16.3
Saudi Arabia	7.1	19.6	34.6	60.1	35.7
United States	18.3	23.6	33.7	58.8	18.1
France	10.8	17.4	23.3	43.5	22.0
Germany, Federal Republic of	12.9	12.7	13.9	37.2	16.3
Syria	16.8	24.3	23.6	33.0	10.1
Jordan	29.5	17.9	25.0	32.3	1.3
Total	317.6	428.1	534.8	793.1	14.0

Source: Ministry of Tourism.

Tourist Nationalities

Libyans are the most numerous single nationality visiting Egypt.
Their visits grew at a rate of 15.4 percent a year on the average
between 1968 and 1977 and at 24.9 percent up to 1974 (see table
14-4).

The most spectacular growth has been in the number of Saudi
Arabians (nearly 36 percent a year on the average between 1968 and
1976) and of visitors from other smaller Persian Gulf States. As in
the case of Libyans, this is attributable mainly to the unprecedented
increase in incomes. The ebb and flow of tourists from socialist
countries can be attributed more directly to political factors.[8] Tourist arrivals from the United States and the main Western European
countries have increased quite rapidly since 1967, but it was only
in 1975 that they surpassed the 1966 figures (see table 14-5).

Mode of Travel

Roughly 70 to 80 percent of foreign tourists come by air. Arrivals by sea climbed back in 1974 and 1975 to more than 10 percent of the total. Arrivals by road, which are linked to fluctuations
in Libyan tourism, were around 20 percent of total arrivals in the
early 1970s but fell to around 10 percent in 1975. The resumption
of traffic in the Suez Canal will probably increase the share of sea
traffic slightly, and the normalization of relations with Libya could

8. During the last few years, only about 30,000 to 35,000 socialist tourists a
year have visited Egypt.

TABLE 14-5. VISITOR ARRIVALS BY NATIONALITY, 1954-78

Year	Arab		European		American		Other		Total	
	Thousands	Percent	Thousands	Percent	Thousands	Percent	Thousands	Percent	Thousands	Percent
1954	38	33.3	49	43.0	20	17.5	7	6.2	114	100.0
1955	43	28.9	71	47.7	27	18.1	8	5.3	149	100.0
1956	62	36.5	75	44.1	24	14.1	9	5.3	170	100.0
1957	67	52.3	41	32.0	11	8.6	9	7.1	128	100.0
1958	80	49.1	44	27.0	17	10.4	22	13.5	163	100.0
1959	129	53.7	69	28.8	18	7.5	24	10.0	240	100.0
1960	127	44.6	91	31.9	37	13.0	30	10.5	285	100.0
1961	107	37.7	106	37.3	43	15.1	28	9.9	284	100.0
1962	116	39.9	87	29.9	40	13.7	48	16.5	291	100.0
1963	151	37.4	133	32.9	61	15.1	59	14.6	404	100.0
1964	208	41.9	165	33.2	66	13.3	58	11.6	497	100.0
1965	246	45.4	179	33.0	63	11.6	54	10.0	542	100.0
1966	256	44.2	197	34.0	73	12.6	53	9.2	579	100.0
1967	167	48.5	112	32.6	31	9.0	34	9.9	344	100.0
1968	184	57.9	82	25.8	23	7.2	29	9.1	318	100.0
1969	194	56.2	85	24.6	33	9.6	33	9.6	345	100.0
1970	231	64.5	66	18.4	25	7.0	36	10.1	358	100.0
1971	260	60.7	95	22.2	30	7.0	43	10.1	428	100.0
1972	314	58.0	132	24.4	44	8.1	51	9.5	541	100.0
1973	333	62.2	119	22.2	41	7.7	42	7.9	535	100.0
1974	412	61.7	144	21.6	56	8.4	56	8.3	668	100.0
1975	438	55.3	214	27.0	76	9.6	65	8.1	793	100.0
1976	535	54.4	298	30.3	84	8.5	67	6.8	984	100.0
1977	475	47.4	331	32.9	109	10.9	89	8.9	1,004	100.0
1978	455	43.3	359	34.1	146	13.9	92	8.7	1,052	100.0

Source: Ministry of Tourism.

293

increase the road traffic. Air traffic is expected to predominate, however, especially if charter flights, which now account for only about 10 percent of visitor arrivals, become more common. Since the total cost of travel to Egypt from, say, the United Kingdom or West Germany is reduced by as much as 50 percent for a one-week charter tour, the tourists' demand for Egypt and the share of air travel in the flows would tend to increase if charter flights become more readily available and hotel capacity expands.

Seasonality

Tourism in Egypt displays less seasonal variation than in most Mediterranean countries because of the relatively low proportion of beach-oriented tourists, especially among Westerners, and the shortage of accommodations. While half the Arabs arrive in the summer (June–September), only a third of the Europeans and 41 percent of the Americans do so. Tourists from the socialist countries come mostly during the off-season (only 31 percent visit during June–September). Years ago, rich European visitors traveled to Egypt to escape the winter; later as the proportion of Arab visitors increased, the seasonal pattern changed in favor of the summer months. But even among European visitors, there were fewer arrivals in winter months because of the "massification" of tourism that allowed blue-collar workers to travel abroad during their vacations, usually in summer. By the late 1960s and early 1970s, as much as 44 percent of the total yearly arrivals was concentrated in the June–September period. In 1974 and 1975 the lack of accommodations caused arrivals during the four-month summer peak period to drop significantly (to only 41 and 38 percent of the annual total, respectively). Arrivals in January and February are now the lowest for the year (see table 14-6).

Motivation of Travel

Although most Arabs visit Egypt on a single-destination trip, European and American tourists usually make their visits as part of a multiple-stop package tour. This would normally include other countries in the Middle East (such as Jordan, Israel, or Syria), North Africa (such as Tunisia), or East Africa (such as Kenya). Among Americans, tours to Western Europe and Greece along with Egypt are also popular. Such tours normally include three to four days in Egypt and, almost without exception, cover the Pharaonic attractions of Upper Egypt. An estimated 70 percent of Western visitors to Egypt are part of organized tours.

No statistics are available on tourist motivation to visit Egypt, but interviews with travel agents and hoteliers provide some rough estimates. Visitors engaged in business represent about 15 percent

TABLE 14-6.   SEASONALITY OF VISITOR
ARRIVALS, SELECTED YEARS

(Seasonality index = $\dfrac{\text{Yearly total}}{12}$ = 100)

Month	Average 1968-72	1973	1974	1975
January	71	84	62	69
February	79	85	72	75
March	82	96	91	99
April	84	106	93	80
May	82	89	82	91
June	115	127	137	113
July	161	163	138	144
August	134	149	117	129
September	116	130	101	76
October	100	44	115	119
November	78	53	97	98
December	98	75	110	107

Source: Ministry of Tourism.

of those from the West and about 5 percent of those from Arab
countries; most of the rest are on vacation.

TOURIST ACCOMMODATIONS

In late 1978 there were about 10,000 rooms in hotels suitable for
foreign visitors in Egypt. These are classified as deluxe (five star),
first class (three to four star), and second class (two to three star)
(see table 14-7). In addition, there were more than 2,000 hotel
rooms classified as third class and tourist class and about 10,000
rooms in boarding houses (popular class). International-class hotels cater mostly to foreigners (77 percent of total lodgers) while
those in the lower categories cater mostly to Egyptians (95 percent).
Foreigners staying in these low-category hotels are mostly Sudanese.
The availability of international-class hotel rooms was reduced
by the 1967 war from 7,500 rooms in 1965 to 6,200 in 1970, and
most of the hotels affected were in the Suez Canal area and on the
Red Sea coast. Capacity did not begin to expand again until after
1970, but the total increase between 1965 and 1975 was only 20 percent, or at an average rate of only 1.9 percent a year. This has
resulted in an acute shortage of accommodations. More than half

TABLE 14-7. INTERNATIONAL-CLASS HOTEL ROOMS
AVAILABLE, SELECTED YEARS

Accommodation	1965		1970		1975		Rate of increase, 1965-75 (percent)
	Number	Percent	Number	Percent	Number	Percent	
Type							
Deluxe	1,234	16.5	1,478	23.7	2,002	22.3	62.2
First class	3,420	45.9	2,472	39.6	3,513	39.1	2.7
Second Class	2,798	37.6	2,288	36.7	3,465	38.6	23.8
Total	7,452	100.0	6,238	100.0	8,980	100.0	20.5
Place							
Cairo	3,987	53.5	3,760	60.3	4,569	50.9	14.6
Alexandria	868	11.6	765	12.3	1,754	19.5	102.1
Luxor	535	7.2	602	9.6	749	8.3	40.0
Aswan	698	9.4	671	10.8	859	9.6	23.1
Other	1,364	18.3	440	7.0	1,049	11.7	-23.1
Total	7,452	100.0	6,238	00.0	8,980	100.0	20.5

Source: Ministry of Tourism and Central Agency for Public Mobilization and
Statistics.

the international-class hotels are in Cairo, roughly 20 percent in
Alexandria, and 10 percent each in Luxor and Aswan; the rest are
scattered throughout Egypt. Most of the hotel expansion during the
1965-75 period took place in Alexandria, and in the deluxe category.
    Since most Arab visitors prefer to stay in furnished apartments
and villas, their availability is as important as that of hotels. Unfortunately, there is no information relating to the number of such
accommodations available or the changes that have occurred. Most
of the available apartments or villas are normally lived in by Egyptians who rent them to foreigners or local tourists for short periods.
According to very tentative estimates, as many as 30,000 apartments
in Cairo and Alexandria are rented to Arab visitors during the high
season. The number of apartments available for rent seems to have
declined since the 1960s owing to Egypt's population growth and, in
particular, the rapid growth in demand for middle-class housing.

Hotel Ownership and Investment

    As a consequence of Egyptian economic policies from the late
1950s to 1973, most of the international-class hotels are owned by
the government through the Egyptian General Organization of Tourism and Hotels (EGOTH). Many are operated by private hotel companies under long-term management contracts. The larger and better hotels are all government-owned but managed by foreign companies, such as Hilton, Sheraton, and Meridien. The new economic

policies of 1973 opened the door to private sector investment in tourism. Although a few purely private hotel projects are now being implemented, new hotel projects are typically under mixed private and public ownership, with EGOTH in partnership with foreign investors. Hotel investments by the government were stepped up sharply after the 1973 war, when the number of nights spent by Western tourists began to increase rapidly.

Because of the predominance of the public sector in hotel development, the financial arrangements for hotel construction in the past were purely a budgetary exercise. The new private or semi-private hotel projects, however, are beginning to rely on private equity capital and on the international capital market. Private banks, the most active of which have been the Arab African Bank, Arab International Bank, and Misr-Iran Development Bank, usually participate with loan capital on a syndicated basis and sometimes provide equity capital as well. Most private investors are Arabs, but there are a few active European- and Asian-based hotel developers.[9] Loans finance roughly 60 percent of total capital cost at the going Eurodollar market rate (LIBOR, the London Inter-Bank Offered Rate, plus some 2 percent), with repayment periods of up to ten years, including a two-year grace period. More than US$100 million has already been committed by the private sector to several hotel projects to be implemented during the next few years. The guarantees and incentives provided by the government encourage investment, but investors are attracted primarily by the high rates of occupancy and profitability of hotels at this time.

Occupancy Rates

Hotels in Egypt have had extremely high occupancy rates since 1974. Occupancy rates in 1976 were estimated to be more than 90 percent in Cairo, 70 percent in Upper Egypt, and 65 percent in Alexandria. Hotels in Cairo are fully occupied almost year-round,[10] and so are hotels in Upper Egypt during the winter and in Alexandria during the summer. The seasonal variation of rates of hotel occupancy is much less pronounced than that of visitor arrivals because the bulk of hotel lodgers are Western tourists, who are more evenly distributed throughout the year than are the Arabs. Occupancy rates also reflect the shortage of accommodations. Hotel occupancy in Upper Egypt has traditionally been highly seasonal, and many hotels used to close during the summer. With modern air-conditioning, however, tourists are interested in visiting this part of Egypt any time that adequate hotel accommodation is available, and average

9. The participation of American companies in most of the larger hotel projects is limited to little more than a management role.

10. Normally, a hotel with 90 percent occupancy is considered full from an operational standpoint.

occupancy rates during summer have been increasing with the provision of better accommodations.

Hotel Profitability

The profitability of hotels in Egypt is difficult to document, and
comparisons are hard to draw because financial results are not uni-
formly recorded. Nevertheless, they are readily available for the
large hotels, which are considered among the most profitable in
the world. Not only is the ratio of gross operating profit to sales
(about 45 percent) outstanding, but because hotels in general have
low debts, net profits are even more exceptional. Although small
hotels (usually defined as those with less than a hundred rooms)
were somewhat less profitable, they still enjoyed good financial results. It is estimated that the breakeven point in annual room occupancy in 1976 was around 40 percent for small hotels and around
35 percent for the larger ones. The main difference between large
and small hotels of similar categories is that payroll costs as a
percentage of sales, although still quite low by international standards, are somewhat higher for the small ones. While average
wages and the number of employees per room are similar in both
types of hotels, sales per room are lower for the small ones. The
number of employees per room in Egypt depends more on the category than on the size of the hotel. Deluxe hotels average 1.5 employees per room, first-class hotels 1.3, and second-class hotels
0.6.[11] By mid-1976 wages in hotels in Cairo amounted to about
LE25 a month for unskilled workers, LE50 for semiskilled, and
LE100 for skilled; in addition, tips may amount to as much as 50
percent of wages. Wages for the skilled and semiskilled are about
20 percent higher outside Cairo, and all these wage levels are on
the high side compared with other sectors in Egypt. The financial
returns of travel agencies, tour operators, transport companies,
restaurants, and other enterprises operating in tourism also appear
to be quite good.

The cost component of goods sold in Egyptian hotels compares
well with international standards, in spite of the fact that the food
and beverages served are priced lower than in other tourist areas.
This is so because the prices of many goods procured by hotels,
particularly foodstuffs, are controlled by the government and kept
low by subsidies. If the subsidies were discontinued, it is estimated
that hotels would not have much difficulty in raising the prices of
goods sold, but even if that were not possible, hotels would still remain quite profitable. The question arises whether hotels should
not be allowed to raise prices in any case, if Egypt is to reap
more fully the benefits of tourism.

11. Hotels managed by the private sector have, in general, fewer employees
per room.

A major problem facing hotels is the recruitment of experienced personnel. Even in the best hotels in Egypt, the inadequacy of hotel staff frequently results in poor service. When hotel activities declined after the 1967 war, many experienced middle- and high-level hotel employees emigrated to other Arab countries (mostly to Saudi Arabia and Persian Gulf States) or to Europe, so that the relative abundance of qualified manpower disappeared. Efforts are being made to train workers, but high-paying jobs abroad continue to attract experienced hotel employees. Moreover, the many hotels expected in operation soon will probably aggravate the situation further unless salaries of these employees are raised substantially. There are some signs that the government is considering changes affecting wages, training facilities, and the like, which would ameliorate the situation.

Transport and Travel Services

There is a great shortage of taxis (because of the very low prices charged) and public buses in traffic-congested Cairo. Misr Travel, the government-owned travel agency, operates nearly 250 tourist buses, 50 of which are fully air-conditioned. Tourists take buses to Middle and Upper Egypt more often than in the past, and bus transport could be further expanded because practically all the country's tourist attractions are connected by reasonably well-paved roads. Train service is also used for part or all of the journey to Upper Egypt by many tourists, including those on the cheaper package tours, but there is a shortage of railroad cars between Cairo and Aswan as well as between Cairo and Alexandria. Some domestic airports are still closed to civil traffic, and the shortage of aircraft in domestic service continues to be a problem, but this service has been improved by the addition of several Boeing 737 aircraft to Egypt Air's fleet.

In addition to Misr Travel, several private travel agencies now work in Egypt, including transnationals such as American Express, Thomas Cook, and Wagon Lits. Misr Travel, created in 1934 by Bank Misr, is by far the most important, with offices all over Egypt. It has more than a thousand employees and handles about 100,000 tourists a year, including 50 to 60 percent of those on all-inclusive tours of Egypt.

ORGANIZATION AND POLICIES

The higher priority given to tourism on the part of the government is reflected in the number of governmental agencies now actively engaged in the sector. Responsibility for day-to-day operations lies with the Ministry of Tourism, which plans tourism activities, promotes tourism in Egypt and abroad, and controls the activities of the principal tourism facilities and services, such as hotels, restaurants, guides, and travel agencies. By mid-1976 it had 850 employees.

Under the umbrella of the Ministry of Tourism four agencies play a major role in the sector: EGOTH, Misr Travel, the Egyptian Company for Hotels, and the Misr Grand Hotel Company.[12] Since the 1975 reorganization of the public sector, all four have been relatively decentralized. Although it has the smallest number of employees (less than a hundred), EGOTH is the most important of these agencies. Until 1976 it was the holding company of the other three agencies, and its capital surpasses the US$100 million mark. EGOTH was first organized in 1962 to execute major hotel projects that the private sector would resist because of their magnitude or location, and to create new tourist areas and touristic patterns, such as opening the coasts of the Red Sea and northwestern Mediterranean and introducing bungalow-hotels and Nile steamers. Since 1973 its role has centered on attracting foreign investors to tourism projects through joint ventures to expand the country's accommodation capacity.

In addition, the government created in 1975 the High Council for Tourism, chaired by the premier. It comprises all ministers who have something to do with tourism — the ministers of tourism, interior, maritime transport, economy, housing and reconstruction, finance, war, and civil aviation — the chairmen of Egypt Air, the Antiquities Department, the Union of Tourism Chamber, and the Arab Union for Tourism; and the regional secretary of the International Tourism Association. The High Council defines major policy lines, proposes legislation for the development of the sector, and coordinates tourism-related activities, but because of the multiple responsibilities of its members, the council has been relatively inactive. A new, more active body was created in early 1976, the High Council of Tourism and Civil Aviation, chaired by the minister of tourism (who became the titular minister of civil aviation), and including the chairmen of Egypt Air, EGOTH, Misr Travel, Misr Grand Hotel Company, Egyptian Company for Hotels, General Organization for Civil Aviation, Cairo Airport, and the Institute of Training for Civil Aviation. Its role is similar to that of the High Council for Tourism, but it is not as broad in its approach.

The Tourist Police, under the Ministry of the Interior, also plays a significant role in tourism. This force assists visitors at the principal tourist sites as well as at arrival and departure points. Tourist policemen receive special training and speak more than one foreign language.

12. The Egyptian Company for Hotels was created in late 1975 as an amalgamation of four EGOTH hotel management companies: Shepheard Hotel Company, Upper Egypt Hotels Company, Egyptian Hotels and Tourism Company, and Misr Hotels Company; it manages twenty-one of EGOTH's twenty-nine hotels. The Misr Grand Hotel Company is in charge of the construction of EGOTH's new hotels.

Training

Both the Ministry of Education and the Ministry of Tourism are responsible for training tourism personnel. The Ministry of Education concentrates on medium- to upper-level training at the University of Helwan, where the faculty of tourism and hotel management offers two courses: a four-year course leading to a higher certificate (BSc equivalent) in tourism, hotel management, and guidance, with a total of 350 students and 60 graduates a year; and a two-year course leading to a diploma in kitchen, housekeeping, and services, with 120 students and 60 graduates a year. These courses are very theoretical and suffer from not having a practice hotel, although students are required to work for two months in established hotels before graduating. The faculty's twenty-room practice hotel has remained idle for several years because of lack of funds to complete the building.

The Ministry of Tourism offers vocational training under the direct responsibility of EGOTH, which operates two hotel schools attached to practice hotels. One in Cairo at the Continental Hotel offers three-month vocational courses for 100 students at a time. This school receives aid from the Federal Republic of Germany and the ILO. The second one, which operates in the remodeled Hotel Mediterranée in Alexandria, offers vocational and middle-level courses to 300 students a year, with assistance from the French government. In addition, hotel management companies have their own on-the-job training programs.

Promotion

The main responsibility for tourism promotion rests with the Ministry of Tourism. Its promotion budget is now around LE0.5 million, but the target for promotion expenditure is 1 percent of the foreign exchange revenue from tourism, or roughly twice the level of present expenditure. The ministry has tourist bureaus in the main tourist-generating capitals of the world and operates various tourist information centers throughout Egypt. The government agencies in the tourism sector also undertake promotion activities, as do hoteliers, particularly foreign management companies. Investment promotion in the tourism sector is mainly undertaken by EGOTH.

Legislation

Three important laws govern tourism development. Law number 1 of 1973 entrusts the Ministry of Tourism with regulating hotels and tourist establishments, including fixing the price of their services and determining whether they qualify for incentives. The incentives consist of a five-year income tax exemption (the income tax rate is around 40 percent) and complete exemption from customs duties on the imported component of construction or renovation of such establishments. Under Law number 2 of 1973, the Ministry of Tourism can reserve areas for tourism development. In addition to supervising these areas and planning their development, the Ministry of Tourism coordinates with other government agencies to provide infrastructure for them. Since no person or corporate body may exploit any tourist area without authorization from the Ministry of Tourism, this law is a powerful tool to make private developers comply with the ministry's regulations and building codes and to check land speculation.[13] Law number 43 of 1974 on foreign investment and free-trade zones provides tax exemptions similar to those in Law number 1 of 1973, and guarantees the property rights of foreign investors and the repatriation of profits and capital.

Air Access Policy

Because of severe government restrictions, only about 10 percent of air passengers arrive on charter flights. With the limited accommodations available today, the policy has a certain rationality, but it will probably have to be revised in the future.[14] The government seems to be fully aware of the conflict between the interests of the national airline, which wants to restrict air access to Egypt in order to guarantee its share of the market, and those of the tourism sector in general, whose growth is directly linked to accessibility. Fortunately, the recently established High Council of Tourism and Civil Aviation is in an ideal position to draw a more appropriate balance between these interests.

ECONOMIC AND SOCIAL RETURNS

An examination of tourism activities in recent years shows high financial and economic profitability. Certain weaknesses are evident, however, and some areas have not begun to realize their potential.

Revenues

In the overall balance of payments, tourism revenues in foreign exchange are significant. They represented around 10 percent of

13. This tool has been effectively used only since 1975, and land speculation, which reached high levels in 1974 and 1975, has been somewhat curtailed.
14. With insufficient accommodation capacity, charter flights would merely substitute for scheduled flights instead of generating more traffic, and this would result in lower revenues for the airlines, including Egypt Air. But this policy was not justified when hotel occupancy was at a low level in the late 1960s and early 1970s.

total exports of goods and services from 1966 to 1976 and constitute the third most important item in the exports account, just below cotton and workers' remittances from abroad. Foreign exchange revenues from tourism have fluctuated widely since 1966.[15]   A steep decline followed the 1967 war, and the recuperation that began in 1970 was halted by the 1973 war, but it has made a strong comeback since then.   By 1975 the pre-1967 record had been matched, and by 1978 it was far exceeded.

Average daily expenditures per visitor in 1975 were about US$47.50. No estimate of daily expenditures by nationality is available, but the Ministry of Tourism estimates that they are higher for Westerners, particularly Americans, than for Arab tourists. This, however, may be simply because spending by Arab tourists is only incompletely captured by the statistics. In 1973 and 1974 the average expenditure by all tourists in current prices was US$24 and US$32, respectively. The sharp increases in daily expenditures in 1975 reflect a trebling of apartment rents, which began in 1973, and a 30 to 40 percent increase in hotel rates. This upward trend continued into 1978. In addition, it is likely that shorter lengths of stay have contributed to higher daily expenditures, since tourist expenditures for shopping, local transport, and the like do not rise proportionally with length of stay. No data on the type of tourist expenditures are available. Interviews with hoteliers and travel agents suggest that accommodations represent almost 50 percent of total expenditures, and that when meals in hotels are added, expenditures in hotels reach more than two-thirds of the total in the case of Western tourists.

Costs and Returns

Because of problems of quantification only a sketchy analysis of the economics of tourism can be made. As with most developing countries, domestic prices of goods and services are quite different from international prices as a consequence of price controls, subsidies, import duties, and multiple exchange rates, among other factors.[16] When analyzing the economic returns of tourism activities, it is therefore necessary to make some changes in the financial accounts of tourism enterprises to eliminate the main price

15. In millions of U.S. dollars in 1975 constant prices they are:

1966	1969	1970	1971	1972	1973	1974	1975	1976
275.7	141.2	157.1	191.4	244.0	210.2	229.1	278.0	365.6

As discussed below, statistical series dealing with foreign exchange revenues from tourism lack consistency, and special caution should be exercised in drawing conclusions from time series analysis.

16. While the parallel market rate is used for all foreign exchange transactions of tourists, the official rate applies to many imported goods that are consumed by tourists.

distortions affecting their economic profitability. Unfortunately, few studies have been undertaken in Egypt to make these elements readily quantifiable.

Nevertheless, it can be tentatively concluded that the financial profitability of hotels is somewhat overstated. The effect of subsidies and price controls on supplies and utilities seems to be more important than that of shadow-pricing labor and of indirect taxes — principally because of low taxes on rooms and the exemptions from customs duties for construction materials and equipment for hotels. Operating costs are therefore higher when efficiency is taken into account than when measured in purely financial terms. The benefits to the economy generated by hotels (gross operating profits with distortions netted out) would represent an estimated 40 percent of gross revenues or sales. This ratio is still high and would lead to high economic rates of return on tourism investments.[17] (In most countries, a ratio of around 30 percent for hotels is satisfactory.) Shopping, entertainment, tours, and transport are also estimated to yield high economic returns as well as to be financially profitable.

The economic policies followed by the government should gradually eliminate these distortions, especially those arising from the use of a multiple exchange rate, and consequently the financial profitability of tourism activities may decline. But their economic profitability (calculated at efficiency prices) would not be affected much. It should be borne in mind, however, that the present high economic and financial profitability of tourism is the result of extremely high occupancy rates, which are not likely to last over the long run.[18]

Foreign Exchange Costs

The direct and indirect foreign exchange component of tourism investment costs is estimated to be about 40 to 45 percent of total investment costs, and about 20 to 25 percent of operating costs, including remittances abroad for management fees and commissions. The net foreign exchange revenue from tourism in a year of normal development is around 70 percent of gross foreign exchange revenue. If the investment cost component is excluded, net foreign exchange earnings would represent almost 80 percent of gross foreign exchange earnings.

17. This statement is based on typical projects in the Nile Valley where infrastructure requirements are modest. Although the investment in infrastructure for tourism development on the northwest coast would be much higher, a recent regional development plan determined that tourism projects would still generate satisfactory economic returns in that area.

18. When the economic returns of expanding accommodations were assessed, occupancy rates for hotels were projected at a more normal 75 to 80 percent instead of the present 85 to 90 percent. Egypt should be able to sustain higher rates than other areas because its tourist flow is less seasonal, especially that of Westerners.

Employment

In addition to substantial foreign exchange revenue and income, tourism generated direct employment (that is, employment in activities that sell goods and services directly to tourists, such as hotels, restaurants, nightclubs, tourist shops, airlines; local transport companies, and guides) for about 27,000 people in 1976, at a level of remuneration substantially higher than the national average. Although direct employment in tourism is quite small compared with total employment of about 9 million persons, Egyptian tourism has strong linkages with other labor-intensive sectors such as agriculture and handicrafts. Indirect employment in tourism probably represents 20,000 to 30,000 additional jobs. At least 50 percent of the workers in tourism are estimated to be unskilled and most of the others, semiskilled. In contrast to most other countries, women are estimated to make up less than 20 percent of the total tourism work force, and their employment is almost entirely limited to the highest-class hotels.

With its heavy concentration in Cairo and along the Nile, tourism has not yet played a significant role in backward areas. Should tourism grow along the Mediterranean and Red Sea coasts, however, it could make a major contribution to the development of these areas.

Because of the generous exemptions from income taxes and customs the government does not collect substantial revenues from tourism activities. Sales taxes in hotels are only 2 percent of the total bill plus a local government tax of five piastres a day per person, while other tourism activities go almost untaxed. The government profits substantially, however, from the operation of its own tourist facilities, such as hotels, casinos, and travel agency. Apart from the returns to government, the net economic benefits generated in tourism accrue mostly to the owners of private hotels, apartments, villas, and tourist shops, and to unskilled and semi-skilled workers who earn higher wages in tourism than they could expect elsewhere. The very high rates charged tourists for apartments and villas have resulted in a disproportionate share of benefits accruing to their owners. Foreign hotel management companies have also earned high fees (slightly more than 20 percent of gross operating profits of hotels). On balance, tourism is probably not contributing much toward the improvement of income distribution at present.

PROSPECTS

To establish the growth potential of Egypt's tourism sector, it is necessary to project the likely overall increase in size of the generating markets and then estimate what share Egypt is likely to capture. This double task is particularly difficult in the absence

of specific market studies. The following projections should therefore be looked upon as only a rough indication of the traffic and the
expansion of accommodations in Egypt that were expected for the
early 1980s.

The more important generators of tourists for Egypt are the Arab
countries and those of Western Europe and North America. Arab
tourism is expected to continue its fast growth in the near future
(more than 15 percent a year) owing to a rapid increase in the proportion of people in oil-rich countries such as Saudi Arabia, Libya,
Iraq, Kuwait, and Abu Dhabi who are able to afford vacations abroad.
The number of visitors from Saudi Arabia, for example, increased
at an average rate of 35.7 percent a year from 1968 to 1975. Egypt
should continue to be one of the preferred destinations among Arab
tourists as long as the number of furnished apartments expands,
and growth rates of Arab tourism of 15 percent a year on average
until 1985 seem a reasonable expectation.

Air departures abroad by U.S. citizens grew at a rate of 8.6
percent a year during the 1967-75 period, reaching 7.4 million.
Although this growth was abruptly interrupted in 1974 and 1975 owing to a recession and the energy crisis, the average annual growth
rate between 1967 and 1973 was 13 percent. According to a study
on the prospects of tourism in the Mediterranean basin prepared in
1975 by Battelle, the number of trips abroad by Americans may
reach 12 million in 1980 (an implied growth rate of 10 percent a
year from 1975 to 1980 or 6 percent from 1973 to 1980).[19] Departures abroad from Western Europe grew at a rate of 7.6 percent a
year during the 1964-73 period, to reach a total of about 45 million.
The same study projects the number of departures will reach about
70 million by 1980 (a growth of 7 percent a year on average from
1973 to 1980). At present, Egypt's share of the Western tourist
market is only 0.5 percent, but it could easily be increased if accommodation facilities expand, because there appears to be a substantial unsatisfied demand. A growth rate of 12 percent a year
on the average for the 1975-80 period appears reasonable.

From the demand side, overall yearly rates of growth of 12 to
15 percent in the number of foreign visitor arrivals seem possible
although they would probably fall after 1980.[20] An updating of the
Battelle study in late 1976 projects a growth rate of about 15 percent during the 1975-80 period. The average length of stay of tourists would probably remain around seven days. Although some Arab
visitors have a tendency to extend their stay in Egypt, a greater

19. Battelle Research Centre, "Prospective Study of Tourism in the Mediterranean Basin" (Geneva, 1976).

20. The Battelle study projects a slower growth in the number of Western visit-
or arrivals in the Mediterranean basin after 1980. The Arab tourist market would
also show signs of saturation because of its small population base.

proportion of businessmen among them and a higher demand for apartment rentals will probably prevent a return to the average lengths of stay of the 1950s and 1960s (table 14-3).

MAJOR CONSTRAINTS

Although richly endowed with tourist attractions, Egypt has been restricted in the growth of its tourism sector because of insufficient accommodations.   A joint effort by the government and the private sector is expected to overcome this limitation to a great extent in the near future.   Other constraints relate to the coordination of various ministries and institutions within the sector and to the requirements for trained personnel.

Construction Costs

If construction costs of infrastructure and accommodations continue to be as high as in the last few years, Egypt may lose the competitive advantage it now enjoys in hotels and other facilities, and this may scare away foreign investors.   These cost increases depend to a large extent on local inflation and the overall demand for construction by developers in the long run.   Construction costs will probably continue to increase more than inflation because of the part construction programs play in the 1976-80 plan.   Every effort should be made to minimize future cost increases that would endanger Egypt's competitive advantages.   The Ministry of Tourism and related agencies should avoid overambitious tourism projects in nonestablished areas that require high infrastructure investment.[21]

The present infrastructure along the Nile is generally adequate for tourism development (except for a rather poor telecommunications network), and investment requirements for infrastructure here seem modest.   In contrast, such requirements for tourism development along the northwest coast are quite high.   In Cairo, unfortunately, rapid urbanization has already exhausted the utility system, and a new (and expensive) system has been judged to be the only comprehensive solution.   New hotels now receive good services at the expense of the quality of services offered others.   In order to avoid repetition of this experience, the Ministry of Tourism is preparing new town plans for Luxor and Aswan — two cities where tourism activities predominate — so that the land and the new infrastructure can serve both tourism and the local population.   The same approach should be used in opening up new resort towns and in developing existing towns for tourism.

21. At the macroeconomic level, it is the role of the Ministry of Planning to seek the best use of the limited resources.

Institutional Constraints

The principal weakness of the government structure in the tourism sector is the lack of proper coordination between the unit in charge of the design and implementation of infrastructure (the Ministry of Housing and Reconstruction) and the units in charge of superstructure (the Ministry of Tourism and related specialized agencies). Even if the High Council of Tourism were functioning normally, adequate coordination could not be achieved without continuous rapport at the working level, and this is not easy to secure for two different ministries. As long as most tourism projects consist of city hotels, this shortcoming may not be too serious, but if new tourism resorts are opened and the basic infrastructure becomes an important component of the projects, it will probably be a grave limitation on the efficient use of resources. A possible solution — and one that has been rather successful in other countries — is the creation of a Tourism Development Corporation, possibly amalgamating the expertise of EGOTH, the Misr Grand Hotel Company, and the Planning and Follow-up Department of the Ministry of Tourism. Such a body should coordinate and supervise all tourism projects and either undertake infrastructure and superstructure works itself or entrust this authority to other government agencies.

Manpower

The government's increased efforts in the training field have apparently not satisfied the manpower needs of the tourism sector, particularly in hotels, because as many as 50 percent of the graduates with this training now emigrate. Although the government does not try to dissuade emigrants because they usually remit substantial foreign exchange to Egypt, hotel service can deteriorate as a result. Efforts to provide more formal and on-the-job training should be redoubled. The completion of the training hotel at the University of Helwan should be given top priority because it would increase the carrying capacity of the faculty by almost 100 percent and would also improve its standards of training. The two institutions entrusted with training — the Ministry of Education and the Ministry of Tourism — should be better coordinated to avoid wasting teaching resources and to improve the curriculum. Hotel management companies with good training capabilities could provide on-the-job training, and technical assistance should be given to strengthen the Egyptian Company of Hotels.

Quality of Statistics

A comprehensive assessment of the economic and social returns of tourism in Egypt is limited by the lack of statistics. The most serious problem is the lack of expenditure surveys and the unreliability of the estimates of gross revenues generated by the expenditures of foreign visitors in Egypt. Until 1972 the Ministry of Tourism estimates of foreign exchange revenues from tourism were based on the opinion of some "tourism specialists" and the results of statistically unrepresentative observations of per capita expenditures of particular tourist groups. Independently, the Central Bank estimates revenue on the basis of actual foreign exchange transactions in the banking system, a widely used but still unsatisfactory way of measuring tourist expenditures. [22] In spite of this, the Ministry of Tourism adopted the Central Bank figures in 1973 after the introduction of the parallel market foreign exchange rate substantially reduced the share of black market transactions. Poor information about operation of hotels and other tourist facilities also inhibits proper sector planning and project selection.

ISSUES FOR FUTURE TOURISM DEVELOPMENT

Because investments in tourism can yield high economic returns and provide substantial foreign exchange and well-paid employment, the government's policy of assigning priority to tourism development is not open to question. Tourism is viewed as being capable of providing badly needed foreign exchange. The government owns most of the international-class accommodation capacity in Egypt and is planning continued investments to expand this capacity. The relevant question is whether these investments are necessary or whether the private sector can be counted on to undertake the effort.

Although the private sector has shown some interest in investing in tourism superstructure, it has been reluctant to proceed alone, and the government has been wise to participate. After all, it is only recently that the door was opened to foreign investment and that the government's share in total investment in superstructure began to decline. In the case of several hotel projects, a minority participation of the government was a prerequisite for the private sector to commit its own funds. Furthermore, the government can expect to earn good financial returns on such investments. A gradual improvement of the investment climate would allow the government to reduce substantially its investments in hotels and other tourist facilities and to concentrate its efforts on the infrastructure that will be needed for sustained and balanced growth.

22. Not all visitors' foreign exchange transactions take place in the banking system, especially when there is a black market of foreign exchange as in Egypt. In addition, some foreign exchange transactions attributed to tourism are undistinguishable from those related to workers' remittances from abroad and other transactions.

The government plans to diversify tourism areas in the country by opening beach resorts, mainly along the northwest coast. The Tourism Development Plan proposes that more than 20 percent of all superstructure and more than 60 percent of all infrastructure investments (around LE70 million and LE90 million, respectively) be in that area. In opening the northwest coast Egypt would enter the highly competitive beach-oriented Mediterranean tourism market. Although there is certainly scope for the development of tourism there, the issue is whether it is opportune for Egypt to enter this market at this time or whether it should concentrate its efforts on the development of established Nile Valley tourist areas (Cairo, Luxor, Aswan), which have unsatisfied demand and growth potential.

As stated before, infrastructure costs would be high for massive tourism development of the northwest coast, which is sparsely populated and has a poor resource base. The 100,000 or so nomad Bedouins living in the area might benefit indirectly from tourism development, but they could hardly be expected to provide the manpower to staff the resorts. The cost of mobilizing labor and supplying accommodations and other facilities for tourists and the service population would be much higher than the average in Egypt.

Egypt's archaeological sites are, of course, the principal tourist attractions of the country. Package tours, which combine visits to these areas and beaches, might entice European tourists to Egypt instead of to closer Mediterranean destinations. Nevertheless, it is estimated that few beach-oriented tourists (on a typical four- to fourteen-day stay) are interested in antiquities at all, and those who are might find it possible to combine Egypt's archaeological sites with the beaches of Tunisia, Greece, or Turkey without adding significantly to the cost of an all-Egyptian package. This still leaves open the question whether Egypt, because of its antiquities, could gain a substantial share of the massive Mediterranean beach-oriented tourism market. Egypt would thus be advised to proceed cautiously and on a modest scale with the development of the northwest coast. The case of the Red Sea coast is similar, except that it is closer to Central Europe than most other good winter beaches and could therefore be expected to enjoy a higher year-round occupancy rate. (It would, however, appeal to a smaller segment of the market, though one with high expenditures.) In the meantime, Egypt's established tourist areas along the Nile face substantial unsatisfied demand. To handle this demand would probably require more resources than are available for all tourism investment in the next planning period. Concentrating efforts here where the opportunities are immediately accessible seems most likely to generate higher economic benefits and foreign exchange earnings.

The northwest and the Red Sea coasts have many good beaches scattered hundreds of miles along the seashore. The private sector will probably be interested in developing several of these beaches and will most likely press the government to provide sizable infrastructure works. If the government decides to develop these coastal areas, it should channel private interests to one or two resorts only, in order to capitalize on economies of scale.

Less than 40 percent of total accommodations are of adequate quality for Western tourists, whose demands exceed the existing capacity. There seems, therefore, to be a good case for promoting the international-class rather than the lower-class hotels; the latter will probably develop as small family businesses catering mostly to Egyptians and poorer Arab visitors, such as the Sudanese. The government plan calls for concentrating investment in international-class hotels that will help reestablish Egypt as an area for tourists whose expenditures are likely to be rather high. Egypt's unique attractions and the potential of the market make this strategy financially and economically sound. The government investment plans, however, give priority to deluxe hotel projects, whereas medium-class hotels seem to be more in demand. More attention should be devoted to the "mix" of hotel categories — to add more hotels of the medium class, with proportionately fewer in the highest category.

There also seem to be good prospects for massive development of apartotels (or condotels). These centrally managed apartments can be rented out when not used by the owners, a concept that has proved highly successful in other countries. They might induce important transfers of foreign capital into Egypt by Arab repeat visitors. These schemes could also help relieve pressure on the housing market.

Most of the new hotel projects have contracted with foreign hotel management companies. There is usually a strong case for bringing such companies into nonestablished areas because they have not only management expertise and comprehensive marketing services but also sometimes a captive segment of the market. It is doubtful, however, that this marketing strength has much value in Egypt because several other such companies are already in operation there. It should be remembered that such companies normally require investors to build hotels on deluxe standards, and this might not be in Egypt's interest. Another disadvantage is that these companies capture almost a quarter of the gross operating profits of hotels and seldom contribute to their capital at all.

High priority should be given to strengthening the government's Egyptian Company for Hotels, which now manages twenty-one EGOTH hotels. It is not to be assigned the management of any new ones, however, because the company has just been created and is in the process of settling down. If some foreign experts were hired and the salaries of key personnel raised, it might be possible to divert good managers from emigration or from jobs in foreign-managed hotels in Egypt. As soon as the company is fully consolidated and its management capacity upgraded, the government could assign it new hotels for management. This will probably be possible only in the case of EGOTH-dominated hotel projects because foreign investors tend to rely on foreign management.

Prices of goods and services consumed by tourists in Egypt are low, with the exception of hotel rates and rentals for apartments and villas. This is because internal prices are low in relation to international prices. There is, however, scope for increasing several typical "tourist prices" (airport limousine service, entrance fees to sound and light performances, and so forth) without greatly affecting local price levels and the government's price policies. The issue is whether tourist prices should be kept low in order to attract more tourists once accommodation capacity expands significantly. Increasing these prices would probably not have much effect on occupancy rates of hotel rooms for quite some time, and it would help Egypt reap the benefits of international tourism more fully. In fact, accommodation capacity is not likely to be sufficient for several years for all tourists who wish to visit Egypt.

PART FOUR
Financial Resources and Infrastructure

15
Public Finances

Two major themes run through Egyptian public finances. First, Egypt was in a state of war for nearly three decades after 1948, and this deeply affected the entire process of resource mobilization and allocation. Second, Egypt has represented the largest-scale experiment in "Arab Socialism" since 1962, when the National Charter was adopted. A main objective of this economic policy was greater equity in the distribution of income and in consumption capability, which was to be largely effected through fiscal measures. Another important goal was increased production. With much of the economy dominated by the government, this meant an increase in public investment.

The relative importance of these factors differed over time. In 1959-60 defense expenditures accounted for 5 percent of GDP at market prices; by 1970 they had increased to 16 percent, and by 1978 they were still about 9 percent. The impact of the defense effort on the resource allocation process is indicated by the evolution of public investment (which represents about 80 percent of total investment). In 1959-60 public investment was about 11 percent of GDP; in 1963-64 it rose to 19 percent; in 1970 it declined to 12 percent and rose to 27 percent in 1978.

To achieve greater equity in consumption, many commodities considered essential were subsidized. These cost-of-living subsidies became an important item in the budget after the sharp rise in international wheat prices in 1973; total subsidies rose from less than 2 percent of GDP in 1970-71 to about 5 percent in 1973 and to 10 percent in 1978. Thus, if during the 1960s and early 1970s defense needs had been competing with investment for resources, after 1973 an aggressive new claimant appeared on the scene.

Government domination of the economic system is clearly reflected in the proportion of GDP originating in the public sector, which increased from 13 percent in 1952 to about 50 percent in 1978. Moreover, government intervention in other sectors, particularly agriculture, is so widespread that it virtually determines the level and composition of output. Hence, the government's fiscal actions affecting both revenues and expenditures ramify throughout the economy.

To attain its varied goals, the government has made a major effort to mobilize resources over an extended period. Current government revenue, including receipts of the social security system, has always been high compared with that of other countries of similar per capita income, structure, and degree of openness of the economy.[1] In these comparisons, Egypt has always ranked among the more highly taxed countries. Furthermore, since such a large part of taxes had to be allocated to defense, the effective tax burden has always been substantially greater than in other countries, such as Tunisia and Brazil, which have a similar tax effort but significantly lower defense expenditures.

In spite of this substantial effort, the saving generated by the public sector since 1967 has been inadequate, dropping from 8 percent of GDP in 1967 to -11 percent in 1975, though by 1978 it recovered to about 3 percent. The reasons for this decline, of course, are the major expansion in the defense effort after the war of 1967 and the rapid growth of subsidies after 1973, which outstripped the capacity of the tax system to raise additional revenues.

Direct taxes account for only a small part of total revenues. In 1978 they contributed 29 percent of the total tax revenue and were equivalent to 7 percent of GDP; indirect taxes accounted for 71 percent and were equivalent to 17 percent of GDP. Thus, only a small portion of the tax system is based on the principle of ability to pay. Moreover, although the rates of direct taxes are steeply progressive, there is considerable tax evasion, so that the highest income groups are not actually exposed to the full rigor of the penal rates.

The biggest sector, agriculture, is taxed chiefly by implicit means, especially by procuring produce at prices well below international levels and by not applying the parallel market exchange rates. The main explicit tax on the agricultural sector, the land tax, is uniform for all sizes of holdings and is thus devoid of any element of progressivity. Furthermore, the tax base has not been altered since the mid-1950s despite the vast changes in agricultural cropping patterns, prices, and incomes during that period. Not surprisingly, the yield from the land tax has remained more or less constant at LE15 million a year, falling from 2.4 percent of value added in agriculture in 1955-56 to less than 1 percent in 1978. It is estimated that the burden of the total explicit taxes on agriculture declined from 5.9 percent of agricultural income in 1952 to 3.6 percent in 1974. This is not, however, to minimize the contribution of the agricultural sector to resource mobilization; the net burden

1. Raja J. Chelliah, Hessel J. Baas, and Margaret R. Kelly, "Tax Ratios and Tax Effort in Developing Countries, 1969-71," IMF Staff Papers, vol. 22, no. 1 (1975), pp. 187-205.

of implicit taxation (after adjusting for government-imposed differences in prices and exchange rates) was estimated at about 15 percent of agricultural income in 1972 and about 30 percent in 1975.

There is a wide and growing gap between government expenditure
and revenue. Although total public revenue went up from 28 to about
38 percent of GDP from 1974 to 1978, it is not enough to offset total
public expenditure, which increased from 48 to nearly 63 percent of
GDP in the same period. To finance this gap, the government has
relied on external assistance and borrowing from the banking system. About 40 percent of the deficit is financed by domestic banks
(in 1978 this borrowing reached 11 percent of GDP), thus creating
inflationary pressures in the economy. The overall fiscal deficit
as a ratio of GDP has increased from 19 percent in 1974 to about
24 percent in 1978, and in nominal terms it has increased from
LE813 million to LE2,077 million, an increase of more than 150
percent. Beyond fairly restricted limits, deficit financing in Egypt
adds to the rate of price inflation, constitutes a concealed form of
taxation, and intensifies inequalities in the distribution of wealth
and income.

STRUCTURE OF THE PUBLIC SECTOR

To understand Egyptian fiscal accounts, the government entities
must be defined. Egypt has had a largely government-controlled
economy since the nationalizations of 1961. Moreover, control over
the public sector's fiscal actions has been highly centralized, with
almost no autonomy permitted to local administrations, and with
most of the important decisions affecting public sector enterprises
being made by the central government.

The central government consists of a central administration (the
ministries and the legislature) and agencies referred to as Public
Authorities. For the budget, the latter are divided into Public Authorities (services), which are responsible for general functions of
the government, such as the universities, research institutions,
and the television agency, and Public Authorities (economic), which
are basically nonfinancial public enterprises, such as the Suez Canal Authority and the railways.

Local government consists of the twenty-five governorates and
the various municipal authorities. Their powers to tax and to borrow are minimal and rigidly controlled by the central government;
local expenditures must thus be met almost entirely through transfers from the central budget.

Public sector companies consist of government enterprises that
are not included under the Public Authorities (economic). These
companies are widely dispersed throughout virtually every field
of economic activity and generally dominate the activities of their

respective sectors. They form the chief vehicle for the government's measures to exercise economic control, particularly over prices, wages, and investment.

The extremely complex budget and accounting system of the public sector is composed of many budgets and special financing funds. The state budget is the centerpiece of the system; linked to it are the budgets for the central administration, the local governments, the Public Authorities (services), and the Public Authorities (economic). The special financing funds include the Emergency Fund, which covers defense-related expenditures; the Special Fund for Subsidies; the Investment Fund, which chiefly receives the proceeds from the pension funds and finances most of the investment programs; and the Treasury Fund, which receives the surpluses and meets the deficits of the other budgets. The complexity of this multiplicity of budgets and financing funds is compounded by conceptual differences in the recording of various transactions. For example, the accounts of the central and local governments are on a cash (or near cash) basis, but those of many Public Authorities and the public sector companies are on an accrual basis, as are all investment expenditures.[2] In some cases, such as the Emergency Fund, the details of sources and terms of financing are not released (for security reasons), and only the deficit met from general budget resources is available. Substantial lags in the central government's transfers to cover deficits necessitate direct borrowing by other parts of the public sector from the banking system. Taken together, these factors weaken expenditure control and complicate fiscal analysis.

FISCAL ACCOUNTS

Public Revenue

As shown in table 15-1, between 1974 and 1978 total public revenue as a ratio of GDP increased by 10 percentage points. This increase was almost entirely from taxes on foreign trade, which were estimated to be 5.5 and 10.7 percent of GDP in 1974 and 1978 respectively. This point is illustrated especially by the data for 1977, when the ratio of total public revenue to GDP reached 36.5 percent, about 8 percent higher than in 1974, and the taxes on foreign trade jumped equivalently from 5.5 to 13.0 percent. This increase in foreign trade taxes is due to the rapid growth of imports and the progressive devaluation of the Egyptian pound. Although the ratio

2. A reform bill was passed in 1979 that would put the budget on a cash basis after 1980. The budgets of the Public Authorities (economic) will be excluded from the state budget, but the net surplus or deficit of these entities will be financed from the state budget.

TABLE 15-1. TOTAL PUBLIC REVENUE, 1974-78

Revenue	1974	1975	1976	1977	1978
	Percentage of GDP				
Central government tax revenue					
Personal income	0.8	0.6	0.8	0.7	0.6
Business profit	3.4	4.0	4.4	5.1	6.2
Goods and services	4.6	4.7	4.5	4.5	4.2
Foreign trade	5.5	8.2	8.5	13.0	10.7
Property	0.5	0.6	0.3	0.2	0.3
Other	1.4	1.3	1.3	1.3	1.6
Subtotal	16.2	19.4	19.8	24.8	23.6
Other central and local government revenue	3.9	4.3	3.0	3.0	3.0
Transferred profits					
Suez Canal	0.0	0.3	0.7	0.8	1.3
Petroleum Authority	0.1	0.4	1.3	2.3	2.2
Other	4.4	2.5	1.8	2.0	2.8
Subtotal	4.5	3.2	3.8	5.1	6.3
Self-financing investment	3.6	4.3	5.2	3.6	5.5
Total public revenue	28.2	31.2	31.8	36.5	38.4
GDP at market prices	100.0	100.0	100.0	100.0	100.0
	Millions of Egyptian pounds				
Central government tax revenue					
Personal income	33	31	48	55	52
Business profit	143	195	277	387	538
Goods and services	195	229	284	340	360
Foreign trade	231	400	538	979	920
Property	21	30	19	18	23
Other	59	63	86	97	141
Subtotal	682	948	1,252	1,876	2,034
Other central and local government revenue	164	212	189	227	260
Transferred profits					
Suez Canal	0	14	46	58	107
Petroleum Authority	3	17	84	177	192
Other	185	123	113	149	240
Subtotal	188	154	243	384	539
Self-financing investment	150	210	331	268	473
Total public revenue	1,184	1,524	2,015	2,755	3,306
GDP at market prices	4,197	4,886	6,328	7,551	8,602

Source: Ministry of Finance.

of total public revenue to GDP has been constant over time if taxes on foreign trade are excluded, it does not mean that other taxes and revenues — business profit tax, transferred profits, and self-financing investment — remained unchanged during the period. In fact, an increase in one or more sectors was offset by a decrease in the remaining sectors.

The personal income tax has been constant over time and represents a very low share, less than 1 percent, of GDP. This tax has not been developed into an effective fiscal instrument to control household spending and increase government revenue. Instead, the authorities have taken action to reduce taxable income, setting nontaxable minimum income so high that most of the wages and salaries have become tax exempt.

The share of the business profit tax has increased progressively from 3.4 percent in 1974 to 6.2 percent in 1978, mainly because of the dynamic growth of oil exports and the reopening of the Suez Canal. The taxable private profit assessment, however, is weak, with the result that potentially sizable revenues are lost.

The domestic sales tax system has represented a steady 4.5 percent share of GDP. The system is characterized by a widespread use of specific rates, a narrowly based tax structure (eleven items cover 70 percent of total sales tax revenue), and considerable latitude to public enterprises in sales tax assessment and timing of payments. The government is now considering a more comprehensive manufacturer's sales tax.

In spite of rapid urban development in Egypt since 1974 and the highly inflationary value of new construction, the property tax is still determined on land assessment made in the 1950s. Thus its contribution to GDP has been very low, even declining from 0.5 percent in 1974 to 0.3 percent in 1978.

Public enterprises are required to transfer 65 percent of profits after tax and depreciation to the central government. Overall, the ratio of transferred profits to GDP has slightly improved from 4.5 percent in 1974 to 6.3 percent in 1978, mainly because of the revenues derived from the Suez Canal and the petroleum sector. If these are excluded, profit transfers declined from about 4.4 percent in 1974 to 2.8 percent in 1978. A major factor in this decline has been the virtual elimination of cotton export profits after the fall in the international price of extralong-staple cotton.

Self-financed investment by public enterprises, derived mainly from retained profits and depreciation reserves, show a rising trend between 1974 and 1976. Investments declined to 3.6 percent in 1977 before rising to 5.5 percent in 1978.

Public Expenditure

Total government current expenditures rose from 33.7 percent

TABLE 15-2. TOTAL PUBLIC EXPENDITURE, 1974-78

Expenditure	1974	1975	1976	1977	1978
	Percentage of GDP				
Central and local government expenditure	21.1	21.5	22.8	19.0	21.0
Subsidies					
Food	7.9	10.0	5.1	4.1	5.2
Fertilizer, pesticides, and cotton[a]	—	1.7	0.5	0.5	0.4
Price adjustment[b]	—	—	—	3.0	—
Other	1.9	1.0	1.2	1.0	2.6
Subtotal	9.8[c]	12.7	6.8	8.6	8.2
Public organization deficits	2.0	1.9	1.9	1.8	2.2
Emergency Fund deficit	0.8	5.8	4.8	3.4	4.3
Total current expenditure	33.7	41.9	36.3	32.8	35.7
Public gross fixed investment	13.9	17.7	15.5	20.5	26.9
Total public expenditure	47.6	59.6	51.8	53.3	62.6
GDP at market prices	100.0	100.0	100.0	100.0	100.0
	Millions of Egyptian pounds				
Central and local government expenditure	886	1,050	1,444	1,432	1,806
Subsidies					
Food	329	491	322	313	450
Fertilizer, pesticides, and cotton[a]	—	81	34	35	38
Price adjustment[b]	—	—	—	228	—
Other	81	50	78	74	222
Subtotal	410[c]	622	434	650	710
Public organization deficits	83	93	119	139	185
Emergency Fund deficit	36	284	303	256	370
Total current expenditure	1,415	2,049	2,300	2,476	3,072
Public gross fixed investment	582	863	980	1,549	2,311
Total public expenditure	1,997	2,912	3,280	4,025	5,383
GDP at market prices	4,197	4,886	6,328	7,551	8,602

— Not applicable.

a. This fund is known as the Agricultural Stabilization Fund and includes Treasury Fund payments.

b. Established in 1977 to finance the cost of phasing in the domestic price impact of commodities imported at the parallel rate rather than the official exchange rate.

c. Since the Fund for Subsidies was established in 1975, the 1974 figures are budget estimates.

Source: Ministry of Finance.

of GDP in 1974 to 35.7 percent in 1978, reaching an all-time high of 41.9 percent in 1975 (see table 15-2). These fluctuations are mainly due to direct subsidies and Emergency Fund deficit payments. Before the Special Fund for Subsidies was established in 1975, direct subsidies were included in various sections of the budget. The 1974 payments are budget estimates only and are not representative of the sample; therefore, the analysis is based on 1975 to 1978.

Direct subsidies as a proportion of GDP reached a high level of 12.7 percent in 1975, then dropped sharply to 6.8 percent in 1976, and again rose to 8.6 percent in 1977. This variation stems from the fluctuation in international commodity prices, the shift of some imports from the official exchange rate to the parallel exchange rate, and the abolishment of subsidies for part of 1976 on some key food items. Between 1975 and 1976 the average import price of wheat dropped from about US$4.50 to US$3.90 a bushel, while that of sugar dropped from US$0.25 to US$0.13 a pound. As of May 1976 subsidies on flour, corn, sesame, meat, and coffee were abolished at a saving of LE55 million in 1976. The combined effect of this was a substantial drop in expenditure from LE622 million to LE434 million between 1975 and 1976. The situation was reversed between 1976 and 1977, however, and the subsidy payments increased by about 50 percent, from LE434 million to LE650 million. The increase was primarily because when some imports shifted to the parallel exchange rate, the higher costs were not permitted to be reflected fully in domestic selling prices. Following civil disturbances in January 1977, the measures included in the 1977 budget to reduce subsidies on certain less essential consumption goods were withdrawn. The subsidy payments in 1978 were LE710 million and are expected to be even higher in 1979 because of the shift of imports from the official exchange rate to the parallel market rate.

The Emergency Fund account is also highly variable and ranges from about 1 percent of GDP to almost 6 percent (in 1975). With peace gradually returning to the Middle East, it is hoped that this fund will eventually decrease.

The share of central and local government expenditures in GDP showed a particular stability averaging around 21 percent. These expenditures are expected to increase because of the ongoing decentralization of the Egyptian administration and because of the wage and salary readjustments the government may have to enact to protect the purchasing power of its employees and make the civil service more attractive to the better trained Egyptian labor force.

The losses of the public organizations are directly related to the government's price policy, which severely hampers their ability to operate at a profit, although many of them perform exclusive functions (for example, in agriculture, transportation, and communications). Until 1978 their deficits averaged about 1.9 percent of GDP;

in 1978 they increased to 2.2 percent. This trend is likely to continue unless the government takes action to lift price controls.

Public sector investment spending has accelerated sharply over the 1974-78 period, increasing from an average of about 14 percent of GDP in 1974 to 26.9 percent in 1978. This very high ratio includes large foreign capital transfers and direct foreign investments. During this period, major investments have been made in transportation and communication as well as in the agricultural sector. The present trend of high investment growth performance is expected to continue because major investments (for instance, in housing, utilities, and tourism facilities) are under way.

Summary of Fiscal Operations

Despite the increase from 28 percent in 1974 to 38 percent in 1978 in the revenue-GDP ratio, the overall fiscal deficit increased from some 19 percent of GDP in 1974 to more than 24 percent in 1978 (see table 15-3). The increase has been even more drastic from 1977 to 1978, when the deficit rose from LE1,270 to LE2,077 million. The major cause of this has been a 24 percent increase in the government's current expenditures; of these, wages and salaries increased by about 30 percent because of two nonbudgeted bonuses. Total government current expenditures rose from 34 percent of GDP in 1974 to 36 percent in 1978 and are projected to go over 40 percent in 1979. Such increases relate to the growth of food and nonfood subsidies, public organization deficits, the Emergency Fund deficit, and central and local government expenditures. As a consequence of this expansion of government expenditure, public saving performed rather poorly.

Throughout the 1973-78 period government nonfactor revenues exceeded current expenditures. The fiscal situation during these years did not even allow the financing of current government expenditure, much less public investment in the social infrastructure (education, health, administration, and transportation) without recourse to government borrowing. The deficit increased from LE569 million in 1974 to LE889 million in 1975, then decreased to LE373 million in 1977 and rose again sharply to LE778 million in 1978 (see table 15-3) and is projected to pass the LE1,500 million mark in 1979. As mentioned earlier, this variation is largely because of the fluctuation of subsidy payments with international prices and the shift of some imports from the official to the parallel exchange rate.

The public economic sector's surplus is defined as the sum of transferred profits and self-financing investment. The share of this surplus has increased from 8 percent of GDP in 1974 to 11.7 percent in 1978.

Because of the current government deficit, total public saving

TABLE 15-3. SUMMARY OF FISCAL OPERATIONS, 1974-78

Item	1974	1975	1976	1977	1978
	Percentage of GDP				
Central and local government revenue	20.2	23.7	22.8	27.9	26.7
Public economic sector surplus	8.0	7.4	9.0	8.6	11.7
Total public revenue	28.2	31.1	31.8	36.5	38.4
Current government expenditure	33.7	41.9	36.3	32.8	35.7
Public gross fixed investment	13.9	17.7	15.5	20.5	26.9
Total public expenditure	47.6	59.6	51.8	53.3	62.6
Current operations deficit	13.6	18.2	13.6	4.9	9.0
Total public saving	-5.5	-10.7	-4.5	3.7	2.7
Overall fiscal deficit	19.4	28.4	20.0	16.8	24.1
Foreign financing (net)	2.8	4.3	7.7	6.1	8.2
Domestic financing (net)	16.6	24.1	12.3	10.7	15.9
GDP at market prices	100.0	100.0	100.0	100.0	100.0
	Millions of Egyptian pounds				
Central and local government revenue	846	1,160	1,441	2,103	2,294
Public economic sector surplus	338	364	574	652	1,012
Total public revenue	1,184	1,524	2,015	2,755	3,306
Current government expenditure	1,415	2,049	2,300	2,476	3,072
Public gross fixed investment	582	863	980	1,549	2,311
Total public expenditure	1,997	2,912	3,280	4,025	5,383
Current operations deficit	-569	-889	-859	-373	-778
Total public saving	-231	-525	-285	279	234
Overall fiscal deficit	-813	-1,388	-1,265	-1,270	-2,077
Foreign financing (net)	119	210	488	464	705
Domestic financing (net)	694	1,178	777	806	1,372
GDP at market prices	4,197	4,886	6,328	7,551	8,602

Source: Ministry of Finance.

was negative for 1974, 1975, and 1976 and became positive afterward. Even in 1977, however, total public saving represented less than 4 percent of GDP. This ratio dropped to 2.7 percent in 1978, when total public saving covered about 10 percent of public gross fixed investment, compared with 18 percent in 1977. This disappointing performance of public saving is rooted mainly in the inefficiency of the tax administration and in the much higher responsiveness of government expenditure to domestic and imported inflation than that of government revenue. Sales taxes have very little responsiveness to inflation; property taxes are still based on land value assessments made in the 1950s. Profit taxes outside the oil sector even have a negative responsiveness to inflation, since the prices of many industrial products are controlled by the government, while the cost of production reacts instantaneously to domestic as well as imported inflation. On the expenditure side, wages and salaries are found to react to domestic inflation, and the level of subsidies is directly related to price fluctuations in the international food market. Government expenditures on goods and services are also likely to be sensitive to inflation. Therefore, in any long-term solution to the problem of public saving, the existing tax system should be made more responsive to domestic and imported inflation, and current government expenditure should be rigorously contained.

ISSUES

The foregoing discussion reveals that the increase in the overall fiscal deficit and the inadequate public savings performance during 1974-78 have been much more a problem of expenditure than of revenue. The preceding statistical description also raises some important issues.

Revenue

The first issue is that the tax system is largely inelastic to increases in the values of the variables on which assessments are based; thus, revenues tend to lag behind, particularly in a period of inflation. The main reason is that the tax structure contains many exemptions and specific (as opposed to ad valorem) duties.

Second, the public sector enterprises have not been permitted to raise their prices in line with their costs, which have often been swollen by the employment policy of the government. The question, in essence, turns to the degree of autonomy that the public enterprises are to be permitted, and on how far financial profitability is to be used as the measure of the success of these enterprises. This issue has been discussed in some detail in chapter 4.

Third, the inadequacy of tax administration is an important issue that stems from traditional causes: insufficient staff, a lack of office space and equipment, and corruption among the poorly paid tax officials who often deal with large amounts of tax money. These problems have arisen in administering not only direct (that is, income and profit) taxes, but also customs and excise taxes. Relations between taxpayers and the tax administration are rather poor and based on reciprocal outguessing — a familiar situation that is certainly made more difficult, as in the case of the general income tax, by the extremely high marginal rates of the tax.

The inadequacies of staff relate perhaps more to quality than to number. Working conditions are also poor, especially in the eighty-six regional offices. Lack of space to file tax returns properly — seemingly a trivial problem — is a real bottleneck, as is the lack of equipment, such as calculating machines. Furthermore, poor working conditions have a cumulative negative influence on the staff — bright university graduates, who are brought into the administration by the employment policy of the government, tend to lose their motivation after a few years.

The government has begun to improve tax administration. One measure, which in fact revamps an existing mechanism, is to provide incentives to employees to collect a larger amount of taxes. The incentive is equal to 3 percent of the additional amount collected, with a ceiling equivalent to four times the net monthly salary, a higher limit than the previous one.

Another move has been to reestablish the tax evasion office, which had been abolished in 1972. It consists of a director general, two deputies, and about twenty-five tax inspectors, plus a police subdivision for investigating prime suspects. Tax inspectors, after receiving permission from the judiciary, may seize the books of delinquent taxpayers. Additional measures to improve tax administration include hiring more inspectors and collectors, conducting training courses, and trying to computerize the basic data.

The recent changes in the tax structure, especially the inclusion of agricultural income in the general income tax and the creation of the tax on some capital transactions, will place an additional burden on the tax administration. This burden will become even greater when general sales taxes are introduced and the tariff structure is reformed. In other words, the future problems of tax administration will certainly be more complicated than the present ones.

Expenditure

Three main items of expenditure warrant special attention. First, the government's bill on salaries continues to increase each year, as a result of employing larger numbers and of paying higher salaries, bonuses, and cost-of-living adjustments. The first part of this problem arose largely because until about 1975 it was official policy to provide a job in the public sector to any graduate of an institution of higher education who was unable to obtain one elsewhere within six months of graduation. This policy has not formally been repudiated, but is now pursued with less zeal. As a result of previous actions, however, the public sector is burdened with employees of only limited productivity, and resources are therefore not available to pay the higher salaries required to attract persons of exceptional merit. Further increases in this category of expenditure will have to be held down, for example, by hiring fewer people

than are removed through normal attrition and by restricting the
amounts of the annual bonuses.

Second, defense expenditures (including the deficit in the Emergency Fund) have accounted for nearly 40 percent of current revenues. The level of defense spending is a politically sensitive issue,
and it is hoped that with progress toward a Middle East peace, Egypt
will eventually be able to limit this type of expenditure.

Third, expenditure on subsidies has increased so rapidly and
to such a high level that it merits a separate, detailed discussion.

The System of Subsidies

The subsidy system has become so complex and pervasive that
a recent government report lamented that the real cost of subsidies
could not be estimated with any high degree of accuracy, and that
no public sector expenditure was free from some sort of subsidy.
In the face of this, the concern here is not to offer definitive conclusions, but rather to highlight the contours of the issue, and to make
recommendations for rendering the system more effective in assist-
ing the most vulnerable groups in the population.

Egyptian analysts generally divide subsidies into three types:
(1) direct subsidies, which enable a particular organization to sell
specified items at a price that is often well below cost — for example,
the payments to the General Authority for Supply Commodities for
the provision of wheat, corn, edible oils, and other commodities;
(2) indirect subsidies, which cover the operating losses of various
organizations — for example, the payments to the Cairo Transportation Authority; (3) hidden subsidies, that is, the opportunities
lost because exportable products (for example, raw cotton and petroleum) are sold to other units within the country at less than the
world market price. In fact, the first two are similar in that they
impose a financial cost which is reflected in the budget; the third
imposes a penalty through opportunity costs.

The subsidized commodities and services reach consumers in a
variety of ways. Some, such as bread and transportation fares,
are available to all consumers at a unified price and without any
restrictions; some, such as sugar, tea, and edible oil, are offered
on ration cards distributed according to fixed allocations per individual; some, such as frozen meat, cheese, and dairy products,
are offered to individuals on a first-come, first-serve basis. For
such items the role of the government is confined to importing as
much as its budget allows to try to make up for supply deficiencies
in the market.

Direct subsidies first appeared as a separate item in the general
expenditure budget during the 1950s, generally as a very small
amount; in 1960 it was only about LE9 million. At that time subsidies went to only a few commodities, of which the most important

were wheat, kerosene, and sugar (distributed by ration cards). The total volume of subsidies increased each year with population growth and price increases until they reached about LE20 million in 1970. The most dramatic increase in the subsidy bill occurred after 1973 when world food prices rose steeply; the direct subsidy bill in 1975 was estimated at LE622 million. Despite a decline in world prices of some foodstuffs in subsequent years, the total subsidy bill in domestic currency kept increasing as the parallel market exchange rate was applied to more and more items. As a result, the direct subsidy burden in 1978 was put at LE680 million.

The total subsidy bill gives some indication of the amount of resources that could be available for redirection to more basic items if subsidies to the less important commodities were reduced. The list of basic foodstuffs includes some on which the authorities have placed primary attention, such as wheat, flour, corn, rice, edible oils, beans, lentils, and sugar, and another group of items, such as meat, poultry, fish, and cheese, the availability of which has been determined mainly by the state of the budget.

TABLE 15-4.   BUDGETED SUBSIDY ALLOCATIONS
FOR SUPPLY COMMODITIES, 1973-78
(millions of Egyptian pounds)

Item	1973	1974	1975	1976	1977	1978[a]
Wheat	70.8	194.1	135.1	152.3	117.5	127.6
Flour	8.2	27.0	27.6	25.8	31.6	19.6
Maize	4.4	16.5	29.2	23.1	40.6	49.2
Lentils	0.6	2.2	6.3	9.0	9.4	14.6
Horse beans	0.3	0.7	5.2	6.0	2.0	6.0
Sesame	0.4	0.3	2.7	0.4	0.3	...
Edible oils	16.8	45.2	72.1	41.0	48.4	44.7
Fats	2.9	13.6	19.1	16.4	36.5	51.2
Margarine	1.0	0.2	...	...	...	...
Clarified butter	...	0.4	...	...	...	...
Frozen meat	...	...	...	...	20.4	37.0
Frozen poultry	...	...	0.5	...	...	...
Live sheep	...	0.6	0.3	...	...	...
Frozen fish	0.5	...	2.0	0.2	0.4	2.3
Sugar	...	16.2	19.5	2.0	(9.8)	(26.8)
Coffee beans	...	0.5	0.3	3.3	5.6	...
Tea	...	...	...	...	18.3	45.6
Lumber	1.9	9.4	4.1	...	...	...
Miscellaneous commodities	0.2	0.6	1.1	...	...	...
Other losses	11.7	18.8	31.3	41.7	...	31.0

... Zero or negligible.
Note: For the actual expenditures, which were higher than budgeted, see table 15-11.
a. Estimated.
Source: Ministry of Finance.

TABLE 15-5. AMOUNTS OF MAJOR SUBSIDIZED
COMMODITIES, 1973-78
(thousands of tons)

Item	1973	1974	1975	1976	1977	1978[a]
Wheat						
Imported	2,373	2,877	2,950	2,758	3,297	3,560
Domestic	211	318	332	269	87	150
First-rate flour	452	395	701	541	655	837
Imported maize	609	457	506	435	676	690
Beans						
Imported	...	22	116	83	25	35
Domestic	14	16	26	49	50	50
Lentils						
Imported	12	16	50	17	44	50
Domestic	12	2.6	0.6	12	11	10
Oil						
Imported	138	162	242	222	225	250
Domestic	...	...	...	...	...	125
Food and animal fats	28	126.7	150	163	127	179
Frozen meat	...	2.5	...	...	65	70
Frozen fish						
Imported	32	32.9	40	43	31	50
Domestic	...	...	...	...	...	17
Tea	...	...	...	...	48	37

... Zero or negligible.
a. Estimated.
Source: Ministry of Finance.

A summary of the budgetary allocations for each of the main items
during 1973-78 is shown in table 15-4, the amounts made available
at subsidized prices in table 15-5, and the average subsidy per ton
in table 15-6. These tables show the steep rise in the supply of
most items. For example, wheat went up by 50 percent between
1973 and 1978, flour by 80 percent, lentils by 150 percent, edible
oils by 170 percent, foods and fats by 540 percent, and frozen fish
by over 100 percent. Some items, such as frozen meat, which were
not subsidized in 1973, made a substantial contribution to the subsidy bill in 1978. The 1978 subsidy per ton of wheat was 60 percent
higher than in 1973, the flour subsidy about 100 percent higher, for
corn the increase was over 200 percent, and for frozen fish about
550 percent.

APPENDIX: EFFECTS OF A REDUCTION IN FOOD SUBSIDIES

One of the most debated economic issues in Egypt is to what extent the food subsidy program should be continued. In macroeconomic terms, the subsidies are of course the national dissaving
counterpart of the large balance of payments deficits (and foreign

TABLE 15-6. AVERAGE SUBSIDY PER TON FOR MAJOR COMMODITIES, 1973-78

(Egyptian pounds per ton)

Item	1973	1974	1975	1976	1977	1978[a]
Wheat						
Imported	29.27	66.64	77.6	51.73	34.78⎫	
Domestic	6.43	7.42	18.53	35.57	68.78⎭	47.8
First-rate flour	18.0	68.36	39.33	47.65	47.88	35.34
Imported maize	21.18	32.08	57.8	53.04	58.90	71.2
Beans						
Imported	...	22.86	42.06	58.03	81.88⎫	
Domestic	21.5	14.56	12.8	22.85	0.2 ⎭	70.8
Lentils						
Imported	45.58	134.62	124.08	133.89	208.9 ⎫	
Domestic	8.0	14.61	103.3	3.0	32.45⎭	243.6
Oil	121.43	278.77	297.97	184.5	220.03	119.32
Food and animal fat	105.17	107.37	127.24	100.9	292.62	285.9
Frozen meat	...	2.0	...	...	318.9	528.9
Frozen fish	16.34	54.95	50.77	3.74	14.06	104.7
Tea	...	...	...	...	482.2	1,231.9

... Zero or negligible.
a. Estimated.
Source: Ministry of Finance.

saving) incurred after 1973. In microeconomic terms, one can ask how efficiently they are being distributed to maintain the food consumption levels of the poor.

To address this question, consider a simple model of food consumption demand. Using an asterisk to denote the relative change of variable ($x^* = dx/x$), the shift in demand q for a food when its price changes is

$$q^* = \eta \, (P^D)^*$$

where η is the price elasticity of demand for the population as a whole, and P^D is the demand price. For a vulnerable target group within the population, the appropriate equation is

$$v^* = \eta_v \, (P^D)^*$$

where v is the initial consumption level of the group, and η_v is its price elasticity. Overall supply response is given by the equation

$$q^* = \varepsilon \, (P^S)^*$$

where ε is the supply elasticity, and P^S the price received by the suppliers. If there is a subsidy so that P^S exceeds P^D, its cost C is given by

$$C = (P^S - P^D) \, q.$$

The independent variable in this system is P^D, the subsidized food price set by the government. As it changes, the marginal cost, dC/dv, of delivering a unit of subsidized food to the vulnerable group shifts:[3]

$$\frac{dC}{dv} = \frac{\eta/\eta_v}{v/q}\left(P^S\frac{\varepsilon + 1}{\varepsilon} - P^D\frac{\eta + 1}{\eta}\right).$$

If supply elasticities are high (as they are if marginal quantities of foods come from imports) and demand elasticities are all less than one, the term in parentheses is close to constant for all foods. The dominant terms in determining marginal cost are therefore the share v/q of the food consumed by the vulnerable group, and the ratio of elasticities η/η_v. Marginal cost is low insofar as the vulnerable group has a relatively elastic demand for the food in question and consumes a large share of its total supply.

Tables 15-7 and 15-8 shed some light on the share of consumption. For any given expenditure class, the tables show the shares in total value of consumption taken by consumers in the class. For example, rural consumers in the LE200-249 expenditure range account for 9.16 percent of total value of rural consumption of grains, 8.0 percent of dry beans, and so on. High numbers in the tables in relation to total expenditure shares of the class indicate a commodity with low marginal subsidy costs. By this criterion, grains and starches, dry beans, oils and fats, and vegetables appear to be likely candidates for subsidy.

Price elasticities can be expressed as

$$\eta = -(1/2 + \phi)\eta Y$$

and

$$\eta_v = -(1/2 + \phi_v)\eta Y$$

where ϕ and ϕ_v are the budget shares of the food for the population and vulnerable groups respectively, and ηY is the Engel elasticity. In effect, the Engel elasticity is assumed to be approximately constant across income groups, and the negative of the compensated price elasticity of demand is assumed to be half the Engel elasticity. The income effect in demand is of course represented by ϕ and ϕ_v—the real income of a consumer group goes down more with a price increase of a commodity when it devotes a large share of its budget to that commodity. With these approximations, the elasticity term in the marginal cost of subsidizing a food is

$$\frac{\eta}{\eta_v} = \frac{(1/2 + \phi)}{(1/2 + \phi_v)},$$

so that the subsidy cost is lower as the vulnerable group's budget share for the food is higher in relation to the average budget share.

3. The derivation follows fairly closely from one in Shlomo Reutlinger and Marcelo Selowsky, <u>Malnutrition and Poverty: Magnitude and Policy Options</u> (Baltimore, Md.: Johns Hopkins University Press, 1976).

TABLE 15-7. SHARES IN TOTAL FOOD CONSUMPTION: RURAL EXPENDITURE GROUPS, 1974-75

Expenditure interval[a]	Households[b]	Persons[c]	Expenditure share				Share of total consumption				
				Grain, starch	Dry beans	Meat, fish, eggs	Oil, fat	Milk and products	Vegetables	Fruit	Sugar
5-49	.0200	.0044	.0020	.0033	.0033	.0013	.0017	.0021	.0027	.0013	.0026
50-74	.0270	.0087	.0044	.0061	.0054	.0047	.0047	.0036	.0063	.0039	.0040
75-99	.0350	.0178	.0082	.0123	.0115	.0089	.0087	.0082	.0123	.0093	.0091
100-149	.0779	.0484	.0263	.0384	.0332	.0258	.0292	.0231	.0349	.0215	.0270
150-199	.1119	.0845	.0516	.0669	.0656	.0511	.0561	.0499	.0672	.0447	.0616
200-249	.1179	.1049	.0711	.0916	.0800	.0693	.0778	.0703	.0784	.0605	.0840
250-299	.1259	.1267	.0924	.1131	.0983	.0911	.0968	.0935	.1028	.0812	.0995
300-349	.1019	.1126	.0882	.0995	.1017	.0947	.1027	.0838	.1030	.0943	.0945
350-399	.0889	.0999	.0878	.0992	.0883	.0878	.1010	.0750	.0927	.0843	.0962
400-499	.1129	.1347	.1316	.1377	.1336	.1451	.1430	.1383	.1411	.1352	.1406
500-599	.0440	.0570	.0633	.0609	.0665	.0647	.0605	.0609	.0582	.0577	.0706
600-799	.0649	.0923	.1194	.1107	.1126	.1184	.1176	.1362	.1171	.1365	.1117
800-999	.0300	.0451	.0701	.0649	.0750	.0679	.0752	.0763	.0634	.0793	.0641
1,000-1,399	.0240	.0323	.0769	.0443	.0707	.0767	.0649	.0823	.0617	.0875	.0608
1,400-1,999	.0130	.0231	.0554	.0370	.0312	.0533	.0438	.0739	.0431	.0803	.0535
2,000 or more	.0050	.0077	.0512	.0142	.0229	.0393	.0163	.0227	.0152	.0225	.0200

a. Egyptian pounds a year.
b. Number of households/Total households.
c. Number of persons/Total persons.
Source: Household Expenditure Survey, 1974-75.

332

TABLE 15-8. SHARES IN TOTAL FOOD CONSUMPTION: URBAN EXPENDITURE GROUPS, 1974-75

Expenditure interval[a]	House-holds[b]	Persons[c]	Expen-diture share	Share of total consumption							
				Grain, starch	Dry beans	Meat, fish, eggs	Oil, fat	Milk and products	Vege-tables	Fruit	Sugar
5-49	.0040	.0008	.0003	.0006	.0004	.0002	.0002	.0002	.0004	.0003	.0003
50-74	.0050	.0013	.0006	.0013	.0010	.0006	.0008	.0005	.0009	.0005	.0009
75-99	.0085	.0034	.0013	.0030	.0033	.0014	.0021	.0009	.0019	.0007	.0019
100-149	.0395	.0206	.0091	.0169	.0189	.0088	.0106	.0076	.0131	.0073	.0137
150-199	.0530	.0353	.0166	.0306	.0252	.0170	.0210	.0134	.0242	.0147	.0217
200-249	.0660	.0549	.0266	.0466	.0428	.0251	.0332	.0238	.0358	.0231	.0351
250-299	.0885	.0760	.0438	.0671	.0664	.0410	.0511	.0386	.0579	.0375	.0528
300-349	.0805	.0733	.0470	.0703	.0696	.0483	.0564	.0433	.0620	.0483	.0544
350-399	.0775	.0804	.0523	.0719	.0739	.0510	.0572	.0522	.0674	.0523	.0595
400-499	.1470	.1567	.1134	.1002	.1477	.1135	.1368	.1152	.1394	.1088	.1251
500-599	.1200	.1351	.1185	.1384	.1355	.1156	.1314	.1218	.1320	.1156	.1256
600-799	.1275	.1483	.1565	.1578	.1476	.1649	.1650	.1640	.1589	.1586	.1554
800-999	.0690	.0749	.1103	.0854	.0910	.1169	.1081	.1217	.0978	.1304	.1143
1,000-1,399	.0690	.0846	.1423	.0984	.1077	.1489	.1268	.1470	.1169	.1434	.1322
1,400-1,999	.0295	.0353	.0927	.0880	.0439	.0889	.0589	.0912	.0581	.0900	.0585
2,000 or more	.0155	.0192	.0689	.0232	.0251	.0578	.0407	.0584	.0332	.0685	.0484

a. Egyptian pounds a year.
b. Number of households/Total households.
c. Number of persons/Total persons.
Source: Household Expenditure Survey, 1974-75.

TABLE 15-9. RURAL BUDGET SHARES FOR FOODS, 1974–75

Expenditure interval[a]	All food	Grain, starch	Dry beans	Meat, fish, eggs	Oil, fat	Milk and products	Vege- tables	Fruit	Sugar	Expenditure Per person	Expenditure Per household
5–49	.7265	.3083	.0375	.0912	.0483	.0335	.0590	.0186	.0483	28.6923	37.3000
50–74	.6953	.2507	.0276	.1458	.0600	.0258	.0606	.0246	.0336	32.0577	61.7407
75–99	.7402	.2747	.0317	.1475	.0595	.0317	.0641	.0317	.0408	29.1604	88.3143
100–149	.6955	.2674	.0286	.1341	.0626	.0279	.0568	.0230	.0378	34.2526	126.9103
150–199	.6766	.2381	.0288	.1356	.0615	.0309	.0558	.0244	.0440	38.4583	173.0625
200–249	.6620	.2367	.0255	.1337	.0620	.0315	.0472	.0240	.0435	42.6550	227.2881
250–299	.6449	.2248	.0241	.1352	.0593	.0322	.0477	.0248	.0396	45.9074	275.4444
300–349	.6529	.2070	.0261	.1471	.0659	.0303	.0500	.0301	.0394	45.3393	325.0588
350–399	.6328	.2073	.0228	.1369	.0651	.0272	.0452	.0270	.0403	55.3909	370.9326
400–499	.6308	.1920	.0230	.1511	.0615	.0335	.0459	.0290	.0393	61.5075	437.6283
500–599	.5935	.1766	.0238	.1402	.0541	.0307	.0394	.0257	.0411	69.9324	540.3864
600–799	.5792	.1702	.0214	.1358	.0557	.0363	.0420	.0322	.0344	81.4374	690.3385
800–999	.5780	.1697	.0242	.1326	.0607	.0346	.0387	.0319	.0337	97.9777	878.5333
1,000–1,399	.4922	.1057	.0209	.1366	.0477	.0341	.0291	.0344	.0321	149.7617	1,204.3333
1,400–1,999	.5136	.1227	.0128	.1319	.0448	.0425	.0333	.0408	.0356	150.8189	1,601.0000
2,000 or more	.2748	.0508	.0101	.1051	.0180	.0141	.0127	.0124	.0144	418.6522	3,851.6000
Total	.5943	.1836	.0227	.1370	.0566	.0319	.0428	.0282	.0368	62.9683	375.4195

a. Egyptian pounds a year.
Source: Household Expenditure Survey, 1974–75.

TABLE 15-10. URBAN BUDGET SHARES FOR FOODS, 1974-75

Expenditure intervala	All food	Grain, starch	Dry beans	Meat, fish, eggs	Oil, fat	Milk and products	Vege- tables	Fruit	Sugar	Expenditure	
										Per person	Per household
5-49	.6566	.2290	.0236	.0741	.0337	.0370	.0640	.0370	.0370	33.0000	37.1250
50-74	.6989	.2106	.0250	.1310	.0562	.0359	.0702	.0312	.0468	45.7857	64.1000
75-99	.6773	.2165	.0372	.1387	.0629	.0277	.0609	.0183	.0399	38.8947	86.9412
100-149	.6489	.1793	.0308	.1258	.0466	.0341	.0625	.0287	.0429	43.8782	127.7468
150-199	.6360	.1780	.0225	.1325	.0506	.0328	.0632	.0315	.0371	46.8426	174.1132
200-249	.6134	.1687	.0238	.1227	.0498	.0364	.0582	.0309	.0375	48.3971	224.3864
250-299	.5818	.1476	.0224	.1212	.0467	.0358	.0573	.0304	.0343	57.5691	275.4859
300-349	.5849	.1440	.0219	.1332	.0480	.0375	.0572	.0365	.0329	64.0135	324.8385
350-399	.5626	.1324	.0209	.1265	.0438	.0406	.0558	.0355	.0323	64.8740	375.4323
400-499	.5257	.0851	.0193	.1296	.0482	.0413	.0532	.0341	.0313	72.2610	429.3878
500-599	.5280	.1127	.0169	.1264	.0443	.0418	.0482	.0346	.0301	87.5607	549.8083
600-799	.5126	.0970	.0140	.1365	.0421	.0426	.0440	.0360	.0282	105.3791	683.5176
800-999	.4915	.0745	.0122	.1373	.0392	.0448	.0384	.0420	.0294	147.1042	890.0870
1,000-1,399	.4596	.0666	.0112	.1356	.0356	.0420	.0356	.0358	.0264	167.9979	1,147.9855
1,400-1,999	.4231	.0914	.0070	.1243	.0254	.0400	.0272	.0345	.0179	261.9010	1,748.9661
2,000 or more	.3429	.0324	.0054	.1087	.0236	.0344	.0208	.0353	.0200	358.5935	2,475.4516
Total	.0514	.0963	.0148	.1296	.0400	.0406	.0433	.0355	.0348	99.8483	556.7540

a. Egyptian pounds a year.
Source: Household Expenditure Survey, 1974-75.

335

Tables 15-9 and 15-10 contain the relevant information on budget shares and show grains and starches, vegetables, and sugar to have low subsidy costs.

According to the criteria just discussed, table 15-11 indicates that the Egyptian subsidy program is probably fairly cost-effective in delivering food to poor people. The most important point is that grains are heavily subsidized, essentially to make up the difference between import price and a traditional within-country price. This is cost-effective, since grains make up a large share of the budget of the poor and the poor consume a large part of total supply. By the same criterion, however, the reduction of subsidies for maize (and their absence for consumption of Nili maize and millets in the countryside) is not rational, although reducing the subsidy on consumption of fine flour would do little social harm. Of the other items, edible oil and sugar are usefully subsidized on nutritional grounds, and some items in the "other" category are also. The main expenditures there are on beans, sesame, fats, and meats.

TABLE 15-11. TRADING OPERATIONS OF THE GENERAL
AUTHORITY FOR SUPPLY COMMODITIES, 1973-78
(millions of Egyptian pounds)

Item	1973	1974	1975	1976	1977	1978
Subsidies (losses)	136.2	393.2	423.7	281.4	343.2	452.4
Wheat and flour	79.0	216.4	260.9	171.6	149.1	222.8
Maize	4.4	16.5	31.1	23.1	40.6	53.8
Edible fats and oils (rationed)	16.8	55.3	72.2	43.2	54.6	137.4
Sugar (rationed)	19.0	68.9	20.8	6.1	...	...
Other	17.0	36.1	38.7	37.4	98.9	38.4
Profits	47.2	63.1	15.0	31.2	12.6	29.3
Cottonseed	2.5	2.0	2.1	2.0	2.0	...
Edible oil (nonrationed)	5.0	8.0	...	...	...	...
Tea	14.4	14.0	11.5	13.2	...	...
Sugar (nonrationed)	22.6	36.0	...	...	8.6	26.1
Other	2.7	3.1	1.4	16.0	2.0	3.2
Total net losses	-89.0	-330.1	-408.7	-250.2	-330.6[a]	-423.1

... Zero or negligible.
Note: Total net losses are normally less than total subsidy payments from the Special Fund for Subsidies and the Price Adjustment Fund, the difference representing various administrative costs and, in some years, settlement of arrears.
a. Actual net losses are estimated to have been LE455 million, the additional LE124 million being met from the Price Adjustment Fund. The losses shown above are based on the official exchange rate, whereas during 1977 all subsidized commodities apart from wheat, flour, edible oils, sugar, and tea were imported at the parallel exchange rate.
Source: General Authority for Supply Commodities.

TABLE 15-12. ECONOMIC EFFECTS OF INCREASING
SUBSIDIZED FOOD PRICE TO REDUCE SUBSIDIES
BY LE200 MILLION

Item	Base solution	Solution with price increase	Solution with price and wage increases	Solution with price, wage, and investment increases
GNP in base prices	4.4173	4.1801	4.2572	4.4177
Percentage change in real GNP	—	-5.37	-3.62	0.01
Percentage change in costs				
Rural	—	—	2.73	2.73
Urban	—	—	5.56	5.56
Food	—	—	0.70	0.70
Total	—	—	4.52	4.52
Total imports	1.6204	1.5069	1.5416	1.6314
Food imports	0.5690	0.5103	0.5252	0.5333
Trade deficit	0.4994	0.3858	0.4206	0.5104
Government expenditure	1.7857	1.5495	1.6458	1.6526
Government expenditure on food subsidies	0.4909	0.2608	0.2761	0.2804
Government deficit	0.1429	0.0058	0.0402	-0.0159
Percentage change in cost of living				
Rural	—	2.17	5.99	5.99
Urban	—	8.23	11.66	11.66
Percentage change in real income				
Rural	—	-6.77	-7.19	-6.20
Urban	—	-13.98	-8.80	0.60

Note: The consumer food price increases from 0.5854 to 0.75439 in the last
three solutions. Wage increases in the last two are: rural sector, 0.19213 to
0.19629; urban sector, 0.44652 to 0.48329; food sector, 0.53544 to 0.57953.
In the last solution, gross capital formation increases from LE840 million to
LE1,002 million.
Source: World Bank.

Programmed reductions in meat subsidies, of course, make good
sense.

The subsidies are a major component of government current expenditures, amounting to 27.5 percent of the total. Any significant
reduction would have a major effect on aggregate demand, as can
be seen by comparing the first and second columns in table 15-12,
where the first column summarizes the base 1975 estimates, and
the second column describes a model solution in which the food price
is raised by about 29 percent in an attempt to cut subsidies by
LE200 million.

The food price increases would drive up the cost of living of rural and urban income groups by about 2.2 percent and 8.2 percent
respectively. Given the inelasticity of food demand, most of the

real income loss caused by these price increases would in fact reduce demand for other commodities — the ensuing multiplier contraction would reduce real GNP by about LE240 million. Food imports themselves would fall by no more than LE60 million, although
the balance of payments would improve by LE114 million as a result
of the overall contraction in the economy. Thus, a reduction of food
subsidies would not reduce food imports by very much, but it would
lead to a substantial decrease in economic activity as consumers
cut back on purchases of other goods rather than do without the chief
necessity of life. Could the contractionary impact of the reduction
in subsidies be offset? Two devices present themselves.

First, there would be pressure for increased wages if food prices
went up. The third column in table 15-12 shows what happens when
wages rise enough to offset the real income loss caused by higher
food prices. By assumption, wage increments would be passed on
in further price increases — the first round of a wage-price spiral
that might be touched off by the reduced subsidies. The table shows
that a price index weighted by initial value added levels in the three
sectors would go up by 4.5 percent, while the additional inflation
for rural and urban consumers would be 3.8 percent and 3.4 percent respectively. The wage increases would generate enough demand to make the reduction in real GNP only LE160 million. Further rounds in the wage-price spiral would close the gap more, but
only at the cost of a significant burst of inflation.

A second way to offset the subsidy decrease would be to increase
aggregate demand, say, by an increase in investment. The last
column of the table shows that if gross capital formation rose by
19 percent to LE1,002 million, the higher investment plus wage increases could restore the original level of GNP. But there are still
significant distributional effects — the real income of rural consumers falls by 6.2 percent, while that of urban consumers goes up by
0.6 percent. Moreover, the overall trade deficit widens by about
LE10 million. Investment creates demand mainly for urban workers and imported goods.

Any summary assessment of the impacts of reducing food subsidies would depend on the likelihood of the events inserted into the
various model solutions: a push for higher wages in response to
higher food prices seems quite probable, an increase in real investment perhaps less so. But even if the food price increase were offset in macro terms by higher investment, there would still be a
significant loss in incomes in rural areas. This of course could
be offset by higher agricultural prices, which could be offset by
higher subsidies or higher urban wages — and the story begins again.

16
Balance of Payments and External Resources

Perhaps the most important factor in the post-1973 Egyptian economic situation has been the unprecedented magnitude of the transfer of external resources into the country. The deficit on goods and services (the resource gap) averaged about 11 percent of GDP during 1973-78, compared with an average of 1 to 4 percent of GDP in the previous two decades (see table 16-1). Initially, this was financed through Arab grants and loans and fairly substantial short-term external commercial borrowing. Subsequently, however, large medium- and long-term aid from Arab and OECD countries and international institutions have allowed Egypt not only to sustain this higher deficit but also to retire a large portion of its outstanding short-term debt.

Other significant features of the external situation are the emergence of workers' remittances and petroleum as the major foreign

TABLE 16-1. COMPOSITION OF DOMESTIC EXPENDITURE,
1952-53 TO 1973-76
(annual average percent)

Period	GDP growth rate at current prices	Expenditure as percentage of GDP[a]			Deficit on goods and services as percentage of GDP
		Gross invest-ment	Public consump-tion	Private consump-tion	
1952-53 to 1957-58	7.1	14.2	17.0	69.9	1.2
1958-59 to 1965-66	10.0	16.8	18.7	68.5	4.1
1966-67 to 1971-72	6.2	13.5	23.9	66.5	3.9
1973-76	15.3	21.2	25.4	66.3	12.9

a. Excess of total expenditures over 100 percent equals the deficit in goods and services.
Source: Ministry of Planning, CAPMAS, and World Bank estimates.

exchange earners of the economy (replacing cotton, which is still a major commodity export), the resurgence of tourism, and the reopening of the Suez Canal, which is being widened and deepened. The commodity export sector other than petroleum, however, remains weak and is restrained by capacity and inadequate quality.

Egyptian policymakers are accordingly confronted with the need to strengthen their foreign sector at a time when large amounts of foreign aid are available. This external support presents the opportunity to set the economy on the path of self-sustained growth. This chapter reviews briefly the historical experience of Egypt's external accounts (1952-72), the main problems that faced Egyptian policymakers in managing external finances after the October 1973 war, and the actual developments in this sector during 1973-78.

HISTORICAL EXPERIENCE, 1952-72

The period under review, 1952-72, encompasses three distinct stages in Egypt's financial relations with the rest of the world: the era of economic independence (1952-58), the externally vulnerable command economy (1959-66), and the war years (1967-73). During the 1952-58 period the assertion of political and economic independence took various forms, including the nationalization of the Suez Canal. Management of external finances was directed toward stabilizing the Egyptian balance of payments and the domestic economy, which was still largely dependent on cotton. Earnings from cotton, the Suez Canal, and tourism represented the bulk of Egypt's export revenue. Foreign medium- and long-term capital inflows were nonexistent, and Egypt's foreign exchange gap was met by the foreign exchange reserves of about US$980 million inherited by the Egyptian government. Since these reserves were largely in blocked sterling accounts in the British Treasury, foreign exchange mechanisms were instituted to encourage exports and control imports. These included export bonuses, import entitlements, triangular payment transactions, payments agreements, and direct allocations through the institution of a Foreign Exchange Budget.[1]

Direct control over all major sectors of the economy was exercised in 1959-66. A sweeping series of nationalizations of foreign trade companies, financial institutions, and industrial enterprises together with agrarian reform characterized the period through 1961. By 1962 Egypt's foreign exchange reserves were exhausted, and new measures were required. The most important was the devaluation of the Egyptian pound by about 25 percent in 1962. The

1. For details, see Bent Hansen and Karim Nashashibi, Foreign Trade Regimes and Economic Development: Egypt (New York: National Bureau of Economic Research, Columbia University Press, 1975).

exchange rate adjustment, however, proved ineffectual in encouraging exports and dampening imports because of the rigidly controlled economy. The composition and level of exports remained essentially unchanged, with cotton (including yarn and textiles), the Suez Canal, and tourism continuing to dominate. Imports of both goods and services mounted, with machinery and equipment financed largely by the Soviet bloc and food grains by the United States under the PL 480 program.[2] The total inflow of medium- and long-term foreign assistance averaged US$216 million a year.

The war of June 1967 caused serious dislocations in the Egyptian economy. The cities of the Canal Zone (with a population of approximately 1 million) were rendered uninhabitable; major industries, including oil refineries, were destroyed; and the Suez Canal was closed. Export earnings in the 1967-72 period accrued largely from the traditional mainstay of the economy — cotton. Tourism earnings declined initially but regained some of their strength in later years. Egypt was able to meet its import needs of goods and services during this period only through Arab subsidies, Eastern bloc medium- and long-term assistance, and suppliers' credit from OECD countries.

The Trade and Services Accounts

As this brief discussion indicates, Egypt relied heavily on its three leading export sectors: cotton, the Suez Canal, and tourism. Commodity exports, including cotton, virtually stagnated in 1952-66, however, as an ever-enlarging portion of domestically produced goods was diverted to domestic consumption (see table 16-2). Dependence on the service sectors, particularly the Suez Canal, increased until the 1967 war closed the canal and caused tourism earnings to decline; emphasis in policy was then shifted toward increasing commodity exports. The balance of trade (the ratio of exports to imports) strengthened considerably in 1967-72. The balance on the services account was, however, negative in this period, primarily because of the loss of the canal revenues.

Commodity exports during this period remained heavily dependent on cotton, and efforts at diversification were only partially successful. Some minor quantities of other agricultural products (rice, onions, potatoes) and a somewhat larger quantity of manufactures (cotton textiles and garments, footwear, cement, and chemicals) were exported. Because of institutional and political factors and inadequate quality control, a substantial share of these exports went to bilateral agreement areas, mainly in Eastern Europe. As table

---

2. U.S. Public Law 480 provides surplus agricultural commodities to other countries on concessional terms, with repayment in local currency.

TABLE 16-2. SUMMARY BALANCE ON GOODS
AND SERVICES, 1952-58 TO 1967-72
(millions of U.S. dollars)

Item	1952-58 Cumula-tive	1952-58 Annual average	1959-66 Cumula-tive	1959-66 Annual average	1967-72 Cumula-tive	1967-72 Annual average
Commodity trade balance	-942	-135	-2,475	-310	-2,007	-335
Exports, f.o.b.	2,963	423	4,115	514	4,475	745
Cotton, including yarn and textiles	2,417	345	2,895	362	2,786	464
Imports, c.i.f.	-3,905	-558	-6,590	-824	-6,482	-1,080
Cereals	-365	-52	-968	-121	-782	-130
Services, net	435	62	865	108	-243	-40
Receipts	1,600	229	2,471	309	1,235	206
Suez Canal	617	88	1,314	164	108	15
Travel	706	101	775	97	463	77
Payments	-1,165	-166	-1,606	-201	-1,478	-246
Interest and dividends	-245	-35	-197	-25	-421	-70
Net balance on commodities and services	-507	-73	-1,610	-202	-2,250	-375

Source: Central Bank of Egypt.

16-3 indicates, almost 54 percent of Egypt's total commodity exports were diverted to East European countries during the period. Given the nature of bilateral trade and the fact that most medium-and long-term foreign assistance came from the Eastern bloc, commodity imports were largely from these countries.

TABLE 16-3. DIRECTION OF TRADE,
1952-58 TO 1967-72
(annual average percent)

Item	1952-58	1959-66	1967-72
Exports			
Middle East	7	9	8
Eastern Europe	26	45	54
Other	67	46	38
Imports			
Middle East	6	7	7
Eastern Europe	16	24	34
Other	78	69	59

Source: CAPMAS and World Bank estimates.

TABLE 16-4. FINANCING OF THE EXTERNAL DEFICIT,
1952-58 TO 1967-72
(millions of U.S. dollars)

Item	1952-58		1959-66		1967-72	
	Cumulative	Annual average	Cumulative	Annual average	Cumulative	Annual average
Deficit on goods and services	-507	-73	-1,610	-202	-2,250	-375
Amortization of medium- and long-term debt	-53	-8	-448	-56	-1,496	-240
Foreign exchange deficit	-560	-81	-2,058	-257	-3,746	-624
Supply of funds	73	11	1,636	204	3,564	594
Grants and other transfer payments	...	...	12	1	1,566	261
Loans[a] and suppliers' credits[b]	...	...	1,725	216	1,638	273
Soviet Union	...	...	n.a.	n.a.	810	133
Other inflow, net[c]	46	7	-108	14	255	42
Monetary movements (net), errors, and omissions	27	4	7	1	105	18
Change in reserves	-487	-70	-422	-53	-182	-30

n.a. Not available.
... Zero or negligible.
a. Medium and long term.
b. Almost entirely constituted of Soviet assistance and OECD suppliers' credits.
c. Including use of commercial short-term bank credits (net) and compensation payments.
Source: Central Bank of Egypt and World Bank estimates.

Financing the External Deficit and Foreign Indebtedness

As table 16-4 shows, Egypt's external deficit during 1952-58 was financed almost entirely by drawing on its foreign exchange reserves. The cumulative deficit on current account in this period was US$507 million, and US$487 million were drawn from reserves. The use of these reserves, held largely in sterling, was subject to prolonged negotiations with the British Treasury. Thus at the end of 1952, US$500 million of Egypt's total sterling reserves of US$517 million were blocked; at the end of 1955, US$359 million of a total of US$419 million of Egyptian sterling reserves were blocked, and at the end of 1958, US$121 million of the remaining US$250 million were unavailable for Egyptian use. Egyptian authorities were therefore forced to encourage exports and restrict imports considered unnecessary for development.

In this pre-1958 period two major development agreements were signed with the Soviet Union — US$170 million for initiating the

Helwan Iron and Steel Complex and US$97 million for the construction of the first phase of the Aswan Dam. In addition, an economic cooperation agreement for US$124 million was concluded with the Federal Republic of Germany in May 1958. No disbursements took place under these agreements in this period, and consequently Egypt had virtually no external public debt at the end of 1958.

Egypt became even more dependent on foreign assistance throughout the 1959-66 period. Except for 1962 when substantial assistance was obtained from the International Monetary Fund (IMF) after a formal devaluation, the bulk of Egypt's external financing was from the Soviet Union and the United States. Medium- and long-term loans (including Aswan High Dam deliveries) averaged US$216 million a year in this period. External financial liabilities were limited largely to compensation payments in the earlier years,[3] but the burden of repayments on medium- and long-term debt (largely to the Soviet Union) grew larger in 1963-66. In addition, the use of short-term banking credit facilities became especially important in 1964-65 to 1967-68, when the United States terminated its PL480 assistance for political reasons at a time when Egypt suffered two consecutive bad harvests. Such short-term bank credit amounted to US$244 million in 1964-65, US$221 million in 1965-66, US$171 million in 1966-67, and US$182 million in 1967-68. It is believed that these credits were obtained at exorbitant interest rates.[4]

The 1967-72 period saw a virtual cessation of Western medium- and long-term assistance. The major source of external assistance was the Khartoum Agreement (signed in 1968), in which Saudi Arabia, Kuwait, and Libya guaranteed to replace lost Suez Canal revenues with grant assistance averaging about US$286 million a year. The Eastern bloc continued to be the major source of development assistance (about US$140 million a year), while substantial use was also made of suppliers' credits from OECD countries (about US$95 million a year). By this period, however, Egypt had incurred substantial external debt liabilities. Amortization payments on this debt (on average about US$250 million a year) almost entirely offset all external medium- and long-term capital assistance and suppliers' credit flows (which averaged about US$270 million a year).

Egypt's total outstanding nonmilitary foreign debt on December 31, 1971, was reported at US$1,300 million (disbursed), or US$1,800 million, including undisbursed credits — equivalent to about one-fourth of GNP. An additional US$315 million consisted of the uncommitted parts of frame agreements. The Soviet Union was Egypt's principal creditor, with a debt outstanding and disbursed

3. The compensation was for foreign assets (including the Suez Canal) nationalized by the government of Egypt, and for flooding portions of Sudan when the Aswan Dam created Lake Nasser.

4. Hansen and Nashashibi refer to "interest rates that even the Khedive Ismail would have found immodest" (Foreign Trade Regimes, p. 111).

of US$380 million — 28 percent of the total. Other major creditor countries were the United States, with a debt outstanding of US$205 million (15 percent of the total); Kuwait, US$130 million (9 percent); Italy, US$122 million (10 percent); and the Federal Republic of Germany, US$106 million (8 percent). Foreign governments held 87 percent of Egypt's reported debt, suppliers and private institutions 12 percent, and 1 percent was held by the World Bank. More than half the total medium- and long-term debt outstanding (including undisbursed) was owed to Eastern European countries and China.

DEVELOPMENT OF EXTERNAL FINANCES, 1973-78

The 1973-78 period was marked by preparation for the October 1973 war, the war itself, and the subsequent effort to rehabilitate the economy while remaining prepared for war. The economic requirements of the situation were financed initially through short-term borrowing, largely from Arab banks in the free-trade zones of Egypt. After 1973, however, larger amounts of Arab grants and loans became available, and OECD countries and international institutions again offered substantial medium- and long-term assistance as a result of the changed political situation and renewed economic prospects for Egypt.

Policy Environment

The compulsions of the situation were unique and the foreign exchange requirements enormous. Egypt was heavily dependent on food-grain imports, which had to be purchased for cash or against banking facilities at a time when international wheat prices had tripled. Stocks of intermediate goods and raw materials were depleted and had to be replenished. The Suez Canal had to be reopened and the canal cities, deserted since 1967, rehabilitated. Social and physical infrastructure, run down after almost a decade of war, had to be restored. Economic relations, and particularly trade, had to be shifted from the Eastern bloc countries toward the West.

Egyptian policymakers perceived that in the short term Egypt's needs could largely be met through external financing on concessional terms. The open-door policy enunciated by President Sadat after the October war was aimed specifically at attracting Arab and Western investment (both government and private) in a more liberal and market-oriented Egypt. To institutionalize this assistance, a Gulf Organization for the Development of Egypt (GODE) was created in April 1976, comprising Saudi Arabia, Kuwait, Qatar, and the United Arab Emirates; and a Consultative Group for Egypt was formed under the chairmanship of the World Bank, comprising Arab and OECD countries and international and bilateral institutions (including

GODE). The first meeting of the Consultative Group was held in
May 1977. Assistance was committed to enable Egypt not only to
meet its import requirements but also to retire much of its short-
term debt.

Simultaneously, a variety of mechanisms were adopted to build
up Egypt's ability to earn foreign exchange: (1) The reopening of
the Suez Canal was given top priority. (2) The exchange rate was
devalued to encourage nontraditional commodity exports to convertible currency areas. This parallel market rate was also extended
to earnings from tourism and workers' remittances. (3) Egyptians
were authorized to hold foreign currency accounts and to use these
for own-exchange imports — the intention being to attract residual
foreign exchange earnings of Egyptians working abroad. (4) State
trading corporations, which had monopolized foreign trade, were
abolished and this field of economic activity was opened to private
entrepreneurs. (5) Free-trade zones were opened in the canal
cities and near Cairo and Alexandria.

While some of these policy efforts met with a fair amount of success, others did not. Diversion of trade from Eastern bloc countries to convertible currency areas proved to be difficult — largely
because quality standards were inappropriate for Western markets.
The own-exchange imports scheme also had certain negative effects
because it diverted growing amounts of workers' remittances (whose
foreign exchange accrued directly to the state) to imports of highly
profitable consumer goods over which the government had minimal
control. Finally, as a result of growth and inflation in Egypt, previously exportable surpluses had to be diverted to domestic consumption. Egypt's export potential was therefore not fully exploited in
this period.

Import policies were also only partially successful. The Foreign
Exchange Budget continued to exercise rigorous control over all official imports. Because of uncertainties and delays in the provision
of foreign exchange, there was a continuing tendency to build up excessive stocks. A major step toward dampening import demand was
taken in 1976, however, when all imports, except food, medicines,
and fertilizers, were gradually shifted to the parallel market rate.

Balance of Payments

The government's balance of payments policy after the 1973 war
was aimed at: (1) sustaining the very high level of food requirements of the economy, an effort made much more difficult by the
rapid inflation in world food prices; (2) importing larger quantities
of intermediate and capital goods in order to increase capacity utilization and rehabilitate the economy; and (3) building up stocks of
both food and intermediate goods, which had been dangerously depleted. Despite the increase in the price of raw cotton, exports

TABLE 16-5.   SUMMARY BALANCE OF PAYMENTS, 1973-78
(millions of U.S. dollars)

Item	1973	1974	1975	1976	1977	1978
Exports, f.o.b.	1,003	1,671	1,566	1,609	1,992	1,984
Imports, c.i.f.[a]	-1,664	-3,582	-4,538	-4,627	-4,843	-5,966
Services, net[a]	7	212	357	1,180	1,261	2,219
Deficit on goods and services	-654	-1,699	-2,615	-1,838	-1,590	-1,763
Amortization of medium- and long-term debt	-407	-664	-600	-734	-812	-899
Suppliers' credits	277	-284	-280	-413	-551	-605
Reduction of balance on bilateral agreements	-113	-28	-241	10	-121	-115
Foreign exchange deficit	-1,174	-2,391	-3,456	-2,562	-2,523	-2,777
Supply of funds	1,290	2,384	3,394	2,607	2,718	2,848
Transfers, total	731	1,303	1,076	792	445	345
Medium- and long-term loans	170	726	2,146	1,122	2,612	1,983
Suppliers' credits	160	273	363	500	415	605
Foreign investment		70	140	300	434	440
Short-term commercial bank credits, net	352	584	89	226	-840	-379
Other monetary movements (net), errors, and omissions	-123	-572	-420	-333	-348	-146
Change in reserves[b]	-116	7	62	-45	-195	-71

a. Excludes the market value of own-exchange imports.
b. Minus sign indicates an increase.
Source: Central Bank of Egypt.

were so inadequate, and reserves so negligible, that massive external financing was necessary (see table 16-5).

Export performance continued to be inadequate to meet Egyptian import requirements, and the volume of most merchandise exports virtually stagnated. The increase in the value of commodity exports of about 98 percent between 1973 and 1978 was almost entirely a result of higher international prices and the increase in petroleum exports. The services account began to show substantial gains, however, with the surplus increasing to US$2,219 million in 1978. This was a result of increased tourist receipts, workers' remittances, and — after 1975 — receipts from the reopened Suez Canal. But the country's massive import bill overwhelmed these gains. Commodity imports alone more than tripled in this period, reaching US$5,966 million in 1978.   The deficit in goods and services

TABLE 16-6. BANKING FACILITIES, 1972-78
(millions of U.S. dollars)

| Year | Disbursement (A) | Repayments | | Net use (A - B) |
		Principal (B)	Interest	
1972	371	342	16	29
1973	711	355	24	356
1974	1,542	959	113	583
1975	2,080	1,992	192	88
1976	1,580	1,353	81	238
1977	1,290	2,130	75	-840
1978	821	936	57	-115

Source: Central Bank of Egypt, Foreign Department.

accordingly increased from US$654 million in 1973 to US$1,763 million in 1978.

In the 1973-78 period the deficit was largely financed through grants from Arab countries, capital flows on concessional terms from Arab and OECD countries (particularly the United States, Federal Republic of Germany, and Japan), and multilateral institutions such as the World Bank. During 1973-76, however, Egypt also made substantial use of short-term bank credit. The repayment of this debt created a severe liquidity problem until assistance from GODE enabled it to be cleared in 1977. Thereafter, this type of financing was severely curtailed (table 16-6).

Services Accounts

The directional imbalances in Egypt's merchandise trade were compensated for by a strengthened services sector incorporating workers' remittances, tourist receipts, and the reopened Suez Canal (table 16-7).

Skilled and semiskilled Egyptians continue to be in great demand throughout the oil-rich Arab countries, which have ambitious development plans and limited manpower resources. To take advantage of this situation, the government of Egypt eased emigration procedures, and after the abolition of exit visas in early 1974 the emigration of workers and the flow of workers' remittances accelerated. If the finance provided for Egypt's own-exchange imports is attributed to Egyptians abroad — as is logical — it can be seen that workers' remittances increased from US$86 million in 1973 to US$1,761 million in 1978. Workers' remittances have accordingly replaced earnings from cotton (both raw and processed) as the leading source of Egypt's foreign exchange earnings.

TABLE 16-7.   TRADE AND SERVICES ACCOUNTS, 1973-78
(millions of U.S. dollars)

Item	1973	1974	1975	1976	1977	1978
Trade balance	-661	-1,911	-2,972	-3,018	-2,851	-3,982
Nonfactor services, net	38	92	95	627	572	729
Receipts	301	433	628	1,150	1,545	1,541
Suez Canal	...	...	85	311	428	514
Tourism	158	265	332	464	730	702
Payments	-263	-341	-533	-523	-973	-812
Factor services, net	-31	120	262	553	689	1,490
Receipts	120	276	452	827	1,007	1,905
Workers' remittances	86	189	366	755	894	1,761
Payments	-151	-156	-190	-274	-318	-415
Balance	-654	-1,699	-2,615	-1,838	-1,590	-1,763

... Zero or negligible.
Note: Table excludes own-exchange imports.
Source: Central Bank of Egypt and World Bank estimates.

Capital Accounts

The massive deficits on the goods and services account since 1973 have been financed to a large extent by official Arab grants, loans, and deposits with the Central Bank of Egypt (see table 16-5). Western medium- and long-term capital assistance, which had been reduced to a trickle after the suspension of U.S. PL 480 aid in 1964 and had practically ceased after the 1967 war, was restored after the October 1973 war (see table 16-8). But the slowness of disbursements — inherent in the aid process, particularly for project assistance — has meant that even through 1975 net Western medium- and long-term transfers to Egypt were negative,[5] largely because of heavy repayments on these accounts from past commitments. The commitments from the Western countries have, however, established a strong aid pipeline, which began to have effect in 1976. Meanwhile, worsening political relations with the Eastern bloc have meant almost negligible new commitments of assistance from this source and a sharp decline in disbursements on existing loan agreements, both of which have led to negative transfers on these accounts. The situation was the same with regard to suppliers' credits. There was a net outflow to both the United States and the Soviet bloc, and the only net credit of any significance was extended by the European Economic Community (EEC). The shortfall on Egypt's external accounts in 1973-78 was thus financed largely through Arab (and from

5. Iranian assistance of US$320 million (LE125 million) is not being treated as "Western" in this discussion.

TABLE 16-8. MEDIUM- AND LONG-TERM LOANS:
COMMITMENTS FROM WESTERN COUNTRIES
AND MULTILATERAL INSTITUTIONS, 1973-78
(millions of U.S. dollars)

Country or institution	1973	1974	1975	1976	1977	1978
World Bank	...	85.0	77.0	157.0	316.0	40.0
International Development Association	74.9	55.0	55.0	40.0	54.0	124.0
Denmark	...	9.0	...	6.6	...	18.2
France	...	40.0	81.4	113.0	...	107.0
Germany, Federal Republic of	59.1	83.1	99.8	91.4	107.8	158.1
Japan	11.3	22.7	178.6	39.2	85.9	16.3
Netherlands	...	...	4.4	16.6	9.4	10.7
United Kingdom	24.5	...	...	...	...	...
United States	...	60.8	458.4	731.3	818.5	839.6
Iran	...	...	320.0	...	...	...

... Zero or negligible.
Note: Table excludes suppliers' credits.
Source: World Bank estimates.

1976 on, Western) assistance and, as discussed earlier, until 1976
through short-term borrowing.

Assistance from Arab countries. Grants from Arab countries
to compensate for the loss of Suez Canal revenues became a regular item in Egypt's balance of payments following the closure of
the canal in 1967. Arab financial assistance in the 1973-78 period
was not confined to grants, however, but took many different forms
— cash loans, project and program financing, deposits in the Central Bank of Egypt, guarantees to underpin borrowing from other
sources — and was in large, but varying, amounts. Grants peaked
in 1974 and declined sharply in subsequent years. Cash loans and
deposits in the Central Bank were large in 1975 and 1977-78, en-
abling Egypt to reduce its short-term debt in the latter period. Disbursements from project and program loans increased fairly quickly
as the pipeline was strengthened. These changes in the flow were
a logical consequence of the pattern of Egyptian development, and
resulted from the gradual improvement in Egypt's debt servicing
capacity, the elimination of the heavy cash requirements for meeting short-term banking facilities, and an acceleration of investment
and productive activities among the donors. A breakdown of the
major types of assistance in millions of U.S. dollars is:

	1973	1974	1975	1976	1977	1978
Grants	700	1,243	1,002	700	350	148
Cash loans and deposits	175	360	1,750	285	1,243	573
Project and program loans	30	—	22	87	158	164
Total	905	1,603	2,774	1,072	1,751	885

Non-Arab assistance. The post-October 1973 period is characterized by the opening toward the West and the consequent renewal of aid commitments from Western countries and international aid agencies. The medium- and long-term accounts in 1973-75 show a negative capital flow from both Eastern and Western countries, however, if the US$320 million loan from Iran in 1975 is excluded. This is a result of several factors: assistance from Eastern bloc countries slowed down and heavy repayments were due them; between 1967 and 1973 almost no new commitments were made, which led to no disbursements in 1974 and 1975; repayments due Western countries accumulated; and it was difficult to disburse quickly the new Western commitments of 1974 and 1975.

The deterioration in Egypt's economic relations with the Soviet Union is reflected in the slowing down of disbursements under Economic and Technical Cooperation Agreements, the almost complete withholding of suppliers' credits, and the heavy repayments on these two accounts. As a result, net capital movements from the Soviet Union to Egypt changed from a positive inflow of about US$38 million in 1972 to net outflows of about US$228 million in 1974, about US$67 million in 1975, and about US$148 million in 1976.

Although commitments of assistance from OECD countries and multilateral agencies increased rapidly after 1973, it was some years before disbursements began to reach levels that were comparable to the Arab inflows. The main reason for this lay in the nature of the assistance provided — Arab aid was overwhelmingly in the form of cash or near-cash, while Western aid was largely for projects, or disbursed for commodities. As the project pipeline was developed and as aid programming procedures improved, disbursements from Western assistance increased from about US$350 million in 1973 to nearly US$1,200 million in 1978. The United States was the largest provider of concessional capital, accounting for about two-thirds of the Western total in 1978. The contributions of the major groups are shown in table 16-9.

Egypt's nonmilitary medium- and long-term debt outstanding and disbursed on December 31, 1978, was US$9,968 million. The major creditors were Saudi Arabia and Kuwait, followed by the United States, Soviet Union, and Federal Republic of Germany. The

TABLE 16-9. MAJOR NON-ARAB PROVIDERS
OF CONCESSIONAL CAPITAL, 1973-78
(millions of U.S. dollars)

Concessional capital	1973	1974	1975	1976	1977	1978
Non-Arab grants	38	60	74	92	95	52
Non-Arab project and						
program loans	306	134	324	548	831	1,068
United States	...	19	95	266	416	672
Western Europe	165	45	86	143	148	122
Japan	...	3	23	24	116	133
World Bank	23	12	63	78	79	101
Other countries	118	55	57	37	72	41
IMF drawings	57	49	...	146	130	100
Total	401	243	398	786	1,056	1,220

... Zero or negligible.
Sources: Ministry of Economy, Central Bank of Egypt, and World Bank
estimates.

foregoing figures do not include Eastern bloc military debt on which
Egypt was trying to obtain rescheduling of service payments. A
detailed description of the evolution of external debt is appended to
this chapter.

Policy Reform

Since 1973 Egypt has had a system of multiple exhange rates for
both imports and exports. The resurgence of multiple rates in this
period was brought about by the creation of the parallel market for
foreign exchange in September 1973.[6]

Rationalizing the exchange rate. The coverage of the parallel
market has been gradually enlarged. At its inception, all traditional exports were excluded: cotton, rice, onions, potatoes, garlic,
cotton yarn, textiles, crude petroleum, and petroleum products,
and all official receipts. On the import side, the parallel market
was largely intended for the private sector and was confined to certain categories of imports, largely services and some intermediate
goods.

According to the Foreign Exchange Budget of 1975, about 45 percent of convertible currency exports of goods and services (which
totaled US$1,083 million) and about 9 percent of convertible currency
imports of goods and services (which totaled US$4,564 million)
were channeled through the parallel market. In 1976, however, it
was substantially enlarged when an additional US$1,075 million of

6. See Hansen and Nashashibi, Foreign Trade Regimes.

public sector commodity imports were transferred (US$275 million
in February and US$800 million in May). As a result, about 37 per-
cent of total convertible currency payments in 1976 (which were estimated at US$4,392 million, excluding about US$255 million of own-
exchange imports) were expected to be at the parallel market rate.
The list of commodities to be exported at this rate remained
unchanged until May 1976, when only about 27 percent of total convertible currency exports were expected to go through the market.
This percentage decrease was caused by increased petroleum exports, which were transacted at the official rate. The exchange
rates set by the Central Bank have moved as follows:

Official rate since February 1973   LE1 = US$2.56
Parallel market rate:
        September 1973   LE1 = US$1.70
        February 1975   LE1 = US$1.57
        May 1976   LE1 = US$1.50
        December 1976   LE1 = US$1.43
        December 1978   LE1 = US$1.43

Since the beginning of 1978, almost all foreign exchange transactions (except for a very small amount covered by past bilateral
trade agreements) have been conducted at the parallel market rate.
Table 16-10 indicates the progressive depreciation of the effective
exchange rate with convertible currency areas, which had a significant effect on trade with these areas.

In addition to the official and parallel markets is a third foreign
exchange market associated with own-exchange imports. Under
this scheme, which was introduced in 1974, traders or individuals
who hold foreign exchange eligible for the parallel market may

TABLE 16-10. EXCHANGE MARKET ANALYSIS:
CONVERTIBLE CURRENCY TRANSACTIONS AS
PERCENTAGE OF TOTAL EXPORTS AND IMPORTS
OF GOODS AND SERVICES AT PARALLEL MARKET
RATE, 1974-78

Convertible currency transactions	1974	1975	1976	1977	1978[a]
Goods exported	12.0	9.0	19.0	26.0	100
Goods and services exported	28.5	45.0	44.4	86.0	100
Goods imported	5.5	5.8	43.0	71.0	100
Goods and services imported	8.3	8.5	47.0	63.1	100

a. As of January 1, 1979.
Source: World Bank estimates.

transfer these holdings into imports of goods. This market became extremely popular because a minimum of formalities was required. The original scheme permitted imports of about 380 commodities, with no licensing requirements for values less than LE5,000. In November 1975 all goods became eligible except for eighteen supply commodities and ten others which the government wanted to protect. Goods imported under this scheme are estimated to have been worth about LE70 million (converted at the official exchange rate). The curb rate for the Egyptian pound in this market during 1975 varied between US$1.42 and US$1.25, compared with the parallel market rate of US$1.75. During 1976, however, as foreign exchange shortages again became apparent, a system of licensing was imposed on all own-exchange imports, with licenses granted primarily for intermediate goods. As a result, the own-exchange rate has moved closer to the parallel market rate.

Reorganizing external trade. The trend away from bilateralism was prompted not only by the post-October 1973 open-door policy and emphasis on trading with the West, but also by the accumulation of excessive balances against Egypt, which affected the volume of trade with bilateral agreement countries. At the end of 1973 Egypt was engaged in bilateral trade relations with more than thirty countries. These bilateral payments agreements were steadily eliminated until by the end of 1978 agreements with only ten countries were left.

Trading structures. More important than the trend away from bilateralism was the effect of abolishing the monopoly of the state trading companies and opening external trade to private enterprise. The Egyptian General Organization for Foreign Trade, the holding company for the six state foreign trading companies, was abolished on January 1, 1976, along with other public economic organizations as required by Law no. 111, September 18, 1975.[7] This decentralization was further reinforced by allowing the private sector to engage in most types of foreign trade. The private sector could export and import all commodities to free currency areas (with the exception of the supply commodities) and could also import in free currency from bilateral agreement areas items without quotas or those with quotas that had been exhausted.

POLICY REQUIREMENTS

The policy actions discussed in this chapter — namely, the adoption of a multiple exchange rate, incorporating substantial exchange rate

7. The six companies were the Arab Foreign Trading Company, Nasr Import and Export Company, Misr Import and Export Company, Arab Foreign Trade Company, and Alwadi and Nile Companies, which specialized in the export of agricultural products.

depreciation, and the reorganization of trading and tariff structures — were largely ad hoc responses to the changing external situation, particularly the availability of foreign assistance. This was in large part understandable, given the uncertain nature of the international political situation and the desire to avoid the internal political repercussions of adopting difficult policies. In addition, there was a reluctance to abandon traditional instruments of control, such as the Foreign Exchange Budget, in favor of freer market mechanisms, the effects of which were unknown and unstudied. Increasingly, however, reassured by the progress toward peace and the prospects of a continuing foreign aid cushion, Egyptian authorities began to move toward integrated longer-term policies for strengthening the external sector. Some important areas in which policies need to be strengthened are sketched out below.

Because exports are vitally affected by many different factors in the economy (national production, consumption patterns, investment policies, factor productivity, marketing, and so forth) an export promotion program needs to be comprehensive, including exchange rate and tariff adjustments. Consideration should be given to the potential offered by the Arab common markets as well as other markets of the East and West.

Maximization of the growth of national production, control over consumption, and creation of exportable surpluses would have to form the basis of any successful export growth program. In the short term efficient utilization of existing capacity is required; over the medium and long term success depends on the quality of the investment program. Fiscal and monetary policies would have to set limits on consumption and to encourage investment. All this will have to be reinforced by appropriate policies for domestic prices and the price of foreign exchange.

Decontrol of prices in the economy, adjustment of the exchange rate, and effective use of tariffs (including export taxes and subsidies) would be important. Windfall gains accruing to the agricultural sector could be taxed at source; if that is a problem, export taxes could be imposed on certain agricultural products and on cotton textiles. The tariff system should be rationalized to achieve economic efficiency. Export taxes for certain infant industries should be considered, but they should be designed to be phased out over time.

Foreign exchange receipts from the services sector should also be maximized. The Suez Canal is now being expanded to allow the passage of ships with a 53-foot draft by 1981. At the moment canal tolls have not been adjusted for inflation, largely because of abnormal conditions in the international tanker market. If the Suez Canal Authority were to revise its tariff structure or tariff levels upon completion of the expansion project, and if the shipping market were to recover by then, it is reasonable to expect that revenues could be increased substantially.

The tourism sector could be strengthened substantially, depending largely on the policies adopted (see chapter 14). The growth of workers' remittances could be further encouraged by systematic manpower training to meet the specific needs of the Arab countries and by appropriate incentives (including the rate of exchange and investment opportunities) to encourage repatriation of Egyptian earnings overseas.

Institutional constraints to better export performance must be identified and remedied. The shortage of foreign exchange for imported inputs or investment is commonly blamed for the inadequacies of the export performance, but many other causes are of equal or greater importance. Industrial enterprises are often unable to compete in world markets because of inefficiencies stemming from uncertain management, inappropriate technological processes and equipment, lack of incentives and accountability, an administratively controlled and inexperienced marketing capability, and suspension of an entrepreneurial spirit.

A systematic study is needed of the products for which Egypt now has a comparative advantage or, with some assistance and correctives, could have in the future. The result of this operational analysis would be a comprehensive list of products with production costs that were competitive on world markets and that were also economical in view of their domestic resource cost.

Every successful trading country has had an incentive system that was revised as conditions changed. It is important to provide a solid basis of incentives (in addition to the exchange rate adjustment) that are least costly and most effective in promoting exports. Many measures could be employed: (1) exemption from customs of imported goods that are to be directly incorporated in exports; (2) preferential credit for financing or investing in exports; (3) direct export incentives with percentage payments based on the value added of exports (targets might be established and the incentive applied only to the exports above target); (4) promotional and marketing programs to exploit market opportunities, including identification of foreign markets that are most favorable for the expansion of Egyptian exports. This would include evaluating market conditions (prices, competitors, delivery requirements, quality of products needed, and so forth) in all the product lines and in a variety of countries. Special attention could be given to other Arab countries.

APPENDIX: EXTERNAL DEBT

At the beginning of 1955 virtually all of Egypt's external public debt had either been converted into internal issues or paid off through the Debt Conversion Plan of 1943. The only amount known

to be outstanding was approximately US$482,000 due on the 4 per-
cent City of Alexandria 1902-63 bonds. During the ensuing decade
the picture changed rapidly as a large-scale development program
was implemented and Egypt received substantial amounts of foreign
aid. By the end of 1965 the total external debt amounted to slightly
more than US$2,000 million, of which US$1,516 million were already
disbursed. The most important creditors were the U.S.S.R. and
the United States, followed by the Federal Republic of Germany,
Italy, and Kuwait. In addition, short-term liabilities against banking facilities stood at US$103 million.

Medium- and Long-Term Debt

From 1956 to 1965 general agreements totaling some US$1,450
million were signed with the Sino-Soviet bloc; of this, the U.S.S.R.
accounted for US$900.5 million. Major agreements with the
U.S.S.R. for rubles 149.5 million and rubles 300 million were concluded, in 1958 and 1964 respectively, for the financing of industrial projects, in particular the Helwan Iron and Steel Complex,
and two 1958-59 agreements of rubles 295 million for the construction of the Aswan Dam. All these agreements, like the majority
of those with the Sino-Soviet countries, were at 2.5 percent interest and called for repayment through bilateral accounts in twelve
years, payments to commence one year after completion of the project. Despite this seemingly enormous program of assistance from
the Sino-Soviet countries, there was a considerable gap between
bloc agreements and actual disbursements. Thus, by the end of
1965, although two-thirds of the agreements had been firmly
committed, only some US$320 million had been disbursed; the
U.S.S.R.'s share being US$625 million committed and US$266 million disbursed.

Up to the mid-1960s, Egypt was also the recipient of substantial
amounts of Western aid, and by December 1965 the Western countries, with the addition of Kuwait, accounted for 76 percent of the
total debt disbursed and outstanding. The United States was by far
the most important of the Western creditors, Egypt at this period
being the largest PL 480 signatory in Africa and the third largest
in the world (behind India and Pakistan). Of the US$662 million com-
mitted and US$537 million disbursed from the United States by 1965,
more than 85 percent was accounted for by local currency loans.

The evolution of Egypt's external debt during 1966-73 was markedly different from that of the earlier part of the decade. Severe
balance of payments difficulties in 1966 and the Middle East war
of June 1967 added to the problems of an already heavy debt burden
and considerably weakened Egypt's ability to borrow abroad. Diplomatic relations with the United States were broken off in 1967, and
new commitments of long-term aid from the West practically ceased.

Egypt was almost entirely dependent on assistance from the Eastern bloc countries, and even here new agreements accounted for relatively little (approximately US$100 million) during 1966-70. The bulk of this bilateral assistance (quite apart from military deliveries) was related to specific projects, agreed upon before 1965.

By the end of the 1960s, Egypt had managed to complete rescheduling or refinancing with almost all of its Western creditors, and these arrangements made some additional, though limited, borrowing possible. The new facilities, however, were almost entirely in the form of suppliers' credits with short maturities, and resulted in another rapid accumulation of medium-term debt. Egypt also received US$250 million annually from the Arab countries under the Khartoum Agreement as compensation for losses of Suez Canal revenues (the canal was closed in June 1967), and there was some additional assistance from this quarter in the form of bank deposits and grants. Nevertheless, Egypt's development in 1968-72 continued to be financed largely by assistance from the Eastern bloc. New economic cooperation agreements totaling US$500 million (80 percent from the U.S.S.R.) were concluded in 1971-73, thus bringing the overall nonmilitary assistance from these countries to well over US$2,000 million shortly before the 1973 war; of this more than US$1,500 million had been utilized.

In 1973 Saudi Arabia, Libya, and the Gulf States provided US$725 million (inclusive of the Khartoum pledges) in economic assistance. Unfortunately, however, 1973 was the year of the oil crisis, and the rapid rise in world prices of food and other essential commodities, coupled with an almost total lack of non-Arab aid, forced Egypt to resort heavily to short-term borrowing. The overall use of one-year banking facilities, including rollovers, amounted to US$1,100 million, and before the year was out Egypt's already substantial debt problems had been severely compounded. Of the US$3,509 million of total debt outstanding in December 1973, 32 percent was accountable to short-term banking facilities and 61 percent of the outstanding debt was due in the next three years.

After the 1973 war, strengthened relations with Arab countries, in conjunction with progress toward peace in the Middle East and the restoration of diplomatic relations with the United States, profoundly affected Egypt's ability to mobilize private and official capital. New commitments of medium- and long-term aid rose to US$1,500 million and US$3,100 million in 1974 and 1975 respectively, in contrast to an average of US$350 million (inclusive of refinancing loans) for 1971-73. Of this total of US$4,600 million, the OPEC countries accounted for 55 percent (Saudi Arabia, 17 percent; Kuwait, 15 percent; Iran, 9 percent; Abu Dhabi, 7 percent; Qatar, 3 percent; Arab Fund, 3 percent; Libya, 1 percent); the United States, 10 percent; Japan, 5 percent; and the Federal Republic of Germany, 5 percent. The World Bank share was 6 percent.

Because of the continuing steep rise in the price of imports and a much slower than anticipated rate of disbursement on new commitments of concessional assistance, together with a cessation of Eastern bloc inflows, Egypt was forced once again in 1974 to rely heavily on banking facilities to meet the cost of critical imports. Given the onerous terms of these facilities, the effective cost of debt servicing and the liquidity requirements of the economy were significantly increased; in 1975 about US$2,000 million in repayment of banking facilities fell due. In the same year, Egypt's total nonmilitary external debt rose considerably from a disbursed and outstanding amount of just over US$4,000 million at the end of 1974 to US$6,300 million by December 31, 1975. With an additional US$2,900 million still undisbursed, the total civilian debt amounted to US$9,100 million. Overall disbursements during 1975 stood at US$4,700 million, US$2,100 million being accountable to short-term banking facilities. The average yearly inflows for the related periods are shown in table 16-11.

By December 31, 1976, Egypt's medium- and long-term public debt was US$8,349.5 million, of which US$5,858.3 million were disbursed and outstanding. In addition, US$1,395.8 million disbursed and US$873.6 million undisbursed were outstanding on banking facilities. Disbursements on medium- and long-term debt fell quite markedly from the very high level attained in 1975 because very little was committed as cash from the OPEC countries. Actual disbursements were US$1,490.0 million.

TABLE 16-11. AVERAGE YEARLY INFLOW OF LOANS (NET), 1956-60 TO 1976-78

(millions of U.S. dollars)

Loans	1956-60	1961-65	1966-70	1971-75	1976-78
Medium- plus long-term loans	71.5	77.2	81.2	424.5	1,446.2
Western countries	45.0	16.0	21.1	46.0	649.0
Eastern bloc	26.5	36.4	51.2	41.1	-14.3
Arab countries	—	24.8	8.9	337.4	811.5
World Bank and IDA	6.2	2.5	-4.3	15.2	85.9
Suppliers' credits	20.0	32.2	22.1	64.6	-10.0
Eurocurrency loans	—	—	—	45.2	100.0
Banking facilities	2.8	14.3	5.0	215.8	-242.0
Total	100.5	126.2	104.0	765.3	1,380.1
U.S. loans repayable in Egyptian pounds	16.8	76.7	-24.4	-15.1	-12.6

— Not applicable.

Sources: World Bank, Ministry of Economy, and Central Bank of Egypt.

TABLE 16-12. OUTSTANDING EXTERNAL DEBT, DECEMBER 31, 1978
(millions of U.S. dollars)

External debt	Undisbursed[a]	Disbursed[a]	Payments schedule (disbursed)				
			1979	1980	1981	1982	After 1982
Convertible currencies	3,857.6	9,263.7	1,914.1	921.9	812.3	845.3	4,770.1
Official loans	3,740.9	5,919.0	340.1	352.4	437.5	517.6	4,271.4
Rescheduling agreements	...	107.4	24.8	20.2	19.6	19.6	23.2
Suppliers' credits	116.7	636.2	276.4	171.0	63.7	54.5	70.6
Loans from financial institutions	...	610.3	119.4	117.6	134.9	133.6	104.8
Official deposits	...	1,990.8	1,153.4	260.7	156.6	120.0	300.1
Clearing currencies	389.9	703.8	83.1	96.3	87.4	59.0	378.0
Official loans	389.9	666.8	66.1	89.5	84.7	58.1	368.4
Suppliers' credits	...	37.0	17.0	6.8	2.7	0.9	9.6
Total medium- and long-term debt	4,247.5	9,967.5	1,997.2	1,018.2	899.7	904.3	5,148.1
Bank credit facilities	551.7	443.4	381.7	60.8	0.5	0.4	—
GRAND TOTAL	4,799.2	10,410.9	2,378.9	1,089.0	890.2	904.7	5,148.1

... Zero or negligible.
Note: Does not include bilateral payments agreement liabilities, foreign deposits with Egyptian commercial banks, liabilities under compensation agreements, or military debts.
a. Excluding interest.
Sources: Ministry of Economy and Economic Cooperation and the Central Bank of Egypt.

Egypt's medium- and long-term public debt increased substantially in subsequent years to US$8,107.3 million disbursed and outstanding at the end of 1977 and US$9,967.5 million by December 31, 1978 (see table 16-12). Of this outstanding amount, US$6,585.3 million or 66 percent represented borrowing from official sources and US$1,424.2 million or 14 percent borrowing from private sources. The remaining US$1,958.0 million or 20 percent was accounted for by medium-term deposits from the oil-exporting Arab countries. Major creditors were GODE, 16 percent; United States, 16 percent; Saudi Arabia, 19 percent; Kuwait, 11 percent; and the Federal Republic of Germany, 6 percent. A further US$2,932.9 million of committed but undisbursed debt brings the overall total of medium- and long-term public debt on the civilian account to US$12,900.4 million at December 31, 1978. The medium- and long-term debt since 1970 (in millions of U.S. dollars) can be summarized as:

1970	1973	1974	1975	1976	1977	1978
1,640	2,483	2,810	5,101	5,858	8,107	9,968

Banking Facilities

Egypt has long relied on correspondent bank facilities, in the form of trade-related lines of credit, for the opening and confirmation of letters of credit and acceptance of drafts arising out of export-import transactions. These have normally been for periods of 90 to 180 days, but in recent years maturities have been extended for as long as eighteen months to two years. It is somewhat difficult to assess the overall usage of banking facilities during the early years under review, although it is known that the amount disbursed and outstanding rose from US$14.2 million in 1955 to US$103.0 million by December 1965. Substantial increases in consumption, prompted by rising incomes and population growth, the absence of adequate, quick-disbursing foreign aid, and the willingness of correspondent banks to provide short-term financing on imports required for development projects led to a considerable reliance on banking facilities as a source of financing. By 1964 net usage of these facilities had increased to US$66.7 million annually.

By December 1965 outstanding liabilities of US$103.0 million represented more than 10 percent of the total external public debt disbursed and outstanding. By this time, persistent balance of payments difficulties, coupled with an already substantial debt service burden on the medium- and long-term debt, had already resulted in payments difficulties, and arrears against short-term banking facilities were starting to accumulate. Nevertheless, prompted in part by the creditors' opinion that these payments difficulties were temporary, the flow of additional commercial credits from Western countries continued unabated. As a result, by June 1966, shortly

TABLE 16-13. BANKING FACILITIES, 1970-78
(millions of U.S. dollars)

| Year | Outstanding at end of period | | During period | | Repayments | |
	Including undisbursed	Disbursed only	Utilization	Disbursement	Principal	Interest and bank charges
1970	267.8	147.8	313.5	n.a.	281.3	14.1
1971	245.3	112.7	251.9	305.1	320.1	14.8
1972	345.4	141.3	246.6	371.0	342.4	15.6
1973	1,125.0	496.9	1,100.4	710.5	354.9	24.3
1974	2,696.0	1,080.5	2,327.0	1,542.2	958.6	112.7
1975	2,467.8	1,169.4	1,789.0	2,080.8	1,991.9	192.1
1976	2,122.9	1,396.0	1,392.0	1,579.5	1,353.1	81.2
1977	1,131.1	555.7	1,129.8	1,289.8	2,129.8	74.7
1978	995.1	443.4	797.5	821.2	933.5	57.4

Note: Correspondent bank trade financing against lines of credit established in favor of Egyptian commercial banks. The authorization of the opening of the letter of credit by the Central Bank constitutes "utilization." Disbursement occurs when shipping documents are received, at which point the credit period begins. Eurocurrency loans are not included in these series, although some of the trade financing included is medium term.
Source: Central Bank of Egypt.

before the crisis came to a head and the lending banks were forced to step in with new overdraft facilities and lengthened maturities, the total outstanding liabilites had risen to around US$135.0 million. A rescheduling agreement in July 1966 provided for an extended repayment schedule for arrears, and in the meantime the lending banks continued to make available additional facilities within the limit of amounts repaid. The exact cost of this rescheduling agreement is unclear, but interest rates were said to be possibly as high as 8 to 10 percent.

During 1967-71 Western creditors' hardening position in relation to Egypt, chronic balance of payments difficulties, and the 1967 war served, if not substantially to reduce, certainly to control the overall use of short-term commercial credits. Thus, while utilizations continued at an average of US$30 million, additional credits were extended only in strict relation to amounts repaid, and consequently net yearly inflows averaged only US$5 million, or approximately one-third of the comparable inflows recorded for 1961-66.

After 1971 the use of banking facilities again increased (see table 16-13). The 1973 war, the sharp rise in world prices for food and other commodities, and the lack of adequate quick-disbursing foreign aid all compelled Egypt to resort heavily to borrowing short-term funds to meet the cost of essential imports. Net use (that is, disbursement minus repayment of principal) of banking facilities amounted to US$355.6 million in 1973 (as opposed to US$28.6 million in 1972); and while outstanding liabilities had averaged US$134.0 million for 1970-72, by December 1973 these had risen to US$496.9 million.

In 1974 borrowing against short-term banking facilities continued at an unprecedented rate. With a net usage of US$583.6 million the outstanding liabilities by December 1974 stood at US$1,080.5 million disbursed, or equal to approximately 27 percent of the total external debt disbursed and outstanding. The rapid build-up of short-term liabilities was considerably facilitated by the absence of any control mechanism within Egypt over this type of borrowing, and coincided with a gradual move toward establishing sizable lines of credit with Middle East banks, heavily dependent on Arab financing. Thus, while the traditional ties with Western European and American banks continued and to some extent were strengthened, after 1971 banks such as the Arab African Bank and the Arab International Bank became a major source of short-term financing.

In 1975 Egypt adopted strict measures to reduce the use of banking facilities and to prevent outstanding bank credits from spiraling even higher. Thus, new commitments fell, but because of time lags and the large amounts in the pipeline, the actual disbursements rose. At the same time, however, the large repayments made possible almost entirely by substantial cash loans from OPEC countries[8]

8. Namely, Iran, Kuwait, Qatar, Saudi Arabia, and the United Arab Emirates.

TABLE 16-14. STRUCTURE OF EXTERNAL PUBLIC DEBT
OUTSTANDING AND DISBURSED, 1960-78
(percent)

External public debt	1960 Excluding short term	Total	1965 Excluding short term	Total	1970 Excluding short term	Total
Loans from governments	73	71	71	65	74	68
Western countries	46	45	29	27	26	24
Eastern bloc	27	26	30	28	37	34
Arab countries	...	...	12	10	11	10
World Bank and IDA	6	6	4	3	1	1
Suppliers' credits	21	20	25	23	25	23
Eurocurrency loans	...	...	...	...	...	...
Total medium- and long-term debt	100		100		100	
Banking facilities		3		9		8
Total external public debt		100		100		100

... Zero or negligible.
Note: All figures are as of December 31.
Sources: Central Bank of Egypt and Ministry of Economy.

reduced the net use of banking facilities from US$583.6 million in 1974 to US$88.9 million in 1975.

In 1976 additional cash loans from the OPEC countries were not nearly so abundant as in 1975. Consequently, while authorizations and disbursements were significantly lower than in 1975, low repayments brought the net usage to US$226.4 million, nearly two and a half times the comparable 1975 figure. At the same time, these low repayments, added to the short maturities on the bulk of the outstanding banking facilities, produced a very rapid accumulation of arrears, from US$32.9 million at December 31, 1975, to US$452.9 million by December 31, 1976.

Arrears on short-term banking facilities continued to increase substantially in the first half of 1977 to a peak of almost US$1,000 million by midyear. But sizable inflows of cash aid, principally from GODE, enabled the Egyptian authorities not only to clear all payments arrears but also significantly to reduce reliance on costly short-term facilities. The amount disbursed and outstanding dropped to US$555.7 million at the end of 1977 and still further to US$443.4 million at December 31, 1978.

| 1975 | | 1976 | | 1977 | | 1978 | |
Excluding short term	Total	Excluding short term	Total	Excluding short term	Total	Excluding short term	Total
76	59	80	67	82	78	82	80
15	12	19	15	22	21	27	27
18	14	12	10	8	7	6	6
43	33	49	42	52	50	49	47
2	2	3	2	3	3	3	3
17	13	12	9	8	7	8	7
5	4	5	3	7	6	7	6
100		100		100		100	
	22		19		6		4
	100		100		100		100

Growth and Structure

Egypt's external debt has risen on average by 17 percent a year for the past fifteen years. The rate of growth has accelerated considerably in recent years, and the total debt disbursed and outstanding has increased on average by 28 percent annually since 1971, as opposed to 13 percent during the preceding decade. Medium- and long-term debt outstanding increased on average by 9 percent from 1960 to 1970, rising to 23 percent yearly from 1971 to 1975, 15 percent in 1976, 38 percent in 1977, and a further 23 percent in 1978. Short-term liabilities, which were already growing at 25 percent a year up to 1970, rose thereafter at an average annual rate of 55 percent up to and including 1975. There was an additional increase of 19 percent in 1976 but a sharp decline thereafter of 60 percent in 1977 and a further 20 percent in 1978.

The most significant elements to surface as Egypt's external debt increased were: until mid-1977 a sharp rise in the use of short-term banking facilities, which had been a major source of financing since 1970, and especially since 1973; sizable shifts over time among major creditors (Western, Eastern bloc, and Arab countries); and for medium- and long-term debt, a relatively steady distribution among various categories of lending, that is, loans from bilateral and multilateral sources and from private creditors.

Table 16-14 reflects the changing structure of outstanding, disbursed debt, both including and excluding short-term liabilities, by categories of lending. The outstanding liabilities against short-term banking facilities increased from US$103.0 million, or approximately 9 percent of the total debt disbursed and outstanding in 1965, to US$1,169.4 million, or some 19 percent in 1975. At the same time, the share of loans from bilateral sources and those from private creditors (suppliers' credits and private bank loans) decreased in roughly the same proportions, from 65 to 59 percent and from 23 to 17 percent, respectively. Explanations for this can be found in the low level of new commitments from foreign governments during 1965-70; the slow rate of disbursements (with the exception of the large cash loans received in 1975) on loans from bilateral sources despite rising commitments after 1971; and the difficulty of obtaining suppliers' credits because of past payment difficulties and the resultant restricted coverage by the creditor guaranteeing agencies.

By 1976, however, the cumulative effect of disbursements made on the substantial bilateral and multilateral commitments since 1971, particularly quick-disbursing commodity loans, coupled with a concerted effort by Egyptian authorities to reduce reliance on banking facilities, began to be reflected in the total debt outstanding. Thus by December 31, 1978, bilateral and multilateral loans accounted for 86 percent of the total medium- and long-term debt outstanding, while the share of suppliers' credits and private bank loans had dropped to 14 percent.

Creditor Composition

The creditor country composition of the medium- and long-term debt has changed significantly over time, most markedly among loans from governments. Sizable inflows, totaling US$772.5 million during 1955-65, from Western countries resulted in their share of the total disbursed and outstanding debt being 62 percent by December 1965. This declined steadily to 59 percent by 1970 and then dropped sharply to 25 percent in 1975, rising again to 30 percent by December 1976. Comparable figures for amounts of disbursed debt due to Eastern bloc countries indicate a rise from 25 percent in 1965 to 36 percent in 1970, falling thereafter to 16 percent by 1976.

The United States was Egypt's foremost creditor up to 1970 with 34 percent of the disbursed debt in the category "loans from governments," followed by the U.S.S.R., 26 percent; Kuwait, 8 percent; Italy, 6 percent; and Federal Republic of Germany, 6 percent. Despite the fact that net inflows from Western countries were, on average, negative from 1965 to 1970, the increased inflows from the Eastern bloc countries, notably U.S.S.R., Czechoslovakia, and East Germany, were not enough to offset the extremely high level of lending from the West (particularly the United States) before 1965.

The Eastern bloc countries remained Egypt's major source of fresh bilateral assistance until 1973, but then the picture changed rapidly as large inflows in the form of loans and medium-term deposits from the OPEC countries became a major factor. With commitments of US$2,300 million in 1974-75 and disbursements (mostly in cash) of US$1,700 million during the same period, by December 1975 amounts due to Arab countries accounted for 56 percent of the total disbursed and outstanding loans from governments. Increased flows from the West made the United States, the Federal Republic of Germany, and Japan next with 20 percent, slightly behind the Eastern bloc with 24 percent. By December 31, 1978, the distribution had shifted again. Sizable disbursements that year by the Western countries, particularly the United States and the Federal Republic of Germany, increased to 25 percent the Western countries' share of disbursed and outstanding government loans. Continued negative flows from the Eastern bloc countries resulted in a further decline in their share to 13 percent, while the OPEC countries increased their share to 62 percent.

Within the category of suppliers' credits, debt due in nonconvertible currencies has always been relatively unimportant. It averaged 10 percent of the total up to 1965, rose to a peak of 17 percent by 1970, and declined thereafter to 5 percent of the total disbursed and outstanding on suppliers' credits at December 1978. The principal source of suppliers' credits has traditionally been the Western European countries, notably the Federal Republic of Germany, France, Italy, and the United Kingdom, as well as Japan, the United States, and Australia.

One of the more surprising elements to surface from table 16-14 is that, despite substantial increases from US$1,048.0 million disbursed and outstanding medium- and long-term debt in 1965 to US$3,679.3 million by December 1975, the distribution among various types of lending has remained relatively stable since 1960. Loans from bilateral sources consistently accounted for about three-fourths of the disbursed and outstanding debt, with the remaining one-fourth made up of loans from private creditors.

The use of suppliers' credits declined during 1970-75 because of some rescheduling into medium-term debt and a further buildup of arrears, with a consequent reduction in coverage by the creditor guaranteeing agencies. This decline was largely offset by the use of medium-term Eurodollar loans, Egypt's first venture into this category of borrowing. World Bank and IDA loans and credits also oscillated from 6 percent of the total debt disbursed and outstanding in 1960 to 1 percent in 1970, rising to 2 percent by 1975. Only in 1976 was there any real change in distribution, with bilateral and multilateral loans rising to 83 percent of the total medium- and long-term debt outstanding, while loans from private creditors dropped to 17 percent. This shift was the result of the extremely large bi-

TABLE 16-15.   CURRENCY DISTRIBUTION
OF FOREIGN DEBT, 1960-78
(percent)

Debt	1960	1965	1970	1975	1976	1977	1978
Loans from							
governments	73	71	74	76	81	82	82
Convertible	31	11	19	52	65	70	74
Nonconvertible	27	30	37	18	12	8	6
Local currency	15	30	18	6	4	2	2
Suppliers' and							
bank credits	21	25	25	22	16	15	15
Convertible	20	23	21	20	15	14	15
Nonconvertible	1	2	4	2	1	1	...
World Bank and							
IDA	6	4	1	2	3	3	3

... Zero or negligible.
Note: The table includes only debt with a maturity of more than one year. All
short-term debt is due in convertible currencies. Percentages are calculated
on the disbursed and outstanding debt.
Sources: Central Bank of Egypt and Ministry of Economy.

lateral and multilateral commitments in the period since 1974, and
the trend continued through 1979.

Currency Composition

Table 16-15 is intended to complement table 16-14 by dividing
Egypt's external debt according to convertible and nonconvertible
currency areas. In particular, it brings out clearly the impact of
the large U.S. PL 480 program of the early 1960s under which loans
were repayable in local currency, as well as the significant drop
in recent years of payments due in nonconvertible currencies, a direct consequence of the considerable decline in borrowing from the
Eastern bloc countries since 1973.

The greater part of the agreements concluded with the Eastern
bloc countries provided for repayment through bilateral accounts
in Egyptian exports, notably cotton. Amounts due in nonconvertible currencies accounted for 41 percent of all debt outstanding in
1970 and remained sizable up to 1973. Moreover, these proportions are significantly understated in that they encompass only the
civilian debt. Similar payments arrangements were common in
agreements concluded with Eastern bloc countries for defense
purposes.

The percentage of debt repayable in convertible currencies rose
sharply by 1978 because, in addition to disbursements from the
Western countries, the large loans and medium-term deposits from
OPEC countries received since 1974 are, almost without exception,
denominated and repayable in U.S. dollars.

Time Profile of Debt

The time profile of Egypt's total debt service has been extremely unfavorable since 1965. Between 1970 and 1974 it became particularly severe, largely as a result of an excessive use of short-term banking facilities with short maturities and very high interest rates. At the end of 1965, 44 percent of the outstanding debt had to be repaid within the following three years; this share rose to 50 percent by 1970, increasing rapidly to 61 percent by 1973, and thereafter declining slightly. Since 1976, however, improvements in the debt profile reflect a serious and successful attempt by the Egyptian authorities to substitute long-term loans from bilateral and multilateral sources for banking facilities and suppliers' credits.

17
Physical Infrastructure: Current Situation and Development Issues

The pervasive impression is that physical infrastructure in Egypt is seriously underdeveloped.[1] Despite the acceleration in investment since 1973, the capacity of port facilities, railways, the inland water transport system, and telecommunications is seriously limited. The road transport system is not seriously deficient, however, and has experienced rapid growth since 1965. Although Egypt has adequate facilities to generate power, the distribution system is deficient. About 40 percent of the population has access to electricity, but in the rural areas this figure is about 20 percent. About one-third of the total population has no access to safe water, and the per capita supply of water in most urban areas is less than the minimal adequate level. Sanitation facilities are still worse.

This situation is a direct consequence of underinvestment in physical infrastructure (see table 17-1). The real volume of investment expenditures declined from 1965-66 to 1973 in electricity, construction, and housing. The two significant exceptions have been transport and communications and public utilities (principally water supply and sewerage). The figures are highly biased in favor of road transport, however, and conceal the neglect of other modes of transport. The current low level of water supply and sanitation services underscores the need for further acceleration in investments in this area. Since 1973 investments in all the subsectors listed above have increased rapidly and somewhat ameliorated the situation. The government has recognized the need to sustain the present pace of investment expenditures and allocated about 45 percent of the public investments in the 1978-82 five-year plan to the various infrastructure subsectors. About 9 percent went to power, 27 percent to transport and telecommunications, and the rest to construction and housing.

1. Petroleum and gas are an exception and have been separately analyzed in chapter 13.

TABLE 17-1. GROSS FIXED INVESTMENT IN PHYSICAL
INFRASTRUCTURE, 1965-66 TO 1976
(millions of Egyptian pounds)

Subsector	1965-66	1973	1976	"Real" increase (percent)[a] 1965-66 to 1973	1973-76
Electricity	61.1	30.3	48.5	-60.2	29.1
Petroleum and gas	n.a.	26.8	52.4	n.a.	57.7
Construction	6.8	5.0	48.0	-41.0	774.2
Transport and communication	53.1	123.0	347.9	85.9	228.1
Housing	47.5	40.3	109.3	-32.0	217.7
Public utilities	12.4	22.8	44.6	47.6	157.8
Aggregate	180.9	248.2	650.7	n.a.	211.4

n.a. Not available.
a. Based on the estimated increase in the GNP deflator of 24.6 percent
between 1965-66 and 1973 and 24.0 percent between 1973 and 1976. Because the estimated GNP deflator probably understates actual price movements, real increases and decreases estimated above are overstated and
understated respectively.
Source: Statistical Appendix table 9.

Apart from operational inefficiency caused by past underinvestment, the sector is debilitated by general overemployment and a
severe shortage of technical and managerial manpower. This direct consequence of the government's policy of guaranteed employment contributes to the poor financial performance of the public
sector institutions.
   Distributive price policies are another concern because prices
are frequently set below marginal costs and what the market will
bear. Major examples are found in the electricity, telecommunications, railway, petroleum, and gas subsectors, which conform to
the general pattern of subsidized pricing in public sector institutions.
Recently the government has sought more appropriate price policies
to improve resource allocation as well as the financial performance
of the public sector institutions. Some progress has been made by
revising the tariff structure in some of the subsectors.
   A major impediment to the sustained development of the sector
is the lack of coordination in investment programming, notably in
the energy and transport sectors. At present, Egypt's energy program does not extend beyond the general aim to develop indigenous
resources. Little has been done to relate the patterns of national
demand to an optimal mix of the delivery modes. In transport, the
pattern of past investment created some excess capacity in the road

subsector, but severe undercapacity exists in all other subsectors. Among other things, investment programming must address this disequilibrium.

Part of the problem in investment programming originates in the complex organizational responsibility for management and development in the various sectors. For example, responsibility for the transport sector is divided among five ministries and thirty public sector companies. The Transport Planning Authority was created to improve coordination in investment and policy planning, and the transport survey currently underway will provide the basis for the modal choice in investment. Similarly, the creation of the Ministerial Committee on Energy in 1974 was a necessary first step in coordinating the work of the various energy agencies.

ENERGY AND POWER

The principal indigenous energy resources are petroleum and natural gas (see chapter 13) and hydropower; small coal deposits also exist in the Sinai. No conventional deposits of low-cost uranium ore have been discovered so far. In the long run solar energy may be another important source, but it has not been tapped because present knowledge and technology are limited. Noncommercial fuels, in the form of animal and vegetable wastes, may be another significant energy source in rural areas, but no information is available on their use.

Energy Resources (Other than Petroleum and Gas)

The main conventional hydropower resources are on the Nile and have been largely developed. The principal hydropower stations are at the Aswan Dam, which were commissioned in 1960-61, and the Aswan High Dam, which came into service in 1967-70. Installed capacities are 345 megawatts (MW) and 2,100 MW, respectively, but total available capacity varies from about 800 MW in the winter months to about 1,400 MW in the summer. Although the reservoir was filled in 1976, the maximum effective capacity in 1977 was only 1,300 MW because of transmission limitations. Improvements are expected to raise this figure to 1,800 MW by 1983.

Between Aswan and Cairo a further 635 MW could be developed, using the seventy meters of head in the flow of the Nile, if existing barrages were strengthened and additional ones constructed. The high plateau overlooking the Gulf of Suez and plateaus bordering the Nile near Cairo and Nag Hammadi are potential sites for pumped-storage schemes. The only other potential source of hydropower is the Qattara Project, which would channel water from the Mediterranean to the Qattara Depression, about 160 kilometers southwest of Alexandria. It could have a firm capacity of about 640 MW while the depression is filling (estimated to take twelve years) and 340 MW thereafter as water is lost by evaporation.

Systematic prospecting for nuclear fuel materials, which began in 1961, indicates three possible sources of uranium: conventional deposits, uranium-bearing monazite in the heavy mineral beach sands, and phosphate rock. About 13 to 14 percent of the total land area of Egypt has been surveyed from the air, and ground surveys have been made of about 10 percent of this area. A considerable number of conventional deposits have been discovered, especially in the central part of the Eastern Desert, but subsurface exploration has been too limited to estimate ore reserves. Geological indications in both the Eastern and Western deserts suggest that intensified prospecting may find economic deposits of uranium ore. The main problem is to obtain financing, and the possibility of joint exploration and exploitation agreements, along the lines of the oil agreements, is now being pursued with U.S., German, and French companies.

The heavy mineral beach sands of the Nile Delta and Mediterranean coast are an important potential source of nuclear fuel material (both uranium and thorium, in the forms of U_3O_8 and ThO_2). Approximate reserve estimates to a depth of twenty meters are: heavy minerals, 600 million tons; monazite, 6 million tons; ThO_2, 370,000 tons; and U_3O_8, 28,000 tons. Because of the low percentage content of uranium and thorium, it would be feasible to produce them from this source only as by-products. Whether this operation would be economic depends on the successful development of the whole beach sands industry and the marketing of the principal products. An industry with an annual throughput of one million tons of heavy minerals, for example, could theoretically provide annually forty to fifty tons of U_3O_8 and about 600 tons of ThO_2.

An estimated 100,000 tons of U_3O_8 may exist in the country's rich phosphate deposits, estimated at 4,000 million tons, of which about 1,000 million tons may be economically exploitable. Again, U_3O_8 would be a by-product, completely dependent on the installation of a triple-superphosphate plant. Such a plant handling 500,000 tons of raw phosphate rock a year could theoretically produce twenty-five tons of U_3O_8. Any realistic estimate of the need for nuclear power by the year 2000 calls for many thousands of tons of uranium fuel. The above figures make it clear that most of the future requirements would have to be met by imports unless significant amounts of uranium deposits are discovered.

The most important potential applications of nuclear energy are in the production of electricity and desalination of sea water. The possibility of combining electricity generation with water desalination at nuclear power stations has been under study for some time, particularly in relation to the use of desalted water for irrigation.

The desalination technology is well established, but it has not yet been economic to apply it in agriculture. Special techniques for using the desalted water (for example, trickle irrigation) would have to be developed to overcome this problem.

Coal deposits estimated at about 80 million tons have been discovered in the Sinai near Suez, but there is no information on their quality and no plans to develop them.

Energy Consumption

Annual consumption of oil, natural gas, and hydroelectricity averaged around 230 kilograms oil-equivalent (kgoe)[2] per capita during 1960-72, which is low compared with other countries. In 1972 the figure for Egypt was 249 kgoe, while average world consumption was 1,526 kgoe and the average for Africa, 279 kgoe; world consumption ranged from 8 kgoe in Burundi to 8,032 kgoe in the United States.

During the 1960-72 period total energy consumption increased around 4 percent a year, slightly less than the average rate of growth of real GDP, yielding an average energy coefficient of 0.93 (ratio of energy to GDP growth rate). With an expected annual growth rate of real GDP of about 8 to 9 percent between 1975 and 1980, energy consumption could grow at about 8 to 10 percent a year during the plan period. This assumes a slightly higher energy coefficient than the above.

The above analysis is too aggregated to shed much light on the balance of different types and uses of energy. A more complete and useful discussion would address the question by disaggregating the different kinds of energy to reveal their availabilities and uses and by allowing for possibilities of interfuel substitution. Even on the aggregated level, however, it appears that the country should have enough overall energy resources to sustain the anticipated growth of production through the early 1980s, given a degree of fuel substitutability. Such growth would imply an increase in per capita energy consumption, but the average level would still be very low compared with other countries. Should industrialization proceed at a more accelerated rate, the requirements for energy sources would necessarily increase.

Domestic distributive prices of energy products are highly subsidized. The present price structure is intended to provide production subsidies to public entities as well as direct subsidies to consumers. In both cases, it tends to perpetuate the underpricing of

2. This assumes 1,000 kilowatt hours of generated hydroelectricity is equivalent to 0.096 tons oil-equivalent, in accordance with the standard UN convention, which measures the fuel equivalent of hydro- (or nuclear) electricity in terms of its heat value (860 kilocalories per kilowatt hour) rather than of the amount of fuel which would be required to generate one kilowatt hour.

publicly distributed goods in Egypt. This is not desirable because
of the adverse effect on resource allocation and mobilization and
the bias against low-income brackets in the use of energy.

Electric Power Subsector

Electricity was first introduced in Egypt in 1895. Isolated diesel
and some oil-fire steam units were installed in major population
centers by various government, private, and municipal organizations. The supply in Cairo was in the hands of the privately owned
Lebon Company until 1949, when the government-owned Cairo Electric and Gas Department took over the responsibility. In Alexandria the assets of the Lebon Company were nationalized in 1961, and
a government corporation, the Alexandria Electric and Gas Authority, took control.
    In 1964 the Ministry of Electricity and Energy (MEE) was formed
to consolidate all electricity organizations under state ownership.
In 1965 the General Egyptian Electricity Corporation (GEEC) was
established to own, operate, and expand the public power system.
In 1971 the General Rural Electrification Authority was created to
plan and supervise the construction of rural electrification projects.
Early in 1976 the sector was reorganized through the establishment
of four new authorities: the Egyptian Electricity Authority (EEA)
replacing GEEC, the Rural Electrification Authority (REA), the
Nuclear Power Plant Authority (NPPA), and Qattara Depression
Authority.

    Existing facilities. Since 1970 all important hydro- and thermal-
generating stations in Egypt have operated through EEA's unified
power system. The system has a total installed generating capacity of 2,445 MW of hydro in the South and 1,370 MW of steam and
gas-turbine units, mostly in the Delta. A 500-kilovolt, double-
circuit transmission line, 838 kilometers long, connects the Aswan
station to the Delta region and is the backbone of the interconnected
system.
    Excessive outages experienced during early operation of the 500-
kilovolt system caused EEA to impose unusually severe restrictions
on the maximum load assigned to the hydro stations. This limitation on the power transmitted from Aswan to the large load centers
in the Delta has delayed full utilization of available High Dam generation. Although load growth averaged 17 percent annually during
1974–76 and is estimated at 13 percent annually for 1976–80, existing capacity and committed construction are ample to serve the
short-term needs if expected improvements in system operation
are realized.

    Tariffs. EEA's existing tariffs are based on a 1970 study by
Electricité de France, which provided an appropriate basis for

calculating the costs of supply. The current tariffs do not realistically reflect the costs of supply in economic terms, however, because
fuel is charged to EEA at subsidized prices, that is, pre-1973 prices,
and not at its export value or at international prices. Using international prices for fuel oil, the cost of generation from EEA's new
steam plant has been estimated to be 14.4 milliemes (one-thousandth
of an Egyptian pound) per kilowatt hour (kWh), of which 8.5 milliemes
would be for fuel alone. This position will improve once the changeover to associated gas firing is accomplished.

In 1975 EEA's average revenue per kWh sold was about 9 milliemes, barely sufficient to cover the fuel cost in new thermal plants.
Industry, which consumes about 60 percent of the electricity sold,
paid on average only about 7 milliemes per kWh despite a tariff increase of 20 percent that was introduced in January 1975 for all
consumers except municipalities and residential customers. Certain larger industrial customers are on special tariffs, the two
most important being the aluminum smelter at Nag Hammadi, which
paid about 2.5 milliemes per kWh, and the Kima fertilizer complex
near Aswan, whose tariff was increased from about 1.8 milliemes
per kWh in 1974 to about 5.0 milliemes per kWh in 1975. The prices
paid by these consumers and other industrial consumers are clearly
less than the marginal cost of supply from Egypt's newest baseload
steam plants. To the extent that these tariffs are below the long-
run marginal costs of supply, these consumers are being subsidized.

The municipalities, which buy power in bulk from EEA at 10.5
milliemes per kWh (that is, 9.0 milliemes per kWh for power and
1.5 millimemes per kWh for system operation and maintenance),
bill all medium- and low-voltage consumers in the cities, towns,
and villages beyond Cairo and Alexandria. By law, the prices they
charge may not exceed those in Cairo and Alexandria, and in practice they are the same. No doubt the cost of supply to rural consumers is higher than in Cairo and Alexandria, but the government
is anxious to improve conditions in rural areas and thus established
a uniform tariff for low-voltage residential and commercial consumers who cannot afford higher costs.

Nearly all medium- and low-voltage rates are based on declining
block tariffs. As consumption increases, the price to the consumer
is reduced, but the cost of incremental supplies may not be declining. As a result, larger consumers who often can afford to pay
more may in fact be paying less than the cost of supplying them.

Changes in electricity prices can be secured only through a time-
consuming and cumbersome process. First, EEA must determine
its basic costs, which are then checked by the Central Auditing Organization and the Price Planning Authority. They are then submitted to the Higher Council of the Electricity Sector and finally approved
by the Council of Ministers and issued as a presidential decree. In
June 1976 EEA set up a committee to study the costs of generation,

transmission, and distribution up to 1980, to recommend rate increases, and to establish a fair basis for determining costs on which a tariff structure could be formulated. The committee recommended that the cost of electricity include depreciation of the High Dam electrical assets and the 500-kilovolt transmission and assets transferred to EEA by REA for operation and maintenance; interest on all local and foreign loans; and a 3 percent return on total invested capital as approved by the Council of Ministers July 25, 1973. The committee also proposed that consumers in the duty-free zones in Alexandria, Port Said, and Suez should pay tariffs that include the international price of fuel (calculated at the parallel market rate of exchange), and that local price changes for fuel and other costs should be reflected in tariffs for all categories of consumers. Increases in tariffs of about 10 percent were submitted to the government and, with some exemptions and changes, were accepted.

Main Issues and Government Policy in the Energy Sector

A national energy policy in the sense of an explicit statement of national objectives in the energy field and specific plans for achieving them does not exist. The implicit aim of Egypt's energy policy in the early 1970s was to develop and exploit indigenous energy resources as rapidly as possible and to supplement these internal resources by increasing recourse to nuclear power in the early 1980s. After the 1973-74 oil price increases, however, Egypt's ambitious plans for economic development called for a more clearly defined national energy strategy. The first important step was the formation in 1974 of the Ministerial Committee on Energy, with the minister of electricity as chairman. The committee's main responsibilities are to coordinate the work of the different energy agencies in light of economic and social development needs; to review the present organization of the energy sector with a view to its improvement; to consider the most economic way of meeting the country's energy requirements; to consider legislation on energy matters; and to make decisions on joint issues concerning the ministries and agencies engaged in the energy field.

Before the completion of the High Dam and the discovery of natural gas fields and the large oil fields in the Gulf of Suez, Egypt relied on fuel imports to satisfy domestic demand. Under those circumstances, it made sense to develop domestic sources as fast as possible. The completion of the High Dam substantially increased the country's electrical power capacity, and the discovery of domestic crude oil enabled the country to substitute for imports of refined products to fire thermal power stations and to use for transportation and houses. With the continued increase in oil production and the availability of natural gas, Egypt's energy sources are in excess of its immediate needs. Thus the generating capacity of electrical

energy is adequate for the short term, and sufficient new plant is
being added to take care of planned load growth.

With the transition from an energy-deficient to an energy-surplus
country and the availability of new forms of energy (gas and possibly
nuclear in the near future), the need for an overall program of energy
management has become more important. The possibility for substitution among new kinds of energy raises the question of the most
optimal fuel mix for both social and economic ends. A further question concerns the best rate of development of new sources of energy.
It seems likely that Egypt will continue to develop its energy resources (especially crude oil) at the fastest rate possible and that
it will export larger volumes in order to relieve the severe balance
of payments problems (this assumes a modest rate of discovery of
new sources). In the case of very large discoveries, however, the
optimal rate of extraction becomes operationally more significant.
Optimal fuel-mixes are already being discussed. The use of gas,
especially in associated form but also in its nonassociated form, to
fuel electrical generators releases more crude oil for export. Such
a shift may prove beneficial as long as associated gas is being flared,
but the long-term implications need further investigation to take account of alternative uses for gas (see chapter 13).

A comprehensive energy management program should address
the question of the location of new power generation plants in relation to load centers and transmission and distribution networks.
Thermal plants could be located close to load centers by using liquid
or gaseous fuel that has alternative uses, or the plants could utilize
the excess capacity of the High Dam if the transmission network
were reinforced so that outages were minimized. A more complete
answer would be possible if the question were addressed within an
overall framework for the development of energy resources. A related problem is that EEA plans a large number of new generating
units, and this additional capacity will require an adequate transmission and distribution network.

TRANSPORT

The demand for transport is concentrated along the 1,000 kilometer Alexandria-Cairo-Aswan corridor, which contains Egypt's economic activities and the bulk of its population. The Suez Canal area
is being reconstructed and developed and will need transport services. The flat topography of the Nile Valley has encouraged the
development of railways as a main mode of inland transport, supported by inland waterways. Roads are the most important means
of transport of freight and passengers, however, and are crucial
for short-distance hauls. Continuing hostilities have prevented the

full utilization of air and coastal shipping, which have considerable
growth potential. Egypt has one major international airport in Cairo
and nine domestic airports, only three of which have the scheduled
services of Egypt Air, the only domestic carrier. It also has four
major ports, two the Mediterranean and two on the Red Sea. Following is a summary of the principal features of the various transport subsectors.

Roads and Motor Vehicles

In 1978 roads carried more than 80 percent of the total freight
tonnage and around 75 percent of passenger kilometers. Of about
27,000 kilometers of roads in the country, about 12,000 were paved
(see table 17-2). Favorable climatic conditions have kept them in
relatively good condition, and the regional roads are all usable for
normal motor vehicles.
About 2,810 kilometers of roads are under construction, which
also includes resurfacing, widening, doubling, and such minor improvements as shoulder paving. New construction alone amounts
to only 1,700 kilometers or 60 percent of the total. The other main
projects consist of doubling or widening 700 kilometers of roads,
including those from Ismailia to Cairo, Port Said, and Suez, as well
as the Cairo-Suez and Alexandria-Marsa Matruh roads. Total
traffic on Egypt's roads is expected to increase at an annual rate
of about 12 percent between 1978 and 1985. The growth of freight
is put somewhat lower, at around 8 percent annually.

Railways

Egypt has a total railway route of 3,905 kilometers, extending
from the Aswan High Dam northward through the Nile Valley to the
Mediterranean and including an extensive system between Cairo and

TABLE 17-2. ROAD AND HIGHWAY NETWORK, 1978

Category	Length (kilometers)	Percentage of total	Paved (kilometers)
Divided highways	238	1	238
Main highways	11,244	42	10,857
Regional roads	15,039	57	1,799
Total	26,521	100	12,894

Source: Ministry of Transport, 1978.

Alexandria. A main line travels eastward to the Suez Canal and ends at Ismailia, where it intersects with the line that parallels the canal from Suez to Port Said. Another line runs westward from Alexandria to the Libyan border. In addition, there is a direct line from Cairo to Suez and a new 360 kilometer line that runs from the iron ore area at Bahariya oasis in the Western Desert to the steel works at Tibein. The railway network in Egypt is standard gauge (1,435 millimeters), with double track for about 951 kilometers of the total.

The Egyptian Railway Authority, established in 1956, is responsible for the operation of the railway network in Egypt. Although a semiautonomous agency under the Ministry of Transport, the authority does not enjoy commercial freedom since it has to abide by government policies and procedures governing staffing and tariffs.

Freight traffic on the railways decreased after 1973. The shortage of locomotives (mainly because of poor maintenance), cancellations of trains, and the unreliability of service led customers to switch from rail to other modes of transport. Despite some recovery in 1977 and 1978, tons per kilometer were still less than in 1973. In contrast, passenger traffic continued to grow rapidly, and in 1978 was about 30 percent higher than in 1973.

Inland Waterways

The inland waterways, particularly the Nile, constitute a main transport mode in the densely populated area of the Delta and the Nile Valley. Because of their relatively low hauling cost and high transport capacity, they are expected to be a major factor in Egypt's industrial development.

The inland waterways include the Nile River and the canal network, which consists of two classes of waterways. Class 1 is a narrow line beginning at Alexandria, which is linked by a canal to Cairo, and runs from there down the Nile to Aswan. Lake Nasser is navigable as far as Sudan, but because of the difference in altitude at the Aswan High Dam, there is no shipping connection between the lake and the Lower Nile. This class of waterway is 1,495 kilometers long and is navigable by vessels with a capacity of up to 920 tons. The class 2 waterway is mainly located in the Delta, and caters only to sailing boats and small barges with a capacity of up to 200 tons. The length of this class is 1,849 kilometers.

Information on freight movement on inland waterways is incomplete. But since the two large companies of the Roads and Waterways Authority (RWA) are believed to handle nearly 75 percent of all such freight, a description of their activities gives a general impression of waterways traffic. Both tonnages and ton-kilometers of the two RWA companies have been increasing; between 1974 and 1975 total tonnage increased from 1.9 to 2.6 million tons.

Numerous commodities are handled, the most important ones being petroleum, iron ore, phosphate, clay, cement, fertilizer, and
coal.

Traffic is expected to increase rapidly during the coming decade.
Between 1980 and 1985 volume is projected to rise from 6.4 million
tons to 18.1 million tons and from 2.3 million to 5.7 million ton-
kilometers. The relatively abundant capacity makes it likely that
it will be able to meet the increase in demand at relatively low
cost. Moreover, the expansion of the main waterways proposed
in the five-year plan will permit the use of larger vessels, which
in turn will benefit the development of basic industries.

Ports

Egypt is bordered on the north by the Mediterranean Sea and on
the east by the Red Sea and the Gulf of Suez, but because of inland
geographical conditions, it has only one major port, Alexandria,
at the western corner of the Nile Delta on the Mediterranean. The
development of other ports is inhibited by the sparse population and
low level of economic activity in the coastal areas, as well as by
the lack of adequate transport links with the densely populated areas
in the Nile Valley. Other geographical constraints are the vast desert, and the mountain chain separating the Red Sea coast from the
rest of the country.

Only after the Suez Canal was constructed about a century ago
were seaports of any significance developed on the eastern coast:
Port Said on the Mediterranean end of the Suez Canal, and Suez on
the Red Sea end. Both ports are near the densely populated areas
of the Delta and Cairo. Two small ports, Safaga and Quseir on the
Red Sea, specialize in bulk traffic of phosphate and other minerals.
On the Mediterranean is another small port, Marsa Matruh, located midway between Alexandria and the Libyan border. Other small
ports handle nominal traffic but have good prospects for future development. Egypt also has specialized oil ports.

The hostilities in 1967 and 1973 badly affected the operations of
Port Said and Suez, so that Alexandria's share of traffic increased
from 76 percent in 1966 to 90 percent in 1975. The total number of
ships calling at the port in that year was 2,926. Both Port Said and
Suez partly resumed operations in late 1974, and additional reconstruction work increased their capacity in 1978. Some traffic in
food grain, fertilizer, timber, and general cargo has already been
diverted from Alexandria to Port Said. Since reopening, Port Said
and Suez have handled a fair volume of trade, reaching 1.3 million
tons and 1.8 million tons, respectively, in 1975.

The decline in exports from Alexandria was substantial — from
2.6 million tons in 1971 to about 1 million tons in 1975. The capacity of the port has been deficient since 1969 because of insufficient

and poor equipment, inadequate storage facilities, inadequate dock
transport, and insufficiently trained manpower. Serious congestion increased the average waiting time for general cargo ships from
3.3 days in 1974 to 6.2 days in 1975.

In view of this congestion and the projected increase in traffic for
Egyptian ports, there are many proposals for increasing port capacity,
including the construction of new ports (for example, in Marsa Matruh,
Dekheila, Damietta, Ismailia, and Berenice) and the rehabilitation
(for example, Port Said) and further development (for example,
Suez-Adabiya) of existing ports. Many of these proposals are still
nothing more than ideas; others have been subjected to prefeasibil-
ity studies. Apart from the port of Alexandria, the only project under implementation is the construction of a new port at Marsa Matruh. The initial proposal was reduced owing to a lack of funds and
the doubtful economic justification for the project. So far, a quay
twelve meters deep has been constructed to a length of 575 meters,
sufficient for four or five ships.

On the basis of the economic prospects of the Egyptian economy,
port traffic over the coming decade is forecast to increase considerably. Dry cargo exported and imported through Egypt's four main
ports (Alexandria, Port Said, Suez, and Safaga) is expected to reach
28.3 million tons in 1985. This is largely related to the expected
increase in imports of wheat, flour, corn, and coal as well as to
the imports needed for Egypt's development programs.

Shipping

Although Egypt lies at the crossroads of international shipping,
the nationalization of its shipping industry in the early 1960s and
the closure of the Suez Canal in 1967 resulted in a sharp decline in
shipping activities. Since the reopening of Suez and recent government measures to encourage private shipping, Egypt has been passing through a period of transition that makes it difficult to formulate policies to promote shipping. The country's development is not,
however, critically dependent on its shipping industry.

Egyptian shipping is handled by one state-owned company and
two private companies, both of which were established in the 1970s,
one by the Arab League. A third private company is being formed.
The public company was formed in 1963 after taking ownership of
five private companies. It operated obsolete fleets for a long time,
but foreign investment has enabled the company to renew and expand
its fleet. Prior to nationalization, the Egyptian fleet consisted of
thirty-three ships (twenty-one general cargo, five passenger, and
seven tankers), with a total of 225,000 deadweight tonnage. By
1976 the public company's fleet had expanded to forty-five ships
with a total of 307,000 deadweight tonnage; this is about 81 percent
of the ships of the Egyptian fleet, and they carry 84 percent of the
tonnage.

Air Transport

Cairo has the only international airport in Egypt. It is the main
center of all flight activities and the base of Egypt Air, the national
airline and the only domestic carrier. Of the nine domestic airports,
only three (Abu Simbel, Aswan, and Luxor) are included on Egypt
Air's regular schedule. The others are Alexandria, Asiut, Cairo
Embaba, Ghardaga, Marsa Matruh, and Port Said. Air transport
to and within Egypt is largely for tourists because only a small
segment of the population can afford to fly. About 80 percent of the
passengers on internal routes are foreign tourists.

Apart from a slight decline in 1973 owing to the war, air traffic
has been growing since 1971. Between 1971 and 1978 aircraft movements grew at an annual rate of 11 percent. The growth of passenger traffic (domestic and international) has also been rapid, amounting to about 16 percent annually; freight traffic has been growing
since 1971 at a rate of over 10 percent annually.

Major Issues in the Transport Sector

Investment program. The 1978-82 plan envisages the following
public sector investment program for the various transport subsectors (in millions of Egyptian pounds):

Roads	
Construction	100
Vehicles and equipment	310
Railway	310
Waterways and river transport	74
Ocean transport and ports	144
Air transport	169
Suez Canal	495
Total	1,602

This allocation does not adequately address the present disequilibrium in the capacity, that is, the excess capacity in the roads while
serious limitations exist in the railways. In the light of this, a major road transport program as envisaged in the plan is inadvisable.
Similarly, there seems to be excessive emphasis on building up the
number of publicly owned trucks and buses, while very little emphasis has been put on maintenance. A high proportion of the fleet
is now unserviceable but could be repaired. Greater emphasis on
proper repair and maintenance could substantially reduce the estimated investment needs for road transport. In contrast, investment
in railways is well conceived, involving track renewal and expansion, replacement of unserviceable equipment, maintenance of equipment, and training facilities to relieve the shortage of technical

manpower. Similarly, the proposed investment in inland water transportation seems appropriate; this and railways probably represent the most cost-effective modes for internal transportation.

Organization and management. Responsibility for the transport sector is distributed among at least five ministries and about thirty public sector companies. Areas of responsibility and jurisdiction among these institutions are not clear and often overlap, and there is disguised unemployment. An example of the lopsidedness of responsibility is that the Ministry of Housing and Reconstruction has a larger budget for highway construction than the Ministry of Transport, the primary ministry in the sector. A significant step in the right direction is the recent establishment of the Transport Planning Authority (TPA) in the Ministry of Transport to bring about a well-integrated transport plan for the country. To achieve its objectives, the agency will need to examine all existing organizational and decisionmaking mechanisms and ensure the flow of information on a continuous basis and the coordination of planning efforts. Moreover, the planning and policy responsibilities of various governmental organs should be clearly defined to eliminate duplications. It should be understood that TPA has the primary responsibility for coordinating planning and policymaking activities of all transport-related agencies at the working level. Finally, TPA should be supported by technical assistance programs and resources adequate to its role.

Tariffs. The structure of tariffs in the various transport subsectors follows the general pattern of underpricing of public goods and services. Prime examples are railway freight tariffs, which have not been changed since 1957, and passenger tariffs, which were last raised in 1967. Combined with the decline in freight traffic, these low tariffs largely account for the Egyptian Railway's 1977 operating deficit of about LE22 million. Similarly, the road users' charges determined by the government bear no relation to the costs of services. The effect is to defer private investment, which might otherwise have helped expand capacity in urban transportation. Admittedly, the break from this pattern of underpricing of transport services can be only gradual, but a change of direction is important.

TELECOMMUNICATIONS

The high population densities in the valley of the Nile, the Delta, and the canal area have considerably strained telecommunications facilities in Egypt. Although the habitable area has many attractions for industries that wish to supply the growing domestic and regional markets, the inadequacy of the telecommunications system is a significant constraint on the development process.

The Arab Republic of Egypt Telecommunications Organization (ARETO), attached to the Ministry of Communications, is responsible for the operation, management, and development of all public telecommunications facilities in the country. The Suez Canal Authority, defense service, railways, and civil aviation authorities do, however, maintain telecommunications facilities for their own specialized needs.

Some items of telecommunications equipment and cables are manufactured in Egypt. The state-owned Egyptian Telephone Company, attached to the Ministry of Communications, produces crossbar telephone switching equipment and telephone instruments under license from L. M. Ericsson of Sweden. The state-owned Electro Cable, attached to the Ministry of Industry, produces wires and underground cables for telecommunications and electric power. Production of the factories does not, however, cover the full range of needs, and ARETO has to import a great deal of equipment and cable.

Access to Telephone Service

Egypt's density of 1.34 telephones per 100 population is significantly lower than that of other Middle Eastern countries (Iran, 2.00; Turkey, 2.52; Syria, 2.30; Iraq, 1.69). The telephone density in Cairo is about 5.0 and in Alexandria, 3.4, compared with Algiers, 9.5; Teheran, 8.2; and Manila, 23.2. The overall average for the country, excluding Cairo and Alexandria, is only 0.44. As many as 1,000 villages do not have even primary access to telephone service, for example, a public call office.

Telephone availability in Egypt has been deteriorating at a rapid pace during the last decade.[3] It declined from 96.9 percent in 1968 to 56.8 percent in 1976. According to the registered telephone waiting list of ARETO, the number of waiting applicants rose during the same period from 15,500 to 268,000,[4] which is about 76 percent of the number of existing connections. Actual unsatisfied demand is likely to be higher, however, because registered telephone waiting lists tend to understate demand (lists are not kept in areas without telephone service and long waiting periods discourage many potential subscribers from registering). An ordinary applicant in Cairo may have to wait as long as fourteen years before getting a telephone. The situation is slightly better in Alexandria and the principal cities of Upper and Lower Egypt.

---

3. Telephone availability is defined as the ratio of direct exchange lines (DELs) to the sum of DELs and waiting applicants.

4. This estimate does not include waiting applicants in small towns currently served by manual exchanges.

In places where telephone availability is less than 10 percent, connections are allocated to applicants by a committee composed of the chairman and top officials of ARETO. Priority is given to categories that are felt to be of greatest benefit (hospitals, doctors, schools, police, army, press, government offices, airlines, and offices of engineers, lawyers, and accountants). Nonpriority requests are filled on a first-come first-served basis; as a result, these applicants wait many years for service. Most business firms desiring a telephone have no designated priority and therefore must press for special consideration from the committee, rent a furnished office or apartment in which a telephone is already installed, or wait many years on a list. The price mechanism is not used by ARETO to ration new connections or to maximize the benefits of telecommunications investment.

Users of Telephone Service

Overall statistics of telephone usage by classification of user are not available. A breakdown by type of subscriber for Cairo at the end of 1976 shows that, officially, business subscribers represent 47 percent of the total; government, 10 percent; and residential subscribers, 43 percent. The number of residential subscribers is unrealistically swollen, however, because ARETO's present tariff structure allows them many free calls, and an uncertain number of nonresidential subscribers are listed in this category to take advantage of this saving. Furthermore, as in other developing countries, a sizable portion of the usage of residential telephones is for business or business-related matters; many are used for business purposes during off-peak hours. ARETO estimates that in Cairo approximately 95 percent of all calls during business hours are business-related. The situation in Alexandria is similar to Cairo. In the smaller towns and villages, the subscribers are almost entirely business- or government-related.

Constraints

In addition to the inadequate quality and quantity of telephone service, the sector suffers from several other constraints. Some stem from the financial and administrative relationship between ARETO and the government and affect the financing and development of programs, their execution, and staff control in ARETO. Other weaknesses within ARETO itself affect its day-to-day operational efficiency.

The major constraint that has impeded progress in the telecommunication sector has been the lack of adequate investment.[5] Like

5. In 1973, 1974, and 1975, Egypt invested respectively an estimated 0.19, 0.18, and 0.39 percent of GDP in telecommunications through ARETO. In contrast, a tabulation of forty-four developing countries by the Telecommunication

all government boards in Egypt, ARETO must turn over to the Ministry of Finance any operating surplus in lieu of dividends, and the Ministry of Finance in turn provides ARETO with budgetary funds for capital investment. As a result, ARETO's investment programs and works have been dictated by the availability of funds, which has been far from adequate. This piecemeal arrangement also distorts the capital structure of ARETO, which in turn increases its debt burden and debt service. Compounding this is the fact that ARETO's tariffs have not been changed since 1966 despite domestic price inflation.[6] The unit revenue per direct exchange line has also been low. ARETO was able to contribute only about 18 percent of its capital investment to a relatively modest investment program during the 1973-76 period. It is also required to absorb personnel over and above its needs by the government's mandatory employment policy.

WATER AND SEWERAGE

The predominant source of water for Egypt is the Nile River, which provides an assured supply of some 55,000 million cubic meters of water each year. Increasing demands on the Nile — principally for agriculture, which accounts for 95 percent of water use — has called into question the continuing adequacy of this source. A master plan for the use of water resources has been prepared by the World Bank with UNDP financing. This study provides a long-term perspective for water resource development in the context of which local potable water needs can be realistically evaluated.

Potable water is drawn from two sources: artesian wells or directly from the Nile and irrigation canals. South of Cairo, artesian water is usually of good quality although it sometimes contains iron and manganese salts. To the north of Cairo and in the Fayoum Depression, artesian water is characteristically brackish and may require filtration and blending with sweeter surface water. Artesian water in the coastal areas of the Delta is generally not suitable for human consumption, and communities depend entirely on surface water. The recent discovery of apparently substantial groundwater reserves in the Qattara region has yet to be evaluated.

Institutional Arrangements

Provision of drinking water in Egypt is the responsibility of four public institutions. In Cairo and Alexandria, separate authorities that began as private utility companies in the nineteenth century are

---

Union revealed that in 1972 three-fourths of the countries invested more than 0.4 percent of GDP in telecommunications, more than half invested more than 0.6 percent, and one-fourth invested more than 1.0 percent.

6. The only exception is annual rentals for telex, which were increased in July 1976.

now responsible to the local governor. The Canal Zone cities of
Port Said, Ismailia, and Suez are served by the Suez Canal Authority. Water production and supply in all other governorates, both
urban and rural, is the responsibility of the General Authority for
Potable Water (GOPW). Operations and maintenance of the facilities are generally carried out in townships by the local municipal
authorities and in villages and rural areas by the GOPW itself.

The responsibility for the provision of sewerage services throughout Egypt lies with the General Authority for Sewerage and Sanitary
Drainage (GOSSD). The authority designs, constructs, and maintains sewerage and drainage facilities in all towns, including the
maintenance of the Alexandria and Cairo sewerage systems. Its
technical services are made available to the governorates, which
operate and maintain provincial sewerage and drainage systems.
In addition to Cairo, Alexandria, and the Canal Zone cities, ten
cities in Lower Egypt and four cities in Upper Egypt have sewerage
systems. Drainage systems without any form of treatment facilities exist in another twelve Delta towns. All the authorities in the
water supply and sewerage sector are supervised by the Ministry
of Housing and Reconstruction (MOHAR). Within MOHAR, the Advisory Committee on Reconstruction (ACR) is responsible for long-
range planning of infrastructure.

Sector Constraints and Policies

A 1977 World Health Organization (WHO)-World Bank report on
the water supply and sewerage sector estimates that between 10 and
20 percent of the urban population, accounting for about 45 percent
of the country's total population, is not adequately served with safe
water; in the rural areas more than 50 percent of the population fall
into this category. This implies that about 14 million inhabitants
(37 percent of the total population) lack access to safe public water
supplies. The potable water distribution systems are often old and
underdesigned, and there are heavy losses because of leakage as
well as poor plumbing and waste at public standpipes. Consequently, only about 60 percent of the total production capacity is available for consumption. Furthermore, excessive central government
involvement in planning and program implementation has stifled
local accountability and initiative. Water tariffs are low, and 65
percent of the revenues generated revert to the central budget,
from which funds for new construction and operating costs must be
obtained by the authorities. To improve the situation, new effective organizations must be created, operating procedures changed,
investments must be increased substantially, and qualified staff
has to be trained. Although the needs of water supply and sewerage
in the main urban centers of Cairo, Alexandria, and the Suez Canal
Zone have started to be addressed, very little has been done to help

the rural areas and the secondary provincial cities of between 5,000 and 500,000 inhabitants. A special effort will be necessary to ensure that these parts of the country obtain their due share of the allocations.

The government is fully aware of the sector's shortcomings, and substantial funds have been allocated for the planning period 1976-85. This includes LE545 million (US$1,400 million) for water and LE358 million (US$916 million) for sewerage. This ambitious program can be implemented effectively only if there are major organizational changes and increased training. The WHO-World Bank sector report therefore recommends the decentralization of GOPW into effective regional authorities with integrated rural and urban responsibilities. A similar approach would later be adopted for GOSSD.

Statistical Appendix

SA TABLE 1.   POPULATION AND RATES OF
BIRTH, DEATH, AND NATURAL INCREASE,
1952-77; AGE STRUCTURE, 1960-70

Year	Population (thousands)	Rate per thousand population		
		Birth-rates	Death-rates	Rate of natural increase
1952	21,437	45.2	17.8	27.4
1953	21,943	42.6	19.6	23.0
1954	22,460	42.6	17.9	24.7
1955	22,990	40.3	17.6	22.7
1956	23,532	40.7	16.4	24.3
1957	24,087	38.0	17.8	20.2
1958	24,655	41.1	16.6	24.5
1959	25,237	42.8	16.3	26.5
1960	25,832	43.1	16.9	26.2
1961	26,579	44.1	15.8	28.3
1962	27,257	41.5	17.9	23.6
1963	27,947	43.0	15.5	27.5
1964	28,659	42.3	15.7	26.6
1965	29,389	41.7	14.1	27.6
1966	30,139	41.2	15.9	25.3
1967	30,907	39.2	14.2	25.0
1968	31,693	38.2	16.1	22.1
1969	32,501	36.8	14.4	22.4
1970	33,329	35.6	15.0	20.6
1971	34,076	35.1	13.2	21.9
1972	34,839	34.4	14.5	19.9
1973	35,619	35.7	13.1	22.6
1974	36,417	35.7	12.7	23.0
1975	37,233	37.7	12.2	25.5
1976	38,228	37.6	11.7	25.8
1977[a]	39,860	37.6	12.0	25.8
1978[a]	40,896	n.a.	n.a.	26.0

Age Structure

Age group	Population (thousands)			Percentage distribution	
	1960	1965	1970	1960	1970
0-14	11,013	12,458	14,019	42.6	42.1
15-24	4,915	5,576	6,350	19.0	19.1
25-49	7,175	8,143	9,276	27.8	27.8
50-64	2,014	2,288	2,611	7.8	7.8
65-80	715	924	1,073	2.8	3.2

n.a.   Not available.
a.   Preliminary estimates.
Source: Central Agency for Public Mobilization and
Statistics (CAPMAS).

SA TABLE 2.   POPULATION DENSITY IN CENSUS YEARS,
1882-1976

Census year	Population	Density of total area (per square kilometer)	Inhabited area (square kilometers)	Density of inhabited area (per square kilometer)	Index of density
1882	6,806,381	6.8	34,701	196.1	100.0
1897	9,714,525	9.7	34,716	279.8	142.7
1907	11,287,359	11.3	34,710	325.2	165.8
1917	12,750,918	12.7	34,397	370.7	189.0
1927	14,217,864	14.2	34,708	409.6	208.9
1937	15,932,694	16.0	34,185	466.1	237.7
1947	19,021,840	19.0	34,815	546.4	278.6
1960	26,085,326	26.1	35,580	733.2	373.9
1966	30,083,419	30.0	35,580	845.5	431.1
1976	36,656,180	36.5	35,580	1,030.2	525.3

Note: Population figures exclude Egyptians abroad.
Source: CAPMAS.

SA TABLE 3.   LABOR TRANSFER AMONG GOVERNORATES, 1969

Governorate	Labor force born in the region (thousands)	Total labor force (thousands)	Percentage of labor force born in the region and residing elsewhere	Percentage of resident labor force born elsewhere
Cairo	652	1,196	9.6	50.7
Alexandria	342	490	7.4	36.8
Lower Egypt				
Damietta	132	139	11.3	15.9
Beheira	629	590	8.8	2.7
Charbia	554	505	16.1	8.0
Kafr el-Sheikh	332	340	6.3	8.7
Menufia	525	377	30.6	3.3
Dakahlia	738	668	13.2	4.1
Sharkia	602	566	11.0	5.4
Kalyubia	356	339	14.7	10.3
Upper Egypt				
Giza	500	589	6.4	20.5
Beni Suef	271	250	11.6	4.2
Fayoum	304	290	8.5	3.9
Minya	521	496	7.3	2.8
Assiut	458	393	18.5	5.1
Souhag	574	465	20.7	2.1
Kena	446	380	18.1	3.8
Aswan	158	154	24.7	22.9

Source: CAPMAS, Labor Force Sample Survey, May 1969 (Cairo, 1972).

SA TABLE 4. OCCUPATIONAL STRUCTURE
OF THE LABOR FORCE, 1947-72

(percent)

Occupation	1947	1960	1972
Professional, technical, scientific	2.7	3.7	5.5
Administrative, executive, and managerial	0.9	1.1	1.5
Clerical	2.0	3.7	5.1
Sales	6.8	8.1	6.9
Transport	2.4	3.1 ⎤	
Crafts, production, and processing	13.3	16.2 ⎦	18.4
Farmers and related	60.5	53.1	51.6
Service	9.0	8.9	8.3
Not classified	2.5	2.2	2.7
Total	100.0	100.0	100.0

Sources: CAPMAS, 1947 and 1960 Population Censuses, and Labor Force Sample Survey, 1972.

SA TABLE 5. AVAILABLE RESOURCES AND EXPENDITURES AT CURRENT PRICES AND PERCENTAGE SHARE OF MAIN AGGREGATES IN GDP, 1952–53 TO 1978

Item	1952-53	1955-56	1960-61	1965-66	1966-67	1967-68	1968-69	1969-70
	Millions of Egyptian pounds							
Total resources	883.7	1,066.6	1,477.9	2,572.1	2,581.4	2,669.9	2,767.0	3,151.6
GDP at current factor cost	806.0	965.0	1,363.5	2,138.2	2,194.9	2,202.7	2,339.4	2,663.0
Net indirect taxes	62.4	88.9	95.8	321.3	350.1	356.5	342.2	375.7
GDP at market prices	868.4	1,053.9	1,459.3	2,459.5	2,545.0	2,559.2	2,681.6	3,038.7
Exports	234.0	258.2	280.4	375.7	378.8	258.1	322.6	434.4
Imports	249.3	270.9	299.0	488.3	415.2	368.8	408.0	547.3
Total consumption	765.1	894.5	1,252.3	2,126.0	2,195.8	2,327.6	2,448.8	2,705.8
Public	142.8	182.0	255.9	486.9	499.8	584.1	619.3	713.9
Private	622.3	712.5	996.4	1,639.1	1,696.0	1,743.5	1,829.5	1,991.9
Gross domestic investment	118.6	172.1	225.6	446.1	385.6	342.3	318.2	445.8
Fixed investment	n.a.	n.a.	n.a.	377.3	358.8	292.3	333.2	350.8
Change in stocks	n.a.	n.a.	n.a.	68.8	26.8	50.0	-15.0	95.0
Total expenditure	883.7	1,066.6	1,477.9	2,572.1	2,581.4	2,669.9	2,767.0	3,151.6
	Percentage share of main aggregates in GDP							
Total consumption	88.1	84.9	85.9	86.4	86.2	90.9	91.3	89.0
Public	16.4	17.3	17.6	19.8	19.6	22.8	23.1	23.5
Private	71.7	67.6	68.3	66.6	66.6	68.1	68.2	65.5
Total investment	13.6	16.3	15.5	18.1	15.1	13.4	11.9	14.6
Domestic saving	11.9	15.1	14.1	13.6	13.8	9.1	8.7	11.0
Exports	26.9	24.5	19.2	15.3	14.9	10.1	12.0	14.3
Imports	28.7	25.7	20.5	19.8	16.3	14.4	15.2	18.0
Net indirect taxes	7.2	8.4	6.6	13.0	13.8	13.9	12.8	12.4

SA TABLE 5 (continued)

Item	1970–71	1971–72	1973	1974	1975	1976	1977	1978
	Millions of Egyptian pounds							
Total resources	3,355.7	3,597.3	4,003.4	4,702.0	5,834.7	6,565.0	8,380.0	9,779.0
GDP at current factor cost	2,820.2	3,047.3	3,464.5	4,111.0	4,779.0	5,455.0	6,761.0	7,809.0
Net indirect taxes	382.4	382.2	341.8	86.0	82.0	373.0	813.0	793.0
GDP at market prices	3,202.6	3,429.5	3,806.3	4,197.0	4,861.0	5,828.0	7,551.0	8,602.0
Exports	447.1	457.2	532.2	890.0	947.7	1,143.0	1,447.0	1,475.0
Imports	600.3	625.0	729.3	1,395.0	1,920.4	1,880.0	2,276.0	2,652.0
Total consumption	2,940.2	3,157.3	3,503.0	3,972.0	4,506.0	5,160.0	6,470.0	7,379.0
Public	821.4	926.1	1,074.2	1,101.0	1,213.0	1,361.0	1,697.0	1,812.0
Private	2,118.8	2,231.2	2,428.8	2,871.0	3,293.0	3,799.0	4,773.0	5,561.0
Gross domestic investment	415.5	440.0	500.4	730.0	1,328.7	1,405.0	1,910.0	2,400.0
Fixed investment	355.5	365.0	462.4	640.0	1,228.7	1,325.0	1,805.0	2,183.0
Change in stocks	60.0	75.0	38.0	90.0	100.0	80.0	105.0	217.0
Total expenditure	3,355.7	3,597.3	4,003.4	4,702.0	5,834.7	6,565.0	8,380.0	9,779.0
	Percentage share of main aggregates in GDP							
Total consumption	91.8	92.1	92.0	94.6	92.7	88.5	85.7	85.8
Public	25.6	27.0	28.2	26.2	25.0	23.3	22.5	35.4
Private	66.2	65.1	63.8	68.4	67.7	65.2	63.2	64.6
Total investment	13.0	12.8	13.1	17.4	27.3	24.1	25.3	27.9
Domestic saving	8.2	7.9	8.0	5.4	7.3	11.5	14.3	14.2
Exports	14.0	13.3	14.0	21.2	19.5	19.6	19.2	17.1
Imports	18.7	18.2	19.1	33.2	39.5	32.3	30.1	30.7
Net indirect taxes	11.9	11.1	9.0	2.1	1.7	6.4	10.7	9.2

n.a. Not available.
Source: Ministry of Planning.

SA TABLE 6. AVAILABLE RESOURCES AND EXPENDITURES AT CURRENT MARKET PRICES AND CONSTANT 1965 PRICES, 1950-78

(millions of Egyptian pounds)

Item	1950	1955	1960	1965	1966	1967	1968	1969
				Current market prices				
GNP at market prices	918.0	1,046.5	1,445.8	2,321.9	2,455.5	2,500.3	2,584.8	2,793.4
Net factor income from abroad	-11.9	-9.5	2.6	-18.2	-18.3	-22.6	-29.9	-40.5
GDP at market prices	929.9	1,056.0	1,443.2	2,340.1	2,473.8	2,522.9	2,614.7	2,833.9
Imports of goods and nonfactor services	n.a.	n.a.	290.0	499.5	492.2	448.1	444.5	496.3
Exports of goods and nonfactor services	n.a.	n.a.	281.7	410.4	419.3	369.5	344.9	402.7
Total resources	901.9	1,047.0	1,451.5	2,429.2	2,546.7	2,601.5	2,714.5	2,927.5
Private consumption	656.0	707.4	1,017.5	1,559.8	1,653.5	1,719.0	1,782.5	1,881.7
Public consumption	136.4	185.4	242.0	455.4	477.3	518.6	601.6	678.6
Total consumption	792.4	892.4	1,259.5	2,015.2	2,130.8	2,237.6	2,384.1	2,560.3
Gross domestic investment	109.5	154.2	192.0	414.0	415.9	363.9	330.2	367.2
GNP growth rate (percent)	n.a.	n.a.	4.5a	12.5	5.8	1.8	3.4	8.1
GDP growth rate (percent)	n.a.	n.a.	4.3a	12.6	5.7	2.0	3.6	8.4
				Constant 1965 prices				
GNP at market prices	1,213.9	1,332.5	1,701.4	2,321.9	2,336.2	2,303.1	2,333.9	2,486.8
Net factor income from abroad	-14.8	-11.6	6.4	-18.2	-17.3	-20.8	-26.9	-36.0
GDP at market prices	1,228.7	1,344.1	1,695.0	2,340.1	2,353.5	2,323.9	2,360.8	2,522.8
Imports of goods and nonfactor services	n.a.	n.a.	306.3	499.5	508.7	469.1	466.9	524.5
Exports of goods and nonfactor services	n.a.	n.a.	317.9	410.4	409.8	349.4	306.6	338.8
Total resources	1,228.7	1,344.1	1,683.4	2,429.2	2,452.4	2,443.6	2,521.1	2,708.5
Private consumption	n.a.	n.a.	1,214.5	1,559.8	1,601.6	1,625.1	1,663.7	1,753.4
Public consumption	n.a.	n.a.	258.7	455.4	462.3	489.9	561.5	632.3
Total consumption	n.a.	n.a.	1,473.2	2,015.2	2,063.9	2,115.0	2,224.2	2,385.7
Gross domestic investment	n.a.	n.a.	210.2	414.0	388.5	328.6	295.9	322.8
GNP growth rate (percent)	n.a.	n.a.	3.4a	6.9	0.6	-1.4	1.3	6.7
GDP growth rate (percent)	n.a.	n.a.	3.3a	7.0	0.6	-1.2	1.6	6.9

398

SA TABLE 6 (continued)

Item	1970	1971	1972	1973	1974	1975	1976	1977	1978
				Current market prices					
GNP at market prices	3,006.6	3,180.4	3,380.1	3,625.5	4,085.0	4,713.0	5,674.0	7,758.0	9,089.0
Net factor income from abroad	-51.8	-60.7	-9.8	-19.1	-112.0	-148.0	-154.0	207.0	487.0
GDP at market prices	3,058.4	3,241.1	3,389.9	3,644.6	4,197.0	4,861.0	5,828.0	7,551.0	8,602.0
Imports of goods and nonfactor services	573.5	612.3	648.6	714.7	1,395.0	1,920.4	1,880.0	2,276.0	2,652.0
Exports of goods and nonfactor services	433.8	447.0	452.5	519.2	890.0	947.4	1,143.0	1,447.0	1,475.0
Total resources	3,198.1	3,406.4	3,586.0	3,840.1	4,702.0	5,834.0	6,565.0	8,380.0	9,779.0
Private consumption	2,015.8	2,139.0	2,258.7	2,371.3	2,871.0	3,293.0	3,799.0	4,473.0	5,561.0
Public consumption	755.7	838.7	909.0	1,022.5	1,101.0	1,213.0	1,361.0	1,697.0	1,812.0
Total consumption	2,771.5	2,977.7	3,167.7	3,393.8	3,972.0	4,506.0	5,160.0	6,470.0	7,373.0
Gross domestic investment	426.6	428.7	418.3	446.3	730.0	1,328.7	1,405.0	1,910.0	2,400.0
GNP growth rate (percent)	7.6	5.8	6.3	7.3	12.7	15.4	20.4	36.0	17.0
GDP growth rate (percent)	7.9	6.0	4.6	7.5	15.2	15.8	19.9	29.5	13.9
				Constant 1965 prices					
GNP at market prices	2,637.4	2,741.7	2,838.0	2,909.7	3,104.0	3,367.0	3,670.0	4,055.0	4,542.0
Net factor income from abroad	-45.4	-52.4	-8.4	-15.3	-60.0	-80.0	-100.0	92.0	82.0
GDP at market prices	2,682.8	2,794.1	2,846.3	2,925.0	3,164.0	3,447.0	3,770.0	4,147.0	4,624.0
Imports of goods and nonfactor services	613.9	690.7	703.0	722.4	1,030.0	1,360.0	1,220.0	1,327.0	1,479.0
Exports of goods and nonfactor services	355.5	372.2	379.2	389.7	660.0	670.0	740.0	813.0	906.0
Total resources	2,941.2	3,112.6	3,170.1	3,257.7	3,534.0	4,137.0	4,250.0	4,661.0	5,197.0
Private consumption	1,901.0	2,033.4	2,068.5	2,094.5	2,126.0	2,330.0	2,460.0	2,697.0	3,007.0
Public consumption	701.3	781.7	795.2	805.2	815.0	860.0	880.0	966.0	1,077.0
Total consumption	2,602.3	2,815.1	2,863.7	2,899.7	2,941.0	3,190.0	3,340.0	3,663.0	4,084.0
Gross domestic investment	338.9	297.5	306.4	358.0	593.0	947.0	910.0	998.0	1,112.0
GNP growth rate (percent)	6.1	4.0	3.5	2.5	6.7	8.5	9.0	10.5	12.0
GDP growth rate (percent)	6.3	4.2	1.9	2.8	8.2	8.9	9.4	10.0	11.5

n.a. Not available.
Note: Data for 1973 differ slightly from those in SA table 5 because different sources were used.
a. Average annual growth rate for 1950–60.
Source: The World Bank, World Tables 1976 (Baltimore: Johns Hopkins University Press, 1976); and World Bank estimates.

SA TABLE 7. GROSS DOMESTIC PRODUCT AT CURRENT PRICES AND AS PERCENTAGE OF GDP, WITH ANNUAL GROWTH RATES, BY ECONOMIC ACTIVITY, 1955-56 TO 1978

Economic activity	1955-56	1960-61	1965-66	1966-67	1967-68	1968-69	1969-70
	Millions of Egyptian pounds						
Agriculture	312.0	402.7	608.5	612.3	644.4	688.3	779.9
Industry, petroleum, and mining	170.0	285.6	461.1	477.4	460.3	503.9	542.0
Electricity	n.a.	12.2	24.3	25.2	35.1	35.7	41.8
Construction	27.0	44.2	94.9	94.3	81.7	110.3	123.7
Transport and communication	62.0	102.2	196.1	204.8	115.6	116.3	130.9
Trade and finance	92.0	145.1	181.5	195.9	205.0	215.9	239.0
Housing	94.0	107.0	108.0	111.0	113.1	115.5	118.2
Public utilities	n.a.	6.8	9.2	9.4	9.9	10.8	11.7
Other services	208.0	257.7	454.1	464.6	537.6	542.6	683.8
GDP at factor cost	965.0	1,363.5	2,138.2	2,194.9	2,202.7	2,339.4	2,663.0

Economic activity	1955-56	1965-66	1970-71	1975	1976	1978
	Percentage of GDP at current factor cost					
Agriculture	32.3	28.5	27.5	29.6	28.5	28.7
Industry, petroleum, and mining	17.6	21.6	22.7	20.9	23.8	24.1
Electricity	n.a.	1.1	1.4	1.5	1.4	1.2
Construction	2.9	4.4	4.2	4.8	4.6	4.3
Transport and communication	6.4	9.2	5.1	4.7	6.5	8.4
Trade and finance	9.5	8.5	9.7	11.3	12.5	11.7
Housing	9.7	5.1	4.3	2.7	2.5	1.9
Public utilities	n.a.	0.4	0.5	0.4	0.4	0.3
Other services	21.6	21.2	24.6	24.1	19.8	19.4
All sectors	100.0	100.0	100.0	100.0	100.0	100.0

SA TABLE 7 (continued)

Economic activity	1970–71	1971–72	1973	1974	1975	1976	1977	1978
	Millions of Egyptian pounds							
Agriculture	774.1	854.3	1,062.4	1,280.0	1,406.9	1,553.0	2,038.0	2,241.0
Industry, petroleum, and mining	640.1	663.1	689.5	842.8	1,013.7	1,302.6	1,581.0	1,881.0
Electricity	40.0	47.8	44.8	48.0	71.9	77.5	83.0	93.0
Construction	118.9	127.8	118.1	134.9	230.5	249.0	285.0	336.0
Transport and communication	143.6	147.8	158.6	167.4	224.2	355.3	455.0	657.0
Trade and finance	274.2	294.1	349.3	466.5	538.5	680.0	809.0	910.0
Housing	120.2	121.1	124.0	127.1	130.0	136.3	140.0	149.0
Public utilities	14.1	14.5	16.1	17.4	17.8	21.7	24.0	25.0
Other services	695.0	777.0	901.7	1,026.9	1,145.5	1,079.7	1,326.0	1,517.0
GDP at factor cost	2,820.2	3,047.3	3,464.5	4,111.0	4,779.0	5,455.1	6,741.0	7,809.0
	Annual growth rate (percent)							
Agriculture	-0.7	10.4	24.3	20.5	9.9	10.4	31.2	10.0
Industry, petroleum, and mining	18.1	3.6	4.0	22.2	18.0	28.5	21.4	19.0
Electricity	-4.3	19.5	-6.3	7.1	49.8	7.8	7.1	12.0
Construction	-4.0	7.5	-7.6	14.2	70.9	8.0	14.5	17.9
Transport and communication	9.7	2.9	7.3	5.6	33.9	58.5	28.1	44.4
Trade and finance	14.7	7.3	18.8	33.6	15.4	26.3	19.0	12.5
Housing	1.7	0.8	2.4	2.5	2.3	4.9	2.7	6.4
Public utilities	20.5	2.8	11.0	8.1	2.3	21.9	10.6	4.2
Other services	1.6	11.8	16.1	13.8	11.6	-5.7	22.8	14.4
All sectors	5.9	8.1	13.7	18.6	15.8	14.2	23.6	15.8

n.a. Not available.
Source: Ministry of Planning. For 1955–56 data, see Donald C. Mead, Growth and Structural Change in the Egyptian Economy (Homewood, Ill.: Richard D. Irwin, 1967).

SA TABLE 8. GROSS DOMESTIC PRODUCT AT CONSTANT PRICES AND GROWTH RATES BY ECONOMIC ACTIVITY, 1955-56 TO 1978
(millions of Egyptian pounds)

| Economic activity | 1955-56 | 1960-61 | 1964-65 prices | | | | |
			1965-66	1966-67	1967-68	1968-69	1969-70
Agriculture	414.5	491.4	588.1	576.7	595.2	601.5	640.8
Industry, petroleum, and mining	214.2	314.1	433.8	436.9	416.3	457.2	486.9
Electricity	n.a.	12.6	24.3	25.2	35.4	36.6	44.3
Construction	28.3	44.2	94.9	88.5	76.9	105.0	114.1
Transport and communication	72.9	114.1	194.7	201.3	113.3	115.2	127.8
Trade and finance	133.3	162.0	180.2	190.7	191.5	198.9	209.6
Housing	87.8	100.0	108.0	111.0	112.9	115.3	118.0
Public utilities	n.a.	7.2	9.1	9.4	10.0	10.8	11.7
Other services	254.8	313.6	462.1	462.4	479.2	522.4	559.1
GDP at factor cost	1,205.8	1,559.2	2,095.2	2,102.1	2,048.7	2,162.9	2,312.1

	1956-61	1961-66	1966-71[b]
	Average annual growth rate (percent)		
Agriculture	3.5	3.7	1.6
Industry, petroleum, and mining	8.0	6.6	4.7
Electricity	n.a.	14.0	15.3
Construction	9.3	16.6	3.0
Transport and communication	9.4	11.3	-6.0
Trade and finance	4.0	2.2	3.4
Housing	2.6	1.5	2.1
Public utilities	n.a.	4.8	6.4
Other services	4.0	7.6	5.6
GDP at factor cost	5.3	6.1	2.9

SA TABLE 8 (continued)

Economic activity	1970 prices					1975 prices		
	1970–71	1971–72	1973	1974	1975	1976	1977	1978a
Agriculture	774.1	791.6	815.4	817.5	837.5	1,491.0	1,480.0	1,524.0
Industry, petroleum, and mining	640.1	650.2	647.4	671.8	751.8	1,138.0	1,294.0	1,450.0
Electricity	40.0	47.8	56.0	60.4	69.8	78.0	83.0	94.0
Construction	118.9	121.5	112.3	83.3	128.5	244.0	274.0	296.0
Transport and communication	143.6	152.1	163.5	180.2	241.3	412.0	448.0	537.0
Trade and finance	274.2	282.5	313.6	350.3	386.5	662.0	722.0	795.0
Housing	120.2	121.1	124.0	127.1	130.0	136.0	140.0	149.0
Public utilities	14.1	14.8	16.5	18.7	20.0	22.0	24.0	25.0
Other services	693.8	755.4	826.6	863.3	919.1	1,085.0	1,184.0	1,250.0
GDP at factor cost	2,819.0	2,937.0	3,075.3	3,172.6	3,484.5	5,268.0	5,654.0	6,120.0

Annual growth rate (percent)

Economic activity	1971–72	1973	1974	1975	1976	1977	1978a
Agriculture	2.3	3.0	0.3	2.5	1.5	-0.7	3.0
Industry, petroleum, and mining	1.6	-0.4	3.8	11.9	14.0	13.7	12.1
Electricity	19.5	17.2	7.9	15.6	8.3	6.4	13.3
Construction	2.2	-7.6	-25.8	54.3	13.5	12.3	8.0
Transport and communication	5.9	7.5	10.2	33.9	67.5	8.7	20.0
Trade and finance	30.3	11.0	11.7	10.3	4.1	9.1	10.1
Housing	0.8	2.4	2.5	2.3	4.6	2.9	6.4
Public utilities	5.0	11.5	13.3	7.0	15.8	9.1	4.2
Other services	8.9	9.4	4.4	6.5	9.2	9.1	5.6
GDP at factor cost	4.2	4.7	3.2	9.8	10.2	7.3	8.2

n.a. Not available.
a. Provisional.
b. Average annual growth rate for this period is calculated on the basis of old figures for 1970–71 at 1964–65 prices.
Source: Ministry of Planning.

403

SA TABLE 9. GROSS FIXED INVESTMENT AT CURRENT PRICES AND PERCENTAGE DISTRIBUTION BY ECONOMIC ACTIVITY, 1955–56 TO 1978

Economic activity	1955–56	1960–61	1965–66	1966–67	1967–68	1968–69	1969–70	1970–71
				Millions of Egyptian pounds				
Agriculture	7.0	16.6	30.7	31.3	24.9	25.6	27.0	27.9
Irrigation and drainage	11.7	21.6	51.6	50.9	31.6	42.0	34.3	25.4
Industry, petroleum, and mining	49.8	67.8	100.6	98.4	80.8	101.1	123.1	125.7
Electricity	9.7	5.6	61.1	69.3	62.9	31.9	27.3	23.1
Construction	n.a.	n.a.	6.8	3.9	2.0	2.6	3.4	8.9
Transport and communication	25.1	74.8	53.1	46.1	38.3	69.5	71.4	81.2
Trade and finance	n.a.	n.a.	2.7	2.6	0.7	2.7	3.6	9.5
Housing	54.6	19.1	47.5	42.3	41.7	46.9	36.5	26.5
Public utilities	5.1	7.7	12.4	8.6	4.2	5.8	10.9	16.8
Other services	13.9	19.8	17.3	12.4	10.9	15.4	18.0	16.0
Less expenditure for purchased land	-4.8	-7.4	-6.4	-7.0	-5.6	-10.3	-5.2	-6.0
Gross fixed investment	172.1	225.6	377.3	358.8	292.3	333.2	350.8	355.5
Public	n.a.	n.a.	349.6	329.4	266.0	290.9	312.9	314.5
Private	n.a.	n.a.	27.7	29.4	26.3	42.3	37.9	41.0
				Percentage of gross fixed investment				
Agriculture	4.1	7.4	8.2	8.6	8.5	7.6	7.7	7.9
Irrigation and drainage	6.8	9.6	13.6	14.2	10.8	12.6	9.8	7.1
Industry, petroleum, and mining	28.9	30.1	26.7	27.4	27.6	30.3	35.1	35.4
Electricity	5.6	2.5	16.2	19.3	21.5	9.6	7.8	6.5
Construction	n.a.	n.a.	1.8	1.1	0.7	0.7	1.0	2.5
Transport and communication	14.6	33.1	14.1	12.9	13.1	20.5	20.4	22.9
Trade and finance	n.a.	n.a.	0.7	0.7	0.2	1.0	1.0	2.7
Housing	31.7	8.5	12.6	11.8	14.3	14.1	10.4	7.5
Public utilities	3.0	3.4	3.3	2.4	1.4	1.6	3.1	4.7
Other services	8.1	8.7	4.6	3.5	3.7	4.5	5.1	4.5
Less expenditure for purchased land	-2.8	-3.3	-1.8	-1.9	-1.8	-2.5	-1.4	-1.7
Gross fixed investment	100.0	100.0	100.0	100.0	100.0	100.0	100.0	100.0
Public	n.a.	n.a.	92.6	91.8	91.0	87.3	89.3	88.5
Private	n.a.	n.a.	7.4	8.2	9.0	12.7	10.7	11.5

404

SA TABLE 9 (continued)

Economic activity	1971-72	1972	1973	1974	1975	1976	1977	1978
			Millions of Egyptian pounds					
Agriculture	22.3	28.3	35.2	32.7	42.4	99.4a	139.0a	179.0a
Irrigation and drainage	21.6	22.0	22.4	21.5	41.7	n.a.	n.a.	n.a.
Industry, petroleum, and mining	140.0	119.7	154.3	234.0	394.1	560.8	742.0	759.0
Electricity	21.3	26.3	30.3	30.3	49.3	48.5	103.0	148.0
Construction	5.5	3.9	5.0	10.6	24.8	48.0	46.0	37.0
Transport and communication	79.6	100.1	123.0	187.0	385.5	347.9	442.0	382.0
Trade and finance	11.0	3.0	2.7	5.2	9.8	23.2	30.0	41.0
Housing	29.8	40.0	40.3	51.5	169.3	109.3	176.0	147.0
Public utilities	16.9	13.0	22.8	28.7	39.3	44.6	64.0	86.0
Other services	21.5	26.0	29.2	43.9	71.8	62.6	98.0	182.0
Less expenditure for purchased land	-4.5	-4.0	-3.2	-4.9	...	-19.3	-23.0	-42.0
Gross fixed investment	365.0	378.3	462.4	640.0	1,228.0	1,325.0	1,805.0	2,183.0
Public	325.0	337.3	424.4	612.5	1,051.5	1,089.0	1,439.0	1,823.0
Private	40.0	41.0	38.0	27.5	176.5	236.0	366.0	360.0
			Percentage of gross fixed investment					
Agriculture	6.1	7.5	7.6	5.1	3.5	7.5a	7.7a	8.2a
Irrigation and drainage	5.9	5.8	4.9	3.4	3.4	n.a.	n.a.	n.a.
Industry, petroleum, and mining	38.4	31.6	33.4	36.6	32.1	42.3	41.1	34.8
Electricity	5.8	6.9	6.6	4.7	4.0	3.7	5.7	6.8
Construction	1.5	1.0	1.1	1.7	2.0	3.6	2.5	1.7
Transport and communication	21.8	26.5	26.6	29.2	31.4	26.3	24.5	17.5
Trade and finance	3.0	0.8	0.6	0.8	0.8	1.7	1.7	1.9
Housing	8.1	10.6	8.7	8.0	13.8	8.3	9.8	6.7
Public utilities	4.7	3.4	4.9	4.5	3.2	3.4	3.5	3.9
Other services	5.9	6.9	6.3	6.8	5.8	4.7	5.4	8.3
Less expenditure for purchased land	-1.2	-1.1	-0.7	-0.8	...	-1.5	-1.9	-1.9
Gross fixed investment	100.0	100.0	100.0	100.0	100.0	100.0	100.0	100.0
Public	89.0	89.2	91.9	95.7	85.6	82.2	79.7	83.5
Private	11.0	10.8	8.1	4.3	14.4	17.8	20.3	16.5

n.a. Not available.
... Negligible.
a. Includes irrigation and drainage.
Source: Ministry of Planning and CAPMAS.

SA TABLE 10.   SAVING AND INVESTMENT AT CURRENT PRICES, 1950–78

Item	1950	1955	1960	1965	1970	1971
			Millions of Egyptian pounds			
GDP at market prices	929.9	1,056.0	1,443.2	2,340.1	3,058.4	3,241.1
Net factor income	-11.9	-9.5	2.6	-18.2	-51.8	-60.7
GNP at market prices	918.0	1,046.5	1,445.8	2,231.9	3,006.6	3,180.4
Consumption	792.4	892.4	1,259.5	2,015.2	2,771.5	2,977.7
Resource gap[a]	-28.0	-9.4	8.3	89.1	139.7	165.3
Gross domestic saving	137.5	163.6	183.7	324.9	286.9	263.4
Gross investment	109.5	154.2	192.0	414.0	426.6	428.7
Current account deficit[b]	-16.1	0.1	5.7	107.3	191.5	226.0
Gross national saving	125.6	154.1	186.3	306.7	235.1	202.7
			Percentage of GDP			
Gross investment	11.8	14.6	13.3	17.7	14.0	13.2
Resource gap	-3.0	-0.9	0.6	3.8	4.6	5.1
Gross domestic saving	14.8	15.5	12.7	13.9	9.4	8.1
			Percentage of GNP			
Gross investment	11.9	14.7	13.3	17.8	14.2	13.5
Current account deficit	-1.8	0.0	0.4	4.6	6.4	7.1
Gross national saving	13.7	14.7	12.9	13.2	7.8	6.4

a. The resource gap is defined as the difference between gross investment and domestic saving; it is also identical to the difference between imports and exports of goods and nonfactor services. Hence a negative sign indicates a savings (or export) surplus.

b. The current account deficit is defined as the difference between gross investment and national saving; it is also identical to the difference between imports and exports of goods and all services. A negative sign indicates a savings (or export) surplus.

Source: Calculated from SA table 6.

1972	1973	1974	1975	1976	1977	1978
			Millions of Egyptian pounds			
3,389.9	3,644.6	4,197.0	4,861.0	5,828.0	7,551.0	8,602.0
-9.8	-19.1	-112.0	-148.0	-154.0	207.0	487.0
3,380.1	3,625.5	4,085.0	4,713.0	5,674.0	7,758.0	9,089.0
3,167.7	3,393.8	3,972.0	4,506.0	5,160.0	6,470.0	7,379.0
196.1	195.5	505.0	973.7	737.0	829.0	1,177.0
222.2	250.8	225.0	355.0	668.0	1,081.0	1,223.0
418.3	446.3	730.0	1,328.7	1,405.0	1,910.0	2,400.0
205.9	214.6	617.0	1,121.7	891.0	-622.0	-690.0
212.4	231.7	113.0	207.0	514.0	1,288.0	1,710.0
			Percentage of GDP			
12.4	12.3	17.4	27.3	24.1	25.2	27.9
5.8	5.4	12.0	20.0	12.6	10.9	13.6
6.6	6.9	5.4	7.3	11.5	14.3	14.2
			Percentage of GNP			
12.4	12.3	17.9	28.2	24.8	24.6	26.4
6.1	5.9	15.1	23.8	15.7	8.0	7.5
6.3	6.4	2.8	4.4	9.1	16.6	18.8

SA TABLE 11. SUMMARY OF FISCAL OPERATIONS, 1962-63 TO 1978

(millions of Egyptian pounds)

Item	1962-63	1963-64	1964-65	1965-66	1966-67	1967-68
Total revenue	458	527	598	660	753[a]	643
Central government revenue	359	440	514	560	666	510
Tax revenue	214	272	317	342	423	414
Transferred profits[b]	68	71	84	86	69	26
Other nontax revenue	77	97	113	132	174	70
Local government revenue	31	44	44	50	46	55
Investment self-financing[c]	68	43	40	50	41	78
Total expenditure[d]	710	896	906	1,022	971	894[e]
Current expenditure	437	527	612	722	700	626
Central and local government	437	527	612	722	700	611
Public authority deficits	n.a.	n.a.	n.a.	n.a.	n.a.	14
Subsidies	...	...	...	...	...	1
Investment expenditure[f]	273	369	294	300	271	268
Emergency fund deficit (-)[g]	n.a.	n.a.	n.a.	n.a.	n.a.	n.a.
Overall deficit (-)	-252	-369	-308	-362	-218	-251
Financing (net)						
External borrowing (net)	28	83	81	67	57	24
Domestic borrowing (net)	226	287	227	295	161	227
Banking system[h]	70	150	72	116	75	50
Social insurance and pension funds	60	70	100	109	123	145
Savings certificates	...	...	6	18	25	14
Postal savings	8	11	9	5	1	1
Other[i]	88	56	40	47	-63	17

n.a. Not available.
... Negligible.
a. Split between transferred profits and investment self-financing estimated on the previous year's allocation.
b. Mandatory transfers under the legal requirement that 65 percent of net profits after tax and depreciation be transferred to the Treasury.
c. Investment resources generated by the public authorities and public sector companies.
d. Excludes Emergency Fund deficit.
e. Split between public authority deficits and subsidies based on 1970-71 allocation.

1968-69	1969-70	1970-71	1972	1973	1974	1975	1976	1977	1978
<u>675</u>	<u>750</u>	<u>869</u>	<u>903</u>	<u>1,018</u>	<u>1,184</u>	<u>1,524</u>	<u>2,015</u>	<u>2,755</u>	<u>3,306</u>
565	658	726	745	830	968	1,222	1,595	2,373	2,692
451	524	564	584	616	683	948	1,251	1,876	2,034
32	40	101	81	137	188	154	243	384	539
82	94	61	80	78	97	120	101	113	119
48	56	56	58	60	66	92	89	114	141
62	36	87	100	127	150	210	331	268	473
<u>880[e]</u>	<u>956</u>	<u>1,063</u>	<u>1,218</u>	<u>1,404</u>	<u>1,961</u>	<u>2,628</u>	<u>2,977</u>	<u>3,769</u>	<u>5,013</u>
568	604	705	804	953	1,379	1,765	1,997	2,220	2,702
562	604	661	731	765	886	1,050	1,444	1,431	1,806
6	...	41	62	188	83	93	119	139	185
...	...	3	11	...	410	622	434	650	710
312	352	358	414	451	582	863	980	1,549	2,311
n.a.	n.a.	n.a.	n.a.	-148	-36	-284	-303	-256	-370
-205	-206	-194	-315	-534	-813	-1,388	-1,265	-1,270	-2,077
-13	-15	...	18	51	119	210	488	464	705
218	221	193	297	483	694	1,178	777	860	1,372
48	80	79	77	185	219	731	437	471	827
151	159	188	214	224	245	253	295	353	381
14	22	23	32	38	43	50	54	76	135
5	5	3	9	10	18	17	19	16	25
...	-45	-100	-35	26	169	127	-28	-76	4

f. Consolidated public sector investment adjusted for known arrears in 1975 and 1976.

g. Adjusted for Emergency Fund domestic revenue, which is consolidated with other central government revenue.

h. From monetary accounts. Counterpart funds, which previously had been classified as government deposits, have been reclassified and excluded from these deposits. The figure for 1977 is adjusted for differences in the valuation of development bonds between the fiscal and monetary accounts.

i. Reflects primarily the discrepancy between domestic bank financing in the fiscal and monetary accounts.

Sources: Ministry of Finance and World Bank estimates.

SA TABLE 12. GOVERNMENT REVENUE, 1962-63 TO 1978
(millions of Egyptian pounds)

Item	1962–63	1963–64	1964–65	1965–66	1966–67	1967–68	1968–69	1969–70
Central government								
Tax revenue	213.8	271.9	317.3	341.8	423.0	414.0	451.3	523.9
Net income and profits	34.8	47.3	70.7	88.9	114.2	90.1	110.9	130.4
Business profits	22.4	32.8	53.8	70.5	93.0	68.5	87.9	104.3
Personal income	12.4	14.5	16.9	18.4	21.2	21.6	23.0	26.1
Property	7.9	11.2	8.7	9.2	12.2	11.7	16.0	18.8
Estate duties	3.2	3.6	2.0	2.1	2.0	2.2	2.2	2.7
Immovable property	4.7	7.6	6.7	7.1	10.2	9.5	13.8	16.1
Goods and services[a]	23.2	49.6	48.5	45.9	115.0	127.5	145.1	161.4
Excise duties	—	—	—	—	n.a.	n.a.	n.a.	42.7
Price differentials								118.7
International trade	121.1	144.3	164.5	172.2	154.2	144.3	134.0	173.9
Stamp duties	8.5	11.0	14.3	17.0	15.3	24.3	28.0	31.7
Other taxes	18.3	8.5	10.6	8.6	12.1	16.1	17.3	7.7
Nontax revenue	145.5	168.0	197.0	217.9	242.6	96.0	114.2	134.1
Fees	33.5	43.4	36.9	54.1	67.7	17.4	16.8	22.1
Miscellaneous	44.0	53.6	76.1	77.8	105.9	52.6	65.4	72.0
Transferred profits	68.0	71.0	84.0	86.0	69.0	26.0	32.0	40.0
Total central government	359.3	439.9	514.3	559.7	665.6	510.0	565.5	658.0
Local governments	30.5	44.0	44.1	49.5	45.8	54.7	48.1	56.0
Total current revenue	389.8	483.9	558.4	609.2	711.4	564.7	613.6	714.0

SA TABLE 12 (continued)

Item	1970–71	1972	1973	1974	1975	1976	1977	1978
Central government								
Tax revenue	564.4	583.6	616.0	682.9	948.0	1,251.5	1,876.3	2,034.1
Net income and profits	143.5	146.1	160.8	176.4	226.3	325.3	442.1	590.3
Business profits	115.3	120.2	128.5	142.5	195.2	277.6	387.2	538.4
Personal income	28.2	25.9	32.3	32.9	31.1	47.7	54.9	51.9
Property	19.2	23.8	16.7	21.3	29.6	19.2	17.9	22.5
Estate duties	2.4	2.1	2.5	2.7	2.6	3.6	3.8	4.1
Immovable property	16.8	21.7	14.2	18.6	27.0	15.6	14.1	18.4
Goods and services[a]	166.0	181.2	190.7	195.3	229.0	283.6	339.7	360.3
Excise duties	62.7	68.2	68.0	78.3	82.0	98.1	143.9	155.2
Price differentials	103.3	113.0	122.7	117.0	147.0	185.5	195.8	205.1
International trade	196.3	193.7	205.1	231.4	399.9	537.8	979.4	919.8
Stamp duties	34.3	33.6	39.0	55.9	60.6	82.2	89.8	126.2
Other taxes	5.1	5.1	3.7	2.6	2.6	3.4	7.4	15.0
Nontax revenue	161.8	161.0	214.1	285.2	274.4	343.9	497.1	658.3
Fees	17.5	16.5	19.4	19.7	26.2	37.6	46.8	53.8
Miscellaneous	43.3	63.5	58.2	77.5	93.8	63.4	65.9	65.2
Transferred profits	101.0	81.0	136.5	188.0	154.4	242.9	384.4	539.3
Total central government	726.2	744.6	830.1	968.1	1,222.4	1,595.4	2,373.4	2,692.4
Local governments	55.7	58.4	60.0	65.5	91.8	88.9	114.0	141.2
Total current revenue	781.9	803.0	890.1	1,033.6	1,314.2	1,684.3	2,487.4	2,833.6

— Not applicable.
n.a. Not available.
a. As of 1966–67 it includes revenue from price differentials, a specific levy on certain consumer durables. A breakdown is available only after 1969–70.
Source: Ministry of Finance.

411

SA TABLE 13. MONETARY SURVEY, 1974–78

(millions of Egyptian pounds)

Item	1974	1975	1976	1977	September 1978	December 1978 Old basis[a]	December 1978 New basis[b]
Foreign assets (net)	-184.4	-973.7	-922.0	-644.8	-466.5	-694.3	-2,188.2
Foreign assets	608.8	744.7	1,020.5	1,677.5	1,887.7	2,001.1	2,314.3
Foreign liabilities	-749.7	-1,685.3	-1,862.4	-2,206.4	-2,208.9	2,553.2	-4,235.7
IMF position (net)	-43.5	-33.1	-80.1	-115.9	-145.3	-142.2	-266.8
Claims on public sector	2,337.8	3,527.4	4,123.4	4,774.7	5,457.4	6,035.1	7,855.1
Central and local government	1,707.1	2,436.1	2,896.2	3,382.3	3,975.2	4,284.1	5,954.5
Counterpart of Treasury coin and notes	15.5	28.4	28.4	30.3	30.3	29.9	29.9
Public authorities	196.8	445.9	342.7	297.1	420.6	544.8	692.7
Public sector companies	433.9	645.4	884.5	1,095.3	1,061.6	1,206.2	1,207.9
Cotton financing	109.2	118.3	181.4	204.0	96.9	267.2	267.2
Claims on private sector	148.5	230.0	251.2	433.8	508.3	571.7	576.4
Claims on cooperatives	4.7	5.5	10.9	7.6	6.2	5.6	5.6
Claims on specialized banks	201.1	211.9	179.4	205.7	297.9	232.3	237.8
Agricultural Credit Bank	177.3	188.7	154.9	156.3	225.6	148.4	153.9
Unclassified assets	110.7	150.1	246.9	327.9	412.3	378.3	418.1
Assets = Liabilities	2,618.4	3,151.2	3,889.9	5,104.9	6,215.6	6,528.7	6,904.8

Money and quasi money	1,514.6	1,883.1	2,416.7	3,184.8	3,778.0	4,091.0	4,108.3
Currency in circulation	947.6	1,155.9	1,387.8	1,749.5	2,019.9	2,183.3	2,183.3
Demand deposits	305.4	406.3	546.4	782.4	837.1	896.4	909.7
Private sector	296.2	393.8	527.7	760.9	810.0	862.8	876.1
Cooperatives	6.8	11.5	12.2	19.8	24.7	26.1	26.1
Specialized banks	2.4	1.0	6.5	1.7	2.4	7.5	7.5
Time and savings deposits	261.6	320.9	482.5	652.9	921.0	1,011.3	1,015.3
Private sector	255.5	313.0	471.7	615.7	884.1	975.1	978.1
Cooperatives	3.4	7.6	10.4	10.1	17.2	20.5	20.5
Specialized banks	2.7	0.3	0.4	27.1	19.7	15.7	16.7
Public sector deposits	704.4	795.0	931.4	1,330.3	1,525.0	1,655.6	1,793.0
Central and local government	118.1	116.6	139.8	154.6	186.4	229.2	263.7
Public authorities	100.5	131.7	147.3	257.7	341.7	391.4	432.5
Public sector companies	485.8	546.7	644.3	918.0	996.9	1,035.0	1,096.8
Counterpart funds	141.7	170.7	155.6	141.6	129.7	125.2	125.2
Capital accounts	172.0	191.6	231.8	274.5	354.4	375.6	485.4
Unclassified liabilities	150.2	197.3	265.6	349.9	538.4	415.0	470.7
Interbank items (net)c	-64.5	-86.5	-111.3	-176.2	-109.9	-133.7	-77.8

a. Foreign currency assets and liabilities valued at official and parallel exchange rates.
b. Foreign currency assets and liabilities valued at unified (established) exchange rate.
c. Commercial banks' deposits with Central Bank (Central Bank balance sheet) plus commercial banks' borrowing from Central Bank (commercial banks' balance sheet) minus commercial banks' deposits with Central Bank (commercial banks' balance sheet) minus Central Bank's claims on commercial banks (Central Bank balance sheet).
<u>Sources:</u> Central Bank of Egypt and International Monetary Fund (IMF).

SA TABLE 14. AREA OF MAIN CROPS BY SEASON, 1950–54 TO 1975–78

(thousands of feddans)

Season and crop	1950– 54	1955– 59	1960– 64	1965– 69	1970– 74	1975– 78
Winter						
Wheat	1,571	1,501	1,387	1,268	1,362	1,344
Barley	122	135	128	110	81	103
Broadbeans	328	353	365	349	283	259
Lentils	74	80	77	65	64	52
Onions	26	36	44	45	32	28
Vegetables	70	104	149	170	184	214
Berseem	2,184	2,362	2,444	2,630	2,801	2,801
Orchards	94	114	147	208	255	313
Sugarcane	96	111	122	145	197	239
Other	103	140	165	146	147	188
Subtotal	4,668	4,936	5,028	5,136	5,406	5,541
Summer						
Rice	505	641	791	1,028	1,095	1,051
Maize	1,746	1,850	1,727	1,510	1,593	1,846
Millets	438	451	469	507	493	451
Cotton	1,765	1,791	1,751	1,694	1,551	1,302
Vegetables	189	291	398	498	573	699
Sugarcane	96	111	122	145	197	239
Orchards	94	114	147	208	255	313
Other	101	117	125	164	189	233
Subtotal	4,934	5,366	5,530	5,754	5,946	6,134
Total cropped area	9,602	10,302	10,558	10,890	11,352	11,675

Source: Ministry of Agriculture.

SA TABLE 15.   PERCENTAGE DISTRIBUTION OF LAND OWNERSHIP IN EGYPT, 1900–65

Size of plot (feddans)	1900			1952 (pre–Revolution)			1965		
	Owners (percent)	Area (percent)	Average plot (feddans)	Owners (percent)	Area (percent)	Average plot (feddans)	Owners (percent)	Area (percent)	Average plot (feddans)
Less than 5	83.3	21.8	1.5	94.3	35.4	0.8	94.5	57.1	1.2
5–10	8.7	10.9	7.0	2.8	8.8	6.6	2.4	9.5	7.9
10–20	4.4	10.8	13.8	1.7	10.7	13.6	1.9	8.2	8.6
20–50	2.2	12.2	32.0	0.8	10.9	29.1	0.9	12.6	28.1
More than 50	0.9	43.8	187.0	0.4	34.1	174.6	0.3	12.6	84.5
Total number (thousands)	914	5,114		2,802	5,982		3,211	6,462	
Average size of total (feddans)			5.6			2.1			2.0

Source: CAPMAS; see also Charles Issawi, Egyptian Revolution (London: Oxford University Press, 1963), p. 156.

SA TABLE 16. PRODUCTION OF MAJOR CROPS, 1972-73 TO 1978-79

Crop	Agricultural year ending October 31						
	1972-73	1973-74	1974-75	1975-76	1976-77	1977-78	1978-79[a]
Winter crops							
Wheat							
Production	1,837	1,884	2,033	1,960	1,697	1,933	1,856
Area planted	1,248	1,370	1,394	1,396	1,207	1,381	1,391
Yield	1.47	1.38	1.46	1.40	1.41	1.40	1.33
Horsebeans[b]							
Production	273	234	234	254	270	231	236
Area planted	270	244	246	260	292	239	250
Yield	1.01	0.96	0.95	0.98	0.92	0.97	0.94
Onions[c]							
Production	230	359	229	240	263	223	157
Area planted	27	39	27	31	37	29	23
Yield	8.5	9.2	8.5	7.8	7.1	7.7	6.7
Berseem (clover)							
Area planted	2,874	2,797	2,812	2,787	2,854	2,782	2,777
Summer and autumn crops							
Cotton							
Production (lint)	490	441	382	396	399	435	n.a.
Area planted	1,600	1,453	1,346	1,248	1,423	1,187	n.a.
Yield	0.306	0.304	0.284	0.317	0.280	0.366	n.a.
Rice (paddy)							
Production	2,274	2,242	2,423	2,300	2,272	2,351	2,511
Area planted	997	1,053	1,053	1,078	1,040	1,031	1,040
Yield	2.28	2.13	2.30	2.13	2.19	2.28	2.41
Maize							
Production	2,507	2,640	2,781	3,047	2,724	3,117	2,938
Area planted	1,654	1,755	1,830	1,891	1,765	1,878	1,885
Yield	1.52	1.51	1.52	1.61	1.54	1.66	1.56
Millet (sorghum)							
Production	853	824	775	759	648	681	635
Area planted	487	499	489	475	408	434	407
Yield	1.75	1.65	1.58	1.60	1.59	1.57	1.56
Sugarcane							
Production	7,349	7,018	7,902	8,446	8,721	8,296	n.a.
Area planted	198	208	218	242	250	248	n.a.
Yield	37.1	33.7	36.2	34.9	34.9	33.5	n.a.
Groundnuts							
Production	26	25	28	28	30	26	27
Area planted	29	29	32	32	36	31	31
Yield	0.90	0.86	0.88	0.88	0.83	0.83	0.87

SA TABLE 16 (continued)

Crop	Agricultural year ending October 31						
	1972–73	1973–74	1974–75	1975–76	1976–77	1977–78	1978–79
Fruits and vegetables							
Citrus fruits							
Production	923	963	1,013	889	797	990	1,216
Area planted	n.a.	155	169	178	182	186	190
Dates							
Production	380	396	415	417	461	377	406
Area planted	n.a.	34	33	35	35	33	n.a.
Other fruits							
Production	515	612	640	705	644	718	754
Area planted	n.a.	118	123	135	138	144	150
Potatoes							
Production	796	709	720	893	1,010	772	1,019
Area planted	106	95	98	128	152	128	142
Yield	7.5	7.5	7.3	7.0	6.6	6.1	7.2
Other vegetables							
Production	4,982	5,297	5,800	6,029	5,791	6,357	6,917
Area planted	707	725	797	801	778	822	887

n.a. Not available.

Note: Production in thousands of metric tons; area planted in thousands of feddans; yield in metric tons per feddan.

a. Preliminary estimates.

b. Excludes crops consumed green as vegetables and forage.

c. Winter (export) crop only.

Source: Ministry of Agriculture.

SA TABLE 17. AREA OF MAJOR CROPS, 1960-78
(thousands of feddans)

Crop	1960	1961	1962	1963	1964	1965	1966	1967	1968	1969
Cotton	1,873	1,986	1,657	1,627	1,611	1,900	1,859	1,626	1,464	1,622
Maize	1,821	1,603	1,832	1,721	1,660	1,450	1,575	1,485	1,554	1,484
Sorghum	453	457	455	484	495	501	518	523	533	474
Beans	362	328	369	360	408	402	398	300	306	338
Rice	706	537	830	959	962	848	844	1,075	1,204	1,191
Wheat	1,456	1,384	1,455	1,345	1,295	1,144	1,291	1,245	1,413	1,246
Lentils	85	63	79	78	79	89	75	66	51	46
Fenugreek	62	40	59	59	56	51	41	32	28	36
Lupins	20	14	18	18	18	16	11	11	11	11
Chick-peas	15	7	10	12	14	12	8	10	10	6
Barley	148	121	131	121	121	125	98	107	117	103
Onions a	40	36	42	52	48	46	54	37	35	52
Vegetables	496	507	535	585	608	623	652	641	708	714
Berseem	2,413	2,448	2,442	2,435	2,480	2,493	2,532	2,716	2,679	2,726
Sugarcane	111	112	121	133	134	129	133	137	156	170
Fruit	131	138	145	152	167	178	195	207	225	232
Total netb	10,174	9,772	10,163	10,087	10,135	10,006	10,259	10,191	10,470	10,430

SA TABLE 17 (continued)

Crop	1970	1971	1972	1973	1974	1975	1976	1977	1978
Cotton	1,627	1,525	1,552	1,600	1,453	1,346	1,248	1,423	1,189
Maize	1,504	1,522	1,531	1,654	1,755	1,829	1,891	1,747	1,899
Sorghum	500	494	483	487	499	489	474	408	433
Beans	302	261	336	270	244	246	298	325	272
Rice	1,142	1,137	1,146	997	1,053	1,048	1,074	1,037	1,025
Wheat	1,304	1,349	1,239	1,248	1,370	1,394	1,396	1,207	1,381
Lentils	47	65	67	74	66	58	64	48	35
Fenugreek	31	26	24	26	31	32	33	24	26
Lupins	10	9	10	9	6	8	n.a.	n.a.	n.a.
Chick-peas	6	10	10	8	7	6	n.a.	n.a.	n.a.
Barley	83	70	91	84	77	100	104	95	114
Onions[a]	33	37	32	27	29	24	28	31	27
Vegetables	713	719	749	813	820	862	917	911	937
Berseem	2,748	2,770	2,819	2,874	2,797	2,812	2,756	2,815	2,782
Sugarcane	186	193	202	198	208	217	242	250	249
Fruit	244	249	(253)	(258)	273	285	313	321	331
Total net[b]	10,485	10,419	10,544	10,627	10,688	10,756	10,838	10,642	10,700

n.a. Not available.
a. Winter onion only, probably 50 percent of total.
b. Simple sum of indicated area.
Source: Ministry of Agriculture.

419

SA TABLE 18. PRODUCTION OF MAJOR CROPS AND LIVESTOCK PRODUCTS, 1960-78
(thousand metric tons)

Crop	1960	1961	1962	1963	1964	1965	1966	1967	1968	1969
Cotton, unginned	1,380	1,004	1,335	1,313	1,436	1,501	1,289	1,208	1,210	1,480
Maize	1,691	1,617	2,004	1,867	1,934	2,141	2,376	2,163	2,297	2,366
Sorghum	603	631	659	629	740	806	859	881	906	813
Beans	290	161	328	263	366	344	381	188	283	297
Rice (paddy)	1,486	1,142	2,039	2,219	2,036	1,788	1,679	2,279	2,586	2,557
Wheat	1,499	1,436	1,593	1,493	1,500	1,272	1,465	1,291	1,518	1,269
Lentils	50	34	56	47	52	61	44	34	35	24
Fenugreek	43	23	44	42	42	37	30	21	19	22
Lupins	13	9	12	13	13	12	7	7	7	6
Chick-peas	11	5	7	8	10	9	6	6	7	4
Barley	155	133	146	134	141	130	102	100	121	105
Onions	504	470	558	661	647	669	703	588	445	567
Vegetables	3,424	3,569	3,917	4,320	4,378	4,636	4,928	4,505	5,141	5,214
Sugarcane	4,555	4,195	4,819	5,164	4,898	4,747	5,200	5,269	6,083	6,878
Citrus fruit	315	240	402	441	475	485	631	699	623	785
Dates	424	479	401	440	327	386	317	319	264	355
Other fruit	320	304	351	335	342	350	400	370	378	382
Livestock products										
Meat	238	241	245	249	253	257	262	267	271	279
Milk	1,360	1,381	1,423	1,423	1,445	1,467	1,495	1,518	1,542	1,564
Poultry	78	72	75	78	80	86	90	95	90	94
Eggs	32	32	33	36	40	40	45	50	53	47
Livestock (thousand head)										
Cows	1,867						1,608			
Buffaloes	1,781						1,855			
Sheep	2,220						1,855			
Goats	1,583						787			
Camels	184						175			
Pigs	22						11			
Chickens	21,841						23,013			
Donkeys	1,010						n.a.			

SA TABLE 18 (continued)

Crop	1970	1971	1972	1973	1974	1975	1976	1977	1978
Cotton, unginned	1,404	1,418	1,422	1,368	1,204	1,061	1,084	1,260	1,381
Maize	2,393	2,342	2,417	2,507	2,640	2,781	3,047	2,724	3,117
Sorghum	874	854	831	853	824	775	759	648	681
Beans	277	256	361	273	234	234	254	270	231
Rice (paddy)	2,605	2,534	2,507	2,274	2,247	2,423	2,300	2,272	2,351
Wheat	1,516	1,729	1,616	1,837	1,884	2,033	1,960	1,697	1,933
Lentils	33	50	54	62	51	39	38	24	16
Fenugreek	22	19	17	20	23	24	n.a.	n.a.	n.a.
Lupins	6	6	7	6	4	5	n.a.	n.a.	n.a.
Chick-peas	5	7	7	6	5	4	n.a.	n.a.	n.a.
Barley	83	76	107	96	89	118	123	111	132
Onions	437	582	487	528	730	572	652	723	599
Vegetables	5,159	5,232	5,415	5,688	6,006	6,520	6,922	6,750	7,746
Sugarcane	6,945	7,498	7,713	7,349	7,018	7,902	8,446	8,379	8,296
Citrus rruit	706	883	825	923	963	1,013	889	797	990
Dates	294	340	396	380	396	415	417	461	377
Other fruit	384	441	522	515	612	640	705	644	718
Livestock products									
Meat	284	288	295	299	302	n.a.	313	321	324
Milk	1,589	1,614	1,640	1,666	1,692	n.a.	1,750	1,780	1,801
Poultry	90	98	102	102	112	n.a.	129	121	115
Eggs	50	53	54	58	56	n.a.	76	n.a.	n.a.
Livestock (thousand head)									
Cows	2,115			2,127			2,392		2,341
Buffaloes	2,009			2,135			2,236		2,299
Sheep	2,066			1,994			1,878		2,100
Goats	1,155			1,264			1,372		995
Camels	127			113			113		125
Pigs	15			14			16		22
Chickens	24,236			35,000			n.a.		n.a.
Donkeys	1,362			1,400			n.a.		1,635

n.a. Not available.
Source: Ministry of Agriculture.

421

422   Statistical Appendix

SA TABLE 19. AREA, PRODUCTION, AND AVERAGE YIELD OF THE PRINCIPAL CROPS, 1950-78

Year	Wheat			Maize		
	Area harvested[a]	Production[b]	Average yield per feddan[c]	Area harvested[a]	Production[b]	Average yield per feddan[c]
1950	1,371	1,017	742	1,451	1,306	900
1951	1,496	1,209	808	1,655	1,421	858
1952	1,402	1,089	777	1,679	1,506	882
1953	1,791	1,547	865	2,017	1,853	920
1954	1,795	1,729	961	1,905	1,568	823
1955	1,524	1,451	953	1,833	1,714	932
1956	1,571	1,547	982	1,836	1,652	899
1957	1,514	1,467	978	1,769	1,498	848
1958	1,426	1,412	991	1,955	1,758	899
1959	1,476	1,443	974	1,860	1,500	806
1960	1,456	1,499	1,029	1,821	1,691	929
1961	1,384	1,436	1,037	1,603	1,617	1,009
1962	1,455	1,593	1,095	1,832	2,004	1,094
1963	1,345	1,493	1,110	1,721	1,867	1,085
1964	1,295	1,500	1,158	1,660	1,934	1,165
1965	1,144	1,272	1,111	1,450	2,141	1,476
1966	1,291	1,465	1,135	1,575	2,376	1,509
1967	1,245	1,291	1,036	1,485	2,163	1,456
1968	1,413	1,518	1,074	1,554	2,297	1,478
1969	1,246	1,269	1,018	1,484	2,366	1,594
1970	1,304	1,516	1,163	1,504	2,393	1,592
1971	1,349	1,729	1,282	1,522	2,342	1,539
1972	1,239	1,616	1,304	1,531	2,417	1,579
1973	1,248	1,837	1,472	1,654	2,507	1,515
1974	1,370	1,884	1,375	1,755	2,640	1,505
1975	1,394	2,033	1,459	1,830	2,781	1,520
1976	1,396	1,960	1,404	1,801	3,047	1,611
1977	1,201	1,697	1,406	1,747	2,724	1,559
1978	1,381	1,533	1,400	1,899	3,117	1,641

a. Area in thousands of feddans.
b. Production in thousands of metric tons.
c. Average yield in kilograms per feddan.
Source: Ministry of Agriculture.

Year	Rice Area harvested[a]	Rice Produc- tion[b]	Rice Average yield per feddan[c]	Cotton Area harvested[a]	Cotton Produc- tion[b]	Cotton Average yield per feddan[c]
1950	700	1,242	1,776	1,974	1,226	620
1951	488	620	1,275	1,979	1,165	589
1952	374	517	1,381	1,966	1,364	693
1953	424	652	1,541	1,323	920	695
1954	610	1,118	1,835	1,578	1,021	647
1955	600	1,309	2,179	1,816	983	541
1956	690	1,573	2,280	1,652	964	583
1957	731	1,709	2,335	1,819	1,182	649
1958	519	1,082	2,083	1,904	1,298	681
1959	729	1,535	2,108	1,759	1,312	745
1960	706	1,486	2,105	1,873	1,380	737
1961	537	1,142	2,126	1,986	1,004	506
1962	830	2,039	2,456	1,657	1,335	806
1963	959	2,219	2,313	1,627	1,313	806
1964	962	2,036	2,117	1,611	1,436	891
1965	848	1,788	2,109	1,900	1,501	791
1966	844	1,679	1,989	1,859	1,289	693
1967	1,075	2,279	2,121	1,626	1,208	743
1968	1,204	2,586	2,147	1,464	1,210	827
1969	1,191	2,557	2,146	1,622	1,480	912
1970	1,142	2,605	2,280	1,627	1,404	863
1971	1,137	2,534	2,228	1,525	1,418	929
1972	1,146	2,507	2,189	1,552	1,422	917
1973	997	2,274	2,281	1,600	1,368	855
1974	1,053	2,247	2,129	1,453	1,204	828
1975	1,048	2,423	2,312	1,346	1,061	788
1976	1,074	2,300	2,142	1,248	1,084	844
1977	1,037	2,272	2,101	1,423	1,260	885
1978	1,025	2,351	2,294	1,189	1,381	1,161

SA TABLE 20. PRICES RECEIVED
BY FARMERS FOR WHEAT, MAIZE,
AND COTTON, 1950-78
(Egyptian pounds per metric ton)

Year	Wheat	Maize	Rice	Cotton
1950	21.3	16.4	17.4	95.5
1951	21.3	16.4	16.0	95.5
1952	21.3	16.1	15.8	95.5
1953	30.3	16.9	12.2	95.5
1954	30.2	17.7	16.9	95.5
1955	26.6	21.5	17.9	95.5
1956	26.6	26.0	17.9	95.5
1957	26.6	22.0	17.9	95.5
1958	26.6	22.0	17.9	95.5
1959	26.6	23.3	18.0	95.5
1960	28.6	27.8	18.0	95.5
1961	28.3	26.2	18.0	92.5
1962	28.5	25.4	18.0	94.2
1963	28.7	22.9	18.0	96.7
1964	27.3	26.8	19.1	106.9
1965	30.2	27.9	21.3	102.3
1966	32.8	26.7	26.8	101.9
1967	37.3	31.9	30.1	108.8
1968	32.2	36.8	31.5	110.0
1969	32.7	28.9	31.0	114.5
1970	38.6	32.7	28.4	115.4
1971	35.4	33.4	27.5	115.8
1972	35.0	34.3	26.8	125.7
1973	38.1	42.0	28.0	123.8
1974	46.9	42.0	36.0	149.2
1975	51.3	42.0	45.0	161.9
1976	47.1	50.3	50.0	203.2
1977	54.1	76.1	56.2	218.3
1978	61.7	71.4	66.1	221.4

Source: Ministry of Agriculture.

SA TABLE 21. EGYPTIAN POUNDS PER FEDDAN RECEIVED BY FARMERS, 1950-78

Year	Wheat	Maize	Rice	Cotton	Short berseem[a]	Long berseem
1950	15.8	14.7	31.0	59.2	6.7	18.0
1951	17.2	14.1	20.5	56.2	6.7	18.0
1952	16.5	14.2	21.9	66.2	7.4	19.9
1953	26.2	15.5	18.9	66.3	7.0	18.8
1954	29.0	14.5	31.0	61.8	6.7	17.8
1955	25.3	20.0	39.2	51.6	6.7	18.0
1956	26.1	23.3	40.0	55.6	6.7	18.0
1957	26.0	18.6	42.0	61.9	6.8	18.1
1958	26.3	19.7	37.4	65.1	6.6	17.7
1959	25.9	18.8	37.9	71.7	7.7	20.7
1960	29.4	25.8	37.9	70.4	7.6	20.4
1961	29.4	26.5	38.3	46.8	11.9	21.4
1962	31.2	27.8	44.2	75.9	9.6	25.6
1963	31.9	24.8	41.6	77.9	13.0	34.6
1964	33.9	31.2	40.6	92.5	15.3	41.0
1965	33.5	41.2	44.9	80.9	16.6	44.4
1966	37.2	40.4	53.4	70.7	17.9	47.8
1967	38.6	46.4	63.9	80.9	15.0	40.0
1968	34.6	54.4	67.8	91.0	14.2	38.0
1969	33.3	46.1	66.5	104.4	15.6	41.8
1970	45.0	52.0	64.7	99.6	17.2	46.0
1971	45.3	51.5	61.3	107.6	24.0	64.0
1972	45.7	54.2	58.7	115.3	30.0	80.0
1973	56.1	63.7	64.0	105.9	37.5	100.0
1974	64.5	63.3	76.6	133.5	45.0	120.0
1975	74.9	77.2	92.5	126.9	52.0	140.0
1976	65.9	81.0	106.5	178.6	57.0	152.0
1977	76.3	117.2	123.1	169.4	72.8	194.0
1978	86.4	118.5	150.7	224.5	124.7	332.0

a. Prices per cut are available for only some years. For the missing years the price series computed by the Food and Agriculture Organization/Institute for National Planning (FAO/INP) using the meat price index has been taken (see FAO/INP progress reports on agricultural sector analysis of the Arab Republic of Egypt).

Source: Ministry of Agriculture.

SA TABLE 22. FARM-GATE PRICES OF AGRICULTURAL PRODUCTS, 1965–78
(Egyptian pounds per ton)

Crop	1956	1970	1971	1972	1973	1974	1975	1976	1977[a]	1978[b]
Wheat	30.20	38.62	35.40	35.03	38.13	46.93	51.33	47.13	54.13	61.66
Barley	25.73	34.31	41.98	32.48	39.33	49.17	54.59	51.50	60.33	64.08
Maize	26.91	33.41	33.34	36.77	45.07	50.78	50.80	50.30	76.14	71.42
Rice	21.25	28.42	27.46	26.84	28.17	34.11	42.24	50.00	56.18	66.10
Beans	49.79	47.40	57.40	54.63	53.87	86.00	84.71	104.97	105.35	134.51
Lentils	70.06	104.75	101.25	98.25	111.75	131.25	150.00	152.31	166.94	209.06
Cotton	99.60	115.38	115.64	125.97	123.87	149.21	161.91	203.17	218.35	222.10
Groundnuts	90.77	86.64	87.17	88.37	92.53	119.33	n.a.	112.92	224.53	249.33
Sesame	99.29	123.53	124.61	125.11	133.58	158.33	200.00	206.42	224.16	350.16
Flax seed	58.36	74.18	82.38	89.26	98.93	119.26	133.28	137.40	147.54	187.05
Sugarcane	2.83	2.89	2.72	3.07	3.72	6.45	7.50	8.42	8.20	9.34
Onions, winter	13.15	14.00	15.78	13.63	19.47	19.04	24.58	29.16	31.42	32.90
Onions, other	14.31	13.71	15.61	14.44	17.12	n.a.	36.16	37.57	36.05	41.51
Vegetables										
Winter	17.31	24.34	22.40	26.15	38.64	44.85	n.a.	n.a.	n.a.	n.a.
Summer	14.60	17.66	18.98	20.90	22.42	30.06	n.a.	n.a.	n.a.	n.a.
Nili	21.10	24.47	25.39	37.22	40.51	55.53	n.a.	n.a.	n.a.	n.a.

Fruits									
Citrus	22.99	24.09	24.06	26.22	30.85	31.28	n.a.	n.a.	n.a.
Dates	25.00	25.00	25.00	28.00	30.00	40.00	n.a.	n.a.	n.a.
Other	43.25	39.10	49.46	50.44	52.27	56.57	n.a.	n.a.	n.a.
Livestock products									
Milk	50.00	57.70	62.70	65.80	73.00	85.80	n.a.	n.a.	n.a.
Cattle meat	382.00	478.00	483.00	502.00	551.00	612.00	n.a.	n.a.	n.a.
Poultry meat	365.00	362.00	389.00	401.00	446.00	488.00	n.a.	n.a.	n.a.
Eggs	212.50	262.50	275.00	315.00	345.00	400.00	n.a.	n.a.	n.a.
Wool	298.00	350.00	360.00	375.00	404.00	424.00	n.a.	n.a.	n.a.
Honey	230.00	252.00	262.00	277.70	292.00	389.00	n.a.	n.a.	n.a.

n.a. Not available.

Note: Prices are fixed for rice, wheat, horsebeans, lentils, sesame, and sugarcane. Cotton prices are fixed on the basis of variety, grade, and extraction rate.

a. Updated April and October 1978.

b. Updated April 1979.

Source: Institute of Agricultural Economic Research, Ministry of Agriculture.

SA TABLE 23. ESTIMATED COSTS OF PRODUCTION OF MAJOR CROPS, 1972–73 TO 1974–75
(Egyptian pounds per feddan)

Crop and year	Rent	Wages	Draft power	Machinery	Seeds	Fertilizer Organic	Fertilizer Chemical	Pesti-cides	Other costs	Total costs
Cotton										
1972–73	25.27	24.39	2.64	4.96	1.27	3.75	8.37	4.70	1.15	76.50
1973–74	26.10	30.98	3.35	5.53	1.29	4.37	8.10	6.07	1.19	86.98
1974–75	26.11	40.70	3.37	6.52	1.32	5.83	8.46	9.40	2.05	103.76
Wheat										
1972–73	15.52	7.24	3.65	4.49	3.19	0.93	6.48	...	0.69	42.19
1973–74	16.45	8.07	4.06	5.13	3.64	0.77	8.31	...	1.06	47.49
1974–75	17.07	13.25	3.47	9.62	4.71	2.55	7.12	...	1.54	59.33
Rice (paddy)										
1972–73	11.90	13.32	4.23	7.37	4.40	2.67	5.98	0.55	0.35	50.77
1973–74	13.43	16.33	4.11	8.80	4.86	3.16	6.46	0.47	0.86	58.48
1974–75	14.82	21.96	5.10	10.39	5.18	4.18	6.14	0.36	2.00	70.13
Maize										
1972–73	12.58	11.36	3.83	2.59	1.20	5.75	7.20	...	0.53	45.04
1973–74	13.29	13.65	4.33	3.53	1.57	6.24	7.55	...	0.89	51.05
1974–75	15.02	18.23	4.49	4.00	1.58	7.43	7.63	...	1.19	59.57
Millet (sorghum)										
1974–75	10.60	23.96	3.25	7.43	0.84	0.87	6.90	...	1.71	55.56
Sugarcane										
1972–73	22.27	23.03	5.80	9.05	4.11	0.44	15.66	...	1.51	81.87
1973–74	22.42	33.61	9.91	9.48	5.81	0.21	15.83	...	1.84	99.11

... Negligible.
Note: Agricultural years end October 31.
Source: Ministry of Agriculture.

428

SA TABLE 24. OUTPUT OF SELECTED INDUSTRIAL PRODUCTS, 1973-78

(thousands of metric tons unless otherwise stated)

Product	Previous peak output (and year)		1973	1974	1975	1976	1977	1978
Spinning and weaving								
Cotton yarn	179	(1972)	182	179	181	193	210	212
Cotton textiles (million square meters)	808	(1972)	829	829	843	873	905	918
Foodstuffs								
Sugar	610	(1972)	633	577	526	576	614	629
Cheese	135	(1972)	135	135	153	147	149	161
Preserves, fruits, vegetables	26	(1971–72)	24	18	24	48	41	40
Cottonseed oil	158	(1971–72)	160	170	161	160	166	169
Oilseed cakes	733	(1965–66)	600	540	720	417	430	431
Soft drinks (million bottles)	751	(1964–65)	600	660	784	960	984	1,613
Beer (million liters)	30	(1972)	32	29	29	30	39	42
Cigarettes (billions)	23	(1972)	23	23	21	28	25	27
Chemicals								
Sulfuric acid	227	(1967–68)	23	30	36	28	27	30
Superphosphate	522	(1971–72)	419	465	520	493	513	502
Ammonium nitrate[a]	438	(1967–68)	210	320	400	530	622	698
Tires (thousands)	927	(1972)	860	814	923	859	920	857

(Table continues on the following page.)

429

SA TABLE 24 (continued)

Product	Previous peak output (and year)	1973	1974	1975	1976	1977	1978
Engineering products							
Cars (units)	6,130 (1972)	5,590	8,169	11,576	9,799	13,991	14,562
Trucks and tractors (units)	2,956 (1972)	2,761	2,342	2,825	3,807	4,451	4,101
Buses (units)	1,155 (1965–66)	413	360	305	307	475	465
Refrigerators (thousands)	68 (1969–70)	39	55	109	112	129	138
Television (thousands)	84 (1966–67)	49	68	77	88	147	166
Metallurgical products							
Reinforcing bars	251 (1969–70)	226	232	219	202	230	249
Steel sections	135 (1968–69)	87	81	106	151	128	152
Steel sheets	179 (1972)	167	125	211	156	235	229
Cast iron products	54 (1962–63)	53	55	66	63	78	109
Aluminum	—	—	—	—	54	90	101
Mining products							
Phosphate	748 (1967–68)	540	499	428	392	468	483

— Not applicable.
a. Thirty-one percent nitrogen.
Source: Ministry of Industry.

SA TABLE 25. WHOLESALE PRICE INDEX, 1974-78

(1965-66 = 100)

Item	Commodity weight	End of period 1974	1975	1976	1977	1978
Agricultural commodities	33.7	172.3	178.7	205.0	240.6	258.9
Foodstuffs and beverages	19.9	168.9	190.1	213.2	236.1	241.4
Tobacco and tobacco products	7.1	122.6	122.7	122.7	122.9	122.9
Yarn, textiles, etc.	20.5	122.3	122.4	125.3	128.1	163.9
Petroleum and fuels	7.4	138.3	148.7	157.8	159.5	168.6
Paper	1.2	258.4	258.7	257.2	241.0	248.1
Wood	1.2	225.9	225.9	358.6	370.7	361.9
Construction materials	2.6	151.7	179.2	188.6	212.1	250.3
Medicines	1.6	107.9	110.2	110.2	158.3	158.3
Chemical products	2.8	118.5	125.3	130.8	130.8	132.1
Metal and metal products	1.0	165.8	178.1	190.7	213.8	228.7
Transportation equipment	1.0	173.9	173.9	173.9	195.8	218.2
All items	100.0	152.7	161.8	178.5	196.9	214.1

Source: CAPMAS.

SA TABLE 26. CONSUMER PRICE INDEX FOR URBAN POPULATION, 1974-78

(1966-67 = 100)

Item	Commodity weight[a]	End of period 1974	1975	1976	1977	1978
Food and beverages	52.5	161.3	181.9	209.2	231.3	254.7
Cereals	11.2	120.9	121.5	125.8	135.8	139.3
Pulses	6.6	186.1	202.1	218.1	256.9	273.9
Meat, fish, and eggs	13.1	190.3	234.2	287.8	316.2	331.8
Dairy products	5.9	173.3	216.6	240.9	279.6	315.4
Vegetables	3.8	210.4	218.5	276.8	241.3	331.7
Fruits	2.9	154.2	187.6	230.2	283.6	362.2
Housing	15.7	106.5	108.6	109.1	109.5	110.2
Furniture and other durables	1.3	109.0	128.4	136.3	156.3	181.1
Clothing	8.4	129.9	140.1	147.4	188.1	239.1
Transport and communication	4.4	123.1	122.6	136.0	144.7	145.1
Services	9.9	127.3	140.5	144.0	180.8	203.8
Personal expenses	7.8	120.4	125.0	128.1	133.9	160.7
All items	100.0	141.0	155.2	171.2	191.1	212.6

a. Indicative commodity weights are based on the commodity weights employed in five regional subindexes and population for these regions. The regional weights are based on a family budget survey of 1964-65 and the sample population census of 1966.
Source: CAPMAS.

Index

432